Contents

Abbreviations

AJIL	*American Journal of International Law*
CEEC	Committee for European Economic Cooperation
CIA	Central Intelligence Agency
CPSU	Communist Party of the Soviet Union
CSO	Central Statistics Office
DRV	Democratic Republic of Vietnam
EDC	European Defence Community
EEC	European Economic Community
EFTA	European Free Trade Association
EMPPO	European and Mediterranean Plant Protection Organization
FDP	Free Democratic Party
FRG	Federal Republic of Germany
GA	General Assembly
GATT	General Agreement on Tariffs and Trade
GDR	German Democratic Republic (Deutsche Demokratische Republik, DDR)
GNP	Gross National Product
ICF	Irish Christian Front
IDA	Industrial Development Agency (Ireland)
IFMC	International Folk Music Council
ILO	International Labour Organization
ISRAT	Israel Export and Trust Company
ITU	International Trade Union
IUGG	International Union of Geodesy and Geophysics
LNTS	League of Nations Treaty Service
NATO	North Atlantic Treaty Organisation
NFA	National Farmers' Association
NSC	National Security Council
OECD	Organization for European Cooperation and Development
OEEC	Organization for European Economic Cooperation
PCC	Palestine Conciliation Commission
PRC	People's Republic of China
PSORG	Public Service Organization Review Group

ROC	Republic of China
TD	Teachta Dála – member of the Oireachtas
UNO	United Nations Organization
UNSCOP	United Nations Special Committee on Palestine
UPU	United Postal Union
WHO	World Health Organization
WMO	World Meteorological Organization

Note: The Chinese proper names, places and terms used in this text follow the *pīnyīn* system developed in China in 1958. However, in quotations containing primary sources, the spellings remain true to the original document.

The grammar and spellings of original documents and secondary sources have not been altered.

Acknowledgements

Between 1995 and 1997 I spent many hours researching in the Reading Room of the National Archives, Dublin – an endeavor that led to this book. The exhausting daytrips by train from Mallow Co. Cork to Dublin would have been overwhelming if not for the exceptional ability of the staff of the National Archives in the preservation, maintenance, and delivery of the diplomatic files. I often felt that somewhere in the back rooms Freddie Boland's old desk sat untouched, or Con Cremin's filing cabinet, from which the files would magically appear.

During the past ten years several universities have been gracious in allowing me to research in their libraries. My study of Irish history began at UCC's Boole Library and Trinity College's Berkeley Library. In the United States, I am grateful to the research staffs of the Arthur W. Diamond Law Library at Columbia University and the Tarlton Law Library at the University of Texas. There is no finer library in existence than the Perry-Castañeda Library at the University of Texas where I gathered material from the rare diplomatic recognition texts. Living in Davidson, North Carolina, allowed me access to the excellent E. H. Little Library at Davidson College. In the Washington DC area, I am grateful to the staffs at the University of Maryland, Baltimore County Albin O. Kuhn Library, the Georgetown University Lauinger Library, the Johns Hopkins University Milton S. Eisenhower Library, the Mullen Library at the Catholic University of America, and the Paul H. Nitze School of Advanced International Studies.

Thank you to Lisa Hyde, my editor, for turning my cumbersome manuscript into this fine book. Thank you, also, to Jenny Oates for superb subediting. Numerous friends and colleagues have reviewed the manuscript and encouraged me to write. Thank you especially to my colleague George McLoone. From my former professors Lawrence H. Eaker, Jr. and Michael W. Mullane, I gained a passion for scholarship and teaching. Graduate seminars with Professor Robert A. Divine and the late Professor Walt W. Rostow in diplomatic and economic history at the University of Texas, Austin, further stimulated my interest in researching and writing history. Numerous discussions with Professor Alan W. Ertl of Ramstein, Germany in 1989 changed the course of my life and career.

I am grateful to Professor Dermot Keogh, above all others, for gently encouraging me to follow a dream, even when I imagined the world to be conspiring against me. My father, to whom this book is dedicated, gave me 'room to make some big mistakes' by supporting my efforts in every way. The gratitude I feel for his imprint on my life is infinite and I miss him. My children, Brooke and Callan Bower, patiently and trustingly journeyed with me to Ireland, arriving for the first time in Shannon Airport on a cold, wet January morning in 1994. They cheerfully lived the Irish life and were never afraid of a new adventure. Friendships they made in Killavullen National School became lasting ones. Our lives were touched by all we met during those years in Ireland. The gratitude and love I feel for my longtime friend, John F. Brosnan, cannot be expressed in words. John has provided inspiration and guidance far beyond the bounds of friendship.

Foreword

Dr Paula Wylie's *Ireland and the Cold War – Diplomacy and Recognition 1949-63* is to be warmly welcomed. This highly original work represents a new generation of studies on the history of Irish diplomacy. It breaks new ground, is innovative in its methodology, interdisciplinary in its approach and rigorous in its research. The author succeeds in using the corpus of contemporary international relations literature without subjecting the reader to the unexplained and very often incomprehensible prose that sometimes characterizes writing in that field. This book will serve as a model for future investigations in the area of Ireland and the Cold War.

The book began life as a doctoral thesis. Here I must declare an interest. The work was conducted under my supervision in the History Department at University College, Cork. Dr Wylie was one of a number of MA, M. Phil and Ph.D. students in the mid-1980s who have now published extensively in the area of Irish diplomatic history. Dr Mervyn O'Driscoll published a monograph on *Ireland, Germany and the Nazis: Politics and Diplomacy, 1919–1939*. Dr Mark Hull wrote a book entitled: *Irish Secrets: German Spies in Wartime Ireland, 1939–1945*. Dr Bernadette Whelan has published a volume: *Ireland and the Marshall Plan, 1947–1957*. Dr Maurice Fitzgerald has written a monograph entitled: *Protectionism to Liberalism – Ireland and the EEC, 1957–1966*. Other works were also published in monograph and article format. A number remain to be published, such as Aengus Nolan's excellent study of the long-serving Secretary of the Department of External Affairs, Joseph Walshe, and studies by other students on a range of Irish diplomats, foreign ministers and foreign policy issues.

Dr Wylie's work was part of that pioneering generation of historians who had access from the mid-1980s to the newly opened files of the Department of Foreign Affairs and who set that material in a comparative international context by exploring relevant material in the National Archives in Washington and London, as well as the foreign ministries of Germany, France, Italy and Spain. They also used a wide variety of personal papers belonging to diplomats and politicians in the same countries and beyond.

Dr Wylie, coming from outside the Irish university system, brought an added academic strength to her work. She had an MA in Law and had studied international relations as an undergraduate. Her approach to the study of Irish foreign policy first led her to focus upon Ireland and the search for membership of the EEC in the 1960s. While her research reached an advanced stage in this area, Dr Wylie's interests veered towards the question of Irish recognition policy during the Cold War. Primary research in that area did not exist. The relevant files, as the author observes, remained virtually unopened in most cases since the last diplomat worked on them in the early 1960s.

However, I do not wish to give the impression that the subject of this book was an obvious area of research. It took considerable historical imagination to conceive the subject and structure the scope of the inquiry. Dr Wylie chose wisely to focus upon case studies dealing with East Germany, Israel and China and Tibet. This comprises the latter three chapters of her book. These are preceded by three very valuable and wide ranging chapters on 'the convergence of Irish foreign policy and international law', 'Ireland in the world system 1949–1963' and 'Irish recognition policy and practice'.

Dr Wylie formulated her primary research question as follows: 'When, in the course of defining Ireland's international interests, does Ireland open the way to bilateral diplomatic relations by recognizing an entity as a state?' When pulling the various strands of the evidence together from scores of files, the writer concluded that Irish policy in this area was not *ad hoc*. There was a logic and a coherence to the Irish stance throughout the period under review. Irish national interest was advanced during the early years of the Cold War.

The Dublin government recognized states and not governments. That was consistent with the position adopted by Eamon de Valera, as illustrated most strongly during the Spanish Civil War. It was independent-minded in the way that it approached the issue of granting only *de facto* recognition to Israel from 1948 until the early 1960s. The files reveal the masterly by the relevant Irish diplomats of the intricacies of international law. Ireland had much greater latitude regarding recognition during the period 1948-1955. The author writes: 'In the difficult atmosphere of the early Cold War years, Irish foreign policy objectives existed metaphorically below the level of radar – present but unnoticed in the international political arena.'

Dr Wylie illustrates how Ireland, after joining the United Nations in the mid-1950s, was obliged to work in a more complex multilateral world engaged in a struggle for rapid decolonization. Dr Wylie teases out those complexities, examining a range of issues in a wide geopolitical context.

This book provides the first coherent study of Irish recognition policy between 1948 and 1963.

Professor Dermot Keogh
Cork
January 2006

Preface

> The State is bound by minute rules to respect the sovereignty and independence of other States. But as... it is left to its free discretion, by availing itself to the unlimited right of war, to assail the very existence of other States, so, in the light of the predominant doctrine of recognition, it is free to decide, according to its unfettered discretion and by consulting its own interests only, whether another community shall enjoy the rights of sovereignty and independence in statehood.
>
> Sir Hersch Lauterpacht, *Recognition in International Law*[1]

In 1986 the National Archives of Ireland were opened for public inspection, clearing the way for diplomatic historians in Ireland. Although many Irish scholars were given access to documents before 1986, the opening of the archives allowed students, journalists and the general public the similar entrée. After 1986 a flurry of diplomatic historiography occurred in Ireland that documented the moving from dependence upon Britain to the independence of statehood within the twentieth century. While the foreign policy interests of Ireland have been studied at length (such as neutrality, European integration and United Nations diplomacy), there is a lack of scholarly publication on the general administration of Irish foreign policy during the period. In other words, how did a small Department of External (and later, Foreign) Affairs, manage Ireland's international policy issues?

Since Irish foreign policy objectives often fluctuated in the Cold War environment, the conventional assumption is that the administration of Irish foreign policy was conducted in a haphazard manner. With its many labels – ambivalent, unprincipled, *ad hoc* – Irish foreign policy since 1949 has had its share of deprecatory press. Yet the present research in the area of Ireland's diplomatic recognition toward emerging and reconstituted states demonstrates the highest level of professionalism, commitment and administrative consistency within the diplomatic corps in the administration of foreign policy. This work presents the difficulties in balancing the interests of Ireland within the complicated framework of the early Cold War years. While specific issues were not conducted within the framework of conventional models of larger states (for example, British or American policy and practice), the files on diplomatic recognition issues demonstrate that the Department of External Affairs consistently acted in what Irish decision-makers perceived as Ireland's national interest – a conclusive determinant of statehood.

This study also demonstrates the Irish perception of autonomy within an indifferent world system. Conflicted with two antithetical desires – to participate in the world system yet to remain aloof from it – Ireland's foreign policy often seemed to lack strategy and consistency. Ambivalence in diplomacy causes criticism, where many assume that other 'principled' approaches to achieving foreign policy goals will be more palatable to the international community.[2] However, one of the most striking features of our international system of states is that principles are readily cast aside for the achievement of specific interests. For survival, small states need excessive latitude in policy space. Flexibility and caution during the period 1949–63 by the Department of External (Foreign) Affairs averted careless judgement errors and allowed policy formulation that is arguably not ambivalent. Irish foreign policy-making existed in the Cold War environment of *pro tempore et pro re*.[3]

The stereotype of small states in the world system since 1945 has included the notion of 'passive and reactive' foreign policy, explained by the lack of economic resources to pursue and establish diplomatic relations.[4] The study of Ireland's diplomatic recognition decisions shatters the assumption that weaker, cooperative governments within the world system invariably follow the path of least resistance. Although Ireland could not meet many of its foreign policy objectives during the period and did not achieve a resolution to partition of the North, diplomatic recognition issues were resolved with confident policies that continued to strengthen and improve Ireland's position within the world system as an independent state.

RESEARCH METHOD AND ARCHIVAL EVIDENCE

The research for this project began in 1994, originally an effort to gather material for the study of bilateral interaction of Irish foreign policy and the foreign policies of the founding six member states of the European Economic Community. Only eight years after the National Archives Act of 1986, there were many avenues of unpublished research to pursue. The files of the Department of External (Foreign) Affairs were rich with research possibilities and these became the primary sources for this work.

In 1995, while examining records from the postwar period of the Federal Republic of Germany, the research revealed a massive amount of unpublished material on the policy of non-recognition of the Soviet-controlled eastern territory of Germany (formerly East Germany). Similar voluminous files existed on the non-recognition of China and the issue of Taiwan. Most intriguing were the documents on the policy of non-recognition toward recognition of Israel. Noting the volume of official records on recognition, it became apparent that the maintenance of non-recognition required continuous administrative effort on the part of the Department of External Affairs. The questions became more intriguing concerning how External Affairs managed recognition problems on a day-to-day basis with a limited staff and other more urgent issues. Relying on E.H. Carr's dictum that 'facts speak only when the historian calls on them', the discovery of unpublished material opened the way for an historical narrative on the maintenance of recognition policies by External Affairs.[5]

Although the files on East Germany and the China/Taiwan problems were quite large and fell naturally within the period of study [1949–63], the Israel diplomatic recognition files were the most intriguing for the length of time in which the Department of External Affairs maintained non-recognition toward Israel – a period of fifteen years after the State of Israel was declared in 1948. Ireland's relationship with Israel stands uniquely within the time period studied. The fact that no serious international legal consequences developed during the early period of Ireland's independent foreign policy is quite remarkable in light of the trade that continued to exist between Ireland and the non-recognized states.

The intersection of international law and foreign policy became the focus of the research, converging in the study of diplomatic recognition. In approaching the subject, the larger questions of *what is a state* and *when does an entity become a state* could be examined from within Ireland on an administrative level, evaluating what the Department of External Affairs *perceived* to be relevant to recognition issues. The theoretical tension that dominated the field of diplomatic recognition in the first half of the twentieth century, the interplay between constitutive and declaratory theories, clearly existed in the files of External Affairs. After reviewing numerous recognition files, one specific question emerged: *When, in the course of defining Ireland's international interests, does Ireland open the way to bilateral diplomatic relations by recognizing an entity as a state?* The materials housed in the National Archives are an accurate and accessible means of examining *how* foreign policy decisions concerning recognition were made during the years 1949–63.

A unique feature of the diplomatic recognition files is their administrative elegance. Upon viewing the documents, one is aware of their utilitarian nature. The files are surprisingly orderly and complete, with much of the material chronologically intact. In contrast to purged records, the files on recognition seem to have been removed directly from the offices of those working with them and placed intact and undisturbed into the archival system. The changing role of External Affairs within the Irish government is evident in the amount of information collected, analysed, compiled and distributed by the department after 1945. Ronan Fanning, the first scholar to thoroughly examine the files of the Department of Finance, remarked on the 'explosive growth in the volume of [Finance's] records from 1946–47' that he attributed to the 'additional documentation' originating from the Department of External Affairs.[6] After the Second World War, Ireland's participation in international affairs expanded considerably, and much of this growth is documented in the files of the National Archives. This unprecedented documentation by the Department External Affairs in the period 1949–63 provides rich material for an historical narrative of small, independent Ireland trying to establish and manage diplomatic recognition policy within the framework of the early Cold War years.

NOTES

1   Sir Hersch Lauterpacht, *Recognition in International Law* (Cambridge 1947), p. 3.
2   See Trevor Salmon, *Unneutral Ireland: An Ambivalent and Unique Security Policy* (Oxford, 1989).
3   A Latin phrase meaning 'to suit the time and circumstance'. www. perseus.tufts.edu
4   See Paul Sutton, 'Political aspects', in Colin Clarke and Tony Payne (eds), *Politics, Security and Development in Small States* (London 1987), pp. 19–20.
5   E.H. Carr, *What is History?* 2nd edn (London, 1987), p. 11.
6   Ronan Fanning, *The Irish Department of Finance 1922–58* (Dublin 1978), pp. 407–8.

1

The convergence of Irish foreign policy and international law

Law is a process for making decisions. It is distinguished from coordinate political processes in that it seeks to conform in high degree to the expectations of authority... regarding who should make decisions, and by what criteria decisions ought to be made, and in that it insists that reasons for those decisions relating them rationally to community goals be made explicit.

W. Michael Reisman and Eisuke Suzuki, 'Recognition and Social Change in International Law: A Prologue for Decisionmaking'[1]

INTRODUCTION

In the post-1945 era, when Ireland formally disassociated from the British Commonwealth but had not joined the European Economic Community, Irish foreign policy did not have the constraints of colonialism or the responsibilities of integration to inhibit the establishment of its own foreign policy. Setting policy in these circumstances had two effects. First, in a positive sense, Irish foreign policy decisions did not have any measurable impact on the greater powers that resulted in unintended consequences for newly independent Ireland. Second, in a more negative sense, due to Ireland's limited involvement in international organizations, the greater powers did not establish close diplomatic relationships with the Irish, hindering the advancement of Ireland's own foreign policy goals. Ireland remained outside the framework of the North Atlantic Treaty Organization (NATO) from its creation, and was not accepted into the United Nations (UN) until 1955.

The research for this study reveals four persistent international interests after the Second World War that anchored Irish foreign policy decisions: the desire to end partition; the commitment to neutrality as a security and economic policy; the transition from protectionism in economic policy to the expansion of international trade; and an exaggerated need to achieve prestige in the international system. In the area of diplomatic recognition of other states, Ireland asserted these four international interests time and again during the period 1949–63 with mixed success.

In contrast to other former dominion states such as Canada and Australia, Ireland's announcement of independent statehood in 1949 did not constitute a crisis within the diplomatic department of the Irish government. For thirty years beforehand, the Department of External Affairs (now called Foreign Affairs) began its slow evolution with the establishment of the first Dáil Éireann in January 1919. The primary objective of the first Dáil under Eamon de Valera was to have the Irish Republic recognized in the international community. Creating an organization to undertake the task of establishing critical diplomatic contacts with other states, de Valera subsumed the old Sinn Féin propaganda unit into the new Publicity Department in 1919.[2] Recognition for Ireland did not come until thirty years later. In the interim, the Irish developed their own style of diplomacy while shaking off the constraints imposed by the former British system.

The External Relations of Act of 1936, passed during the abdication crisis of Edward VIII, had severed Ireland's technical dependence on Britain in the field of foreign policy, putting diplomatic relations in the hands of Ireland's Executive Council instead of the King of England. Essentially, any decisions concerning diplomatic recognition of other states could be made by the Executive Council without interference from Britain. From 1936 until full statehood in 1949, the Irish diplomats working within the Department of External Affairs acted as if the Department *was* independent of Britain, although the perception and reality of independence were distinct. During these years, Ireland relied on Britain exclusively in trade and national security, especially intelligence. The Department of External Affairs did not have the personnel or financial budget to undertake many foreign policy initiatives. Recognition policy generally dovetailed with Britain or the United States, as most Irish international interests could not avoid being filtered through London or Washington in one way or another, especially in the early Cold War years.

The year 1936, apart from its importance in the Anglo-Irish relationship, is the point of departure for independent recognition policy in Ireland. The Department of External Affairs found itself in the uncomfortable position of supporting a non-interventionist policy in the Spanish Civil War, while facing fierce criticism from the Irish Christian Front (ICF) and the opposition party, Fine Gael, in the Dáil.[3] The ICF's amplified criticism of 'suffering inflicted upon the unhappy Catholics of Spain' played well with the Irish public and the pressure placed on de Valera's government for recognition of Franco's regime grew substantially.[4] British foreign policy, under the leadership of Foreign Secretary Anthony Eden while Prime Minister Stanley Baldwin was preoccupied with the abdication crisis, centred on a non-interventionist policy in Spain as well. The British, however, placed strategic and military concerns at the forefront of policy during the early Spanish crisis, not ideological ones. The British joined with the French 'to prevent foreign support reaching Franco' because Eden believed any effort at helping the Republic would only encourage Hitler and Mussolini to aid the Nationalists.[5]

Under the leadership of de Valera, who held the dual portfolio of Taoiseach and Minister for External Affairs, Fianna Fáil had been in power since 1932. Responding to the demand for recognition of the *de facto* government of Spain, de Valera found the answer in asserting Ireland's independent diplomatic approach through his own partisan *Irish Press*:

> To those public bodies, however, and to others who have requested the government to sever diplomatic relations with the Spanish government, the government of Saorstát Éireann would point out that diplomatic relations are primarily between States rather than governments, and that the severance of diplomatic relations between the two countries would serve no useful purpose at the present time.[6]

The practice of maintaining recognition of a state without cognizance to its changing government became popular with diplomats and practitioners of international law beginning with the announcement of the Estrada Doctrine in 1930. Although de Valera did not formally incorporate *Estrada* into Irish foreign policy in the manner of many states on the American continents, he applied its principle tenet: recognition of a state is irrevocable and anterior to recognition of a government. Ireland's non-intervention policy in Spain was fundamentally different from most European states, including Britain, as Irish national interests were centred on its affinity with Catholic Spain. A major qualifier in de Valera's decision was the lack of an immediate threat to the Irish government, its commerce or territory. Diplomatic relations with Spain were eventually severed during the war, but Ireland did not withdraw recognition of the state. President de Valera simply withdrew the Irish diplomat there. In March 1939, when it was clear Franco was the *de facto* ruler of Spain, the Irish envoy Leopold Kerney returned to his post in Madrid.[7]

De Valera's subtle diplomatic posturing during the era of European dictatorships set a precedent for future recognition decisions. Ireland's foreign policy years afterward continued to hold to de Valera's approach of recognizing states rather than governments. The Taoiseach was considerably adept in taking a point of law and applying its strict construction in policy. For a small state like Ireland, de Valera's approach was useful. As this study will show, when international law did not conform to Ireland's interests, Irish foreign policy required pragmatism rather than a legalistic approach. During the early years of the Cold War, the American diplomat George F. Kennan wrote that a purely legalistic approach to diplomatic behaviour ideally would rectify 'awkward conflicts of national interest'.[8] The deficiency in this theory, Kennan argued, is that 'even under a system of world law the sanction against destructive international behavior might continue to rest . . . on the alliances and relationships of the great powers themselves'.[9]

While smaller states might not overtly circumvent standard diplomatic practices, a flexible approach to international issues (and in this case, diplomatic recognition) more effectively serves the interests of the state. The tension created by trying to marry policy choices with legal justifications is especially poignant in states whose diplomatic behaviour is not under scrutiny, either at home or by greater powers in the system. During 1949–63 in Ireland, the policy-oriented approach often proved difficult as well. In foreign affairs, where the legal rules were at odds with the requirements of Irish international interests, members of the Civil Service did not want to violate the only operational rules available for issues of state recognition that had no precedence in Irish diplomatic practice. The Department of External Affairs relied on international legal principles as much as possible in proposing policy but came under pressure from the ministers of various departments, as well as the Taoiseach, to find alternatives that best suited perceived national interests. As a result, foreign policy decisions concerning recognition appear *prima facie* to be loose and indecisive, but significant deliberation existed behind each decision.

Studying Ireland's recognition issues provides an opportunity to see the unfettered formulation of decisions. The decision-making inhibitors that did influence Irish recognition policy were not the result of external influences, such as the will of more dominant states like Britain, or the stringent application of normative international legal principles. Rather, the constraints on recognition in Irish foreign policy came from within the government itself. The decisions of whether to recognize Israel, or East Germany, or China or Poland were based on strategy and were decided in terms of what Irish interests could be served in withholding or granting recognition.

Another complicating factor in the decision-making process stemmed from the hostile international political environment of bipolarity. In practice, Ireland's diplomatic recognition policies were actually ahead of their time in reacting to the systemic change caused by the Cold War. The fascinating feature concerning Ireland's recognition policies was the ability to bend international legal principles far enough to suit the imperative interests of the government and/or the policy-makers, yet not so far that Irish foreign policy would be questioned or denounced by other states with hostile consequences. The ability to 'dance on the ropes' between arbitrary policy and the law makes the historical study of Irish diplomatic recognition practice intriguing.[10] Ireland's maintenance of *de facto* recognition policy toward certain states from 1949–63 against a current of superpower diplomacy, makes Ireland's recognition practice remarkable.

REVIEW OF DIPLOMATIC RECOGNITION LITERATURE

In its broadest definition, recognition in international law is 'the acceptance by a state of any fact or situation occurring in its relations with other states'.[11] The practical application of recognition in foreign policy, however, is a political act of the state granting recognition toward a particular body in a particular capacity, usually a community with the attributes of a sovereign state. With the advent of the Estrada doctrine (1930), the political nature of recognition within some states of the international community became codified, for *Estrada* delimited recognition to the general principle of recognizing *states* rather than *governments*, noting that a change of government is an internal matter for each state.[12]

By 1933 the Montevideo Convention established the legal requirements for statehood: (a) a permanent population; (b) defined territory; (c) a government; and (d) capacity to enter into relations with other states.[13] *Montevideo* also provided that recognition should be declaratory rather than constitutive, stating 'the political existence of the State is independent of recognition by other States' (Art. 3) and 'the recognition of a State merely signifies that the State which recognizes it accepts the personality of the other with all the rights and duties determined by International Law' (Art. 6).[14] The practice of recognizing states instead of governments, as well as accepting the declaratory nature of recognition, altered the concept of diplomatic recognition, moving away from the personal approach of the nineteenth century and earlier, toward the bureaucratic environment of the twentieth century.

An additional consequence of *Estrada* and *Montevideo* was the application of normative international law to the principle of recognition, enforcing the idea that recognition should be *unconditional* and *irrevocable*. These changes in the definition of recognition of states had two practical effects. First, governments setting recognition policy did not have to contend with the internal changes of other states, a consequence that made application of the policy much more flexible. However, the second effect – the unconditional and irrevocable nature of the recognition decision – caused states to consider and to withhold recognition using more caution. Although the Estrada doctrine and the Montevideo Convention were predominantly supported by North and South American governments in the early part of the twentieth century as guides in recognition policy and practice, the basic tenet of granting diplomatic recognition in matters of state formation gradually has been accepted by non-American states, including Ireland.

In 1995 jurist Clive Symmons highlighted the lack of academic analysis on Ireland's foreign policy of diplomatic recognition. 'Irish policy and practice on the topic of recognition of States, governments and illegal acquisition of territory appears never to have been researched in Ireland, let alone written up'.[15] Symmons' comments express the dearth of analysis on the subject of Ireland's recognition policy, from both the legal and historical perspectives. Prior to this study, readers of Irish foreign policy may have concluded that recognition was neither of interest to, nor the subject of, policy analysis by the Irish government. Irish Teachta Dálas (TDs) did not generally regard recognition as a public issue, although Symmons' review of Dáil Debates found a slight mention of the subject.

Symmons' article for the *Irish Jurist* was written without the benefit of historical documents. Without researching the archival materials, Symmons concluded that 'Irish policy on recognition has proceeded *sub silencio* in an *ad hoc* fashion with periodical ministerial statements... fleshing out the picture'.[16] Although the statement may be correct in describing the general public's knowledge of how recognition issues were decided, the Department of External Affairs (as well as other governmental departments) certainly did not ignore recognition policy, nor was policy made in an *ad hoc* fashion, two propositions upheld by the wealth of material on the subject in the National Archives in Dublin. Members of the Dáil did not discuss recognition issues primarily because decisions were held closely to the departments of the Taoiseach and External Affairs.

Diplomatic recognition applied as a tool of foreign policy lost its threatening nature in the latter half of the twentieth century, during a time when the acceleration of state membership in international organizations such as the United Nations created cohesion in policy-making for existing states. However, non-recognition in the Cold War environment played an important role in the foreign policy of many states, including Ireland, requiring considerable effort on the part of civil servants and diplomats to navigate specific policies between the pragmatism of politics and the ideals of international law.

In Ireland, recognition decisions were held closely in the departments of the Taoiseach and External Affairs and generally were not articulated to the public during the years 1949–63. Symmons' article is 'the tip of the iceberg' in presenting an analysis of Ireland's recognition policy and suffers from the lack of an historical analysis based on government archival documents. Symmons wearily concluded:

> The impression one gets from the periodic references in the parliamentary debates... is that Irish practice on recognition... has to a large extent followed British practice in the theoretical approach to the basic situations of international law where recognition decisions have to be made; but without a clear and comprehensive statement on the issues ever being made in the same mould as in the famous UK 'Morrison' statement of 1951.[17]

Symmons' work underestimates the depth of the recognition issues and the wealth of historical archives available. One may agree that Irish practice on recognition has followed British practice in its theoretical approach in tackling recognition issues. After all, Ireland's status as a sovereign state in western Europe since 1949 compels it to abide by the principles of international law in theory and in practice. However, any study of Irish policy and practice in recognition must include historical research within the governmental departments concerned, not simply a study of the Dáil Debates in general. As will be shown in this study, the archives of the Taoiseach and the Department of External (Foreign) Affairs represent sources rich in policy formulation and practice. The present study also includes the decisions of Irish courts on recognition questions.

Simply put, Symmons overstates the comparison of Irish policy to British policy. To compare the foreign policy interests of twentieth-century Britain to Ireland's, and to conclude they are 'similar', does not help in defining Irish policy and practice. First, how is it possible to reach conclusions without researching the decision-making process of the individual governments? Policies on diplomatic recognition are traditionally made at the highest levels of government, usually within the executive office and often without the benefit of discussions within legislative bodies or with the public. One must look behind the scenes to know how and why decisions were made.

Second, a leading line of reasoning in Symmons' thesis is that diplomatic recognition policy was not critical to Irish foreign policy in general, as there has been only one legal case reported that involved a question of recognition.

> The *Zarine* case evidences another curious feature relating to Irish recognition practice; that this has been the *only* case, which has ever come to the Irish courts involving a problem of recognition. (In contrast, British courts have handled many such cases.) For this reason, the effects in Irish *municipal* law resulting from *non*-recognition of an entity have never been fully examined in more recent times; but no doubt Irish practice here would follow UK precedents, especially as in the *Zarine* case such existing British precedents were cited with approval.[18] (italics in original)

A precursory study of the index to Irish Reports shows another case, *Carl Zeiss Stiftung* v. *Hempenstal Trust Ltd.* (HC) 1963 IR 221, in which a trademark registered in the Soviet-controlled area of Germany (East Germany) was found to be illegally on the Irish trademark register. This case predated the well-known *Carl Zeiss Stiftung* v. *VEB Carl Zeiss Jena* (1970), 61 ILR 36, landmark litigation in international law in establishing that 'decisions handed down by the courts of East Germany...[should be given] such weight as they appear to merit'.[19] A Carl Zeiss Stiftung case may be found in almost every western European state in the 1960s, sponsored by the government in East Germany, daring each national court to recognize the claims of the Zeiss companies, and ultimately, recognizing East Germany.[20]

The two Zeiss cases mentioned above – one from the Irish High Court in 1963 and the second from the United States Court of Appeals, 2nd Circuit in New York (1970) – deal directly with the question of succession in trademark law and are important in the history of recognition of East Germany as a 'sovereign' state. Whereas *Zeiss* in the United States upheld East German law without the United States government's recognizing the German Democratic Republic (GDR) as an independent state, the Irish trial court judge either did not understand the recognition problem inherent in the case, or refused to address it. The British did not address the problem until 1965 in the case *Carl Zeiss Stiftung* v. *Rayner and Keeler, Ltd.*[21] Symmons asserts that there has been only one case in Irish legal history concerning a question of recognition. It is submitted that there were at least two: one, which formally addressed the problem (*Zarine*), and one, which ignored it altogether (*Carl Zeiss* v. *Hempenstal*). Both cases, however, show independence apart from Great Britain in setting Irish policy.

DE FACTO AND *DE JURE* DISTINCTIONS

In reviewing the recognition practice of states during the twentieth century, one is aware of the usage of the terms *de facto* and *de jure* to describe the level of diplomatic recognition afforded to new states and governments. The *Encyclopedia of International Law* notes the distinction of the two terms 'has always been a source of difficulties'[22] while *Oppenheim's International Law* characterized *de facto* and *de jure* as 'convenient but elliptical'.[23] The Irish government, however, made an absolute distinction in practice between the terms *de facto* and *de jure* recognition, although defining those terms in ways which were politically convenient rather than in a strict legal sense. In 1963 international legal scholar J.L. Brierly refined the distinction between the two terms:

> Recognition either of a state or a government may be recognition *de jure* or *de facto*. The latter meets the case where a state, either because the position is obscure or for political reasons, is reluctant to recognize definitely some entity claiming to be a state or government, but yet finds it necessary for practical reasons to enter into some sort of official relations. Recognition *de facto* is provisional; it means that the recognizing government offers for the time being to enter into relations, yet ordinarily without cordiality, and without the usual courtesies of diplomacy.[24]

Brierly noted, however, that 'the terminology is misleading in more ways than one'.[25] When used as political tools, the terms become blurred. While *de facto* is most often used as a term of transition, *de jure* implies that the state being recognized meets all the necessary criteria for statehood and is in compliance with international law. During the years 1949–63 the members of the Irish government responsible for recognition policy were often misled by the confusing nature of the terms *de facto* and *de jure*. As Brierly explained, 'it is not the act of recognition that is *de jure* or *de facto*, but the state or the government, as the case may be, that is recognized as existing either *de jure* or *de facto*'.[26] As shown in the case of Israel (Chapter 6), a foreign policy of strict *non-recognition* was consistently termed *de facto* recognition.

GENERAL DIPLOMATIC RECOGNITION SCHOLARSHIP

The inviolability of a state, once it has met the criteria of statehood, was addressed in the nineteenth century by author J.T. Abdy. In the wake of the US

Civil War, Abdy wrote in 1878 that 'a state neither loses any of its rights, nor is discharged from any of its duties, by a change in the form of its civil government'.[27] For these reasons, the granting of *de jure* recognition is undertaken by states only when it certain that the state to be recognized has met the criteria for statehood. Fifty years later, Taylor Cole echoed Abdy's principle: 'the state...has a continuing personality which is not affected by changes in government'.[28] Although these authors were primarily interested in diplomatic recognition practice toward changes in government, the absolute concept of a state remained a cornerstone in international legal principles throughout the nineteenth and into the twentieth centuries.

Prior to 1945, the heart of the recognition dilemma in foreign policy was whether a state, having met the qualifications of statehood, had a right to be recognized and whether other states had a duty to recognize it. In international law, the distinction is drawn between the *constitutive* nature of recognition (a state exists because other states have recognized it) and the *declaratory* nature of recognition (a state exists when the criteria for statehood have been met under codified international law). In recent times, constitutive recognition has declined and objective tests such as the Montevideo Convention of 1933 have contributed to the declaratory nature of recognition.

International legal scholars today continue to debate whether states have a duty to recognize in all circumstances, once the requirements of statehood have been met.[29] In 1928 American scholar John Hervey stated that 'recognition is not compulsory. It is voluntary or optional. Each state judges for itself whether a new state or a new government with an old state merits recognition.'[30] Hervey's comments were seen as justifying the United States' position of non-recognition toward the government of the Soviet Union after 1917. Then, in 1933, Louis Jaffe articulated the leading criticisms of the United States government for its refusal to recognize the USSR.

> The failure or refusal of the political branch of government to accord recognition has been held to demonstrate the international non-existence of the unrecognized state or government, thus equating the practice known to the states as 'recognition' with the...constitutive recognition of the positivists; ignoring the infinite gradation of relations which may and do exist *infra* recognition; and treating recognition as white and non-recognition as black and exiling the whole world of unresolved color.[31]

Jaffe's book was published the same year the United States finally recognized the USSR *de jure*. The United States pursued a foreign policy of non-recognition of the Soviet Union from 1917–33. As an explanation, John Lewis Gaddis offered the following:

> Traditional American policy would have been to enter into diplomatic relations with the Bolshevik government once it had become clear that it

controlled Russia. But Wilson had departed dramatically from normal practice in 1913, when he refused to recognize the Huerto government in Mexico because it had come to power through unconstitutional means. Two years later... Secretary of State Bryan had declined to take official cognizance of any treaty arrangements imposed by Japan or China which might threaten the principle of Open Door. Hence, by the time of the Bolshevik Revolution, there was precedent for the view that recognition was not a neutral act, that it carried with it the connotation of approval, and that where such approval did not exist, recognition should be withheld.[32]

By 1948 Sir Hersch Lauterpacht, the pre-eminent British scholar on diplomatic recognition in the twentieth century, clarified the principles of *right* and *duty* in the recognition debate. Lauterpacht reasoned that the 'right and duty' question was valid only if one prescribed to recognition as a *legal* construct and not a *political* one. He was not willing to concede in 1948, however, that recognition had lost all legal definition, or that it had become strictly political in nature. In fact, his writing stressed the importance of holding to the legal nature of recognition:

[Recognition], as taught by writers, constitutes one of the weakest links in international law. The science of international law can no longer avoid the task of inquiring whether this state of affairs is due to a clear defect of the law of nations as expressed in the practice of States or whether it is attributable to the failure of lawyers to give an accurate account of the practice of States and to analyze it by reference to jurisprudential principles of order as distinguished from amorphous maxims of policy. An inquiry of this nature is of special urgency at a time when the foundations are being laid of an improved international order.[33]

In the aftermath of two world wars in less than thirty years (as well as the *precipitate* recognition of Israel by the United States in May 1948), Lauterpacht urged a return to recognition as a legal concept. He considered the ideals put forth by the Kellogg-Briand Pact of 1928 and questioned the state's unlimited right to pursue its own interests without regard to established principles of international law. Clearly, the concept of 'national interest' was driving a change in international law. Although he did not entirely place the blame on the 'unfettered discretion of states',[34] Lauterpacht saw the mechanisms of international law failing to prevent abuses in the name of national interest, namely the Second World War after Kellogg-Briand and many other safeguards in international law. Giving the political act of recognition one final blow, he stated:

[The] view that recognition is not a function consisting in the fulfilment of an international legal duty but an act of *national policy independent of binding legal principle*, has had the further result of divorcing recognition from the scientific bases of fact on which all must ultimately rest ... Law must be based on facts – in so far as such facts are not in themselves contrary to law.[35] (emphasis added)

In supporting his position that recognition must be based on principles of international law and not simply *ad hoc* state practice, Lauterpacht cited four guiding principles of recognition:

1. To recognize a political community as a state is to declare that it fulfils the conditions of statehood as required by international law.
2. If these conditions are present, the existing states are under the duty to grant recognition.
3. This legal rule signifies that in withholding or granting recognition states do not claim and are not entitled to serve exclusively the interest of their national policy and convenience regardless of the principles of international law in the matter.
4. Although recognition is thus declaratory of an existing fact, such declaration, made in the impartial fulfilment of a legal duty, is constitutive, as between the recognizing state and the community so recognized, of international rights and duties associated with full statehood.[36]

Lauterpacht was perhaps overly idealistic in 1948. Only the year before, Robert Langer argued that under specific circumstances there was not only sufficient reason *not* to recognize particular states, there also existed an international legal *duty* for *non-recognition*.[37] Langer cited the Stimson Doctrine of 1932 in which the United States refused to recognize Japan's territorial claims in Manchuria. Clearly states could, and often did, manipulate diplomatic recognition principles to serve imperative interests. The strict guidelines that Lauterpacht offered were never adopted as general principles of recognition in international law. During the period 1949–63, Ireland, as well as other states, would supplant Lauterpacht's rational approach with more emotive reasons based on imperative international (and national) interests, although the documents in the archives of the Department of External Affairs prove that the legal adviser often consulted (and quoted) Lauterpacht's 1948 treatise.

THE DEMISE OF RECOGNITION OF GOVERNMENTS

Limiting recognition to the state rather than to the state's government was well established by 1948. Beginning in 1907, questioning the right of *de facto* governments in Central America to be recognized, the Tobar Doctrine brought changes in recognition policy for many states. Carlos Tobar, then Minister of Foreign Affairs in Ecuador, suggested to the Bolivian consul in Brussels: 'the American Republics ... should intervene in an indirect way in the internal

dissentions of the republics of the continent. This intervention might consist...
in the non-recognition of *de facto* governments which have come into power by
revolution against the Constitution.'[38] The Central American republics codified
the Tobar Doctrine in 1907 and again in 1923.[39] *Tobar* was conveniently applied
'particularly by the United States in Central America to protect American
interests in or near the Panama Canal'.[40]

With the academic use of the term 'self-determination'[41] as a guidepost for
managing change in the state system after the First World War, the Tobar
Doctrine eventually led to an extremely flexible approach in the recognition of
governments. In an arbitration decision between Britain and Costa Rica in 1923,
US Chief Justice (and former President) William Howard Taft (the sole
arbitrator), found the short-lived government of Federico Tinoco in Costa Rica,
between 1917 and 1919 to be 'an actual sovereign government' even though the
'leading powers of the day' refused to recognized Tinoco's government *de facto*
or *de jure*.

> The non-recognition by other nations of a government claiming to be a
> national personality is usually appropriate evidence that it has not attained
> the independence and control entitling it by international law to be classed
> as such. But when recognition *vel non* of a government is by such nations
> determined by inquiry, not into its *de facto* sovereignty and complete
> governmental control, but into its illegitimacy or irregularity of origin,
> then non-recognition loses something of evidential weight on the issue
> with which those applying the rules of international law are alone
> concerned... The question is, has [the government] really established
> itself in such a way that all within its influence recognize its control, and
> that there is no opposing force assuming to be a government in its place?
> Is it discharging its functions as a government usually does, respected with
> its own jurisdiction?[42]

Prompted by the irregularity of the United States' decision for non-recognition toward the Soviet Union, many scholars saw Taft's decision as an indication
of the waning usefulness of recognizing *de facto* regimes rather than the state
itself. However, the United States stood firm in its policy toward the Soviet
Union until 1933. In the meantime, Foreign Secretary Estrada of Mexico
contributed to the demise of recognition for governments in 1930 by stating that
in order to avoid the 'insulting practice' of pronouncing judgement on the right
of other states to maintain or replace their governments, the government of
Mexico would no longer give grants or denials of recognition of governments.
Instead, the government of Mexico would limit itself 'to the maintenance or
withdrawal, as it may deem advisable, of its diplomatic agents, and to the
continued acceptance, also when it may deem advisable, of such similar
accredited diplomatic agents as the respective nations may have in Mexico'.[43]
The Estrada Doctrine simplified recognition considerably. Individual state

practice eventually accepted the concept of *Estrada*, although many governments still do not refer to the policy in those terms. As a consequence, the idea of recognizing governments has virtually disappeared in diplomatic relations. Instead, foreign departments withdraw diplomatic representatives from states to show disapproval of governments or government actions.

NON-RECOGNITION AS A FOREIGN POLICY

In Ireland's foreign policy practice during the period 1949–63, overt non-recognition is used in three specific cases – Israel, East Germany and China. Each of these cases contained a different rationale for non-recognition. The complexities of recognition problems will be discussed in the following chapters. The purpose here is to discuss the general rationale for applying non-recognition as a foreign policy.

Oppenheim's International Law describes the principle of non-recognition as 'hesitant and incomplete' in solving recognition problems.[44] Von Glahn argued that non-recognition has evolved to represent an 'effective method of intervening in a country's internal affairs, without violating, technically, the duty of non-intervention'.[45] Burns Weston argued that 'non-recognition would be an indication of severe disapproval'.[46] Non-recognition as a principle of international law falls between jurisprudence and political realities, echoing the problems found in *de facto* and *de jure* usage in policy formulation.

Since 1945 the definition of what constitutes non-recognition has changed as a result of state practice. Many states delay recognition decisions and over time, non-recognition becomes the policy by default. Non-recognition is difficult in a legal sense. On the one hand, the principle of *ex injuria jus non oritur* prevails (an illegality cannot become a source of legal right to the wrongdoer). If a state comes into existence through illegal or unconstitutional means, the fact that it eventually qualifies as a state does not mean other states are obliged to recognize it, and non-recognition may be justified, even though violating international legal principles. On the other hand, *ex factis jus oritur* (law is a product of social reality) is used to justify foreign policy conduct, which might be *prima facie* illegal. These principles are not opposites; the latter may flow out of the former to adjust to international realities or individual state interests. For example, the establishment of East Germany as a satellite state under the USSR in 1949, and its recognition by West Germany and the international community in 1972, seems to turn the concept of *ex injuria jus non oritur* on its head.

Lauterpacht argued that although illegal conduct may inevitably change international law, it does not necessarily contribute to strengthening international law.

International law, being weak law, is fully exposed to the impact of the phenomenon to which jurists have referred to as the 'law-creating influence of facts'. But unless law is to become a convenient code for malefactors, it must steer a middle course between the law-creating influence of acts and the principle, which is the essence of law, that its validity is impervious to individual acts of lawlessness. Law is a body of rules operating under the aegis of a system of force actually operative in society. This does not mean that all branches of the law, if successful, become part of the legal order. A balance must be achieved somewhere. It cannot be found in the immediate validation of the illegal act; it must be sought in considerations of a general nature, which would justify the legislator in incorporating the result of the illegality as part of the law.[47]

Lauterpacht admitted that 'a provisional balance may be found, in the international sphere, in *de facto* recognition combining the necessities of international intercourse with the maintenance of an essential legal principle'.[48] Essentially, *de facto* and non-recognition had the same impact on diplomatic relations. Other authors, writing after Lauterpacht, understood non-recognition to imply something beyond the acceptance of a state *de facto*. Jennings and Watts explained that since the development in the twentieth century of international laws proscribing war as an instrument of foreign policy, non-recognition is often used as a political tool to show disapproval.[49] Similarly, Chen found that 'non-recognition [may] be used as a legal tool which might replace war and other similar retaliatory measures'.[50]

The United States' position toward the Japanese conquest of Manchuria in 1931 is an example of non-recognition used to discourage 'the fruit of illegal conduct'.[51] In 1947 author Robert Langer examined non-recognition as found in the Stimson Doctrine. Langer concluded that if a state chooses to apply a doctrine of non-recognition toward a state which it believes has come into existence illegally, the non-recognizing state does so at its own peril.[52] First, a state must answer to problems encountered in 'diplomatic and consular representation and have international agreements', which fall into the realm of external affairs.[53] Second, a state must deal with situations, which arise domestically concerning the non-recognized state – personal status, property and the 'validity of acts effected by, or under the authority of, the dispossessing sovereign'.[54] Although Langer specifically addressed the Stimson Doctrine, the effects of non-recognition as an active foreign policy may be found in Ireland's practice toward Israel from 1949–63.

In the 1950s the Federal Republic of Germany, to prevent or delay the acceptance of East Germany into the international sphere, applied non-recognition through doctrinal practice. The Hallstein Doctrine (1955) threatened the suspension of relations with any state that recognized East Germany as sovereign. Although this policy will be discussed at length in Chapter 4, the doctrinaire approach to non-recognition established by *Hallstein* provided further evidence that diplomatic recognition had evolved into a convenient political tool of foreign affairs. The concept of non-recognition, used in a practical sense by larger states such as Germany and the United States, effectively undermined the legal principles of diplomatic recognition.

In fact, many jurists began to wonder if express diplomatic recognition ought to be abolished altogether. In 1953 the Inter-American Council of Jurists submitted a report advocating the abolishment of the practice on the grounds that it violated principles of non-intervention. The council found:

> The circumstance that, quite frequently, recognition has been used in the American Continent as a means of coercion, has sometimes led to the thought of the advantage of abolishing the institution itself, on the grounds that the act of recognition or non-recognition actually constitutes an overt intervention by one State in the internal affairs of another.[55]

In 1956, Thomas and Thomas countered the negative approach of abolishing recognition altogether, saying that if enough legal grounds may be found for granting or refusing to grant recognition, then intervention is not an issue.[56] Admittedly they found that 'confusion, misinterpretation, misunderstanding, contradiction between words and deeds dot the landscape of recognition'.[57]

By the 1960s, scholars had turned from the issue of non-recognition as intervention toward the effects of non-recognition on more specific, technical areas of international legal relations. In 1968, B.R. Bot addressed the principle of non-recognition in treaty relations. Using the case studies of East Germany and China, he found that 'unrecognized states and governments often abrogate existing treaties according to criteria that are not always acceptable to third parties'.[58] More importantly, Bot provided a definition for what diplomatic recognition provides in the relationship between states: '[recognition] opens the way to negotiations in order to decide by common agreement which categories of treaties can be considered annulled as a result of the changed situation'.[59] As Bot's analysis focused on the technical aspects of applying the principles of diplomatic relations, his work demonstrated how the academic study of non-recognition had changed in the late 1960s, moving beyond ideological issues and Lauterpacht's normative approach into more practical applications.

Also in 1968, Max Sørensen provided a broad explanation of the effects of non-recognition. He concluded that 'the principle of non-recognition has been criticized chiefly on the ground that it is ineffective as a sanction'.[60]

> [That] the refusal to recognize can be used in the role of a sanction in cases where the act or situation in question is contrary to international law is of dubious legality. When recognition of the situation or act is withheld, such an act or situation becomes a standing illegality before the courts of the states withholding recognition. It is therefore suggested that the greater the number of members of the community of states that withhold recognition in such a case, the greater the chance of ensuring that such an act or situation will remain illegal unless the delinquent state agrees to rectify it.[61]

One may argue that non-recognition as a foreign policy tool was used to a large extent in the beginning of the Cold War, but increasingly subsided from international practice throughout the third quarter of the twentieth century, with the exception of the United States' attitude toward the People's Republic of China from 1949 until 1979.

In 1972 Gene T. Hsiao examined another practical area of international affairs affected by non-recognition of states – international trade.[62] Hsiao highlighted the contradictions of trade with a non-recognized state. In studying Sino-Japanese trade agreements, he found that in each negotiation for trade, 'China sought to maximize its potential for implicit diplomatic recognition, and Japan sought to minimize that potential'.[63] In spite of a policy of non-recognition in the diplomatic sphere, by 1972 China had become Japan's leading trade partner. Hsiao noted that 'interstate trade demands orderly arrangements for transactions, mutual concessions in matters relating to national sovereignty – such as the freedom of entry, travel, and residence, and other pertinent rights of individual traders in the receiving state'.[64] The result of non-recognition is that when trade occurs in spite of foreign policy, 'it denies to mutually unrecognized states the possibility of making legal transactions and thereby deprives the traders of both states the usual legal protections'.[65] In this study, one will note that trade existed between Ireland and the states it did not recognize, allowing the risks to be taken by businesses and individuals who would have no recourse to Irish courts in the event of a dispute with the non-recognized state.

P.K. Menon wrote the most recent comprehensive treatise on diplomatic recognition in international law in 1994. In chapter 7 of his work, Menon provided the following definition: 'non-recognition is the absence of recognition; it is the negative condition wherever the positive procedures do not exist for whatever reason'.[66] Menon found that non-recognition is 'a kind of sanction or pressure' which 'is dictated more on the ground of policy and political expediency than the assessment of existing facts'.[67] In the current international political environment, diplomatic recognition perhaps has become obsolete, even when used as a tool in foreign policy, although the proponents for the states of Taiwan and Palestine wholeheartedly disagree. Because recognition of a state is seen as permanent and irrevocable, other recognizing states undertake decisions in an earnest manner. Seen as antiquated in the current practice of withdrawing diplomats from rogue governments, one author has argued that diplomatic recognition should be abolished as a concept.[68] Most recently, another author from Oxford University has examined recognition of governments once again.[69] Clearly, the interest in diplomatic recognition as a historical subject is considerable. In contemporary foreign policy, the recent disturbances in the Middle East demonstrate that the issue of recognition is still viable in world politics.

In the period of this study, recognition of states played a large role in foreign policy decision-making. Not only were territories being reorganized in a bipolar framework, east versus west and communist versus capitalist, but also the policy of decolonization generated many recognition problems. Upon reviewing the documents concerning recognition in the National Archives, one is acutely aware of the large amount of time spent on diplomatic recognition issues with the Department of External Affairs. The following chapters will show how officials in the various government departments responded to recognition problems, navigating the frenetic relationship between policy and law, while actively pursuing the ephemeral foreign policy interests of Ireland in an often uninterested (but unforgiving) bipolar system of states between 1949–63.

NOTES

1   W. Michael Reisman and Eisuke Suzuki, 'Recognition and social change in international law: a prologue for decisionmaking', in W. Michael Reisman and Burns H. Weston, eds, *Toward World Order and Human Dignity* (New York, 1976), p. 414.

2   See Dermot Keogh, *Ireland and Europe 1919–1989: A Diplomatic and Political History* (Cork, 1990), p. 286.

3   Taoiseach Eamon de Valera had dismissed Fine Gael's former leader, General Eoin McDuffy, from his post as Commissioner of the police force, Garda Síochána. In 1933, O'Duffy became the leader of the 'Blueshirts', or the Army Comrades Association, a group supporting the aims of Mussolini's theory of the corporate state. With support from the Catholic hierarchy, O'Duffy raised enough funds to support 700 of his Irish troops to Spain where they quarrelled with Spanish officers, engaged in an episode of friendly fire, and 'returned to Dublin in a welter of acrimony and recrimination'. Dermot Keogh, *Twentieth-century Ireland: Nation and State* (Dublin, 1994), p. 95. See also Keogh, *Ireland and Europe*, pp. 63–97.

4   Keogh, *Ireland and Europe*, p. 72.

5   Antony Beevor, *The Spanish Civil War* (London, 1999), p. 110.

6   Keogh, *Ireland and Europe*, p. 67.

7   Keogh, *Twentieth-century Ireland*, p. 96.

8   George F. Kennan, 'Diplomacy in the modern world', in John A. Vasquez, ed., *Classics of International Relations* (Upper Saddle River, NJ, 3rd edn, 1996), p. 28.

9   Kennan, 'Diplomacy in the modern world', p. 30.

10   From Jonathan Swift's *Gulliver's Travels* (1726) from Part 1, 'A Voyage to Lilliput', in M.H. Abrams *et al.*, eds, *The Norton Anthology of English Literature*, Vol. 1 (New York, 1986).

11   Robert Jennings and Arthur Watts, eds, *Oppenheim's International Law* (Harlow, 9th edn, 1992), p. 127.

12   See AJIL Supp 203 (1931) for the English translation of Foreign Secretary Estrada's press statement made on behalf of the Mexican government on 27 September 1930.

13   Convention on the Rights and Duties of States, Done at Montevideo, 26 December 1933, 165 LNTS 19. Burns H. Weston *et al. Basic Documents in International Law and World Order* (St Paul, MN, 2nd edn, 1990), p. 12.

14   Sixteen states, including the United States and several states in Central and South America, eventually ratified the Montevideo Convention. The treaty was entered into force on 26 December 1934.

15   Clive R. Symmons, 'Irish policy and practice on recognition', *Irish Jurist*, 28, 175 (1995), pp. 175–99. Symmons' research was based exclusively on Dáil Debates and Irish Supreme Court reports.

16   Symmons, 'Irish policy and practice on recognition', p. 175.

17   Ibid., p. 199.

18   Ibid., p. 178.

19   *Carl Zeiss Stiftung* v. *VEB Carl Zeiss Jena* (1970), 61 ILR 36 citing 433 F. 2d 686 (1970).
20   Symmons, 'Irish policy and practice on recognition', p. 175.
21   Rudolf Dolzer *et al.* eds, *Encyclopedia of Public International Law* (Amsterdam, 1987), pp. 529–30.
22   10 *Encyclopedia of International Law* (1987), pp. 340–47 in Burns H. Weston *et al.*, *International Law and World Order*, 2nd edn (St Paul, MN 1990), p. 845.
23   Jennings and Watts, eds, *Oppenheim's International Law*, pp. 154–5.
24   J.L. Brierly, *The Law of Nations: An Introduction to the International Law of Peace* (Oxford, 6th edn, 1963), pp. 146–7.
25   Ibid.
26   Ibid.
27   J.T. Abdy, *Kent's Commentary on International Law* (Cambridge, 1878), p. 95.
28   Taylor Cole, *The Recognition Policy of the United States Since 1901* (Baton Rouge, LA, 1928), p. 4.
29   For example, see Stephen D. Krasner, 'Making peace agreements work: the implementation and enforcement of peace agreements between sovereigns and intermediate sovereigns', *Cornell Int'l. L. J. 30*, 651 (1997).
30   John Hervey, *The Legal Effects of Recognition in International Law* (Philadelphia, PA, 1928), p. 11.
31   Louis L. Jaffe, *Judicial Aspects of Foreign Relations: In Particular of the Recognition of Foreign Powers* (Cambridge, MA, 1933), p. 122.
32   John Lewis Gaddis, *Russia, the Soviet Union, and the United States: An Interpretive History* (New York, 1978), pp. 93–4.
33   Lauterpacht, *Recognition in International Law*, p. 3.
34   Ibid., p. 4.
35   Ibid., p. 5.
36   Ibid, p. 6.
37   Robert Langer, *Seizure of Territory: The Stimson Doctrine and Related Principles in Legal Theory and Diplomatic Practice* (Princeton, NJ, 1947).
38   Inter-American Council of Jurists, *Recognition of* De Facto *Governments* (Washington, DC, 1953), p. 10.
39   Ibid.
40   Weston, *et al.*, *International Law and World Order*, p. 854.
41   The word *self-determination* was in limited usage as early as 1911. Lloyd George referred to 'all principles of self-determination' in his statement of war aims in January 1918. Woodrow Wilson did not use the term *per se* in his Fourteen Points speech on 8 January 1918, but employed the concept in his Four Principles speech on 11 February 1918: 'National aspirations must be respected: peoples may now be dominated and governed only by their own consent. "Self-determination" is not a mere phrase. It is an imperative principle of action which statesmen will henceforth ignore at their peril.' Martin Wight, *Systems of States* (Leicester, 1977), p. 161.
42   Arbitration Between Great Britain and Costa Rica (Tinoco Case), [1923], 18 AJIL 147 (1924) in Weston *et al.*, *International Law and World Order*, pp. 851–3.
43   Press statement of 27 September 1930, translated in 25 AJIL Supp. 203 (1931) in Weston *et al.*, *International Law and World Order*, pp. 854–5. For analysis of the reaction in Central and South America, see the Instituto American de Derecho y Legislacion Comparada, *La Opinion Universal sobre La Doctrine Estrada* (Mexico, 1931). Although the United States adopted *Estrada* with its recognition of the USSR in 1933, the United Kingdom and other European states have generally adopted the principles of Estrada, and state practice has evolved to include only recognition of states. For an analysis of contemporary British practice, see Colin Warbrick, 'The new British policy on recognition of governments', *International and Comparative Law Quarterly*, 30 (July 1981), pp. 568–92.
44   Jennings and Watts, eds, *Oppenheim's International Law*, p. 184.

45   Gerhard von Glahn, *Law Among Nations: An Introduction to Public International Law*, (New York, 5th edn, 1986), p. 93.
46   Weston, *et al.*, *International Law and World Order*, p. 856.
47   Sir Hersch Lauterpacht, 'Recognition of states in international law', *Yale Law Journal*, 53, 3 (1944), p. 427.
48   Ibid.
49   Jennings and Watts, eds, *Oppenheim's International Law*, p. 185.
50   Ti-Chang Chen, *The International Law of Recognition: With Special Reference to Practice in Great Britain and the United States* (London, 1951), p. 26.
51   Ibid., p. 27.
52   Langer, *Seizure of Territory*, p. 101.
53   Ibid.
54   Ibid.
55   Inter-American Council of Jurists, *Recognition of De Facto Governments*, p. 10.
56   Ann Van Wynen Thomas and A.J. Thomas, Jr., *Non-intervention, The Law and its Import in the Americas* (Dallas, TX, 1956).
57   Ibid., p. 245.
58   B.R. Bot, *Nonrecognition and Treaty Relations* (Dobbs Ferry, NY, 1968), p. 278.
59   Ibid.
60   Max Sørensen, ed., *Manual of Public International Law* (London, 1968), p. 279.
61   Ibid., p. 278.
62   Gene T. Hsiao, 'Nonrecognition and trade: a case study of the Fourth Sino-Japanese Trade Agreement', Lin Gene T. Hsias, ed., *Asian Studies: Occasional Paper Series* (Edwardsville, IL, 1973).
63   Ibid., p. 24.
64   Ibid., p. 3.
65   Ibid., pp. 3–4.
66   P.K. Menon, *The Law of Recognition in International Law: Basic Principles* (Lewiston, NY, 1994), p. 221.
67   Ibid..
68   L. Thomas Galloway, *Recognizing Foreign Governments: The Practice of the United States* (Washington, DC, 1978).
69   See Stefan Talmon, *Recognition of Governments in International Law: With Particular Reference to Governments in Exile* (Oxford, 1998).

2

Ireland in the world system, 1949–63

The *principle* characteristic of the period before the twentieth century was the absence of a necessary relationship between the economic theory of a nation and that nation's position in the pattern of international power. This explains how a nation as small as Sweden was able to acquire the rank of a great power in the seventeenth century... When coercive dimensions in the power of a nation begin to depend more and more on its economic stature and are allied with technological advancement, the process of differentiation between the nations that distinguishes the actual system of international stratification is initiated. [emphasis added]

> Gustavo Lagos, *International Stratification and Underdeveloped Countries*[1]

The proper usage of the term 'independence' is to denote the status of a state which controls its own external relations without dictation from other states... 'independence' does not mean freedom from law but merely *freedom from control by other states*.

> J.L. Brierly, *The Law of Nations*[2]

THE TERM 'PRINCIPLE' IN IRISH FOREIGN POLICY

A conventional argument in explaining Irish foreign policy behaviour during the period of this study would emphasize the overly reactive nature of policy-making to the influences of other states, or an Irish foreign policy lacking a clear sense of principle. For the decision-makers in Ireland, principle was not the issue. Instead, Ireland lacked an effective mechanism to pursue its strategic international interests, including ending partition, maintaining neutrality, ending protectionism and building prestige in the world system. Describing this failure in terms of *principle* is problematic due to the various meanings of the word. A *principle* may be a basic truth; or it may be a standard of either a legal or ethical nature; or it may mean a predetermined policy inciting a mode of action. In Irish foreign policy decision-making, it may be argued that the meaning of *principle* is derived from two 'modes of action'. First, decisions that required tactical measures in the daily running of government were based on practical standards of behaviour or *principles*. For example, routine issues which occurred frequently were evaluated in an expeditious manner, and decisions were made relying on tactical principles. During the period of this study, the Department of External Affairs was certainly organized in handling the daily tasks of foreign policy.

The second distinct meaning of *principle* occurs in a strategic framework. In this context *principle* takes an additional meaning – the ability to formulate foreign policies based on long-term goals, or the effectiveness in using principles to achieve the national interest. Because the national interests of Ireland during the period 1949–63 were varied and impossible to achieve in the short-term, it is convenient (but inaccurate) to define foreign policy behaviour as *unprincipled*.

Distinguishing the term *interest*

Interests may be defined as the *goals* a state pursues at a specific period in time. These goals may be domestic or foreign pursuits, but they are generally prophylactic measures, protecting values at home or the state's practical interests abroad. In the domestic context of western European states since the 1700s, *national interest* generally refers to the protection of the individuals within society, relying on the core Enlightenment values of life, liberty and property. Interests abroad, or *international interests*, protect the basic components of statehood – territory, population, sovereignty among other states and governance – from interference by outside threats. Interests may include an ideological component, in both the domestic and foreign context, and may be seen as *offensive* or proactive in nature. The interests of other states ultimately delimit a particular state's interests.

Interests may be defined differently in any given situation. They are illusive and transitory, defying lasting definition in any sense. Hans J. Morgenthau, the quintessential realist of the twentieth century, wrote that the *survival* of a political unit (the state) is the 'irreducible minimum' of national interest.[3] In defining Ireland's international interests between the years 1949–63, perhaps the word *survival* was the key to foreign policy decision-making.

The foreign policy decision-makers in Ireland often had difficulty in articulating Irish national interests to other states. For a system engaged in bipolar struggle, small or weak states such as Ireland, acting unilaterally, virtually had no voice. Ireland's representation abroad was only beginning to materialize in the 1940s and 1950s. In the forum of the Council of Europe, or later at the United Nations, the ghostly mutterings of Daniel O'Connell might have been heard when Irish leaders introduced Irish self-interested issues: 'I shall be as brief as I can upon this subject, for it is quite clear, that no man ever yet rose to address a more unwilling audience.'[4] The audiences at international forums during the first years of statehood were not interested in solving the partition dilemma, a fact that Seán MacBride learned the hard way at the

Council of Europe in 1949–50. 'MacBride duly banged the anti-partition drum... [The] Irish insistence on making partition a European issue found little sympathy among continentals who regarded Britain as their liberator from real tyranny... The Americans showed equally little concern.'[5]

THE OPERATING ENVIRONMENT

In studying characteristics of Ireland's stratification within the international system of states, the constraints of a 'small' state become apparent. The rationale for using a systems approach in studying foreign policy behaviour is to distinguish between the possible and the impossible. While a state has certain freedoms as an independent actor within the system, other factors project an opposing force, limiting manoeuverability. Kenneth Waltz (1979) suggested that foreign policy behaviour must be examined in terms of the state's 'operating environment', a combination of external and internal influences and constraints. The external environment concerns the dependent actions of states, while the internal environment considers the factors within the administrative functioning of government, including the state's 'psychological environment'.[6] This chapter borrows from the operational analysis in describing Ireland's position in the world system from 1949–63.

> The external environment (external structure)... has to do with the ways in which states are dependent upon one another. It relates to such matters as: the degree of polarity in the international system, the degree of stability, the extent of the division of labour, the state of technology... The internal environment (internal structure)... refers to the properties of the state itself: its power, its geographical position, the amount of available resources, the extent to which these resources may be mobilized... In a systemic approach of this kind, which is also employed by Theda Skocpol, 'states necessarily stand out at the intersections between domestic socio-political orders and the transnational relations within which they must maneuver for survival and advantage in relation to other states'... Waltz considers the psychological environment [referring to the adaptability of a state]... in other words, the extent to which changes are possible in a state's behavioural repertoire. In particular, it relates to the way in which a state processes information about its environment, the quality of 'theories' it has at its disposal, and its capacity for collective decision making.[7]

The predominant external force that affected Ireland's economic development and position within the world system was the liberalization of trade. A secondary force was the tension created for an anti-communist neutral in the bipolar system of the Cold War. From a psychological point of view, the *perception* by foreign policy leaders of Ireland's relative position in the world system was critical in evaluating issues and setting policy.

Liberalization of trade

After 1945, Ireland attempted to liberalize trade policies and to participate more openly in the world market. The changes were incremental and hampered by de Valera's Fianna Fáil policy of market protection in an ever-increasing liberal trading environment. One effect of the post-war Bretton Woods economic system was to further differentiate the economic capabilities of states in the capitalist world. The *haves* were clearly separated from the *have-nots*. For Ireland, with few natural resources and the legacy of protectionism, this often meant ingratiating itself to the hegemonic system. The terms *core* and *periphery*, popular in international relations theory through the work of Johan Galtung[8] and others, clearly define Ireland's position relative to other capitalist economies after the Second World War.

> This process of uneven growth among national economies in a liberal world economy results in an increasing economic and political differentiation of states and creates an international hierarchy of wealth, power, and dependency relations among emergent core economies and periphery economies dependent upon the former for the major sources of their growth. Powerful nationalistic reactions are stimulated as new centers of economic growth arise and other economies decline. Individual states and economic interests attempt to counter and channel the operation of economic forces.[9]

After sixteen years of de Valera's protectionism the inter-party government of 1948 attempted to bring Ireland into the world economic system by initiating more trading relationships with states other than Britain. Although the system of protectionism was not dismantled until the late 1950s under the guidance of Seán Lemass and T.K. Whitaker,[10] the composition of export destinations changed considerably after 1948. Exports to Germany grew 528 per cent from 1948–49, while exports to the United States and India increased by 291 per cent and 356 per cent respectively. In contrast, exports to Britain increased by a modest 25 per cent in the same period.[11] The pace of free trade increased under Costello's inter-party government, but protectionist policies continued to exist. Robert Gilpin explained why newly independent states cling to economic nationalism:

> In effect, economic nationalism arises in the periphery as a protective measure against those market forces that first concentrate wealth and then divide the international economy into advanced core and dependent periphery. Economic nationalism reflects the desire of the periphery to possess and control an independent industrial core in which wealth, attractive careers, and power are located. Its objective is to transform the international division of labor through industrialization and to transform the peripheral nation into a relatively independent industrial core.[12]

Ireland's status as *periphery* to Britain's *core*, used in this sense to mean the extent of dependence on Britain for Irish imports and exports, was a stumbling block to the liberalization of trade. In 1951 a study was commissioned by the Irish government in order to 'chart the industrial potential of Ireland'.[13] The IBEC Technical Services Corporation in New York conducted the study, in conjunction with the new Irish Development Authority (IDA). The resulting report met with an unfortunate consequence in timing. Presented in 1952, the report appeared after the first inter-party government had already left office and Fianna Fáil was back in power. The report stated in part:

> That the degree of Ireland's economic linkage with the United Kingdom is greater than is consistent with her status of political sovereignty, and that both her stability and her opportunities for economic growth will be forwarded through the taking of progressive measures to broaden her area of trade ... there runs an undercurrent of pessimism or lack of confidence in the prospects for achieving the pronounced aims. The talk is of economic expansion, but the action of Government, business, and labor alike is too often along the lines of consolidating present positions rather than of accepting the hazards inherent in changed practices upon which expansion depends. There are few evidences of boldness or assurance in economic behaviour to give substance to expressed economic aims. In fact, the declarations of expansive purpose are frequently qualified by expressions of a conflicting, anti-materialist philosophy, of an asceticism that opposes material aspirations to spiritual goals, and hence writes down the former as untrustworthy.[14]

The report concluded with the following recommendation: 'The first need in Ireland's economic programming is for a clarification of aims, and for a confident and wholehearted commitment to their fulfillment'.[15] The report expressed the dangers facing Ireland in confronting the economic dilemma, as well as highlighting the risks involved in moving toward a liberalization of the Irish economic system. Without natural resources, military capabilities and diversified trading partners, Ireland's 'relative power' was minute. Rather than strengthening Ireland's position, liberalization of trade in the world system had the effect of emphasizing Ireland's weaknesses. The one escape mechanism available to bring the economy out of its paralytic state was foreign trade, and not simply increased trade with Britain.

BIPOLARIZATION OF THE SYSTEM AND NEUTRALITY

The second feature of the world system that had a profound effect on Ireland's progress in the area of foreign relations was the bipolarization of the system in military and political terms. The advent of the Cold War forced Ireland to continue its wartime stance of benevolent neutrality as a security measure.

Neutral posturing, of course, was advanced through the dogmatic policy statements of de Valera. In a speech produced for the St Patrick's Day broadcast in the United States (1946), de Valera said:

> I am glad to be back again with you on the old terms of freedom. How often during the terrible years that have intervened have I wished that I could speak to you as I am speaking now. For there were those who during these years would have us here in Ireland believe that by our neutrality we had lost American goodwill and alienated the sympathy of our American friends. I have never believed that that could be so. I could never imagine the American friends that I knew expecting us to do what they themselves in similar circumstances would not dream of doing.[16]

De Valera continued by rationalizing Ireland's position through the difficulties of a 'small' state during conflict.

> It is not pleasant to be taunted with ingratitude as we were ... When a small nation engages in a modern war, it runs risks far beyond any incurred by a great power. Great powers, if they lose, may hope somehow to survive, but, if a small state is on the losing side, it can be utterly annihilated. If, on the other hand, a small state is on the winning side, it has no means of insisting that the principles for which it fought and risked everything be put into effect ... A small nation is thus likely to lose both ways.[17]

De Valera had no difficulty in providing the 'underdog' argument when necessary. In 1948, while on a tour of the United States with Frank Aiken, 'with the purpose of explaining the partition issue and Irish neutrality in World War II to the American public',[18] de Valera repeated the argument on the difference in the outcome of warfare for a small state and a great power. He encountered considerable resistance from the American press.

> Speaking to American audiences, Eamon de Valera has defended Eire's neutrality during the war by pointing out that the United States did not fight until attacked ... That is true. Neither the United States nor the Soviet Union fought until they were attacked, and it was not until they were forced into the war that they considered neutrality a crime. The only nations on the Allies' side which fought without waiting to be attacked were those of the British Empire – including Northern Ireland – and France. Eire has the distinction of being the only State in the Empire which refused to fight ... That he would advocate neutrality in future, Mr. de Valera made plain in Washington. Speaking on the proposed union of states in Western Europe, he said Eire's participation would depend on the extent of her obligation to go to war, adding that, if a small State was on the losing side of the war, it was wiped out of existence, while, if it was on

the winning side, it had little hope that the objects for which it fought would be attained.[19]

After 1946 de Valera did not change his rationale for neutrality. The principles of neutrality that de Valera advocated, however, were not necessarily principles of international law.[20] Other states in the system, namely Switzerland and Austria, were guaranteed neutral status by outside powers.[21] Still other states, such as Sweden and Norway, were neutral but armed. Ireland presented a very different case with its self-imposed, unarmed neutrality. Specific conflicts regarding neutrality issues will be discussed in the following sections of this chapter, but here it should be noted that the intensity of the conflict created by the bipolarization of the state system meant that Ireland had difficulty in earning any level of esteem from other states. Trying to earn respect translated into foreign policies that were aimed at increasing prestige and influence within the system. These efforts were satisfying psychologically but did not solve the underlying problem of Ireland's peripheral status.[22]

PERCEPTION OF RELATIVE POSITION WITHIN THE SYSTEM

Another effect of bipolarization of the world system was the tendency of scholars and practitioners to categorize states in absolute terms, as in the core/periphery analysis above. Terms such as strong/weak, rich/poor, north/south, east/west, large/small, and capitalist/communist were easily and frequently applied to various states after the Second World War. Foreign policy-makers in Ireland, no matter the reality of the situation, resisted most of this terminology while relying on the elusiveness of *perception* in describing the Irish state within the system. As Dermot Keogh wrote in *Ireland and Europe 1919–1989*, the first inter-party government of independent Ireland (with John A. Costello as Taoiseach and Seán MacBride as Minister for External Affairs) had a 'rather inflated view of Ireland's potential role in international politics'.[23] Costello, during a visit to Canada in September 1948 (when he confirmed that Ireland would repeal the External Relations Act of 1936 and declare the Republic of Ireland), proposed the following:

> [Though] a small nation [Ireland] wields an influence in the world far in excess of what its mere physical size and the smallness of its population might warrant ... We are sometimes accused of acting as if we were a big nation. In fact we are ... Our exiles who have gone to practically every part in the world have created for their motherland a spiritual dominion which more than compensated for her lack of size or material wealth.[24]

Costello's statement reflected the oppressive influence of the bipolarized world on a small English-speaking state totally dependent on a few limited trading relationships.[25] The perception by Irish politicians that Ireland wielded influence far greater than its borders did not always approach the reality of the situation.[26] For example, Small and Singer (1973) measured the 'diplomatic importance of states'.[27] Their purpose was to determine the 'relative importance of each state ... to others in the system during the half-decade' for the periods 1950–70.[28] Small and Singer's indicator was 'what percentage of the rest of the system's members have established bonds [through missions]' with a particular state.[29] In 1950 Ireland received fourteen missions, not including the Apostolic Nunicature of the Holy See.[30] For 1950, Ireland ranked sixtieth out of 75 states, in the twentieth percentile; in 1955, Ireland was sixty-eighth of 84 states, still in the twentieth percentile. By 1960 Ireland's position changed to seventy-fourth of 89, or the seventeenth percentile. In 1965, the score hit a low of eighty-eighth of 93, or the fifth percentile. The last year figuring in the research (1970) showed a marked increase in the number of states in the system due to decolonisation, and Ireland's position improved to 113 out of 133, or the sixteenth percentile. Although Small and Singer's research must be taken as a thumbnail sketch of the relative importance of states, one cannot ignore the low rankings attributed to Ireland. Ireland had come a long way by 1970, however, since the number of missions received in Ireland actually grew from fourteen in 1950 to twenty-four in 1970.[31] Whether real or imagined, the perception by Irish politicians and civil employees of the country's relative position in the world system challenged and propelled foreign policy decision-making in Ireland.

T.B. Millar suggested that in examining a state's foreign policy, one must not examine objective facts but the subjective perception of the leaders. Millar's salient remarks indirectly describe Ireland's foreign policy position:

> There are no immutable or absolute factors in foreign policy. This is what makes writing theoretically about foreign policy so difficult. Perhaps nations ought to determine their policies in accordance with set principle ... Prime Ministers ought to be rational, however that may be judged, but they are not always so. To find the basis for the foreign policy of a country, therefore, it is necessary to ascertain why relevant decisions were actually made. This means looking at the thinking of the people who make the decisions, their image of the world and of their own polity, of finding which facts were factors to them, and how they took them into account. One can no more explain foreign policy from a basis of 'objective' facts than one can explain Shakespeare from the basis of a grammar book.[32]

CHARACTERISTICS OF THE SYSTEM, 1949–63

The reconstruction of Europe after the Second World War was the central concern of the victorious Allied Powers. The policy makers of the two leading powers, the United States and the Soviet Union, had highly divergent views on how the reconstruction task would be completed, and in whose ideological image. The histories of recovery programmes, ideological differences and institutional change in the postwar system need not be repeated here. The results of change, however, affected every state in the system, including Ireland. Using 1949 as a watershed year, the significance for Ireland was the repeal of the External Relations Act of 1936 and the establishment of the Republic of Ireland Act, which solidified Ireland's political independence vis-à-vis Britain.

The year 1949 also marked significant changes going on in Europe including the signing of the North Atlantic Treaty and the formation of the NATO alliance; the creation of the Council of Europe; the founding of the Federal Republic of Germany through the proclamation of the Basic Law or constitution; and the proclamation of the German Democratic Republic by the Soviet Union. For the remainder of the world system, several new states during the period gained independence from their colonial past, including India (1947) and Vietnam (1949). The ideas of self-determination and decolonisation were running in tandem. Mao Zedong declared the People's Republic of China, exiling Chiang Kai-shek and the Nationalist Government to Formosa in 1949. Vishinsky replaced Molotov as Foreign Minister of the USSR; Adenauer became Chancellor of West Germany; and Nehru became Prime Minister of India.

The results of these changes was a new organizational structure of the world system, from Euro-centric to bipolarity. Walter Lippmann, the American journalist frustrated by the US policy of containment toward the Soviet Union, coined the struggle for hegemony in the system as 'the Cold War', a phrase that dominated political terminology for over four decades.[33] For the purpose of this study, the significant aspect of the Cold War was the division of the system into two economic and ideological groups. Bipolarity in the Cold War environment had two meanings: first, it was a shorthand term for the political polarization of states into hostile camps; and second, it described the distribution of power among individual states, specifically in terms of nuclear weapon capability and economic hegemony.[34] Wagner (1993), described the evolution of bipolarity:

> One state, the Soviet Union, [occupied] in peacetime a position of near-dominance on the Eurasian continent, a position that states in the past had been able to achieve only after a series of military victories... At the end of World War II, everyone's expectations of postwar international politics were influenced by the experience of World War I. Most people assumed that, as before, the war would be followed by complex negotiations that would lead to a peace treaty with the defeated countries and a reconstruction of the international system. Nearly a decade passed before it became clear that such a settlement would not take place, but soon after the end of the war it was apparent that disagreements between the U.S. and the Soviet governments about its provisions were much greater than had been anticipated.[35]

Ireland became a victim of this post-war fallout between the United States and the USSR when its application to join the United Nations was vetoed by the Soviet

Union prior to 1955. As explained by Inis Claude, Jr. in *Swords into Plowshares*, '[the situation of frustrated applications] was the result of...a policy of competitive exclusion' on the part of the United States and Soviet Union.[36]

> States desirous of membership fell into two groups: those supported by the Soviet Union, presumably as potential members of the Soviet bloc in the United Nations, which were denied the necessary support of seven members of the Security Council; and those regarded by the Soviet Union as potential adherents to the Western grouping, which were consistently blocked by the Soviet veto.[37]

In a recent study of Ireland at the United Nations from 1955–65, Joseph Skelly argued the point in a similar manner: 'the USSR actually feared that a pro-Western Ireland would dilute its standing in the General Assembly'.[38] Certainly, Ireland was not alone in the centre of the struggle. As will be shown in the case studies in later chapters, the Cold War infiltrated all areas of international politics. Participation or non-participation in bilateral and multilateral treaties depended on who the players were and from what 'camp' they came. Membership in international organizations, such as NATO and the Warsaw Pact, the Organization for European Economic Cooperation (OEEC) or the General Agreement on Tariffs and Trade (GATT), were exclusionary devices to expand one set of state interests at the expense of the other. The United Nations had been organized in the same way. The difficulty for Ireland (neutral but anti-communist) was that it tried to pursue an *independent* path in foreign policy, a path that appeared more erratic than reasoned, almost schizophrenic.[39] In the difficult atmosphere of the early Cold War years, Irish foreign policy objectives existed metaphorically below the level of radar – present but unnoticed in the international political arena.

IRISH FOREIGN POLICY IN THE COLD WAR CONTEXT

The literature on Irish foreign policy written about the postwar period often explains foreign policy behaviour stemming from Ireland's unique position within the system. Terms such as *sui generis*[40] and *ad hoc*[41] describe a foreign policy operating without comprehensive strategy. In almost coded language, R.F. Foster described the Irish position as 'a public foreign policy that was ostentatiously not constricted'.[42] J.J. Lee argued that 'all the successful small states of Europe took care to construct an intellectual infrastructure' in the post-war period. The Irish failed in this respect. 'The Irish', he concluded, 'often gave the impression that they could not understand the concept'.[43] The essence of these statements is that Ireland's foreign policy did not fit the normative rulebooks on what a foreign policy *ought* to be. As a result, it is difficult to classify Ireland's behaviour in bipolar, Cold War terms.

Aside from the difficulty of placing Ireland in any world system category of
the time period, the problem with such brief statements regarding the nature of
Irish foreign policy is that they tend to be descriptive but not explanatory. If
Ireland's foreign policies were not based on principle, were *ad hoc* and not
defined within common state practice, how was Ireland able to pursue this
unique style of diplomacy and policy-making? Further, how did the system of
states *allow* Ireland to pursue such policies? The answers may be found in the
international political and economic environment after the Second World War.
The pressures from overall liberalization of trade, European integration and the
emergence of the Cold War left room for smaller, less influential states to seek
their own level of survival. Hedley Bull argued that 'the Cold War provided the
tolerance of two systems which were at variance in terms of what constituted an
international society'.[44] For a state pursuing an *independent* political and
economic path, surely the same tolerance could be found.

> [When] the Cold War was being prosecuted most vigorously, the United
> States and the Soviet Union were inclined to speak of each other as
> heretics or outcasts beyond the pale, rather than as members of the same
> international society. However, they did not even then break off diplomatic
> relations, withdraw recognition of one another's sovereignty, repudiate the
> idea of common international law or cause the break-up of the United
> Nations into rival organisations. In both the Western and communist blocs
> there were voices raised in favour of compromise, drawing attention to the
> common interests of the two sides in coexistence and restating, in secular
> form, the principle *cuijus regio, eijus religio* that had provided a basis for
> accommodation in the wars of religion.[45]

In other words, just as the Cold War environment demanded survival
strategies from the two superpowers, it also required self-help for states not
directly involved in the conflict. The methods of self-help were as varied as the
states employing them. The Cold War allowed Ireland to set flexible policy on
issues which did not directly affect superpower diplomacy. The difficulty in
self-help for Ireland was that without a tradition of political idealism, and with
the day-to-day pressures of running the government, flexible policy gave the
appearance of unprincipled policy. Often, Irish foreign policy-makers operated
in an environment of *maintaining* the system left by the British, without the
benefit of clear-cut strategic goals, much like ocean navigation bereft of a map.[46]
However, the themes in Irish foreign policy – partition, neutrality, economic
independence and prestige – were the guiding interests of members of the
government involved in foreign relations, especially the Department of External
Affairs.

As J.J. Lee commented in 1989, 'The general assumption in the early days
[until the 1960s] was that as the British civil service came as close to perfection
as the mind of man could devise, Ireland was fortunate in having a service so

closely modeled on the ideal'.[47] From 1938 until 1966 the idea of maintaining the status quo left by British influence continued, virtually unchallenged by members of the civil service. Lee strengthened his argument with specifics:

> Critics made little impression on the carapace of complacency... [Ken] Whitaker would be the first Secretary of Finance to give sustained thought to the quality of civil service performance, as [Seán] Lemass was the first Taoiseach to seriously ponder the subject. Both were cautious reformers. Both knew the strengths as well as the weaknesses of the existing service.[48]

The system of states generally ignored Ireland's *modus operandi* in setting anomalous policy, but eventually certain factions within Ireland did.

In 1966, Taoiseach Seán Lemass established the Public Service Organisation Review Group (PSORG), led by Liam St John Devlin, which studied the overall methods operating in the Irish governmental departments, and reported on the state of Civil Service policy-making in 1969. The *Devlin Report* 'provoked extensive debate. Many civil servants and politicians devoutly wished to see Devlin buried.'[49] The report summed up the failure of Irish governmental policy-making as a whole, the Department of External Affairs included: 'Decision-makers were so involved in the press of daily business that they had little time to participate in the formulation of overall policy.'[50] The report concluded that no discernible principle in foreign policy existed because Ireland had not articulated strategy beyond the point of independence and the ending of partition. As the Bishop of Clonfert was quoted as stating in 1957: 'our version of history has tended to make us think of freedom as an end in itself and of independent government – like marriage in a fairy story – as the solution of all ills'.[51]

The responsibility for foreign policy did not fall solely on the Department of External Affairs, however. The Department of Finance, presumably a key partner in developing foreign trade, often took the conservative line. Ronan Fanning argued that the Department of Finance was forced into setting long-term economic policy as criteria for obtaining Marshall Aid in 1947.

> The focal point of this development was the publication of Ireland's Long-Term Recovery Programme, published as a White Paper in January 1949 at a time, [John A. Murphy] writes, when the Department of Finance was 'apathetic if not hostile, to the idea of economic programming and it is noteworthy that responsibility for producing the White Paper rested with the Department of External Affairs under Seán MacBride and the department's secretary, F.H. Boland'. Although the senior officials most intimately concerned with the preparation of the programmes in the Department of Finance a decade later would consider Professor Murphy's statement to be, at best, an exaggeration – Dr. Whitaker has noted that 'no one who took part in preparing the Recovery Programme (and that includes myself) ever looked on it as a development programme, but rather

as an exercise that had to be undertaken to persuade the Americans to give us Marshall Aid' – it does illustrate how, after 1948, ministers and government officials alike became increasingly concerned with framing a longer-term financial and economic policy than had previously been contemplated. The days of *ad hoc*, year-to-year, financial management were clearly numbered.[52]

Fanning argued, however, that the Department of Finance in the first inter-party government (1948–51) was being overshadowed in international economic matters by a change in the Department of External Affairs under the new leadership of F.H. Boland as Secretary.

Ireland's thwarted application for membership in the United Nations, her participation in the Paris conference on European Economic Co-operation in July 1947, her interest in the Marshall Plan and consequently in stronger diplomatic representation in the United States – were all factors in [the extension of External Affairs' range of activities and influence]. An inspection of Finance's archives... reveals an explosive growth in the volume of its records from 1946–47 onwards and a notable feature of this development is how much of the additional documentation came from the Department of External Affairs. Another index of that department's new power and confidence was its insistence that all negotiations between Irish government departments and their British counterparts should be conducted under its auspices and that the practice of direct negotiation (which has been especially favoured by Finance and by Agriculture) should cease.[53]

The wrangling between the Departments of External Affairs and Finance often meant inconsistent (and sometimes incompatible) policy-making throughout the 1950s. As late as 1964 there was still confusion on whether international trade-related agreements would first have to be approved through External Affairs. In a question involving a bilateral air transport agreement, it was unclear whether the Minister for Transport and Power or the Minister for External Affairs should negotiate the agreement. The Legal Adviser clarified that in terms of multilateral agreements,

the formal submission of matters relating to the ratification or acceptance of, or the accession to, international treaties, conventions and agreements (other than International Labour Conventions) should be made by the Minister for External Affairs, acting on behalf of the Minister who is principally concerned with the subject matter of the particular treaty, convention or agreement.[54]

For bilateral agreements, the legal adviser sheepishly added, 'other Departments (acting, of course, in consultation with the Department of External Affairs) may have direct dealings with outside Government authorities'.[55] Not surprisingly, during the postwar years of reconstruction and development in Europe, politics and economics were often pursued in the same vein.

THE CAPACITY TO ACT

In comparative foreign policy literature, the term *capacity to act* has been used to describe the level of manoeuverability a particular state has in creating and implementing foreign policy.[56] For Ireland, the term is more relevant than the use of 'relative power' or other attempts to quantify a state's capabilities in the system. 'Capacity to act refers to the amount of resources a nation has and its ability to utilize these resources.'[57] The term *resources* used in this context does not refer exclusively to natural physical resources or national attributes but also to the political resources, which a state harnesses to meet its foreign policy objectives. This is particularly true for a state with few natural resources. Ireland, in the period of disassociation with the Commonwealth (1949) until joining the European Economic Community (1973), relied on political and social organization to replace natural resource discrepancies. To other states in the system, however, Ireland's position was barely noticeable.[58] To examine the range of possibilities (and impossibilities) for Ireland at the time, the next three sections will consider the following advantages and constraints in Irish policy-making: the status of a 'small or weak' power; the establishment of bilateral and multilateral treaty relationships; and the association with international organizations.

SMALL AND WEAK POWERS

During the period of this study, those who tried to make sense of the Cold War through academic analysis, particularly international relations scholars, were compelled to sort, classify and label states within the system, for that seemed the best way to measure capability in foreign policy. Policy-makers and intelligence departments during the Cold War also tried to classify particular states. In his book, *Weak States in the International System*, Michael Handel illustrated the absurdity of trying to categorize states based on their size or relative strength within the system. Handel noted:

> Much of the foreign policy behaviour of [states] is based on intuitive evaluations by policy-makers in trying to assess the relative strength and position of the opposition, including judgments of national morale, quality of leadership, scope of interests, organization, and the other states' perception of relative strength.[59]

The forced classification system on states since the Second World War has both facilitated and hindered the effectiveness of comparative analysis. Handel argued that comparison needs a very large set of criteria. For example, he insisted that the system of states be divided into the international power hierarchy – super powers, great powers, middle powers, weak states and mini-states.[60] He distinguishes a *weak* state as one which is not a 'power' at all, but rather a state characterized by a '*lack* of power or strength, and hence [a continuous preoccupation] with the question of survival' in the international system.[61] Ireland, in Handel's analysis, comes very close to being the ideal *weak* state, although he does not examine Ireland closely. Handel describes the problem of classification as follows:

> Ireland is a weak state in absolute terms but has no threatening enemies. Israel's armed forces are large in absolute terms but small in relation to the combined forces of the Arab states. The power of a state is thus best measured not against all other countries, but in relation to its neighbors, and by the degree to which the strength at its disposal matches its national goals and ambitions.[62]

Handel describes the ideal weak state as having a very small population within a very small area. The Irish Republic, with a population no greater than 3.5 million in the post-war period, fits the category of 'small' in most literature. Handel refers to the upper limits of population in the definition of 'small' by listing the classifications of other authors. Masaryk (1962) and Marriott (1943) set limits under 20 million. Barston (1971) set the maximum at 10–15 million. Ten million was the maximum for Kuznets (1960). Handel admits these levels are 'highly artificial' but in the case of Ireland, the point should be made that in any definition of state population, Ireland would be considered 'small'.[63]

The twenty-six counties of the Republic comprise a total area of 27,138 square miles, slightly bigger than Sri Lanka, smaller than Panama and half the size of Florida. Handel's classification of economic characteristics included: a small gross national product (GNP) in absolute terms; little or no heavy industry; a high degree of specialization in a narrow range of products; a small domestic market with high dependency on foreign markets for exports and imports; research and development very low in absolute terms; and a high dependence on foreign capital.[64] Ireland, during the period 1949–63, also fits Handel's economic classification of 'small'.

Although Handel's economic analysis is useful, the present study is not as concerned with economic factors as with Ireland's *political* strength within the system. The question is: on what political strengths was Ireland able to capitalize to counterbalance its economic and military weaknesses? In foreign policy behaviour, Handel's ideal type shows a limited scope of interests (usually to neighbouring and regional areas); has little or no influence on the balance of power (or the nature of the system); is mainly passive and reactive in foreign policy, tends to minimize risks at all costs, especially vis-à-vis the powers; and shows a strong support for international law and international organizations.[65]

Using Handel's analysis, it may be seen that Ireland fits the classification of both a small and a weak state in terms of capability in foreign policy. Other analysts agree that a state's relative position in the world system affects its foreign policy behaviour, setting limitations on policy-making, no matter its aspirations for affecting change otherwise. Sutton, for example, argued that small or weak states have an inherent avoidance of decision making.

> [The] focus of this work is on constraints, which are the presumed consequence of limited resource levels. Foreign policy reflects this by being limited in range and extent. Diplomatic representation is restricted to the places where a small state believes its major external interests lie, these generally being within the immediate geographical area with one or more of the major powers. Much diplomatic activity will be concerned with the search for development assistance, which is often the priority in the foreign policy arena.[66]

Sutton concluded that small size relied on 'a lack of institutionalization within foreign policy', which could allow 'a high degree of personal intervention and an *ad hoc* approach to issues'.[67] The generalizations of Handel and Sutton are one explanation of Ireland's foreign policy behaviour from 1949–63, explaining *ad hoc* actions as a result of Ireland's relatively weak position within the system. Given the limited range of possibilities for decision-making, it is perhaps too demanding to search for strategic decision-making in Irish foreign policy. Clearly, *ad hoc* and *sui generis* seem to apply.

Allowing for Ireland's relative position within the system, flexible decision-making rather than strategic policy certainly apply. The peculiar aspect of Irish decision-making is that even in areas of foreign policy where decisions could be made unhindered, they were not. Decision-making in Ireland during this period was hindered by a lack of confidence on the part of policy-makers. Diplomatic recognition issues could have been streamlined based on particular guiding principles, but they were not. Instead, Ireland relied on the status quo of dependency behaviour found in other aspects of its foreign affairs. As J.J. Lee noted, the inability to set overall policies may have been a 'problem of scale'.[68] Functional departments, facilitating policy simply by categorizing the decision, often make foreign policy decisions in larger states. In Ireland, however, the governmental organization was much smaller and functional departments did not exist to the same degree as in Britain.

Unfortunately, Britain was the model for Ireland, but the political and diplomatic infrastructure simply did not exist in Ireland to establish normative British decision-making. The influence of British thinking in Ireland's approach to decision-making and strategic planning reflected imitation rather than innovation. Professor Lee argued that small states learn by 'doing' rather than 'planning', rendering a state 'rudderless, like a cork on a wave'.[69] The critical factors in early Irish foreign policy, though, were not administrative elegance and streamlined decision-making; the guiding principle to all Irish foreign policy during the late 1940s and 1950s was *survival*.[70]

An area in which Ireland's independence flourished, however, was in the development of bilateral relationships. After the establishment of the Irish Free State in January 1922, under 'obscure constitutional and administrative circumstances',[71] Ireland's involvement with other states in negotiating treaties was limited. Dermot Keogh wrote of the development of Irish diplomatic representation abroad during the early years of the Irish Free State,[72] beginning with de Valera's eighteen-month trip to the United States in 1919–20. De Valera's aim was first, to secure recognition from President Wilson for the Irish Republic, and second, to raise funds for the Republic. Although the United States refused to become overtly involved, de Valera's efforts certainly brought the recognition issue to the attention of the American public. The initial contacts for recognition ranged from Chile and Argentina in South America to Australia and New Zealand, into the United States and Canada, and throughout Europe and into South Africa. 'There was little prospect of gaining recognition for the Irish Government from those countries. It was much more important, however, to win support from members of the Irish diaspora in those parts of the world.'[73]

Although unrecognized as a sovereign, independent state by the international system, as early as 1924 the Irish Free State entered into formal agreements with other states (registered under the Treaty Series of the League of Nations, which Ireland joined in 1923), generally in the area of postal agreements. These treaties were primarily concerned with the exchange of postal money orders under the Universal Postal Union Convention of 1874. The first recorded bilateral treaty with a state other than Britain was with Portugal in 1929 concerning Commerce and Navigation. After the Second World War, Ireland entered the Convention on International Civil Aviation, and developed an Exchange Note series with various states concerning aviation rights. By 1947, Ireland entered negotiations on the Abolition of Visas with France, Belgium, the Netherlands, Italy, Denmark and Switzerland. The first treaty recording the 'Establishment of Diplomatic Relations' was with Argentina in June 1947. Not surprisingly, this initiative caused an increase in trade with Argentina, which became Ireland's largest trading partner in the Americas during the late 1940s (apart from the USA and Canada). Imports from Argentina rose from IR£4.6 million in imports in 1947 to IR£9.2 million.[74] Exports to Argentina doubled, although the figures were considerably smaller than imports. The rise was short-lived, however, due to the rising costs of Argentine goods under Juan Perón's fascist economy.

The year 1948 saw a heavy rise in Ireland's bilateral formal relations. Exchange of Notes on the issue of trade was accomplished with the Netherlands, France and Belgium. The reason for the activity was Ireland's joining the

Organisation for European Economic Cooperation (OEEC) in June 1948 in order to qualify for Marshall Aid. The Anglo-Irish Trade Agreement of 1948 followed in July, which 'linked the prices of store cattle and sheep to British guaranteed prices for fat stock'; in effect subsidizing the Irish market.[75]

Perhaps the broadest move in 1948 was the Exchange of Notes between Ireland and the United States in the 'Application of Most-Favoured-Nation Treatment to Occupied Areas'.[76]

> For such time as the Government of the United States of America participates in the occupation and control of any areas in Western Germany, the Free Territory of Trieste, Japan or Southern Korea, the Government of Ireland will extend to the merchandise trade of such areas the most-favoured-nation treatment.[77]

Seán MacBride, Minister for External Affairs, signed the treaty. There was also an 'Agreement on Most-Favoured-Nation Treatment for Areas of Western Germany Under Military Occupation Signed at Geneva, on 14 September 1948'.[78] This agreement, which provided for most-favoured-nation treatment to extend to the western sectors of Berlin, was eventually asserted to be illegal under the Potsdam Conference of 1945, based on a complaint by the Soviet Union. The archival file notes all the accessions and deletions from this agreement by other member states. The most-favoured-nation agreement was abandoned when the Federal Republic of Germany became a contracting party to the General Agreement on Tariffs and Trade (GATT) in 1951 and the signatories were instructed they could withdraw. Interestingly, all contracting parties but Ireland withdrew on 14 December 1951.[79] There is no indication that Ireland gave its notice of withdrawal, except for a note saying 'no action'.

After 1948, several agreements were entered into which extended to nationals from other states. After the Republic of Ireland Act of 1949, bilateral treaty-making acquired added significance. Without the benefit or complication of bilateral negotiations being filtered through the British Civil Service, or under the auspices of the Crown, the Irish diplomatic service could use its own discretion in treaty making. In 1949, the Convention of Double Taxation of Income Taxes with the United States was written, as well as a Double Taxation of Corporate Profits agreement with Britain. (Double taxation agreements on personal income tax with Britain were made in 1926.) Abolition of Visa agreements were made with Luxembourg, Iceland and Italy. Trade agreements were completed with Egypt, Switzerland, France and the Netherlands. From 1949–63, Ireland's bilateral relations expanded enormously. The participants were decidedly anti-communist states, and were generally western European. There were agreements, however, with the United States, Canada and Australia. Ireland did conclude a Trade Agreement with Finland in 1951, which was renewed in 1954 and in subsequent years, but there were no formal treaties made with other communist states in the area of trade.

The overall liberalization in the system of non-communist states in the post-war years is reflected in the level of diplomatic relations that Ireland undertook. The Department of External Affairs had established diplomatic missions in most of the western European capitals by 1959.[80] There were also missions established in the United States, Canada, Australia and New Zealand. Representation was lacking in East Asia and Africa, but contacts were made through Catholic missionary efforts. Ireland relied upon India in China for diplomatic contacts. By 1957 Ireland sent a representative to Japan, and by 1961 to Nigeria. Although these bilateral relationships were significant in establishing diplomatic and economic ties with other states, the next section will consider the final step in Ireland's drive toward independence in foreign policy-making, the decision to enter into multiple international organizations.

IRELAND'S ASSOCIATION IN THE WORLD SYSTEM

The terms *cooperation* and *integration* are often used synonymously with the progression of European organizations after 1945. These terms, however, have different meanings based on the level of analysis of any given issue. To *cooperate* means to work toward a common end or purpose. To *integrate* is to make whole by bringing all parts together, or unification. Although Ireland joined nine international organizations during the period 1949–63, facilitating its political and economic movement into continental Europe, the Irish leaning toward involvement did not stem from either cooperation or integration.[81] The concept of *association*, first used in this context by Eamon de Valera in the 1921 treaty negotiations with the British, allows membership without culpability. 'Ireland's non-involvement in World War II, coupled with its geographical location, [meant] that although lip-service is paid to the notion of European union, there is little intuitive understanding of the original motivations that led the countries of continental Europe to opt for integration.'[82]

The original concept of European union imagined by the continental Europeans was indeed based on fear rather than a genuine desire to integrate. The aim of European organizations after the Second World War (including the Congress of Europe [1948] and later the Council of Europe [1949], as well as the grandfather of European union, the European Coal and Steel Community [1952]) was to rebuild while minimizing the threat of conflict between states.

> [The] search for durable peace was certainly an equally important impetus towards unity. For centuries the peace of Europe had been disturbed, most notably by the *Erbfeindschaft*, or hereditary enmity, of French and German peoples. Fear... was *the* prime motivation. Fear of Russia's military might, fear of America's economic might, and the Europeans' fear of themselves. As Barzini says of these Europeans: 'They know anything might happen in Europe because everything has happened.'[83]

As Europe developed regional organization programmes, the opportunities for Ireland to 'associate' or 'participate' in the system grew. In spite of significant opportunities for membership in international organizations, Ireland's self-imposed policy of neutrality did not permit the consideration of participation in organizations with security or military overtones. Mathisen argued that

> the Republic of Ireland has stubbornly pursued a policy of neutrality ever since it severed the constitutional ties with the United Kingdom, and in fact before that. It does not seem to consider it either possible or necessary to establish any formal relations with a third party to balance British influence on the island.[84]

Mathisen is half-correct in his assumptions. Ireland did welcome associations with 'third political forces' to establish its autonomy, which were necessary components of foreign policy. Since NATO was the prominent security initiative in the post-war era, and Ireland chose not to join, the general assumption was that Ireland preferred isolation to association. This, however, was not the case. Ireland chose association with other states when certain interests could be met, first as a method of linkage to end partition and later, to establish a stronger economic base.

While Mathisen's arguments imply that Ireland could have benefited from joining political and military alliances in order to counter the influence of Britain, the Irish saw the situation differently. They saw non-association and selective association as providing leverage in developing independence from Britain. Both Miriam Hederman and Denis Maher wrote extensively on Ireland's involvement in international organizations.[85] For our purposes in studying Ireland's association in the world system, we will examine briefly the major decisions: the Marshall Plan (1947); NATO (1949); and the first application to join the EEC (European Economic Community, 1961–63). Other rather straightforward membership decisions which occurred within this time period significant to Ireland's progress in international organizations (such as the Council of Europe, 1949 and the United Nations, 1955) have been documented at length by other scholars.[86] The more circuitous decisions will be examined below.

THE MARSHALL PLAN

In the immediate post-war period, from 1945–47, the United States stabilized its position in western Europe as occupying military force in the western zones of Germany and Berlin. The restructuring of Germany's economy began relatively late.[87] The American historian and economist Walt W. Rostow, residing in Geneva in the post-war years and working with reconstruction programmes, explained:

This was not merely the result of war damage, the political disarray of occupation, and inflation. It was also the result of a conscious decision that German recovery should have lower priority than that of the rest of Europe. Coal (especially coking coal needed for steel) was in short supply; and, until Ruhr production was fully revived, it was allocated on a priority basis, which discriminated against German recovery. But, with the currency reform of 1948, Germany moved forward; and the governments of Western Europe, as well as the United States, were prepared to acquiesce in or support a policy of rapid German growth.[88]

The rebuilding of western Europe signified the chance for Ireland to benefit from structural investment funds. When Secretary of State George Marshall announced the European Recovery Programme (Marshall Plan) on 5 June 1947, Ireland was invited to participate. 'Both the United States and Britain accepted [Ireland's] participation despite Irish neutrality during World War II, thus acknowledging Britain's heavy dependency upon Ireland for foodstuffs. A healthy Irish agricultural economy could only contribute to the restoration of a healthy *sterling bloc*.'[89] This was the obvious argument for Ireland's participation from the British point of view.

Although the Irish delegation (which was led by Seán Lemass, Tánaiste and Minister for Industry and Commerce and included F.H. Boland, Secretary to the Department of External [Foreign) Affairs] was eager to participate in the initial Committee for European Economic Cooperation (CEEC) sessions held in Paris, the Department of Finance still had reservations. 'We cannot expect any measure of salvation from the so-called Marshall Plan', lamented J.J. McElligott, Secretary to the Department of Finance.[90] The Department of External (Foreign) Affairs, however, had other plans. After two months of negotiation under the CEEC, de Valera (as Taoiseach and Minister for External [Foreign) Affairs] went to Paris on 22 September 1948. He remarked:

> To seek from another what one could supply by one's efforts is always unworthy. It is doubly so when the assistance is requested from a friend who has proved himself generous repeatedly. I am happy to sign this report on behalf of Ireland because I believe it to be an honest report. In it self-help is recognised as a primary duty, and no more aid is sought than is absolutely necessary if the damage of the war years is to be repaired within a reasonable time and the nations of Western Europe restored to a position in which they can provide for their own needs and preserve their traditional civilisation.[91]

Maher reported that over the total period of Ireland's participation in the Marshall Aid Plan (1948–52), 'the aggregate of Marshall Aid amounted to approximately $13 billion'.[92] Ireland's receipts included $146.2 million – $128.2 in loans and $18 million in grants.[93]

As a result of the US commitments to the Korean War (beginning in June 1950), Marshall Aid took a decidedly different tack in 1951. US foreign policy toward Europe gradually linked economic aid to military alliance. The Mutual Security Act of 1951 created considerable difficulty in Ireland's acceptance of aid. The Act stated in part:

> The Congress declares it to be the purpose of this Act to maintain the security and promote the foreign policy of the United States by authorising military, economic and technical assistance to friendly countries to strengthen the mutual security and individual and collective defence of the free world, to develop their resources in the interest of their security and independence and the national interest of the United States to facilitate the effective participation of those countries in the United Nations system for collective security.[94]

Frank Aiken, the new Minister in the Department of External (Foreign) Affairs, after Fianna Fáil returned to power in June 1951, would have nothing to do with the proposed adherence to security policies of the United States. Maher wrote that Aiken sent a letter to the American Ambassador on 24 December 1951, stating:

> The Irish Government will do all in their power to repel or defeat any attack upon the area under their jurisdiction and to prevent any attempt to use their territory as a base for attack against the United States or Britain. Ireland cannot, except in the case of an unprovoked attack, however, consistent with her history and national stability, consider entering into any further military commitment with other countries for joint defence *as long as she is denied the national unity and freedom they already enjoy.*[95]
> (emphasis added)

Aiken took the linkage tactic and applied it against the United States. The logic employed by Aiken did not work, however, resulting in the United States' suspension of Marshall Aid on 8 January 1952. As Maher noted, 'Politically, the exchanges reflected continuing Irish unwillingness to enter into anything savouring of international defence commitments in advance of a solution of the problem of partition.'[96] In spite of the discontinuance of funds in 1952, Marshall Aid had served its purpose for Ireland.[97] Lee (1989) notes that it amounted to 50 per cent of state investment (structural) funds from 1948–51.[98]

Two competing goals (either support the military alliance in Europe or receive Marshall Aid) were less than optimal choices for Ireland, when the primary objective of Irish foreign policy – ending partition – remained unresolved. US policy toward Ireland and military commitments, as well as possible bilateral military arrangements with Ireland in lieu of NATO participation, was spelled out in the National Security Council directive, NSC

83/1 (dated 2 November 1950), discussed at length in the following section. Effectively, this National Security Council decision dispelled any hopes for Ireland's establishing bilateral military relations with the United States, anticipating the Mutual Security Act which followed (1951). To borrow the language of T.S. Eliot, Marshall Aid ended for Ireland 'not with a bang but a whimper'.[99]

NORTH ATLANTIC TREATY ORGANIZATION (NATO)

The option to participate in NATO in 1949 presented a more complicated problem than Marshall Aid. The principle objective both domestically and in Irish foreign policy in 1949 was to end partition. This objective provided ineffective leverage in discussions with the United States on NATO membership. Initially, the inter-party government and Minister for External Affairs Seán MacBride sought the exclusive link of partition in the acceptance of the US proposal for a western European security organization. In essence, it was MacBride's insertion of the partition link, which resulted in the United States' refusal to negotiate with Ireland on a bilateral basis concerning security arrangements, either inside or outside the NATO command. Had Ireland been of critical strategic value to the NATO structure, the negotiations would have continued; instead, the negotiations ended suddenly.

Other sources provide a more detailed analysis of the issues concerning Ireland and NATO than may be explained here.[100] The difficulty arose in the negotiations toward participation when partition and strategic value became the critical negotiating issues. Would Ireland's geographical position be critical enough to the NATO structure to initiate discussions on ending partition? It was this gamble that Seán MacBride certainly miscalculated. The problem faced by Ireland in 1949 was summarized in a memorandum presented ten years later by Con Cremin in 1959, when the issue once more arose whether Ireland should join NATO. Cremin's analysis is as follows:

> On 7th January, 1949, the American Government informed us by *aide-mémoire*, that the seven countries considering the elaboration of the North Atlantic Treaty felt that five other countries (Ireland, Iceland, Denmark, Norway, Portugal) should be 'consulted as to their willingness to consider participating as original signatories of the treaty, and, if prepared in principle to do this, to participate in the definitive drafting of its terms'. Our reply to this communication was by way of an *aide-mémoire* of 8th February which, while recording agreement 'with the general aim of the proposed Treaty', set out the difficulties of our participating in a military alliance with, or comprising, Britain, and urged that it would be in the interests of 'the security of the States of the Atlantic community' to solve the problem of Partition.[101]

Cremin then stated the reason for the lack of positive response from the United States on continuing negotiations:

> This document was presumably interpreted as a refusal on our part to participate in the proceedings in the manner suggested unless an effort were to be made at those proceedings to solve Partition, and we did not in fact receive an invitation to attend the conference that drew up the treaty.[102]

While Cremin's analysis is accurate, it is an oversimplification of how events occurred in the NATO discussions. Ireland did not expect the NATO members to shut their door so securely against the value of Ireland's participation in NATO. Fanning noted that a leading US State Department official 'intimately' involved in preparation of the North Atlantic Pact, Ted Achilles, provided the American reaction to Ireland's linking partition to NATO:

> We did invite Ireland to join the pact as an important stepping-stone in anti-submarine warfare. We doubted that they would accept. They replied that they would be delighted to join provided we could get the British to give back the six Northern counties. We simply replied, in effect, that 'it's been nice knowing you', and that was that.[103]

Achilles' comments, however sardonic, provide a clue to the strategic value of Ireland in the United States' concept of North Atlantic defence planning.[104] After the NATO pact was signed on 4 April 1949, the discussions and exchange of *aide-mémoires* continued. In fact, Seán MacBride met with Secretary of State Dean Acheson on 11 April 1949 to discuss Ireland's participation in the Pact.[105] Ian McCabe writes of their meeting:

> During the meeting MacBride told Acheson that Ireland was strongly in favour of the Atlantic pact and would have liked to join in signing it, but that no Irish government could have lasted two months had it done so. That strategy would have prevented the possibility of the feared 'civil crisis' that might have occurred in [Ireland] had the government joined NATO while Partition remained. However, Acheson repeated the official state department policy that they 'regarded the position as wholly unconnected with the Atlantic Pact and were not willing to become involved in discussions of Partition.[106]

MacBride's miscalculations continued on the NATO issue throughout 1949. In November 1949 a military headquarters secret report outlined Ireland's position on NATO, from a strategic, as well as from a partition, viewpoint. The report contained several faulty assumptions concerning the strategic value of Ireland and partition used as linkage. The Irish military planners were convinced of Ireland's strategic position in the North Atlantic area, although a long-term, full-scale war had ended only four years previously without Ireland. The report stated:

> The creation and implementation of the Atlantic Pact Organisation is, in fact, the development and application in practice of the principles of American strategy as outlined. As a result, American strategists will reach the same conclusions on Ireland as the Planning Groups of the Pact Organisation. These are that, in addition to providing a complete system of local defence, bases for use in naval and air war are, at a minimum, desirable, and, in the conditions of war envisaged, i.e. with hostile submarines and aircraft operating in the Atlantic, absolutely essential.[107]

As noted above, by 1950 NSC 83/1 declared Ireland's lack of strategic importance to the NATO Pact. In terms of a bilateral agreement with Ireland concerning military aid, NSC 83/1 also stated: 'unilateral extension of US military assistance could be justified only on the basis of extreme military necessity and then only after the possibility of Irish adherence to NATO had been fully explored and rejected. This necessity does not exist.'[108]

In spite of the continuing aggressiveness of MacBride on ending partition, the United States dropped the issue of Ireland's participation in NATO by 1950.[109] From a policy perspective, however, it is interesting to note the arguments presented concerning partition from the Irish military point of view. These arguments were never made to the United States, as the discussions did not reach a stage after November 1949 (when the military report was presented) where such arguments were appropriate. The purpose in introducing them now is to show the logic behind Irish decision-making.

> No staff planning defence for this region can regard with satisfaction the situation in which the region's land defences end with the militarily artificial boundary of Northern Ireland. The staff responsible will be equally dissatisfied with a position in which the sea and air defences of this region extend around but do not include the relatively undefended area of the Republic of Ireland. The attack against which the Western European Region is planning will, if launched, come from the east. The Region's only hope of holding that attack is ample and timely aid from across the Atlantic ... Ireland ... occupies a vital position on the direct lines of communication on which depend the success in war of the Western European Region. Consequently, no staff responsible for the defensive plans of the Western European Region can fail to take note of the position of Ireland, more particularly as they are certain to regard it as relatively defenceless.[110]

When Cremin issued the memorandum mentioned earlier, written in 1959 under a growing pressure to re-examine the NATO issue, his evaluation of the security aspects were more subdued (and less egocentric) than the military planners of 1949.[111] Cremin's analysis also seems more sophisticated than the arguments presented in 1949. He provided four reasons why Ireland should continue its resistance to NATO. Interestingly, none of these arguments was based on an overriding policy of ideologic neutrality.

1. In the event of hostilities the country might be more exposed, via NATO bases or otherwise. (The existence of an important NATO aero-naval base in the North already, of course, with the development of long-range missiles, adds to our danger in such an eventuality.)
2. If we were to join NATO, we would almost certainly have to envisage very much higher defence expenditure than we undertake at the moment. The attached Note sets out the proportion of gross national product of this country and of a number of NATO countries devoted in 1956 and 1957 to defence expenditure. It will be observed that of the NATO countries mentioned, the lowest proportion was borne by Denmark. If we were to have to incur expenditure in the same proportion, it would involve an increase in the Defence Vote of between £13 and £14 million, and if our expenditure were to be the average of that of NATO countries (i.e. 5.8%) the increase would be very much higher – twice as great. It is true, of course, that at least some of this higher expenditure would probably be offset by American military aid.
3. We would almost certainly have to envisage the installation of NATO bases. (These bases would probably, however, give employment and might even result in an improvement in some communications media, e.g. airports, harbours and roads.)
4. We would probably have to co-ordinate our foreign policies with those of NATO members and perhaps to some extent subordinate them to the views of our partners. There appears, indeed, to be an increasing demand within NATO in the direction of greater co-ordination of foreign policy.[112]

By 1959 the policy statements concerning membership in NATO gave no hint of MacBride's linkage arguments, or on the principle of neutrality, focusing instead on the possibility of diminishing autonomy in foreign policy-making if Ireland should join. Frank Aiken had developed his 'independent foreign policy' line in the United Nations by then[113] and it seemed Ireland was discarding the cloak of dependence in foreign policy. Ten years of reality had proven that Ireland was not of strategic importance to the NATO structure, as long as the United States had access to RAF locations in Northern Ireland. Ten years also saw Ireland progress from a relatively isolated state to an active member in the international community. In January 1961 a newspaper article in England began:

Ireland can consider itself, temporarily, the most important little country in the world. The United Nations General Assembly is presided over by an

Irishman; the U.N. troops in the Congo are commanded by another. For a country of under three million people, which only joined the United Nations in December 1955, it is a remarkable but not entirely fortuitous, diplomatic double. To its early, but diminishing, surprise, the world has found itself listening to what the Irish have to say.[114]

IRELAND AND THE (FIRST) APPLICATION TO THE EEC

On 31 July 1961 Ireland formally applied for membership to the European Economic Community. The advantages to joining the EEC were first framed under the benefits that would accrue to the agricultural sector of the economy, which had not progressed as fast as industry under the Programme for Economic Expansion devised by T.K. Whitaker of the Department of Finance in 1958. Whitaker's plan stressed shifting from an economy of protectionism toward free trade; encouraging foreign investment in Ireland; orienting agricultural products toward export; and shifting public expenditure from social to productive investment.[115] Agriculture was lagging by 1961, and with the development of the EEC (created by the Treaty of Rome in 1957) and the European Free Trade Association (EFTA in 1959), Ireland found itself in the precarious situation of building its export economy (based mainly on agricultural products) with no preferential trading partners apart from Britain. The National Farmer's Association (NFA) petitioned the government to make an application to the EEC as early as July 1960.[116] The NFA argued that EEC membership would mean 'guaranteed prices at a relative high level for a wide range of agricultural products... [and] access to a large and expanding consumer market which does not aspire to a cheap food policy'.[117] As Maher noted,

> There was a serious flaw in the NFA's argument which was central to the EEC. Ireland's accession to the EEC would almost certainly be followed immediately by the abrogation of the Anglo-Irish Trade Agreements and the consequential elimination of the preferences, both industrial and agricultural, which Ireland enjoyed in the British market.[118]

The fundamental problem in deciding whether to apply for membership was whether the effects of joining without Britain, either as an associate member or as a full member, would be worth the detriment to Ireland's trading relationship with Britain. Fortunately, Ireland did not have to contemplate membership without Britain, for in April and May 1961 'information reaching the Irish Government through diplomatic channels indicated that there was a strong possibility of a British decision within a few months in favour of entry'.[119]

The question of Ireland's membership was debated throughout 1961. Taoiseach Seán Lemass gave the following response on 16 May 1961 when asked in the Dáil whether Ireland would apply for membership:

Until recently, the prospect of a link between Britain and the Common Market [EEC] seemed slight. There have, however, been indications during the past few months that the British Government may be contemplating the possibility of entering the Common Market on certain conditions. It is the Government's view that, if Britain should take this step, we should consider establishing a link with the Common Market and endeavour to secure terms of membership or association, which would satisfactorily take account of our economic circumstances.[120]

Ireland decided to apply for full membership with its application on 31 July 1961. Britain's application followed on 8 August 1961. Until the negotiations were informally halted by de Gaulle's veto in January 1963, Ireland balanced its diplomatic posturing (among the other members of the EEC and the United States) with domestic concerns expressed mainly in Dáil Éireann. Immediately fears began to swell in Ireland over the political implications of the EEC. In a heated debate on 15 November 1961, Seán Lemass fielded questions concerning whether membership in the EEC would involve (ultimately) a NATO commitment.

Dr. Browne: We are not quite yet clear as to whether our association with or membership of the Common Market would mean membership of NATO.

The Taoiseach: I have made it as clear as it is possible to make it. There is no foundation for the suggestion that I am aware of.

Dr. Browne: May I take it that there is no question that we must be a party to any agreement entered into by the NATO Powers as a result of our association with or membership of the Common Market?

The Taoiseach: Any agreement? That seems to be a very different question altogether.

Dr. Browne: It is not a different question altogether.

The Taoiseach: I think it is.

Dr. Browne: Why does the Taoiseach not tell the country what the implications are? This is a most serious thing for the country. Are we going to have bases, polaris and others, on the Liffey?

Mr. Corish: If we are accepted as members of the Common Market for economic purposes, does the Taoiseach now say that our acceptance as members on that basis does not commit us to anything specifically political?

The Taoiseach: On the contrary, I am making it quite clear that membership of the European Economic Community implies acceptance of certain political objectives. These political objectives have not yet been precisely defined and nobody is in a position to state authoritatively what they are. I think it is extremely likely that they will be defined in a more precise form before we have to take a final decision on membership of EEC.[121]

The previous day (in a confidential letter dated 14 November 1961), T. J. Kiernan, Ambassador to the United States, presented the position of the United States concerning Ireland's application:

Starkly stated, the position is... that Ireland's application for membership will be rejected... The United States' attitude is definitely not to favour neutrals, like Sweden and Ireland, as associate members... The US policy is formed by Under-Secretary of State, George W. Ball... and he is frankly working towards a greater Atlantic Alliance, 'with all the works', seeing the economic union as a means to a more solid defence-against-communism organisation than N.A.T.O. has proved to be... Since I understood... that Mr. Ball is not too friendly to our application, I asked him [Sweeney, Officer-in-Charge of UK and Ireland Affairs at the State Department] whether this attitude had arisen as a result of remarks from representatives of other countries concerned, or... [T]he nub of the matter was, it seemed, our refusal to join NATO in the first instance, and our policy of neutrality at the U.N.O. Mr. Ball sees membership of the E.E.C. as being properly confined to countries which are not, and do not profess to be, neutral. This would exclude us.[122]

This letter was followed by an addendum dated 17 November containing a memorandum by Kevin Rush at the embassy in Washington after meeting with Sweeney at the State Department.

As soon as I met Mr. Sweeney he told me that he had been quite surprised to learn this morning that our Minister, Mr. Aiken, had requested an appointment on Friday next (November 17) at 9 a.m. in Paris, with Mr. George W. Ball... [Sweeney] said, quite candidly, that in the short time available to him he had concentrated on trying to ensure that Mr. Ball would approach the meeting with Mr. Aiken at least with an open mind and would adopt a 'fluid' position, rather than the 'frozen' position which Mr. Ball would otherwise have been likely to adopt... [Sweeney] seemed to think that a confrontation at such a high level might have unfortunate consequences because of the lack of sufficient 'briefing' on either side... I asked [Sweeney]... what he thought of the prospects for the interview arranged for next Friday morning in Paris. He was not optimistic. He explained that Mr. Ball... is by no means sympathetically disposed towards Ireland which, quite frankly, does not play any part in his plans for the Western European Federation, or rather "Atlantic-Alliance" type of development... Mr. Ball's personality is such that he often gives an impression of dourness... even though that impression may not necessarily reflect his feelings.[123]

Denis McDonald, Ambassador in Paris, reported the conversation between Aiken and Ball on 17 November. McDonald wrote that 'it must have been understood on the American side that it was the Minister's intention to speak about Ireland's application... but the Minister had decided beforehand that he would not make any direct request for American support'. After several introductory comments concerning an Organization for Economic Cooperation and Development (OECD) Payments Union (which had been discussed at a ministerial meeting of the OECD the day before), finally Ball found an opening to discuss what he believed to be Aiken's purpose in calling the meeting.

> At this point Mr. Ball opened up the question of our EEC application, remarking that we had made an application under Article 237 of the Treaty of Rome. The Minister said we had done so, believing that we could fulfil the political and economic obligations called for by membership. In regard to the political aspect, the Minister remarked that Ireland's difficulty about entering the NATO Pact was, of course, well known and related to the partition problem. We believed that if Britain and ourselves were to enter the EEC as full members, the tariff problem between the North and the South would tend to disappear with a corresponding trend towards unity of political aims which would be good for both parts of Ireland. It was not clear what we would be required to do under the heading of defence, but felt that the partition problem might have taken on a different complexion before we would be called upon to take a decision on a common defence policy.[124]

Aiken described the industrial growth of Ireland in the preceding years, owing to the introduction of industry from the United States and Germany. He stressed that Ireland was committed to agriculture and the 'social pattern of the community'. At the end of the conversation, McDonald accompanied Ball 'downstairs'.

> [Ball] remarked that he had been very interested in meeting the Minister and in hearing what he had to say about the EEC. I took the chance of commenting that we were all for it and that our Prime Minister would be leading the delegation in Brussels in January, which is in itself a testimony of our strong desire to enter the Community. As he put on his coat, Mr. Ball remarked that he was very glad we had applied for *full membership*. I added that his comment was very welcome. (emphasis in original)[125]

An attached note indicates that Lemass received a copy of the memorandum on 21 November, when he also received the note from Kiernan in Washington dated 14 November.

Cremin advised Kiernan in Washington on 22 November not to pursue matters with Sweeney in the State Department.[126] In a follow-up letter dated 28 November, Cremin explained:

> I wish to confirm my telegram No. 105 of 22nd instant concerning Mr. Rush's talks with Mr. Sweeney... My feeling is that it may, perhaps, serve little purpose and might create an impression of undue anxiety on our part

if we were to keep up a more or less continuous approach among the
'foothills' of the State Department now that the Minister did, as you know,
see the Under-Secretary, Mr. George Ball, in Paris on 17th November.[127]

In the same letter Cremin explained that Lemass was informed of Kiernan's 14
November note before the 17 November meeting between Aiken and Ball.
Further, Cremin and Kiernan spoke of the issue on the telephone the evening of
16 November. The first draft of this letter includes the following passage to
Kiernan:

> In a conversation which we had prior to his departure for New York, the
> Minister wondered whether he might not take the opportunity of his
> presence there to go to Washington and have a talk with Mr. Rusk, with the
> general purpose of developing to him the advantages for the Western
> European Community within it a country free to take an independent line
> in international matters and, in particular to contribute positively... to
> United Nations activities. I pointed out to the Minister the risk of giving
> the impression that we would be opposed to a defence commitment and of
> this impression being relayed to the Six and resulting in our not getting
> across the threshold, even if we should in fact (as a condition of entry) be
> prepared to accept such a commitment... I do not know what the Minister
> will do about seeing Mr. Rusk and I mention the foregoing solely for your
> information.[128]

Also on 28 November Cremin sent a note to Washington and Paris, containing
a summary of the interpreted position of Ball and Kiernan's opinion that 'it
might be necessary for the Taoiseach to go to Washington to explain these
matters. It would be important to ensure that the conversation between the
Minister and Mr. Ball would keep the doors open.'[129] Finally, in one last effort
at 'power diplomacy', Cremin suggested the following: 'If it should prove
impossible to move Mr. Ball from his present attitude, it might be necessary
then to go as far as the White House.'[130]

Kevin Rush at the Washington embassy later wrote of the interest in
Ireland's EEC application, verified in George Ball's memoirs, *The Past Has
Another Pattern* (1982).[131]

> In his letter Mr. Cremin makes two points – first, that the Americans are very
> strongly opposed to the admission as 'associate members' into EEC of the
> three EFTA 'neutrals'; and second, that the Americans seem anxious to ensure
> that the Irish authorities are left in no doubt about the strength of the US
> position in this regard... I should like, with respect, to comment on this
> second point... The US State Department authorities concerned, specifically
> Mr. Ball, have not, so far as I am aware, taken any particular interest, either
> positive or negative, in Ireland's application up to this point.[132]

Meanwhile, the debate within Ireland concerning membership continued, notwithstanding the government's preoccupation with the American point of view. Seán Lemass reported to the Dáil on 14 February 1962 that he attended a 'preliminary meeting with representatives of the States members of the Community, at which [he] made a comprehensive statement concerning [Ireland's] application to the Community'.[133] On 28 February, McQuillan (a TD from Roscommon) posed the following question to Lemass in the Dáil:

> **McQuillan**: May I ask the Taoiseach if, in view of his stated approval on a number of occasions recently of NATO and the objectives of NATO, he will state whether it is the Government's intention, if invited, to join NATO?
> **The Taoiseach**: That seems to me to be a different question, of which notice should be given.
> **McQuillan**: No. The situation up to now has been that Ireland is precluded from joining NATO on account of Partition. In view of the altered views of the Taoiseach, as shown in his recent replies to the effect that he approves of NATO and that there is nothing in the NATO Agreement to complicate our position in regard to Partition, would he now state whether it is the Government's intention, if invited, to join NATO?
> **An Ceann Comhairle**: That does not arise on the question on the Order Paper.[134]

In November 1962, the misgivings of the Irish public about joining the EEC in relation to NATO became secondary to the crisis developing between de Gaulle and the EEC. Ireland's application to the EEC was temporarily forgotten in the course of events. F.H. Boland, Ambassador to the United Nations, prepared a comprehensive memorandum concerning the turn of events in the Irish application.

> Nobody here at the UN was surprised at the outcome of the Brussels meeting of EEC Foreign Ministers on the 28th January about Britain's application for membership of the Common Market. Knowing President de Gaulle's inflexibility, the most anyone seemed to expect was a face-saving device in the shape of a review by the Commission of the results of negotiations up to date … France's rejection of Britain's application goes back to the Carolingian concept of Europe's destiny which General de Gaulle outlined in his memoirs. It is possible, and even likely, that in the end France would have blocked Britain's entry in any case. There is a general feeling here, however, that the strains and stresses which have developed in the structure and leadership of the Atlantic Alliance over the past two years undoubtedly had a great deal to do with President de Gaulle's final decision. It is an open secret here that ever since President Kennedy entered the White House, Franco-American relations have been deteriorating. President de Gaulle has become increasingly irritated with the United States' steady

assertion of its position of leadership in the Atlantic Alliance. America's persistent unwillingness to entertain the idea of a Franco-British-American directorate of the Alliance, coupled with a growing resentment of the position of inferiority to which Anglo-American solidarity ('the special relationship') appeared to relegate France, gradually added strength to President de Gaulle's determination to try to make a united Europe a 'Third Force' under French leadership... The ending of the war in Algeria, the consolidation of his own political position, the growing cohesion of the EEC and the unprecedented prosperity of France herself presented de Gaulle with his opportunity. He grasped it with both hands, outmanoeuvring the United States, Britain and his own EEC partners in the process.[135]

Samuel Wells, in Roger Louis and Hedley Bull's *The Special Relationship* (1989), verified Boland's interpretation. Wells wrote:

> The American agreement at Nassau in December 1962 to provide Britain with Polaris missiles and the information to construct the submarines and nuclear warheads to go with them simply confirmed de Gaulle's suspicions. There was a unique relationship between the two Anglo-Saxon powers, he contended, which made the United States unreliable in protecting European interests and essentially meant that Britain could never be fully part of Europe.[136]

Boland's 'inside information' at the United Nations was obtained through a discussion with Ambassador Seydoux of France, who assured Boland that 'President de Gaulle was, and still is, convinced that some such arrangement was concluded between Britain and the United States at the Bahamas meeting'.[137] He continued to describe the de Gaulle perceptions:

> General Norstad, who has just retired from the supreme command of NATO, told Ambassador Nielsen [Norway] and myself at a party last night that, during his farewell visit to President de Gaulle, the President expressed the same conviction to him. He had spoken very bluntly about it. He said that he felt a 'trick' had been played on him and that a 'trap' had been laid for him. The President spoke with every appearance of sincerity. General Norstad didn't believe he was just using the Bahamas agreement as a pretext.[138]

Without considering de Gaulle's motivations for the veto of the British application in January 1963, the decision left Ireland with a considerable dilemma. Should Ireland withdraw its application to the EEC, or continue without Britain? The answer came fairly soon for the Department of External Affairs. Hugh McCann reported in a note that the Irish Ambassador to Brussels had spoken to 'Monsieur Spaak' on 30 January.

Mr. Biggar telephoned from Brussels yesterday evening to report an interview he had with Monsieur Spaak. Spaak appeared exhausted. He expressed the opinion that notwithstanding the breakdown of negotiations with Britain, the EEC will continue although the atmosphere may be unpleasant for a while... On our application Spaak expressed the view that if the French will not accept Britain he could not see how they would accept Ireland.[139]

The first problem that Ireland faced was one of public opinion. The de Gaulle veto forced the Irish government to make a determination on policy. Behind the scenes, the Department of the Taoiseach was gathering information from all quarters. T.K. Whitaker in the Department of Finance supplied a memorandum on recommendations on 'Possible courses of action open to Ireland in the event of a break-down in the British-EEC negotiations'.[140] Finance proposed plans for both a temporary suspension of negotiations and a permanent one. In the event of a permanent breakdown, Finance predicted that Britain might: seek a bilateral deal with the EEC (which Finance described as unlikely); seek greater access to EEC and the USA for her industrial exports by participating actively in the Kennedy negotiations [of GATT]; 'drum up' support for a North Atlantic Free Trade Community with the EEC, EFTA, the USA and Canada; revivify EFTA (which was being dismantled in anticipation of Britain joining the EEC); and revise arrangements for Commonwealth trade which might increase trade overall (which was also considered unlikely).[141]

Finance also pointed out that Lemass had been quoted as laying contingency plans for the failure of the British application as early as September 1962.

If negotiations with Britain should fail we would nevertheless, wish to pursue our application provided it was economically possible for us to do so. That would of course turn upon the question of the relations that would... exist between Britain and the European Community. Britain is, of course, of predominant importance in our external trade. There would also arise the question whether in the event of the British applications not succeeding, the European Community would wish to pursue any other applications for membership.[142]

In the event that the EEC was willing to continue with the Irish negotiations for membership, Finance had doubts as to their outcome. As the trump card, Finance suggested that Ireland could,

[enlist] support from the USA whence the strongest pressure is likely to be exerted on the EEC for reduction of the common external tariff and the modification of the more restrictive aspects of the common agricultural policy... it would be in our interest... to be a member of GATT if a way could be found round our obligation to accord Britain preferences on all new duties, an obligation which is in conflict with GATT rules.[143]

The recommendation on joining GATT was seconded by a report from the Washington Embassy on US policy reactions.

Lemass' office had already drawn up a statement for the Dáil on 30 January 1963. The statement was revised three times, each time de-emphasizing Ireland's reliance on Britain in trade. The final statement referred to the 'importance of trade with Britain in our external economic relations', discounting the earlier drafts, which referred to the 'predominant importance of trade'.[144] Later, on 5 February, Lemass made a comprehensive speech to the Dáil. By this time, the immediate crisis had passed and Lemass took the middle road by saying that 'up to now, the British application for membership of [the EEC] has not been withdrawn, nor has it been decided by [the EEC]. It is still on the . . . agenda, as is ours.'[145] He gave a final explanation:

> We are not withdrawing our application. Our position is still that we wish to become members of [the EEC] if it is economically possible for us, which is something we may not be able to decide finally until the position concerning the British application, and Britain's future commercial policy, are known.[146]

The purpose of examining Ireland's policy performance during the first application to the EEC crisis is to determine how principled Irish foreign policy had become by 1961. As opposed to the problems confronted with the Marshall Aid termination and the NATO issues, in 1961 Ireland seemed to have acquired more self-confidence and less morality in its tone of setting policy. Pragmatism became an effective mechanism. The notion of linkage did not exist in the Lemass government in determining possible solutions for the EEC application crisis. In fact, Lemass showed remarkable control in handling the situation. William Warnock, Ireland's Ambassador in Switzerland at the time, sent a letter on the crisis dated 30 January 1963, which summed up Ireland's situation.

> In the afternoon I called on Professor Wahlen, Head of the Federal Political Department . . . Representatives of small countries, said Professor Wahlen, should be circumspect in their public utterances. An example which [should] not be followed is that of Mr. Spaak of Belgium, who speaks like the Minister of a Great Power, but has not a powerful country behind him.[147]

CONCLUSION

This chapter is meant to be ancillary to the primary study of recognition and non-recognition in Irish foreign policy during the period 1949–63. By examining how Ireland behaved in the world system in general, it becomes easier to understand the influences and outcomes of recognition problems. While Ireland established bilateral relations with many states during these early years of full independence, foreign policies were maintained that helped cement the perception of Irish neutrality within the system. Ireland did this best through its association in multilateral relationships. The issue of partition was used as linkage mainly in Ireland's association in international organizations, especially the early decision in 1949 concerning NATO.

The early years of the First Inter-Party Government and the handling of recognition problems will be shown in stark contrast to the later years of the Lemass/Aiken Government in addressing the same recognition issues. Seán MacBride was influential as Minister of External Affairs in setting the course for Ireland's participation in post-war reconstruction of Europe. MacBride used selective association in international organizations in an attempt to develop independence from Britain, although his efforts had the effect of often alienating Ireland from the rest of Europe as well. Overall, this chapter provides a description Ireland's developing economic and political position through its bilateral and multilateral relationships from 1949–63, following its progress as a 'small and weak' state during a period dominated by bipolarity in the international system.

NOTES

1   Gustavo Lagos, *International Stratification and Underdeveloped Countries* (Chapel Hill, NC, 1963), p. 10.

2   Brierly, *The Law of Nations*, pp. 121–2 as quoted in Marshall R. Singer, *Weak States in a World of Powers: The Dynamics of International Relationships* (New York, 1972), p. 36. Emphasis added in Singer. Singer added his analysis of the relative nature of independence: 'No state ... falls at either extreme [of independence or dependence]. No matter how dependent a colonial possession became, it was never completely subservient to the mentor Power. That is, decision-making that affected the area was never *wholly* taken out of that area. To be sure, many major decisions were made in Paris, London, Madrid, Lisbon, or Washington, but many more decisions affecting the areas concerned were made locally – very often by local people.' (Singer, *Weak States*, p. 37.)

3   Hans J. Morgenthau, 'Another "Great Debate": the national interest of the United States', in John A. Vasquez, ed., *Classics of International Relations* (Upper Saddle River, NJ, 3rd edn, 1996), p. 148.

4   R.F. Foster, *Paddy & Mr. Punch: Connections in Irish and English History* (London, 1993), p. 78. Used out of context in this example, Daniel O'Connell spoke in favour of Repeal of the Union in the House of Commons on 22 April 1834.

5   J.J. Lee, *Ireland 1912–1985: Politics and Society* (Cambridge, 1989), p. 301.

6   See Kenneth Waltz, *Theory of International Politics* (Reading, MA, 1979).

7   Robert H. Lieshout, *Between Anarchy and Hierarchy: A Theory of International Politics and Foreign Policy* (London, 1995), p. 176.

8   See Johan Galtung, *The True Worlds: A Transnational Perspective* (New York, 1980).

9   Robert Gilpin, *The Political Economy of International Relations* (Princeton, NJ, 1987), p. 96.

10   See Fanning, *The Irish Department of Finance*, pp. 606–11. T.K. Whitaker, a leading member of the Department of Finance from 1934, was appointed Secretary of the Department in 1956. His programme of economic development based on long-term

planning was adopted by the government as a White Paper in May 1958 and led to the 'First Programme for Economic Expansion' in November 1958.

11   Other significant increases in export activity from 1948 to 1949 were reported for Greece, Turkey, French West Africa, Iraq, Venezuela and Brazil. Exports to Israel in 1948 were IR£666. In 1949, they climbed to IR£46,860. By 1950, exports soared to a significant IR£141,930. The author compiled these figures from *Statistical Abstracts of Ireland*, various years.

12   Gilpin, *The Political Economy of International Relations*, p. 96.

13   James L. Wiles and Richard B. Finnegan, eds, *Aspirations and Realities: A Documentary History of Economic Development Policy in Ireland Since 1922* (Westport, CT, 1993), p. 55.

14   Ibid, pp. 57–8.

15   Ibid., p. 58.

16   NAI DFA 305/2, 'Extract from Broadcast by An Taoiseach', 17 March 1946.

17   Ibid.

18   NSF Country File, Biography of Eamon de Valera (1964), Document 8, Box 195, LBJ Presidential Archives, Austin, Texas.

19   NAI DT S14291, 'Extract from *Gazette* of 13th April, 1948'.

20   Ireland's pursuance of peacetime neutrality will be discussed at length in Chapter 2.

21   See von Glahn, *Law Among Nations*, pp. 61–2. Switzerland's neutrality was recognized at the Congress of Vienna in 1815. Austria became neutral after the Second World War, and remained neutral after 1955 as a consequence of the Austria State Treaty imposed by the USSR, USA, Britain and France.

22   Robert Gilpin defined *prestige* as 'the reputation for power, and military power in particular. Whereas power refers to the economic, military, and related capabilities of a state, prestige refers primarily to the perceptions of other states with respect to a state's capacities and its willingness to exercise its power. In the language of contemporary strategic theory, prestige involves the credibility of a state's power and its willingness to deter or compel other states in order to achieve its objectives.' Robert Gilpin, *War and Change in World Politics* (Cambridge, 1981), p. 31.

23   Keogh, *Ireland and Europe*, p. 214.

24   Ibid.

25   The trade figures for the years 1949–58 show a dependence on imports from Britain, the United States, Canada, Sweden, the Netherlands and the former West Germany. Exports predominantly went to Britain during this period, from a high of 88 per cent of all exports in 1950, falling only to 75 per cent in 1960. See Kieran A. Kennedy, Thomas Giblin and Deirdre McHugh, *The Economic Development of Ireland in the Twentieth Century* (London, 1988), pp. 55–74 and 178–201. For all the years of this study, 1949–63, Ireland had consistent trade deficits with Europe and the United States, relying heavily on their imports. The deficits were as high as 29 per cent of total trade in 1951 with Europe and 95 per cent of total trade in 1949 with the United States. By 1965, the relative trade deficit with Europe was 18 per cent and with the United States, 52 per cent. (Derived by the author from *Statistical Abstracts of Ireland*, 1948–64.)

26   Seán Lemass, in a 1960 address concerning the role of small nations at the United Nations, commented: 'By preserving a fair-minded and responsible independence, and, while having regard to our own national interests, endeavouring to promote the interests of the United Nations as a whole, we believe we can contribute, even to an extent out of proportion to our size, and our economic and military importance, to the smooth working of the machinery of the major world organisation'. NAI DFA 305/392/1, Part 2, speech to the Cambridge University Liberal Club, 31 January 1960.

27   Melvin Small and J. David Singer, 'The diplomatic importance of states, 1816–1970: an extension and refinement of the indicator', *World Politics*, 25, 4 (July 1973), pp. 577–99.

28   Ibid., p. 579.

29   Ibid., p. 588.

30   The diplomatic representatives in Ireland in 1950 were from Argentina, Australia, Belgium, Canada, Czechoslovakia, France, Britain, Italy, the Netherlands, Portugal, Spain, Sweden, the United States and Switzerland.
31   Derived from *Thom's Directory* (Dublin), various years.
32   T.B. Millar, 'On writing about foreign policy', in James N. Rosenau, ed., *International Politics and Foreign Policy* (New York, 1969), pp. 59-60.
33   See Walter Lippmann, *The Cold War: A Study in U.S. Foreign Policy* (New York, 1947). Lippmann's articles appear frequently in the Department of External Affairs' archives throughout the period of this study. John Lewis Gaddis, in *We Now Know: Rethinking Cold War History* (Oxford, 1997), underscores the Lippmann argument.
34   R. Harrison Wagner, 'What was bipolarity?', *International Organization*, 47, 1 (Winter 1993), pp. 81–2.
35   Ibid., pp. 79–80.
36   Inis Claude, Jr., *Swords into Plowshares: The Problems and Progress on International Organization*, (New York, 4th edn, 1984), p. 89.
37   Ibid., pp. 89–90.
38   Joseph Morrison Skelly, *Irish Diplomacy at the United Nations 1945–1965: National Interests and the International Order* (Dublin, 1997), p. 15.
39   For a provocative discussion on Irish politics and culture since independence, see Liam Greenslade in '(In)dependence, development, and the colonial legacy in contemporary Irish identity', in Peter Shirlow, ed., *Development Ireland: Contemporary Issues* (London, 1995). Greenslade argues that Irish political and economic underdevelopment after independence caused 'double-bind' decision- making (forced to choose between two less than optimal values). Greenslade suggests this survival pattern creates schizophrenic behaviour, wherein 'the schizophrenic *knows* there is something wrong but is prevented from knowing *where* it is wrong and can find no way of escaping the constraints of the context except through psychological withdrawal in a refusal to play the game of normal behaviour and communication', p. 96.
40   See Salmon, *Unneutral Ireland.*
41   See Lee, *Ireland 1912-1985 1600–1972* (London, 1989), p. 570.
42   R.F. Foster, *Modern Ireland.*
43   Lee, *Ireland 1912–1985*, p. 605.
44   Hedley Bull, *The Anarchical Society: A Study of Order in World Politics* (New York, 1977), pp. 200–29.
45   Ibid., p. 43.
46   Thomas Hobbes once described how 'definitions multiply themselves' and 'lead men into absurdities'. By analogy, one may see the dilemma of Irish foreign policy-makers after independence. Not knowing what was wrong with the system in the first place, they had no way to overhaul decision-making. 'From whence it happens, that they which trust to books, do as they that cast up many little summes into greater, without considering whether those little summes were rightly cast up or not; and at last finding the errour visible, and not mistrusting their first grounds, know not which way to cleere themselves; but spend time in fluttering over their bookes; as birds that entring by the chimney, and finding themselves inclosed in a chamber, flutter at the false light of a glass window, for want of wit to consider which way they came in.' Thomas Hobbes, *Leviathan* (London, (1651) 1914), p. 15.
47   Lee, *Ireland 1912–1985*, pp. 547–8.
48   Ibid., p. 548.
49   Ibid.
50   Ibid.
51   Quoted in Foster, *Modern Ireland*, p. 569.
52   Fanning, *The Irish Department of Finance*, pp. 405–6.
53   Ibid., pp. 407–8.
54   NAI DT S14117 B/95, memorandum, 14 October 1964.
55   NAI DT S14117 B/95, memorandum, 16 October 1964.

56   See Maurice A. East et. al., *Why Nations Act: Theoretical Perspectives for Comparative Foreign Policy Studies* (Beverly Hills, CA, 1978).

57   East, *Why Nations Act*, p. 123.

58   One glaring example of Ireland's relative position in the world economy is found in the economic literature concerning the period. For example, Walt W. Rostow's comparative analysis of the world economy in the nineteenth and twentieth centuries omits contemporary Ireland altogether. See Walt W. Rostow, *World Economy: History and Prospect* (Austin, TX, 1978). One may also explain this lack of comparative analysis as caused by the difficulty of obtaining government archival materials. Rostow's work was published eight years before the opening of Irish archives to the public in 1986.

59   Michael Handel, *Weak States in the International System* (London, 2nd edn, 1990), p. 48.

60   Ibid., p. 11.

61   Ibid., p. 10.

62   Ibid., p. 52.

63   Ibid., p. 31.

64   Ibid., pp. 52–3. The research of J.J. Lee indirectly confirmed Handel's analysis of Irish economic performance after independence. Lee argued that Ireland has not significantly improved its standard of living since independence: 'Ireland recorded the slowest growth per capita income between 1910 and 1970 of a European country except the United Kingdom. Every country ranked above Ireland in the early twentieth century pulled much further ahead. Every country below Ireland overtook her, or significantly narrowed the gap. The result was that Ireland slid from being a reasonably representative economy, in terms of income per head, at the time of independence, to a position far below the western European average in 1970.' Lee, *Ireland 1912–1985*, p. 514.

65   Handel, *Weak States*, p. 53.

66   Sutton, *Politics, Security and Development*, pp. 19–20.

67   Ibid., p. 20.

68   Lee, *Ireland 1912–1985*, pp. 628–9.

69   Ibid., p. 630.

70   Dermot Keogh describes the period 1939–40 in Irish foreign policy as 'the diplomacy of survival' in *Ireland and Europe 1919–1989*.

71   Lee, *Ireland 1912–1985*, p. 54.

72   Keogh, *Ireland and Europe 1919–1989*, pp. 7–33.

73   Ibid., p. 7.

74   *Statistical Abstracts of Ireland*.

75   Lee, *Ireland 1912–1985*, p. 302.

76   32 *United Nations Treaty Series* (UNTS) 69.

77   NAI DFA 408/250, Exchange of Notes, 28 June 1948.

78   NAI DFA 408/229. This Agreement also included a Memorandum of Understanding on the application of the Agreement to 'the Western Sectors of Berlin' issued almost a year later on 13 August 1949.

79   NAI DFA 408/229, letter from the UN Legal Department to Minister for External Affairs, 23 November 1951. The contracting parties included Belgium, Canada, Ceylon (Sri Lanka), Denmark, India, the Netherlands, Norway, Pakistan, United Kingdom, USA, Dominican Republic, China, France, Greece, Luxembourg and South Africa.

80   Keogh lists the establishment of missions by date: Great Britain, 1923; Holy See, 1929; France, 1929; Germany, 1929 (West Germany, 1951); Belgium, 1932; Spain, 1935; Italy, 1938 (also to Turkey, 1951); Switzerland, 1940 (also to Austria, 1952); Portugal, 1942; Sweden, 1946 (also to Finland, 1964); and the Netherlands, 1951. Keogh, *Ireland and Europe 1919–1989*, p. 231.

81   Miriam Hederman, in *The Road To Europe: Irish Attitudes 1948–61* (Dublin, 1983), p. 154, lists the following memberships for Ireland: the Food & Agricultural Organization (FAO, 1945); the Economic Cooperation (Act) Administration (ECA, 1948) which

governed the bilateral agreements of the Marshall Plan; the Organization for European Cooperation (OEEC, 1948) and its successor, the Organization for European Cooperation and Development (1960); the World Health Organization (WHO, 1948); the Council of Europe (1949); the European Payments Union (EPU, 1950); the United Nations Organization (UN, 1955); and the International Monetary Fund (IMF, 1957).

82   Brigid Laffan, *Integration and Cooperation in Europe* (London, 1992), p. 195.
83   Miles Hewstone, *Understanding Attitudes to the European Community* (Cambridge, 1986), p.3. Hewstone cites the work of L. Barzini, *The Impossible Europeans* (London, 1983).
84   Trygve Mathisen, *The Functions of Small States in the Strategies of the Great Powers* (Oslo, 1971), p. 102.
85   See Hederman, *The Road to Europe* and D.J. Maher, *The Tortuous Path: The Course of Ireland's Entry into the EEC 1948–1973* (Dublin, 1986).
86   As mentioned above, Miriam Hederman's *The Road to Europe* discusses the Council of Europe membership at length. Joseph M. Skelly, in *National Interests and the International Order*, provides background to the decision of Ireland in 1945 to join the United Nations and in the subsequent delay in membership due to Soviet veto.
87   Rostow, *World Economy*, p. 235.
88   Ibid.
89   Joseph P. O'Grady, 'Ireland', in S. Victor Papacosma and Mark R. Rubin, eds, *Europe's Neutral and Nonaligned States: Between NATO and the Warsaw Pact* (Wilmington, DE, 1989), p. 109.
90   Fanning, *The Irish Department of Finance*, p. 411. McElligott, Secretary of Finance from 1927, had also opposed Ireland's membership in the International Monetary Fund (IMF) and in the International Bank for Reconstruction and Development (IRBD or World Bank) in 1946. His approach to decision-making rested on Ireland's dependence on the British market: 'McElligott then took the line of doubting whether membership could confer any advantages on Ireland since her export trade was mainly with one country only, Britain'. Fanning, *The Irish Department of Finance*, pp. 386–7.
91   Maher, *The Tortuous Path*, pp. 23–4.
92   Ibid., p. 29.
93   Ibid. Maher gives his figures in US dollars. Other scholars have given conflicting figures for Ireland's receipt of Marshall Aid. Fanning (*The Irish Department of Finance*) seems to be in agreement with Maher, stating: 'Marshall Aid [by December 1950] of $144.2 millions had "produced a counterpart in Irish currency" of IR£35.5 millions.' Lee (*Ireland 1912–1985*) relied on the Truman papers, quoting a figure of IR£36 million. Keogh (*Ireland and Europe 1919–1989, Twentieth-century Ireland*) agrees with Maher ($146.2 million), citing the source as NAI DT S14106. Kennedy et al. (*The Economic Development of Ireland*) cite IR£46 million. The calculation of the exchange rate is probably responsible for the confusion. It was be more reliable, in this case, to determine the value in US dollars than in Irish punts.
94   Maher, *The Tortuous Path*, p. 29.
95   Ibid., pp. 30–1.
96   Ibid., p. 31.
97   Ronan Fanning in 'The United States and Irish participation in NATO: the debate of 1950', *Irish Studies in International Affairs*, 1, 1 (1979), p. 48, wrote of the effects of suspension: 'The financial and economic implications were small. Most of the programme had been completed and, in any event, it was intended to wind up by the end of June 1952... The Irish case was not helped by the fact that every other affected country had been "willing to adhere to the new purposes embodied in the Mutual Security Act".'
98   Lee, *Ireland 1912–1985*, p. 305.
99   T.S. Eliot, 'The Hollow Men', *Selected Poems* (New York, 1964), p. 80.
100   See Ian McCabe, *A Diplomatic History of Ireland 1948–49: The Republic, the Commonwealth and NATO* (Dublin, 1991). Also Fanning's 'The United States and Irish

Participation in NATO; The Debate of 1950', pp. 38–48.
101   NAI DT S14291 – A/3, memorandum, 9 November 1959.
102   Ibid.
103   Fanning, 'The United States and Irish participation in NATO', p. 38.
104   Fanning also cites National Security Council directive NSC 83/1 (2 November 1950) and its background analyses as stating the lack of strategic value of Ireland, although the United States 'would welcome use of Ireland's port facilities and the air bases which could be developed there'. Fanning, 'The United States and Irish participation in NATO', p. 41.
105   McCabe, *A Diplomatic History of Ireland 1948–49*, p. 113.
106   Fanning notes in 'The United States and Irish Participation in NATO' that MacBride also visited Acheson in March 1951, when MacBride presented the partition argument with a slightly different bent. '[MacBride] did not think that, by itself, the United Kingdom would do anything about it [partition]' but that with 'American encouragement of the United Kingdom "to do something" might, however, produce results ... Acheson's response was no less traditional. He said he had "always regarded the problem as one which should be decided by his [MacBride's] government, the United Kingdom and the people of the northern counties".' When MacBride replied, recorded Acheson, '"that he realised this was a difficult question for me but he thought it was a shame that there was not some forum in the Atlantic community where a dispute of this nature could be discussed and settled", Acheson "readily assented to his statement that this was a very difficult problem for me"' (p. 43).
107   NAI DFA SF A89, briefing memorandum, November 1949.
108   NSC 83/1 as quoted in Fanning, 'The United States and Irish participation in NATO', p. 42.
109   MacBride presented a White Paper to both houses of the Oireachtas on 26 April 1950 (P. No. 9934), which may be found at NAI DT S14291 – A/1. The following texts were included: the *aide-mémoire* exchanges with the United States, dated 7 January, 8 February, 25 May, 3 June 1949; and the parliamentary question dated 29 March 1949, referring to the constitutional question involved in acceptance of Article 4 of the NATO agreement: 'The Parties will consult together whenever, in the opinion of any of them, the territorial integrity, political independence or security of any of the Parties is threatened.' MacBride concluded that this provision of the Pact was in violation of Article 2 of the Irish Constitution: 'The national territory consists of the whole island of Ireland, its islands and its territorial seas.' MacBride considered that Ireland's acceptance of Article 4 in NATO would cement partition even further. It is interesting that in references to Article 4 in the Irish briefs and memoranda, only the language 'the territorial integrity, political independence or security' is quoted, not the full meaning of 'consultation'. The deletion of the full text made the argument in linking partition to membership more cogent.
110   NAI DFA SF A89, November 1949.
111   Cornelius C. Cremin was the Secretary to the Department of External Affairs from 1 December 1957 to 6 January 1963. Frank Aiken was Minister of External Affairs during 1951–54 and 1957–68.
112   NAI DFA SF A89, November 1949.
113   See Keogh, *Twentieth-century Ireland*, pp. 234–8.
114   Anthony Dorset, 'Ireland – A Great Little Country', *Coventry Telegraph* (11 January 1961), found in NAI DFA 305/392/1 Part 1.
115   Lee, *Ireland 1912–1985*, pp. 344–55.
116   Maher, *The Tortuous Path*, p. 119.
117   Ibid.
118   Ibid., p. 120.
119   Ibid., p. 123. Beginning with the Messina Conference in June 1955, European integration progressed quickly. The conference established the Spaak Committee, named for Belgian Foreign Minister Henri Spaak, to examine proposals for integration

of the 'inner six' – the Benelux countries plus West Germany, France and Britain. The results were the drafting of two treaties setting up the European Atomic Energy Committee (Euratom) and the European Economic Committee (EEC) in 1956.

120   Maher, *The Tortuous Path*, p. 123.
121   *Dáil Debates*, Vol. 192, cols. 145–6, 15 November 1961.
122   NAI DFA CM6 22, letter, T. J. Kiernan to Con Cremin, 14 November 1961.
123   NAI DFA CM6 22, addendum, 17 November 1961.
124   Ibid.
125   Ibid.
126   NAI DFA CM6 22, telegram from Dublin to Washington, 22 November 1961.
127   NAI DFA CM6 22, letter from Cremin to Kiernan, 28 November 1961.
128   NAI DFA CM6 22, draft letter from Cremin to Kiernan, 28 November 1961. This passage was deleted in the final copy. Dean Rusk was the Secretary of State in the Kennedy and Johnson administrations.
129   NAI DFA CM6 22, confidential memorandum, 28 November 1961.
130   Ibid.
131   George W. Ball, *The Past Has Another Pattern: Memoirs* (New York, 1982), p. 219.
132   NAI DFA CM3 117/34/A, memorandum by Kevin Rush, not dated.
133   *Dáil Debates*, Vol. 193, col.1, 14 February 1962.
134   Ibid.
135   NAI DT S17246, letter from F.H. Boland to Hugh McCann, Secretary of External Affairs, 31 January 1963.
136   Samuel F. Wells, Jr, 'The defence of Europe', in Wm. Roger Louis and Hedley Bull, eds, *The Special Relationship: Anglo-American Relations Since 1945* (Oxford, 1989), p. 132.
137   NAI DT S17246, letter from Boland to McCann, 31 January 1963.
138   Ibid.
139   NAI DT S17246, McCann note, 31 January 1963.
140   NAI DT S17246, 'Notes on possible courses of action open to Ireland in the event of a break-down in the British-EEC negotiations', 31 January 1963.
141   Ibid.
142   Ibid.
143   Ibid.
144   NAI DFA 313/2 J, confidential memorandum from Washington to Secretary of External Affairs, 1 February 1963.
145   NAI DFA CM6 22, Speech by the Taoiseach on Debate on Motion to adjourn the Dáil, 5 February 1963.
146   Ibid.
147   NAI DFA CM6 22, letter from Warnock to McCann, 30 January 1963.

3

Irish recognition policy and practice, 1949–63

There are some who maintain that... recognition is a purely discretionary act of policy – an act of grace which may be withheld at pleasure and may legitimately be used as a weapon of political intervention or of economic pressure. There is no support for any such view in the bulk of the practice of... countries. On the contrary, overwhelming authority points to the view that, provided that the conditions presented by international law are fulfiled, there is a legal duty to recognize.

Sir Hersch Lauterpacht 'Recognition of governments:
one of the crucial issues of international law',
The Times, 6 January 1950[1]

The Cold War deformed the traditional international law that had developed over centuries to facilitate and regulate political, economic and other human relationships across national boundaries. It could hardly have been otherwise. For almost half a century, the world lived in a state of neither war nor peace. The independence and rights of choice of smaller states were restricted by larger neighbors in their own interest and, it was often avowed, interest of systemic security.

W. Michael Reisman, 'International Law after the Cold War'[2]

In 1949 US Secretary of State Dean Acheson testified before the House Committee on Foreign Affairs, arguing that new ideas were essential for flexibility in foreign policy. He was defending his right as Secretary of State to accept or reject policy alternatives provided by his staff. Acheson's senior officer on the policy planning staff was George F. Kennan, the architect of containment. Although containment proved to be one of the most inflexible of US foreign policies in the Cold War, early in 1949 Kennan had a new idea to advance policy in Europe. He suggested that 'a carefully phased disengagement might pave the way for German reunification and reduce East–West tensions'.[3] Acheson overruled Kennan's flexible approach. Understandably, the operational units within the State Department, staffed by desk officers, did not always welcome changes in policy. Acheson described the 'rut' in which 'operating fellows' often found themselves:

There are many plans which were formulated and on which the operating people are going ahead. With the passage of time, such plans become no longer useful. However, an operating fellow is not likely to see that. He just drives in every morning at quarter to nine and carries on policy. He may seem to be getting into hot water, but that just calls for more courage and determination. Mr. Kennan is sitting back there and says, 'This thing is outmoded. We shouldn't be doing this anymore. This is a waste of time. Do it differently, or scrap it, or change the whole thing.' He is both fore-warner and foreplanner on problems, and he is the critic. He says, 'What we are doing was fine when we started, but it is no longer a proper answer to the thing we are dealing with.'[4]

The lower and middle level in policy-making of which Acheson spoke accurately describes diplomatic recognition policy and practice in the Irish context during the years 1949–63. In establishing policies and procedures on recognition, the staff of the Department of External Affairs often encountered the 'rut' of maintaining policies that were no longer appropriate in the changing political climate. But the difficulty was not entirely with the 'operating fellow'. In fact, this chapter will argue that the largest deficiency in Irish diplomatic recognition policy and practice in the post-war period was due to the rigid nature of recognition itself. Whereas the position of Ireland in the world system in 1949 called for flexible, non-exclusionary policies that were to be justified by political considerations, the concept of diplomatic recognition was regarded as 'high policy'. Since the time of Grotius and Vattel 300 years earlier, recognition found its roots in both natural and positivist international law, and had remained virtually unassailable in principle until the twentieth century.

There is no doubt that the Cold War period after the Second World War 'deformed' traditional international law, including the concept of diplomatic recognition. The idea of international society based on legal order, expanding and thriving since 1648 and the end of the Thirty Years' War, lay in a tangled heap in 1945. Hersch Lauterpacht, the pre-eminent jurist on diplomatic recognition from Cambridge, wrote that 'law is a product of social reality',[5] but international law could not keep pace with the changes of social reality occurring in post-war Europe. By 1947 Europe was clearly divided between capitalist West and communist East. As one career US Foreign Service officer lamented in July 1947, the time had come to 'drop the pretense of one world'.[6]

In the two-world, Cold War environment, diplomatic recognition suffered multiple injuries. Expedient policy replaced legal principle. The clear distinction between *de facto* and *de jure* recognition was immediately blurred by Cold War politics. How was it possible that non-communist states could accept the *de jure* existence of new governments in Czechoslovakia or Poland under the old principles of international law? When presenting possible solutions to the problem of Czechoslovakia in 1948, Michael Rynne, the legal adviser in the Department of External Affairs, wrote to Taoiseach John A. Costello:

Probably the most modern authority on international recognition is
Professor Lauterpacht of Cambridge... According to Lauterpacht... the
fairly common belief that international recognition is exclusively a matter
of politics – that is, sovereign will divorced from legal rules or limits – is
absolutely untenable. He holds, on the contrary, that Governments are
bound by the tenets of international law, based on years of practice and
precedents, to accord or refuse recognition in certain types of cases.[7]

Rynne perhaps had no other scholarly reference from which to draw, as
Lauterpacht was pre-eminent in diplomatic recognition and international law at
the time,[8] yet political realities demanded flexibility that traditional recognition
policy could not yield. The problem was in the replacement of the former Czech
diplomat with his new communist counterpart. The crisis was inflamed by the
fear at the Vatican that Italy would succumb to the socialist/communist bloc in
the upcoming election.[9] Solidarity behind the Vatican position of opposing the
communists in every direction was key to maintaining Irish prestige. The real
difficulty was in finding the correct legal principle to justify the position:

> If, for example, the Government were to declare their inability for vital
> domestic, ideological reasons to continue in close friendly relations (as
> distinct from strict legal relations) with a Communist-controlled State,
> their position would be virtually unassailable.[10]

Based on the 'national interest' argument, Ireland thus moved upon the
slippery slope of politicizing diplomatic recognition.[11] From 1948 onward,
Lauterpacht's ideal of diplomatic recognition based on principles of
international law receded into the background of Irish foreign policy analysis.
Even Lauterpacht could not dismiss the changing nature of international law
when he presented a lecture on 'International law after the Second World War'
at the Hebrew University of Jerusalem in 1950.

> The reality of [progress in international law] has been obscured by the
> more tangible and menacing reality of the division of the world into two
> opposing groups of States – a cleavage which seems to engulf hope and to
> rule out further improvement. The outlook is dark unless that ideological
> cleavage – otherwise legitimate and, subject to the respect of the sanctity
> of human personality, in some respects beneficent – is contained within the
> secure channels of law. What can international law offer as its own
> contribution to that end? Its help must be limited for the reason that law is
> primarily the function and the result of the will of States.[12]

Lauterpacht urged states to 'make their contribution towards fostering the rule
of law without sacrificing their vital interest at a time when they deem themselves
in peril'.[13] But states were generally not as willing to sacrifice *any* interests in the

perilous time of reconstruction after 1945, and they were especially unwilling to do anything to give advantage to the 'other' side. Clearly, the 'rules of the game' had changed in post-war Europe and 'reciprocally tolerated violations' of accepted international law became the norm rather than the exception.[14]

During this time of uncertainty in international politics, Ireland distanced itself from Britain and the Commonwealth with the Republic of Ireland Act in 1949. At last, Irish foreign policy became completely unbound from British interference and, for better or worse, Ireland headed for full diplomatic independence.

In this chapter diplomatic recognition policy and practice will be examined on three levels. First, the basic rationale for studying recognition policy in Ireland will be presented. That is, recognition policy will demonstrate the degree of independence that existed in Irish foreign policy decision-making during the years 1949–63. Second, various influences on recognition policy will be considered, including the impact of the Cold War, the influence of individuals in the Department of External Affairs and the inevitable evolution in administration of policy which occurred over a fourteen-year period. Last, remembering that detail may be cumbersome, the policy changes in Irish diplomatic recognition will be studied using statements and diplomatic circulars produced by the Department of External Affairs during the period. This chapter on general recognition policy and practice in Ireland provides the background for the three anomalous case studies of East Germany, China and Israel, which come later in this book.

DEFINING *DIPLOMATIC RECOGNITION* IN THE IRISH CONTEXT

The term *diplomatic recognition* is a construct of international law that touts ambiguity at every turn. In defining the infinitive, *to recognize*, one is immediately faced with an etymological dilemma. *Recognize* stems from not one, but two Latin verbs. Not coincidentally, the two verbs mirror the nature of recognition as the term has evolved in diplomatic practice. First, *agnoscere* means 'to acknowledge', as in acknowledging the receipt of a package, or nodding one's head in passing a stranger. In political terms, *to acknowledge* coincides with the concept of *de facto* recognition in practice. The recognizing state acknowledges that the opposing state exists, meeting the functional criteria for statehood, but the recognizing state is indifferent to this knowledge. In other words, the recognizing state accepts the factual reality while remaining aloof to the establishment of a diplomatic relationship with the other state.

The second meaning found in '*to recognize*' is derived from the Latin infinitive, *accipere*. The word *accipere* means 'to admit or accept' in a partial, subjective manner, as in recognizing a person's right to membership in a group, or approving actions by giving an award of 'recognition'. In practice, this form parallels *de jure* recognition. The state conferring recognition *de jure* is not indifferent but welcoming of the other state into international society, and has made the first step toward advancing a diplomatic relationship.

One would not be risking exaggeration to argue that Irish recognition policy used the meanings of *de facto* and *de jure* recognition in every conceivable ambiguous manner. In the early years, relying on Lauterpacht, *de facto* was used primarily as a tentative measure, a 'wait-and-see' attitude. This practice was not uncommon among other recognizing states, especially when the nature of the new state (or government) was not solidified. The common practice of many states was to grant full *de jure* recognition after a relatively short period of time, although in the atmosphere of the Cold War, this practice proved to be exceptional in many cases. Ireland consistently granted *de facto* recognition in the spirit of the word *agnoscere*, maintaining the *de facto* status for long periods. In this way, Ireland recognized the existence of the state but nothing more. This practice seemed anomalous at the time, but provided Ireland with breathing space in many instances. The longest period of *de facto* recognition was the case of Israel, lasting fourteen years.

On the other hand, until 1963, the granting of *de jure* recognition meant that all was clear for Ireland to establish diplomatic relations with the state. Indeed, *de jure* recognition was symbolic of Ireland's approval and willingness to open a diplomatic relationship with the state. Again, Israel was the exception to this general rule, for after Ireland granted *de jure* recognition in 1963, diplomatic relations with Israel were not established until 1974.[15]

Diplomatic recognition has historically been a solemn act because it conveys certain reciprocal rights and duties between the two states involved. *Oppenheim's* lists six important consequences of granting recognition. First, the new state acquires the capacity to enter into diplomatic relations with other states and make treaties with them. Second, if previously existing treaties have been suspended due to the uncertain nature of the state or government, within limitations, these treaties become operative.[16] Third, the new state acquires the right (as do its citizens) to litigate against the recognizing state and/or with its private citizens. Fourth, the recognized state acquires the right of immunity from the jurisdiction of the courts of law for itself and its property from the recognizing state. Fifth, the recognized state may demand and receive possession of its property located within the jurisdiction of the recognizing state. Last, the recognized state's executive and legislative acts will be entitled to acceptance by the courts of the recognizing state, including the certain transfers of property which, absent recognition, would have been treated as invalid. In this instance, recognition may have retroactive effect.[17]

One additional reason for granting recognition to a new state, whether *de facto* or *de jure*, is that after recognition, 'all rules of public international law governing the relations between sovereign states are applicable *ipso jure*. Without recognition that may be a matter of dispute.'[18] The legal consequences of recognition, whether in favour of the state to be recognized, or for the benefit of the recognizing state, facilitate the legal, political and economic affairs of the system as a whole. Reisman and Suzuki (1976) provided this summary:

On the international plane, recognition opens the way for participation in international organizations and conferences, institutions which are used to maximize the interests of the state in question. Within other states, recognition permits diplomatic representatives a high degree of immunity. While it does not assure formal diplomatic relations, it is usually a precondition for their establishment.[19]

Eamon de Valera knew the value of diplomatic recognition. He spent almost eighteen months in the United States during 1919–20 as the new *Príomh Aire* of the Irish Republic trying to secure recognition from President Wilson. Although he was unsuccessful with Wilson, one whom T. Ryle Dwyer has described as 'a staunch Presbyterian of Scots-Irish parentage...with little or no sympathy for the Irish cause',[20] de Valera did speak from the heart in declaring the importance of recognition to the Irish people:

> When the people of a nation have proved beyond question their desire for an independent government of their own by the civilised as well as decisive test of the ballot; when they have, with scrupulous regard to propriety and method, taken all the measures necessary to establish such a government; and when, having established it, they have, through voluntary acceptance of that government's decrees and obedience to them, succeeded in making it the *de facto* ruling authority of their country, functioning every department of civil administration – no state which denies them recognition can maintain at the same time that it upholds the principle of 'government by the consent of the governed'. Particularly is this true at this moment in history when the greatest war of all time has just been fought to establish, as moral and political principles in universal application, the rights of nations, great and small, to life, liberty, and the pursuit of happiness and 'the privilege of men everywhere to choose their way of life and obedience'.[21]

De Valera did not have the experience in 1920 to understand how easily the US government, or any government for that matter, could deny his request for recognition, when the interests he perceived of the Irish Republic were placed head-to-head with the interests of another state. Ironically, in later years, he used recognition as a tool of foreign policy against certain states even when the criteria for statehood had been met, especially in the case of Israel.

IMPORTANCE OF IRISH RECOGNITION POLICY IN THE HISTORICAL CONTEXT

The details of recognition policy are generally not of interest to diplomatic historians. After all, recognition is rather an absolute position once a decision has been made. Historians use archival recognition materials to confirm dates of recognition and principal actors in the process, but generally recognition files may seem mundane to the scholar. The decision-making process in recognition is generally ignored. The files concerning Irish diplomatic recognition policy, however, reveal much more than the process of decision-making. Within the recognition files can be seen the evolutionary change from dependency to independence in Irish foreign policy. As the jurist Brierly noted in 1955, 'The proper usage of the term *independence* is to denote the status of a state which controls its own external relations without dictation from other states . . . independence does not mean freedom from law but merely *freedom from control by other states*'.[22]

One may argue that upon considering the relatively brief period of time in which the National Archives in Dublin have been opened to the public for research purposes (since 1986), many subjects contained in the archival files have yet to be studied. For this author, stumbling upon the massive amounts of material on diplomatic recognition was akin to finding a secret passageway, an underground tunnel, which paralleled every inch of current Irish diplomatic historiography. E.H. Carr's dictum, 'facts speak only when the historian calls on them',[23] implies volumes about research on diplomatic recognition in the Irish context. Justification for this study demands the answer of the 'so what?' question. Why is Ireland's diplomatic recognition policy during the years 1949–63 worthy of study?

First, recognition policy is a measurement of independent thinking. Policy exists to streamline daily activities. Eventually, however, someone is bound to question the efficacy of a policy. The challenge to policy encourages development. Second, recognition policy in Ireland during the years 1949–63 demonstrates the level of interaction with other states in the system, another measure of independence. Third, the ability to manoeuvre recognition policy within the grey areas of international law – to step close to the line of illegality but not cross over – requires agility that only comes from confidence and independence. Fourth, recognition policy serves to confirm the interests of the state and provide measurement of the state's ability to achieve foreign policy goals. In Ireland, recognition policy mirrored four main interests: ending partition, achieving economic growth, maintaining neutrality and increasing prestige. Finally, examining diplomatic recognition policy provides a window into the day-to-day functions of government departments. Reisman and Suzuki, two authors collaborating in 1976 to evaluate recognition in the changing circumstances of the Cold War, noted that 'recognition, as we have seen, is not a single act, but a continuous response of officials as well as by private participants, to claims made by aspiring elites and their adversaries in different situations and with different power bases at their disposal'.[24]

Modern Irish diplomatic historians fight a dual battle in sifting through the historical evidence. First, the archival files are the result of an executive management style, which existed well into the 1950s that Dermot Keogh has referred to as 'closed government' in which secrecy played a key role.[25] Archival evidence does not always present the complete picture. Two of the principal players in recognition policy during 1949-63, Taoiseach Eamon de Valera and Secretary of External Affairs Joseph P. Walshe, have been alternately described by Keogh as both 'parsimonious' and 'extreme' in foreign policy secrecy. In fact, it is difficult to trace de Valera's thoughts on recognition policy at all; much of the written information available resulted from lower-level administrative activities, generally in the Department of External Affairs. Walshe's feelings are much more evident, especially in the letters written to the Department while he was Ambassador at the Holy See from 1946–54. Keogh found the draconian use of secrecy in government as stemming from several sources, including de Valera's revolutionary past, his belief in censorship in general, and the wartime threat of invasion.[26]

In some ways, the style of government was a reflection of the struggle for independence. From 1932 until Fianna Fáil left office in 1948, the team of De Valera and Walshe had dominated foreign policy-making. Closed-government came naturally to both men and served to strengthen the internal core of policy-making, although it created a legacy of negativity in public calls for openness, democracy and transparency in government. This reliance on secrecy, however, makes the maintenance files on recognition policy even more intriguing. The duty of an administrator of recognition policy during this period, the archetypal 'operations fellow', was not to initiate change, or to aggravate the system, but to hold firm to the status quo. Maintenance of the status quo in recognition policy required an enormous amount of administrative effort and paperwork.

The second challenge for scholars researching in the National Archives has both positive and negative components. A unique feature of the diplomatic recognition files is their administrative and utilitarian nature. The files are surprisingly orderly and complete, with much of the material chronologically intact. In contrast to other archival material that sometimes appears to be compiled after the fact, the files on recognition seem to have been removed directly from the filing cabinets of those working with them and placed intact into the archival system. The recognition files appear quite complete, compared to other archival sources in other governments that have been purged at length. The positive elements are quite apparent; however, the volume of superfluous material is extraordinary and perhaps could be seen as a negative feature. Ronan Fanning, the first scholar to examine the files of the Department of Finance at length, remarked on the 'explosive growth in the volume of [Finance's] records from 1946–47' which he attributed to the 'additional documentation' emanating from the Department of External Affairs.[27] Positive or negative aspects aside, the archival records of the Department of External Affairs hold many narratives upon which historians may call for their craft.

EARLY RECOGNITION POLICY – 1948

One week after the first inter-party government took office, headed by John A. Costello, Taoiseach, and Seán MacBride, Minister for External Affairs, Europe faced yet another post-war threat. On 24 February 1948, the Communist Party of Czechoslovakia overthrew the constitutional government of that country. The impact on the West was enormous, 'where there still existed guilty consciences over what had been done to the Czechs at Munich ten years before'.[28] Western governments braced for the worst, having witnessed the terror of absorption on Lithuania, Latvia, Estonia, Albania, Yugoslavia and Rumania, all independent states made satellites by the Soviet Union since 1940. The Soviet takeover of Czechoslovakia had two immediate effects: first, to ensure the passage of the Marshall Plan in the United States Congress; and second, to bring Britain, France and the Benelux countries closer in forming a military alliance.[29]

Efforts of cooperation with the Soviet Union were increasingly difficult after February 1948. The occupation systems for Berlin and the rest of Germany were causing considerable strain on allied relations. As Konrad Adenauer remarked in his memoirs, 'the necessary basis of mutual confidence was lacking in the administration of Berlin as much as in the administration of the zones outside'.[30] From late March until June, the Soviets began closing the routes of the Western Allies to Berlin, first by automobile and train, and finally by water. The Allies responded with the Berlin Airlift beginning on 25 June 1948 and continuing until May 1949.

In this turbulent political environment, the Irish certainly had enough to worry about. Reports arrived almost daily from Ambassador Joseph Walshe at the Holy See concerning the upcoming Italian elections. Walshe was convinced, and subsequently convinced the new Irish government *and* the Catholic hierarchy, that without a massive propaganda effort, the Italian government would also fall to the communists. A total of £57,000 was raised from various dioceses and channelled through Walshe[31] to fund an organization, *Comitato Civico*, headed by a physician, Luigi Gedda. Gedda's efforts were successful. Walshe telegrammed the results home to External Affairs: 'Elections as you have seen from press results is defeat of Communists. Over 90 per cent polling achieved by Gedda's ad hoc propaganda.'

In Dublin, meanwhile, Taoiseach Costello asked the Department of External Affairs Legal Advisers' Office to draft a policy on Czechoslovakia. The responsibility fell to Dr Michael Rynne. Rynne had worked for the department for many years, hired by Joseph Walshe in 1932.[32] After becoming legal adviser in 1939, Rynne became one of the most outspoken voices in the department for continuity in policy. He was the resident expert on the theories of Hersch Lauterpacht and the resulting policy paper on Czechoslovakia exhibited his understanding of diplomatic recognition principles in international law.

In the case of Czechoslovakia, Rynne weighed the possibilities of non-recognition of the new communist government, or the withdrawal of recognition from the Czechoslovakian government altogether. He noted that if only one government remained in Czechoslovakia, and Ireland withdrew recognition from that government, in essence, as far as Ireland was concerned, 'the Republic of Czechoslovakia and its people [would cease] to exist'.[33] Rynne was not quite accurate in his assessment of the law, and as will be shown, would eventually rationalize that withdrawing recognition from a government is not the same as withdrawing state recognition.

Rynne reasoned through a policy of non-recognition. What would be the ramifications if Ireland withdrew recognition of the Czechoslovak government? Three factors were involved. First, if non-recognition were pursued, trade would probably suffer 'but, from our point of view, the loss would probably be negligible'.[34] Rynne cited falling exports to Czechoslovakia, but rising imports.[35] Surprisingly, the trade statistics show that exports from Ireland to Czechoslovakia grew substantially in spite of the changes occurring, from IR£2,036 in 1947 to IR£75,444 in 1948, even after the absorption by the Soviet Union. Czechoslovakia is the first of several instances in which Irish trade continued to develop, in spite of recognition or a diplomatic relationship.

The second factor to be considered in non-recognition was an Air Services Agreement made in Dublin on 29 January 1947. Rynne believed this agreement 'would not raise any practical difficulty, since no air services are actually in operation between the two countries'.[36] The Czechoslovakian government was quite active in establishing air services agreements throughout 1947 and 1948. Secretary of State George Marshall voiced his concern in March 1948 that 'in view of political developments Czech, Dept seriously concerned Czech air expansion to Middle and Near East'.[37] The Czechoslovakian government was aggressively pursuing an air route to Bombay. As will be noted in Chapter 6, by July 1948 the Czech airfields served to arm Israeli warplanes in violation of a UN resolution prohibiting such activity during the Arab/Israeli truce.[38]

Writing in March 1948, Rynne was perhaps aware of the recent joint decision by the United States and Great Britain on 'a course of action vis-à-vis the Soviet Union and its satellite states in matters relating to civil aviation'.[39] The agreement restricted operating rights for the USSR and satellite countries 'to the minimum necessary to secure...essential requirements on a reciprocal basis' and to deny 'all but the minimum facilities necessary' to operate air services.[40] Further, the United States and Great Britain would prevent the export of aircraft and equipment to the Soviet Union and its satellites, and would also prevent the use of their facilities for the 'overhaul, refitting or major maintenance' on Soviet or satellite aircraft'.[41] Rynne commented that the Air Services Agreement 'appears to be the only bilateral treaty we have made with Czechoslovakia'.[42]

In February 1948 the democratic elements in the Czechoslovakian government began to feel 'the crush' pursued by the Soviet Union against them.[43] The Communist Party rapidly replaced the democratic elements within the government, especially within the police force. By 19 February the American Ambassador, Laurence Steinhardt, returned from Washington to Prague with an offer of $25 million in credit, 'to give political support to the democrats in their struggle against the communists'.[44] The trade union movement, backed by their militia, pushed events in Czechoslovakia past the breaking point. On 24 February, over 2,500,000 workers led a one-hour strike to show the strength of the communist-led trade unions in Prague. The next day, President Benes reluctantly submitted a list of the new government in which the communists represented over half the portfolios. Ambassador Steinhardt described the crisis as follows:

> The Communists were aggressive and bold, and were sufficiently organized to take advantage of the situation. The non-Communists had no adhesion as a group, did not recognize the issue as one of Communism against non-Communism and continued to place their individual party loyalties and personal ambitions ahead of their opposition to Communism. This, combined with weak leadership at the top, particularly on the part of the President, caused the debacle.[45]

As Keogh noted in *Ireland and the Vatican*, the Czechoslovakia crisis of February 1948 put the Irish government on full alert due to Ambassador Walshe's suggestion that Pope Pius XII might want 'to make Ireland the home of the Holy See' during 'the period of persecution' in Italy.[46] By 23 March, the date of Rynne's analysis of the Czechoslovakian recognition problem, Secretary Boland and Minister of External Affairs MacBride made a rushed trip to Paris to meet with Walshe. MacBride 'said that he humoured the ambassador and sent him back to his post content that he had got most of his own way'.[47] Walshe certainly felt that the Italian crisis was of primary importance to the Irish government, but at home, this was not the case. Michael Rynne, during the middle of the crisis, had enough time to pursue the Czechoslovakian recognition problem, producing a fifteen-page memorandum.

The third factor that warranted Rynne's consideration in the Czechoslovakian matter was also the most significant in the recognition issue. 'Where the position created by the withdrawal of recognition would produce most inconvenience and, incidentally, disclose the fact that it was unique, would be in relation to judicial proceedings.' Rynne noted that 'if the Government were to cease to recognise the Government of Czechoslovakia, the latter would not be permitted to plead in Irish Courts'. The effect on civilians in Ireland would be the most notable, due to 'the fact that quite a number of Czech citizens (engaged in the beet sugar industry, etc.) have settled here'.[48]

Eventually Rynne suggested the most viable option toward the Czechoslovakian government would be to sever diplomatic relations. But Rynne wanted to pursue something more. Not only did he suggest that diplomatic relations should be suspended, but that the terms of recognition should be downgraded to *de facto* recognition. This approach, first suggested in terms of Czechoslovakia, became a guiding principle in Irish diplomatic recognition policy for the period 1949–63. Rynne explained the position:

> By recognising the fact (because it *is* a fact) that the Communist-controlled

coalition is really the only government administering in Czechoslovakia, we are not thereby necessarily recognising that that government is legally (or constitutionally) entitled to be regarded as a normal Government. In other words, we have actually withdrawn part of our former recognition – the *de jure* part – while, in allowing an appointee of the Czechoslovak government to reside here without diplomatic or consular status, privileges or immunities, we have severed diplomatic relations but not all relations.[49]

Rynne provided support of the position with the British practice toward the Franco régime in Spain during the Spanish Civil War, 1936–39. The British foreign office adopted the position that a writ against the Nationalist Government of Spain 'had to be set aside as tending to implead the government of a foreign sovereign state' but the British government 'had exchanged agents with General Franco's administration on the understanding that diplomatic status for them would not be claimed by either party'.[50] Rynne concluded that the 'greatest drawback' to this position in respect to Czechoslovakia would rest on two points. First, the presence of a communist agent in Ireland would cause anti-government propaganda by the 'ill-informed public'. Second, the withdrawal of *de jure* recognition might be difficult to justify to the Czechoslovakian government. Rynne concluded that, all legal considerations aside, the decision rested with the Irish government in determining national interests.

> [O]nce our Government have convinced themselves on paper that they are, in the exercise of their sovereign right and in the vital interest of the people they govern, taking the proper course with Czechoslovakia, a reasoned statement of their attitude will be convincing – no matter how unpalatable – to the Czechs and to the world at large. If, for example, the Government were to declare their inability for vital domestic, ideological reasons to continue in close friendly relations (as distinct from strict legal relations) with a Communist-controlled State, their position would be virtually unassailable.[51]

Rynne's comments on Czechoslovakia became policy for additional recognition problems that appeared in 1948–50, especially in the cases of Israel and East Germany that are specifically addressed as case studies in the following chapters.

MAINTENANCE OF THE STATUS QUO – 1950–55

From 1950 until 1955 very few new recognition issues appeared in Irish foreign policy. Overall, the period was quiet in terms of new states in the system. Membership in the United Nations had only increased from fifty-one states in 1945 to sixty by 1950. During the first five years of the United Nations' existence, the admission of new members became 'the focus of major political contention'.[52] But only one new member, Indonesia, was admitted between 1950 and 1955. The politics of the Cold War forced the United States and the Soviet Union to adopt a policy of 'competitive exclusion' wherein states applying for UN membership fell into two groups: potential members of the Soviet Bloc and those supported by the 'Western grouping' of states.[53] From its original application to join the United Nations in 1946, Ireland's membership was delayed by the Soviet veto until 1955.

The case of recognition for Indonesia was straightforward in the Irish context. The territory and independence of Indonesia Raya (Greater Indonesia) was under contention from 1945–49 by the republicans (led by Sukarno and Hatta) and the former Dutch colonialists. The local populations perceived the situation as revolutionary, and were intent on overthrowing the elite who had first collaborated with the Japanese and then the Dutch. After November 1945 and the Battle of Surabaya where hundreds of British Commonwealth troops were slaughtered, the Allies were forced to come to terms with the Republic. The resulting agreement, the Linggajati Agreement of 1946, provided for Dutch recognition of republican rule on Java and Sumatra, and the Netherlands-Indonesian Union under the Dutch Crown. The intent was to place the archipelago under a loose federal arrangement. Although the agreement was signed in May 1947, neither the Dutch nor the Republicans were satisfied. Asserting violations of the Linggajati Agreement, the Dutch launched a police action against the Republic in July 1947. Although the Dutch reasserted control over certain areas, the United Nations stepped in. Meanwhile, a leftist faction of the Republican forces called for the population in Madiun (East Java) to overthrow the republican government. Significantly, the Madiun Affair was crushed by loyal military forces of the Republic, and signalled to the Western world (especially the United States) that the republicans were anticommunist. The Hague continued its hard-line policies against the republicans who were exiled into northern and western parts of Sumatra. In January 1949, the Security Council passed a resolution demanding reinstatement of the republican government. The Dutch were pressured to accept a full transfer of authority to the Indonesians by 1 July 1950, except for the territory of Dutch New Guinea. The transfer occurred on 20 December 1949 and many countries accorded *de jure* recognition, including Ireland.[54]

Recognition of Indonesia stands out in the Irish context due to the simplicity with which recognition was accorded. The Dutch authorities requested recognition from the Irish Government and the Department of External Affairs responded with a complete 'memorandum for the government'.[55] The wording of the memorandum included the following statement:

> Considering the specific request made by the Netherlands Government and the particularly friendly and sympathetic attitude which this country would generally be expected to adopt towards a new State created in vindication

of the principles of national independence and self-determination, it appeared [un]desirable [*sic*] that, with so many other States publishing the fact of their formal recognition, Ireland's position should remain in doubt.[56]

The recognition became complete upon the receipt of an acknowledgement by the Minister for Foreign Affairs in Indonesia.[57]

But the procedural simplicity of the Indonesian recognition was exceptional. From 1948 onward, recognition problems were individually defined in terms of Ireland's interests. Answering recognition requests thus became more stylized. The consummate Irish method of handling difficult recognition issues at the public level was basically to ignore them altogether. In the period until 1955, the Department of External Affairs did not establish a formal distinction between the recognition of states and recognition of governments. Trying to establish broad recognition policy was impossible in the Cold War environment; there were simply too many exceptional cases.

By 1950, Sir Hersch Lauterpacht conceded that 'the distinction must be asserted between recognizing a Government and entering into diplomatic relations with it'.[58] Lauterpacht's statement appeared in *The Times* on 6 January 1950, the day Britain extended *de jure* recognition to the People's Republic of China (PRC). Further, Lauterpacht provided the following diplomatic guidelines:

> No State is legally obligated to enter into and maintain diplomatic relations with a State or Government which it recognizes. On the other hand, it cannot enter into full and normal diplomatic relations with a State or Government which it does not recognize.[59]

The People's Republic of China did not answer Britain's formal request for diplomatic relations until 1954. The process had been sidetracked by the PRC's demand of terms to diplomatic relations, which included the stipulation of British support for the PRC at the United Nations.[60] Throughout the Korean Conflict (1950–53), British and Chinese relations remained stable. Harris argued that British opinion never turned against China due to Korea, 'nor was China, in a national sense, seen as the villain'.[61] However, Britain's China policy did provide an inroad for furthering British recognition policy. In March 1951, Herbert Morrison, Britain's Foreign Secretary, answered a parliamentary question in the House of Commons, which bifurcated Britain's recognition practice. Boland, now Ambassador to Britain, sent the text of the Morrison Statement to the Department of External Affairs, which read as follows:

> On the 21st March (1951) the Foreign Secretary was asked to state in the House of Commons 'on what principles he acts when deciding whether diplomatic recognition should be accorded to foreign Governments'. [Mr.

Morrison replied]: 'The question of the recognition of a State or Government should be distinguished from the question of entering into diplomatic relations with it, which is entirely discretionary. On the other hand, it is international law which defines the conditions under which a Government should be recognised *de jure* or *de facto*, and it is a matter of judgment in each particular case whether a régime fulfils the conditions. The conditions under international law for the recognition of a new régime as the *de facto* Government of a State are that the new régime has in fact effective control over most of the State's territory and that this control seems likely to continue. The conditions for the recognition of a new régime as the *de jure* Government of a State are that the new régime should not merely have effective control over most of the State's territory, but that it should, in fact, be firmly established. His Majesty's Government consider that recognition should be accorded when the conditions specified by international law are, in fact, fulfilled and that recognition should not be given when these conditions are not fulfilled. The recognition of a Government *de jure* or *de facto* should not depend on whether the character of the régime is such as to command His Majesty's Government's approval'.[62]

The Morrison Statement amounted to a flat rejection of the principle of legitimacy in diplomatic recognition, requiring only two conditions for recognition of a government within a state: effective control and firm establishment. Corbett argued that 'British thought and practice are marked by the conviction that good relations demand the recognition of firmly established situations regardless of the mode of establishment' and that Britain 'has not followed the American use of non-recognition'.[63]

When Michael Rynne received the Morrison Statement, he made the following notation: 'This may need a new file. It relates to the Recognition of States and Govts. in general.'[64] As the case of Israel will show, Lauterpacht's dictum in 1950 and the Morrison Statement in 1951 provided further rationale for Ireland's pursuit of independent recognition policies. Although the Morrison Statement indicated that if a government is effectively in control of specific territory and firmly established, that government should be recognized *de jure*, the Irish focused on the avoidance of a diplomatic relationship altogether. Choosing the path of non-recognition toward states with whom they did not wish to establish diplomatic relations solved the problem. If a state is not willing to grant full, *de jure* recognition to another state, then in no way may it enter into diplomatic relations with it. This concept in particular provided a fortress for Ireland's policy toward Israel.

From 1951 to 1955, the Irish foreign policy of recognition consisted primarily of maintenance toward non-recognized states, trying to balance issues of trade and economic expansion with political and security aspirations. The Soviet Union continued to veto Ireland's application for membership in the

United Nations, while Eamon de Valera and Frank Aiken, in office from June 1951 until June 1954, tried to establish some kind of military policy over what Keogh has termed 'the anxiety felt... over the relative defencelessness of Ireland'.[65] While Aiken pursued the purchase of US arms in 1952, he confessed to the American Ambassador in France that 'unlike Switzerland and Sweden, Ireland [has] no firm-rooted tradition of neutrality', and that neutrality 'was a tactic designed to achieve unification of Ireland'.[66] The American ambassador replied that he 'did not agree that Irish policy [concerning] collective defense was entirely logical'.[67] Throughout 1952 and into early 1953, the Irish diplomats met the same refusal for arms from the United States. Then in 1953, Seán Lemass went to Washington and met with Secretary of State John Foster Dulles, approaching the security problem in a new way. Lemass asked Dulles for advice on Ireland's application to the United Nations.[68] By the end of 1955, with Fianna Fáil out of office, the Irish had not only been successful with membership at the United Nations, but had also agreed to a CIA liaison in Dublin.[69]

In September 1955, Dr Alfred Kolb of the German Legation in Dublin asked the Department of External Affairs for information about Ireland's diplomatic relations with other states. Kolb's letter was a harbinger of the reconstruction of Irish recognition policy that began with Ireland's membership in the United Nations in December 1955 and was not complete until May 1963. The letter to Kolb, written by T.J. Horan of the department, opened a Pandora's box in recognition issues. The letter is significant for three main reasons. First, the information Horan provided to Kolb was not quite accurate. Although Horan had worked for the department since 1938, he did not have the legal credentials to answer matters of recognition policy, especially with members of foreign delegations. Second, as will be shown in the text of the letter, Horan's subjectivity on states that he chose to *exclude* from the list is puzzling. Last, his letter (inaccuracies and all) became part of the general file on recognition policy, and his mistakes were repeated in other policy statements.

Dear Dr. Kolb:
Some days ago you telephoned me asking for information about Ireland's diplomatic relations with other States, e.g., what are the States with which Ireland has no diplomatic relations, etc., etc.

Ireland, though an ancient nation, is a comparatively young State. Consequently the number of countries with which to date it has formal diplomatic relations is comparatively small. That number, however, is no doubt likely to increase. The fact, therefore, that Ireland has no diplomatic relations with a particular country does not mean that diplomatic relations were not opened with that country for ideological reasons. There are many countries with which in the opinion of the Department it would be in the interests of Ireland to have diplomatic relations but, for one reason or another – very often reasons of a financial order – we have not yet 'got around to it'. A country in this category would, for instance, be Denmark.

There is, of course, another set of countries with which we have no diplomatic relations, and if the question of opening diplomatic relations arose, the question of ideological differences were almost certainly have to be considered, e.g., USSR.

I should, however, point out that Ireland does recognise the USSR, both *de jure* and *de facto* – with this exception however that Ireland does not recognise the territory of the USSR insofar as it includes the three Baltic Republics of Estonia, Latvia and Lithuania.

Neither does Ireland – either *de jure* or *de facto* – give recognition to the following states:

'German Democratic Republic' (East Germany)
North Viet-Nam
South Viet-Nam
Laos
Cambodia
Nationalist China
Red China
North Korea
South Korea
Poland

With regard to Poland, Ireland, in common with some other States, still recognises the former Polish Government. As you are aware the Polish Government in exile has a career Consulate here in Dublin.

Ireland gives only *de facto* recognition to the State of Israel, not *de jure* recognition.

I hope the foregoing gives you the information you wish to have.

[signed] T.J. Horan[70]

An addendum to the letter, dated 10 November 1955, stated:

The position with regard to China and Poland as set out in the attached letter of 5th September, 1955, is not quite accurate. A distinction must be drawn between the recognition of States and the recognition of Governments. Ireland fully recognises the States of China and Poland but in the case of China Ireland recognises neither the Peking nor the Formosa regime and in the case of Poland it recognises the Polish Government-in-exile.[71]

Dr Kolb of the German Legation perhaps was on a fishing expedition. In May 1955 the Paris Treaties had been signed, wherein the Federal Republic of Germany became sovereign and entered an enlarged Brussels Pact and later NATO. The Western Allies agreed to recognize the Federal Republic as the sole legitimate state of the German people, as well as setting out restrictive security arrangements. Behind the scenes the Soviet Union began consolidating economic efforts with the West Germans, a fact which was made public when Chancellor Adenauer went to Moscow by invitation in September 1955. Adenauer achieved the release of 10,000 German prisoners of war and established full diplomatic relations with the USSR. But under no circumstances was Adenauer or the Federal Republic willing to concede recognition to the Soviet-controlled territory of Germany – East Germany. By December 1955, the Foreign Minister, Dr Walter Hallstein, established unilateral foreign policy to prevent the international recognition of the German Democratic Republic. The ensuing Hallstein Doctrine threatened to withdraw diplomatic recognition from states who chose to recognize the GDR.[72] The USSR was the only exception to the rule.

In developing the response to Dr Kolb's inquiry, T.J. Horan prepared a set of working papers on Ireland's diplomatic relationships. The first list, entitled 'States established since Second World War', included states 'recognized by Ireland' and 'not recognized by Ireland'.[73] Horan's original list included the following states:

Recognised by Ireland
Burma, Ceylon, Iceland, India, Indonesia, Israel (*de facto*), Lebanon, Palestine,[74] Philippines, Syria

Not recognised by Ireland
Members of the UN
Cambodia, Laos, Libya, Jordan

Non-members of the UN
Morocco, Tunisia, Sudan, Korea (South), North Korea, Vietnam (South), North Vietnam, People's Republic of China, German Democratic Republic, Mongolian People's Republic.

Attached to the working papers is a series of annotations on specific states, including the cases of Laos, Cambodia and South Vietnam as 'former *associated* States within the French Union'. These annotations were made at least after April 1956, and include Sudan, Libya, Morocco and Tunisia. A revised chart based on Horan's original list in September 1955 served to clarify Ireland's position on 'Established since Second World War'.

Recognised by Ireland
Burma, Ceylon, Iceland, India, Indonesia, Lebanon, Pakistan, Philippines, Syria

Not recognised by Ireland
Members of the UN
Israel (*de facto* recognition accorded), Jordan, Libya, Sudan, Laos, Cambodia, Poland (Warsaw Govt)

Non-members of UN
North Korea, South Korea, North Vietnam, South Vietnam, German Democratic Republic, People's Republic of China, Mongolian People's Republic

In the meantime, T.J. Horan had other concerns. Horan was scheduled to replace the retiring Chargé d'Affaires Matthew Murphy in Buenos Aires at the end of 1955. On 16 September the Argentine Armed Forces launched a revolt against its long-term president, Juan Domingo Perón. On 19 September Perón was forced to resign. Replaced by a *junta* of four generals, the diplomatic corps in Buenos Aires and their respective states wasted no time in recognizing the new government. The telegram to Dublin read: 'Recognition of new government headed by provisional President General Eduardo Lonardi. Recommend early favourable reply.'[75] By the time the Irish government received the telegram the following day, T.J. Horan had taken charge of the situation. Horan showed the telegram to Maurice Moynihan, Secretary to the Taoiseach, on the morning of 26 September. By late afternoon, in spite of the fact that the Taoiseach, John A. Costello, was absent, the Tanaiste William Norton approved recognition of the new Argentine government. Moynihan suggested that no mention be made of whether the recognition was *de facto* or *de jure*.[76]

Moynihan also prudently suggested that the Department of External Affairs should submit a formal 'memorandum to the government' 'with a view to having this decision confirmed, as we did in 1950 after the recognition of the Indonesian Government', a reflection more of Moynihan's professionalism than of evolutionary Irish recognition policy.[77] The new provisional president, General Eduardo Lonardi, managed to stay in power long enough to stabilize the situation, but was ousted in a bloodless coup d'état on 13 November 1955. By 8 November, however, T.J. Horan was steaming toward Buenos Aires with his credentials. Matthew Murphy wrote on 16 November that the new provisional president, General Pedro Eugenio Aramburu, assumed office. Murphy commented that the 'situation is confused and tense' and that as the two former presidents, Perón and Lonardi, both denied their resignations from office, 'there are (in theory) now three Presidents of Argentina'.[78] However, reason continued to rule among the diplomatic corps, and further recognition of the new government in Argentina was not sought.[79]

QUESTIONING RECOGNITION POLICY AFTER UN ADMISSION – 1955–57

After obtaining membership in the United Nations in December 1955, the Department of External Affairs began a new review of diplomatic recognition problems. The case that caught the attention of the Department of External Affairs, and Dr Eoin MacWhite in particular, was the independence of the

Sudan in December 1955. Ambassador Boland in London provided the initial correspondence,[80] but MacWhite provided a memorandum that spelled out the difficulty of recognizing Sudanese independence.[81]

First, MacWhite noted, 'it would appear that the Sudan fulfills the usual requirements for international recognition'. He continued:

> However the Sudan is fundamentally an Arab State and we have withheld recognition from Libya and the Hashemite Kingdom of Jordan[82] because we feared that such recognition would provoke pressure from Israel to which we accord *de facto* recognition but withhold *de jure* recognition pending a satisfactory settlement of the problem of the Holy Places. It would be invidious to accord recognition to the Sudan before we do so for Libya and Jordan which are older states, unless we can defend our reasons for refusing recognition.[83]

Second, MacWhite realized that Ireland's new membership in the United Nations 'gives us added reason for a general reconsideration of our recognition policy in regard to the UN member States which we do not recognise'.[84] Then, in a moment of true lucidity, MacWhite argued:

> In most of these cases we are very much 'the odd man out' in not recognising these new states and our attitude is not what might be expected from a country which won its freedom the hard way not so very long ago. While possibly Jordan and certainly Israel may be complicated by our following of a rigid Vatican line, there is no good reason to stall further on Libya. We held out on Laos and Cambodia because of our missionaries in China who have since been repatriated and the Maynooth Mission has withdrawn its objection.[85]

Finally, MacWhite suggested that 'the time is ripe for a general clearing of outstanding recognition matters on which there are good grounds for changing our present attitude'.[86] The handwritten response to MacWhite's suggestion revealed the unwillingness of the Department of External Affairs to revamp policy, based on the difficulty with maintaining non-recognition toward Israel.

> I agree that we should prepare a case for the recognition of all States [that are] members of U.N.O. which we have not already recognised, including the Sudan which will obviously be admitted to membership next November. To your bid must now be added Tunisia and Morocco.[87] As we clearly could not *publicly* recognise so many Arab States (having just refused full recognition to Israel), our case [illegible] be based on a plan for *tacit* recognition.[88]

The problem of recognition for Israel began to impede other recognition policy. Other members of the Civil Service began to question recognition policy in general after UN membership, including Ambassador Con Cremin at the Holy See. Cremin, who had replaced Ambassador Joseph P. Walshe at the Holy See in 1954, provided a reasoned attitude to recognition problems. His policy advice was offered not to further his own advancement, but to improve the internal coordination of the Department of External Affairs. Cremin spent the years 1946–50 in Dublin, first as Counsellor and then as Assistant Secretary. His career eventually would lead to the ambassadorship in London (1956–58 and 1963) to Secretary of the Department (1958–62). Later, Cremin served as long-term Ambassador to the United Nations (1964–74).

Beginning with a questioning letter in February 1956, Cremin was the most significant influence in Irish recognition policy during the period 1949–63. During his tenure as Secretary of the department, he streamlined and overhauled recognition policy. Due to the status quo nature of the department, however, even Cremin ran into serious obstacles in defining policy. The learning curve that Cremin faced in mastering the legal aspects of recognition was daunting, but he scaled it. With broader interests in mind, the points that Cremin raised in 1956 were seminal in untangling recognition policy.

After T.J. Horan's letter to Dr Kolb was distributed to the Irish missions abroad as a circular note in November 1955, Cremin questioned the statements on recognition from his position at the Holy See almost three months later.

> With reference to your circular note . . . concerning our position in relation to the recognition of certain states and Governments, I should be glad to know, for general guidance, whether the statement that we fully recognize[89] the States of China and Poland is to be taken as meaning that we recognize the present Polish State within the limits claimed by Warsaw, i.e. in particular, including the territories which were German up to the recent war (those generally described as bounded by the Oder-Neisse line), and, if this is not the case, what are the limits of the Polish State recognized by us.

Then, Cremin inadvertently inserted a larger issue to be considered; that is, state succession after the Second World War and the beginning of decolonisation as guiding principles of recognition policy.

> While not conversant with the intricacies of international law on this question of the recognition of States and Governments, I wonder whether the principle enunciated in the note is not perhaps too summary as related solely to our particular case. If it were legitimate to infer a general principle (applicable to our case) from the correspondence under reference it would seem that of the various States, the Governments of which we do not recognize, the only States that we do recognize are those that had a legal international existence before the war. If this is a correct inference, *I wonder if the criterion invoked is really sound.*[90] I assume that we have not,

by a formal decision taken in recent years, decided to recognize the States of Poland and China. In that case our current recognition of States concerned would seem to derive from the fact that Chinese and Polish States were internationally recognized (also by us) prior to the war. Do we thus also continue to recognize States which we recognized before the war and in respect of which we have taken no act that could be deemed to put an end to such recognition? An instance of such States might be the Baltic Republics to which Mr. Horan's letter specifically refers.[91]

In order to clarify his position at the Holy See, Cremin specifically addressed the problem of Poland:

> Dealing with the specific case of Poland, which is as you know of some interest in connection with the behaviour of the Holy See, I wonder whether the two statements that: 1) we fully recognize the State of Poland; and 2) we still recognize the former Polish Government would not to the average reader mean that we would formally recognize Poland within its present limits if (perhaps *per impossible*) the Government in exile were to find itself in power in Warsaw.[92]

Next Cremin asserted the difficulty of the China recognition problem, a situation in which he would become completely familiar during his ambassadorship at the United Nations. Until 1956, however, no one in the department had seriously examined the so-called 'Two-China Problem' in technical recognition terms.

> A somewhat similar question, although of possibly less practical import as far as we are concerned, arises in relation to the limits of the State of China we recognize. There would, on the face of it, appear to be a difference between our attitude towards the Polish and Chinese regimes. In the former case, we continue to recognize the Government in exile although it has no effective control over Polish territory, whereas in the latter case we do not recognize the so-called Nationalist or Formosa regime which is still on active Chinese territory. Did we, in fact, formally refuse to recognize the present Nationalist regime or cease to recognize the pre-Communist Chinese Government of which the Nationalists claim to be the successors?[93]

For the pursuance of his duties at the Vatican, Cremin inserted the final paragraph:

> While these points may seem to be largely of an academic nature they may perhaps have taken on a certain practical aspect now that we are in the United Nations. It would in any case be desirable for this mission to know

more precisely...how we stand in relation to the territories in dispute between Poland and Germany as this matter is of practical concern to the Vatican because of the problem of dealing with vacancies in bishoprics in German areas now under Polish control.[94]

Cremin's comment, 'while these points may seem to be largely of an academic nature', is telling of the situation that Ireland found itself in after joining the United Nations. From 1949 until 1955, Ireland's foreign policies were not subject to the authoritative conditions of 'belonging' to international organizations. Membership in the Council of Europe, in which Ireland's sovereignty was completely respected, was not quite the same as belonging to the United Nations. The civil administration, of which Cremin was a member, was destined to become more circumspect in its operations in the international arena after UN membership. While the international visibility increased Ireland's overall prestige in the system, the cracks in Irish foreign policy also began to appear. Cremin was absolutely correct in his assessment of recognition policy as 'academic in nature' because the execution of recognition policy seemed to rely upon international legal principles. The simple letter that Horan innocently produced for the German Legation was perhaps the catalyst that changed Irish recognition policy, but Cremin brought home the practical issues involved in setting definitive policy.

In March 1956, the question of recognizing Israel appeared once again. The Israeli Ambassador in Washington called upon John J. Hearne, Ireland's long-term Washington Ambassador, submitting a formal request from the government of Israel to exchange diplomatic representatives. A junior staff member of the department prepared a memorandum that summarized the policy toward Israel from 1949. Unfortunately, the memorandum reflected the department line of justifying non-recognition of Israel on the protection of the Holy Places. In the seven years since the decision was made to limit recognition of Israel to *de facto* status, no movement in policy analysis occurred. Once again the message was repeated: 'to meet the just claims of the Christian world for an international régime guaranteeing the safety of the Holy Places and freedom of access to them', a phrase created for Seán MacBride's Estimates Speech on 13 July 1949.[95]

In June 1956, the Canadian Ambassador in Dublin requested that Seán Murphy, Secretary of the Department of External Affairs since May 1955, provide Ireland's position on 'the group of Communist countries admitted in December 1955'.[96] In particular, the Canadians were questioning Ireland's policy toward Albania, Bulgaria, Hungary and Rumania. An unidentified staff member drafted the following reply:

With reference to your letter of the 15th June our position with regard to recognition of the Communist countries admitted to the United Nations last meeting of the General Assembly is that we do recognise them though we have never made any public announcement to that effect. Except in the case of Hungary we have had no dealings on the diplomatic level with these countries and we have, of course, no intention of establishing diplomatic relations with any of them.[97]

Then, to emphasize Ireland's responsibility as a new member of the United Nations, the letter continued: 'In effect we recognise all Governments of the Member states of the United Nations except the Polish Government in Warsaw. Ireland, of course, still recognises the Polish Government in Exile.'[98] On 19 June 1956 an internal memorandum written by Sheila Murphy of the Department of External Affairs identified on-going recognition problems.[99] The text of the elementary memorandum follows:

Jordan   established 1946, has never sought our recognition. As she also is involved in the Holy Places controversy we would not wish to give her more than *de facto* recognition as in the case of Israel.

Libya   sought our recognition on her establishment in 1951. It was decided to take no action partly because Libya was merely a 'puppet' State kept alive by the Western Big Powers and partly because it was thought that formal recognition of this Arab State might give unnecessary offence to Israel which has continually pressed for full recognition.

Sudan   sought our recognition on her establishment a few months ago. As this was a period of rising Arab–Israeli tension, recognition was not considered advisable, more particularly as no action had been taken on the prior Libyan application. Sudan's application for membership of UNO has been approved by the Security Council and it is clear that she will be admitted to membership at the November Assembly.

Tunisia/Morocco   No direct request for recognition has so far been received from these two newly established States. A letter addressed to the Taoiseach by the Tunisian Prime Minister requesting Irish support for Tunisia's application for membership of UNO might be regarded as an indirect request. The Ambassador in Paris [William P. Fay][100] has suggested that we should recognise both States and has ascertained that the French Government would have no objection to our doing so. It is very probable that both will apply for membership of UNO and be admitted at the next Assembly.

Laos/Cambodia/South Vietnam   Of these successor States of Indochina, Laos and Cambodia are members of UNO. Vietnam was provisionally partitioned by the first Geneva Conference (1954) and neither North or South Vietnam was included in the famous 'package' deal. The Ambassador in Paris [Fay] is urging us to recognise all these States, as from time to time he receives communications from one or other of them. On inquiry at the Quai d'Orsey [*sic*] as to whether these would have any objection he was informed that it was a matter of no interest to them – the French Government had washed their hands of Indochina.

Shortly after the establishment of these three States in 1949, the French Government asked us to recognise them. We would have done so but for the fears of St. Columban's Mission that our recognition of Vietnam – where the French were trying to suppress the Vietnam Forces – might prejudice the position of the Irish priests still working in Communist territories. (This objection, of course, no longer applies.) Vietnam, being much the most important of the three States it was felt that we should not recognise Laos and Cambodia until the 'ban' on Vietnam was lifted. By that time the full scale war was raging in Indochina.

In view of our membership of UNO it would seem desirable to obtain the permission of the Government to put our relations with the above States on a normal basis. At present we are obliged to refrain from replying to communications from them. Such communications though now rare, are bound to increase as the UNO Assembly approaches and our Mission to UNO is established in New York.

On account of our policy towards Israel, and of the present Arab–Israeli tension it would obviously be undesirable to accord recognition to several Arab States by means of formal Notes followed by the usual publicity. What I propose is that we should be free to accord tacit recognition of a *de facto* kind to the Arab and other States listed above as and when the occasion arises, that is by replying to any communications which may be received from them on UNO and other affairs or, by initiating communications ourselves. This method of recognition would not involve any publicity but would achieve the purpose of putting our relations with our fellow members in UNO on a normal basis and obviate the necessity of 'snubs' on the part of our UNO Mission...If the Minister agrees with this proposal the Political Section will prepare a Submission for the Government in consultation with the Legal Adviser.

[handwritten post-script]

PS I understand from Mr. Morrissey that it would be desirable to include (South) Korea in our submission as there is some question of appointing an Hon. Consul in Japan to cover also South Korea.

In November 1956 a circular establishing broad recognition policy was distributed to all missions.[101] The circular attempted to simplify recognition issues that had appeared since Ireland joined the United Nations a year earlier. However, the net result was complete confusion, since many of the policies appeared to come out of nowhere.

DC Circular No. 6/56

Recognition of States

1. Missions are hereby advised that, consequent upon the admission of Ireland to the United Nations, the following Arab and Asian States, from which for various reasons *de jure* recognition is still withheld, are recognised *de facto*:

Cambodia
Jordan
Korea (recognition confined to Government functioning in South Korea)
Laos
Libya
Morocco
Sudan
Tunisia
Vietnam (recognition confined to Government functioning in South Vietnam)

2. Accordingly, Missions may henceforth enter into normal relations with representatives of the Governments of the above-mentioned States as and when the occasion arises.

3. For convenience of reference the position with regard to States (apart from Korea and Vietnam), which are at present wholly or partly under Communist control, is set out below.

China Recognition has not been withdrawn from the so-called Nationalist Government functioning in Formosa. Accordingly, we continue to recognise that Government as the Government of the Republic of China.

Germany The Government of the Federal Republic of Germany is recognised as the only Government in Germany. Missions should be particularly careful to avoid any contact with representatives of the so-called 'German Democratic Republic'.

Poland Recognition is still accorded to the Polish Government-in-exile as the lawful Government of Poland as constituted before the Second World War.

USSR Ireland recognises *de jure* the Government of the USSR. We do not, however, recognise the incorporation in the territory of the USSR of the three Baltic States – Estonia, Latvia, Lithuania.

Albania, **Bulgaria**, **Czechoslovakia**, **Hungary**, **Roumania**, **Yugoslavia** – *De jure* recognition is accorded to the Governments of all these States.

4. The Note, with enclosure, circulated to the Missions on the 10th November, 1955, dealing *inter alia* with Ireland's position in regard to the recognition of certain States, is hereby withdrawn.[102]

In no time the inherent mistakes of this circular became evident. Michael Rynne, former legal adviser in the Department of External Affairs, was serving as Ambassador to Spain in 1956. On 27 November 1956 he wrote a scathing response to the Circular. Although his language was quite inflammatory, he did point out the inconsistencies in recognition policy and the inaccuracies of the circular.

With regard to the Department's D. C. Circular No. 6/56 ... I beg to make the following comments:

1. **Jordan** – Would it now be practicable to accord full recognition to this Arab State, seeing that, presumably, we fully recognise *all* the other Arab States (including near-Communist Syria and half-civilised Saudi Arabia)? Our reason for hesitating to recognise Jordan hitherto was that we feared that such action might force the Government's hand with regard to Israel to which (owing to the Holy Places' controversy) we decided not to concede more than *de facto* recognition.

2. Incidentally, I presume our attitude to *Israel* remains unchanged, despite its membership of the United Nations?

3. **Cambodia, Laos, Vietnam, Communist China, Formosa, South Korea** – Our reasons for declining to commit ourselves to recognising any of the above used to be a) that they were either Communist or potentially so and b) that, owing to some Irish missionaries still remaining in the Far East, the better course seemed to be to take no positive action which might prejudice them in communist eyes.

Even if that position no longer pertains, I wonder if it is correct to say, concerning *China*, that 'recognition has not been withdrawn' from the Formosan Government which 'we continue to recognise'.

My recollection is that we firmly declined, during World War 2, to give any recognition to Chang-Kay-Chek, whom we regard as an ex-bandit thrown up by the fortunes of war to become a ruling puppet of the Western Allies with the financial backing of the notorious 'China Lobby' in Washington... In this connection, I note that the Minister suggested at U.N.O. that it might not be possible to withhold recognition from Communist China indefinitely, although he considered that this was not an appropriate moment (in view of the Hungarian crisis)[103] to welcome the Peking Government into UNO.

* * *

So far as I am concerned here, I have so far studiously avoided accepting invitations from my Formosan colleague on whom I have not even called. In view of the new Circular, I suppose I should reverse this attitude and speak of 'the good relations between our two countries' etc.?

4. **USSR and Various Balkan States and Governments**. It is respectfully submitted that we do *not* have to recognise *de jure* the Governments (repeat 'Governments') of these States (e.g. Hungary!) just because we are in UNO. It goes without saying that we were already recognising the States themselves before we entered UNO. But you will recollect (see an exceedingly long memo of mine which was circulated to the Government about 1948 or 1949[104]) that when Czechoslovakia turned Communist following a Russian coup-de-main, we decided to break off relations with a Government which we felt unable to recognise, although, of course, we still continued to recognise the **State** of Czechoslovakia.

5. **Morocco**. This new State did not originate (as did, say Libya) out of World War 2, but attained its independence with the nominal blessing of its former masters, France and Spain. The United States, which has bases in Morocco, is naturally on the best of terms with the Sultan whose Government is, of course, recognised by Britain and probably by all the other leading European, as well as African States. As I am expecting a call one of these days from the new Moroccan Ambassador here, I should be grateful for some background in connection with our denial to his country of full recognition.

6. If I may be permitted a 'legal' view in this matter of UNO and recognition, I should like to suggest that our participation in the activities of that body or any other international organisation does not necessarily compel the Government to accord even *de facto* recognition to all the 'Governments' or 'States' represented there. The right to grant or withhold international recognition is a sovereign prerogative which, although it may be sometimes exercised tacitly, can never be just taken for granted.

* * *

I am not, of course, attempting to solve any of [these issues] but merely aim at pointing out 1) that our entry into UNO need not necessarily commit us to obligatory new recognition policies and 2) that, before making public the various lines laid down in D.C. Circular No. 6/56, it might be worth while reviewing once again each individual case on its merits.

[signed] Michael Rynne
Ambasadóir.[105]

The Circular was not retracted, despite the protests of Michael Rynne. In fact, general recognition issues achieved certain equilibrium throughout 1957, the exception being the case of Poland. The Polish government-in-exile had been headquartered in London since 1940, although after the Yalta Conference in February 1945, there was little hope of its reinstatement. The United States and Great Britain shifted diplomatic recognition from the London government in July 1945, leaving the President of the Polish government-in-exile, August Zaleski, to his own devices. In 1947 the Polish government-in-exile began to lose support abroad, and in 1954 when Zaleski refused to step-down after seven years in office, the government based in London lost its 'pretence of legitimacy'.[106] By 1957 the government of Poland made serious steps toward gaining 'some measure of independence toward the Soviet Union'' and the non-communist West accepted the idea of peaceful evolution toward independence in Poland rather than the crisis provoked in Hungary in 1956.[107]

W.T. Dobrznski from 1939 operated the Polish Consul General in Dublin until his retirement in 1954, at which time the Vice-Consul, Zofia Zaleska, assumed the position of Consul. On 8 July 1957, Mrs Zaleska retired as a result of ill-health, leaving her post unfilled. When the Minister of Foreign Affairs of the Polish government-in-exile proposed to the Department of External affairs that Pawel Czerwinski succeed Mrs Zaleska, the Irish government refused the appointment. Upon hearing of the Dublin refusal, President Zaleski immediately wrote to Eamon de Valera (Taoiseach since Fianna Fáil assumed office in March 1957). Appealing to de Valera's sentiment, Zaleski reminded him of their association at the League of Nations.

> I can hardly believe that such a blow could be delivered to Poland by the Irish people, who certainly understand better than any other nation in the world what national independence means for a people who were for a century and a half under foreign occupation. This seems to me the more impossible at a moment when the Government of Ireland is headed by the founder and chief artisan of its Independence.[108]

Convinced that acceptance of the new Consul would 'involve a formal act of recognition', de Valera pondered over three drafts of a reply to Zaleski.[109] On 23 August, de Valera sent the following explanation:

> My delay in replying has been due mainly to my anxiety to see if it would be at all possible to change our decision concerning the Consulate General. I find, regretfully, that it is not possible for us to do so... It would be wrong to interpret this inability as a desire in any way to hurt the Polish nation or to weaken their effort to re-establish independence... I understand and sympathise with your feelings in this whole matter, and it would give me great personal pleasure if I could say that our decision could be changed. As things are, I can only ask you to try to appreciate our position.[110]

In the case of Poland, the government had been placating the Holy See. Out of respect for the grievances against the Catholic Church in Poland, especially the imprisonment of Josef Cardinal Mindszenty in 1948 and Stefan Cardinal Wyszynski in 1953, allowing the Consulate General to operate in Dublin created goodwill. Apart from other governments-in-exile of states under communism, the Holy See provided the only official recognition for the Polish government in London. Governments-in-exile were meant to be temporary measures, but twelve years after the end of the Second World War, the pretence wore thin.[111] The relationship between the Irish government and the communist-controlled Polish government was cordial at the United Nations. In fact, Conor Cruise O'Brien, while at the United Nations in November 1957, provided intelligence from the Polish delegate concerning recent changes in the internal administration of Poland.[112]

> He did not directly attack Russia at any point in his remarks but it was quite clear he did not think of Russia as the friend and protector of Poland ... It will ... be an enduring necessity for Poland to have friendly relations with the Soviet Union but it is also necessary for them to achieve much better and closer relations with the Western countries.[113]

Ireland's attitude toward trading with the Polish government also changed during 1957. The import trade from Poland (predominantly coal) increased substantially from IR£34,829 in 1957 to IR£805,015 in 1958 and continued to rise in the following years. Exports to Poland, which had been negligible since 1949, soared to IR£144,366 in 1958.

One may argue that de Valera's decision against allowing the Polish government-in-exile Consulate General to continue its presence in Dublin was not meant to be an invitation of recognition of the government in Warsaw as much as it was meant to put an end to the Zaleski charade. Recognition policy toward Poland is not mentioned in the files again until 7 July 1962 in a memorandum dealing with issues in the DC Circular from 1956. Cremin noted that:

> Our discussion then turned to paragraph 3 of the Circular and, in particular, to China and Poland. The Minister [Frank Aiken] feels that we should now record (but not, of course, announce) recognition of the existing Polish Government.[114]

RETURN TO THE STATUS QUO – 1957–62

From 1957–62 Irish recognition policy remained stable. During the summer of 1958, when the Hashemite dynasty of Iraq was overthrown by in an Egyptian-inspired coup, Ambassador Michael Rynne in Madrid was the first to question possible recognition of the new Iraqi Republic.[115] Embarrassed by the Irish attitude of moderation taken toward Algerian independence during the 12th Session at the United Nations in 1957, in which the Irish position had been to side with the Algerians in principle but vote with the French,[116] Dr Eoin MacWhite suggested early recognition for Iraq.

> At this feverish and early moment in the history of the Iraq Republic recognition by us would be much appreciated and remembered by them and other Arab States. It would, I think, pay dividends in UN votes if we recognized now when recognition is valued and not wait until the U.S. and Britain have done so. It would be particularly helpful if we beat the South American States on this.[117]

Conor Cruise O'Brien agreed. 'General recognition seems imminent. We have nothing to gain by holding back (unless we attach importance to the idea of acting in concert with Britain) and may gain useful goodwill by recognition now.'[118] Secretary Con Cremin sent a reply to Rynne's question by telegram on 31 July and a follow-up letter on 5 August, explaining there was no need for 'formal recognition' since Ireland had 'no form of representation in Iraq'.[119] Cremin, singing to the choir, repeated Irish policy:

> In the case of countries where we are not represented, it is, as you are aware, the usual practice of the department not to notify recognition of a new status unless and until such recognition is specifically sought.[120]

The policy 'not to notify recognition of a new status' would land the department in an embarrassing situation four years later with the recognition of South Vietnam in 1962.

RECOGNITION OF VIETNAM – 1962–63

At the Potsdam Conference in July 1945, the United States, the USSR and Great Britain agreed that southeast Asia would be under British influence after a Japanese surrender. The British would be responsible for establishing law and order in the former French colony of Indochina, but were to share the responsibility with the Chinese. Following the defeat of Japan in August 1945, the Vietminh rebels, led by the revolutionary Ho Chi Minh, were opposed to the return of colonialism in Indochina, demanding independence.[121] The communist-led Vietminh controlled only the northern part of the country, a result of the post-war division between the Chinese zone north of the 17th parallel and the British zone in the South.

The Chinese and British established law and order in their respective zones in very differing ways. When Ho Chi Minh declared the Democratic Republic of Vietnam (DRV) in September 1945, the Chinese recognized the Vietminh régime and its new state. The British, on the other hand, wanted to re-establish pre-war colonies to their 'rightful' owners, and began to break up the Vietminh régime in the South in order to restore French rule. France subsequently recognized the DRV as a 'free state' within the French Union, but serious differences erupted between the two governments.

Fighting between the French and Vietminh began as soon as the French resumed control of the area. Between 1945 and 1947, the United States became increasingly frustrated with the tactics of France in forcing the colonial regime upon the Vietminh. Then, in 1948 the Cold War intensified and the United States foreign policy focused on the Chinese communists as aggressors in collusion with the Russians. Just before China came under communist control in October 1949, the Americans initiated support of the French military in Vietnam by providing vast amounts of financial aid. The former emperor Bao Dai was reinstated as ruler in the South.

On 7 February 1950, the United States recognized Vietnam, as well as Laos and Cambodia, as independent republics. On the same day, the British cautiously recognized Vietnam as an 'associated State within the French Union'.[122] The Vietminh in the North continued to infiltrate the southern part of Vietnam, fighting intensely against French troops. By 1954, the United States paid between 50 per cent and 80 per cent of the French cost of the war against the forces of the Vietminh.[123] John J. Hearne, Ambassador in Washington, reported on the United States' concern in Indochina in 1954 only a few months before the Geneva Conference:

> It has always been basic in American strategic planning, that the loss of Indo-China to the Communists would, inevitably, be followed by the loss of Burma, Thailand, and Malaya with all the food and material resources in which those vast regions are so rich. With Indo-China in their control, Moscow and Peiping would be in a position to dominate Indonesia and Pakistan, to draw India further away from the Western Alliance and, above all, threaten American suzerainty in the Pacific Ocean.[124]

On 7 May 1954 French troops, under siege at the village of Dien Bien Phu, surrendered. The Geneva Conference that followed in June and July 1954 partitioned Vietnam at the 17th parallel. The Eisenhower Administration's 'united action' efforts supported the new presidency of Ngo Dinh Diem, a non-communist, Catholic nationalist in the South who had not collaborated with the French. In the new Republic of Vietnam (1955), most of Diem's political support came from the 900,000 Catholic Vietnamese who had fled from the North.[125] By 1960, those in the United States who had vigorously supported Diem (including Francis Cardinal Spellman and Dr Wesley Fishel of a lobby group called 'American Friends of Vietnam') began to have serious doubts about Diem's ability to maintain control of the South.[126] Diem's regime, undermined by the large population of tenant farmers who were angered by

inefficient land reform, appeared unstable.[127] The Vietminh exploited this
discontent by launching a guerrilla campaign against Saigon beginning in 1957
and the 'insurgency was making rapid gains throughout the South' by 1960.[128]

President John F. Kennedy inherited the Vietnam problem from Eisenhower.
Immediately after his inauguration, Kennedy reversed Eisenhower's foreign
policy of intervention in the Laotian civil war, trying to find a diplomatic, neutral
compromise.[129] The solution appeared in June 1961 during a fourteen-nation
conference held in Geneva. The resulting tripartite agreement in effect neutrali-
zed Laos, threatening the communist trail network that supplied insurgents in the
South. When the communists failed to live up to the Geneva agreements,
Kennedy changed the direction of his foreign policy toward intervention.[130]

Kennedy supported Diem during his stay in the United States in the early
1950s. During his tenure as Senator, Kennedy and Senator Mike Mansfield, both
Catholics, became charter members of the American Friends for Vietnam.[131] By
the time of Kennedy's assassination in November 1963, 'the few hundred
American military that Eisenhower had sent had grown to more than sixteen
thousand U.S. soldiers participating in hundreds of armed confrontations'.[132]
Kennedy's successor, Vice President Lyndon B. Johnson, played a limited role in
support of the Diem regime from 1961–63. Early in Kennedy's administration the
decision was made to broaden the role of the United States in Vietnam by
providing political, economic and military logistical support to the South
Vietnamese. Vice President Johnson personally visited Diem in the spring of
1961. Johnson's mission was 'to provide added encouragement to the Vietnamese
Government in its continuing struggle with the Communists'.[133]

Among the various forms of US 'encouragement' was a plethora of State
Department plans for the survival of the Republic of Vietnam. The area in which
Irish and Vietnamese interests coincided during the early 1960s was in the
development of trade.[134] Diplomatically, Ireland had little interest in Diem's
government or in foreign intervention in Vietnam. William P. Fay, the
Ambassador in Paris, asked that recognition be accorded to Vietnam, Laos and
Cambodia in April 1956. Fay's request was more for convenience in conducting
Paris diplomacy than from ideological reasons.

> In general, it is good international law and good diplomatic practice, I
> would submit, to recognise any Government which is in effective occupa-
> tion of a territory, so long as that Government endeavours to maintain even
> a semblance of civilised rule. It is clear that the Associated States are very
> much on the favourable side of that definition. I therefore recommend that
> we can now extend recognition to them, there being no good reason for
> withholding it. It may well be indeed, ironically enough, that the missions
> of the three States are quite unaware of our attitude so far.[135]

The department's DC Circular 6/56 in November 1956 addressed the South
Vietnam recognition problem by providing *de facto* recognition. Ireland's *de*

facto recognition toward Vietnam reflected a non-interventionist attitude, trying to maintain a neutral position vis-à-vis the French and Americans. Still, in 1956 the Irish government had not yet distinguished in practice the difference between recognition of a state and recognition of a government, and anything less than *de jure* recognition signalled Ireland's unwillingness to make a political or ideological statement. To enter into a formal trade agreement, Irish policy required *de jure* recognition, recognition that South Vietnam did not have.

Until 1960, the Vietnamese diplomats did not test Ireland's recognition policy. But on 4 March 1960 the United Nations Permanent Observer of the Republic of Vietnam made a formal *démarche* to the Irish government.[136] On 16 March the request was sent to Dublin. The reply was not sent until 2 July. A handwritten *apologia* explained the delay on drafting a reply:

> I am sorry that I have left this unattended so long. I had intended to prepare a memo on the position in South Vietnam and the extent of international recognition already accorded to it.
>
> My feeling is that at this present juncture...we have absolutely nothing to gain from making a formal statement of recognition, even if such recognition is a fact. I think that the matter might be let rest and the Permanent Mission advised accordingly.[137]

Conor Cruise O'Brien, home from his UN post as Counsellor in the Political Section in July 1960, approved this course of action.[138]

The aggressiveness of the United States in supporting the Diem regime from 1954 to 1960 should not be underestimated. Given the significant involvement of the US State Department in Vietnamese diplomacy, one might assume that the Vietnamese Permanent Observer to the United Nations would most likely have been coaxed by the United States to press Ireland for recognition. Diem's 'governmental machinery' in fact relied upon American expertise, with a significant history in employing private US public relations firms to disseminate 'good news' about South Vietnam.[139] A small bit of guidance at the United Nations would not have been unexpected. However, an assumption of this nature would be utterly invalid in the case of the Permanent Observer to the United Nations. The Permanent Observer was a member of Diem's family and accepted orders only from the top.

The Irish diplomats concerned with the recognition of Vietnam were not aware of the familial complexity of Diem's government. Ngo Dinh Diem was one of six brothers. After dethroning Emperor Bao Dai in 1955, Diem systematically involved most of his family in the government's administration. Ngo Dinh Can, Diem's brother, 'unofficially' oversaw the northern provinces around the city of Hue, controlling most of the trade and a secret police force.[140] Another brother, Ngo Dinh Thuc, Archbishop of Hue, served as liaison to South Vietnam's Catholic community.[141] Ngo Dinh Nhu, Diem's immediate younger brother, was chief political adviser and operated the secret police.[142] Nhu's wife, known as

Madame Nhu,[143] exerted considerable political pressure on her husband and the celibate Diem.[144] Madame Nhu's parents were also involved in Diem's government from 1954 on. Her father, Tran Van Chuong, became a cabinet minister in Diem's first government. Later, Chuong was Ambassador in Washington, DC. At the same time, Madame Nhu's mother, known as 'Mrs Chuong',[145] became Vietnam's Permanent Observer to the United Nations. The Chuongs eventually resigned from their respective positions in August 1963 when Ngo Dinh Nhu called for the Buddhist persecution. The youngest brother of Diem was Ngo Dinh Luyen, an engineer living in France. Luyen obliged his brother by serving as Ambassador in London, a position he held until the 1 November 1963 coup against Diem. After the coup, Diem and Nhu were assassinated. Madame Nhu fled to Rome. The Chuongs distanced themselves from misfortune, and resided in Washington, DC until their own murders in July 1986.[146]

From the date of Mrs Chuong's request as Permanent Observer at the United Nations, the matter of Irish recognition of Vietnam lay dormant for two years. Then in July 1962 Secretary Con Cremin produced a substantial memorandum on the problems that continued to persist from the beleaguered DC Circular 6/56. Cremin's July memorandum will be analyzed more fully below, but the question of recognition of Vietnam appeared as Cremin's initial subject. The Secretary noted that although the circular 'did not have Government authority'; it represented Ireland's position in 1956 but 'might be at variance with the position today'.[147] Cremin's intent was to 'regularise matters' since 'there appear to be definite prospects of a useful trade with Vietnam'.[148] By August 1962, Ambassador Luyen in London demanded that evidence of Ireland's *de jure* recognition be provided before trade talks could continue. Pacification of Luyen fell to Ambassador Hugh McCann in London.

Sheila Murphy tried to head off any conflict with the Vietnamese Permanent Observer to the United Nations by writing to F.H. Boland, Ireland's Permanent Representative. She advised that 'the Political side will be communicating with you later about a recent decision of the Minister that we should regard ourselves as having accorded full recognition to Vietnam'.[149] Forced into the uncomfortable position of continuing the ruse, she explained:

> So far as Vietnam is concerned, we have decided...to inform the Vietnamese Embassy in London through which we are endeavouring to negotiate the exchange of Notes, that it was decided about two years ago that there was no longer any reason to withhold *de jure* recognition from a number of countries, including Vietnam, which had previously been accorded only *de facto* recognition, adding that there was no formal announcement about this. Our reason for thus vaguely antedating the decision to accord full recognition is that we hope thus to avoid any publicity about the matter by the Vietnamese authorities. If the Permanent Observer should again approach the Mission, he could be informed as above.[150]

Sheila Murphy also wrote to McCann in London:

> About two years ago it was decided that there was no longer any reason to withhold *de jure* recognition from a number of countries, including Vietnam... There was no formal announcement about this. The position, therefore, is that for the past two years we have accorded *de jure* recognition to Vietnam. If the Chargé d'Affaires should request confirmation in writing, you may send him a letter in terms of the attached draft.[151]

Not surprisingly, Hugh McCann received another request from Ambassador Luyen, this time in person. Writing to Sheila Murphy, McCann explained the trade talks were centred on 'our desire to obtain minimum tariff treatment for Irish exports to Vietnam'.[152] The Vietnamese Ambassador told McCann that the minimum tariff treatment would be granted 'only to those countries [that] grant full recognition to Vietnam' and 'only on the basis of reciprocity'.[153] The difficulty, Ambassador Luyen said, was that the Vietnamese foreign ministry 'had no piece of paper from us on that subject'. McCann then handed Luyen a letter stating that Ireland recognized Vietnam two years previously, a verbatim text of Sheila Murphy's instructions.

> I understand that your Embassy was enquiring as to whether Ireland had accorded full recognition to Vietnam. I have been in touch with Dublin about the matter and I am happy to confirm that about two years ago it was decided to grant *de jure* recognition to Vietnam and a number of other countries, which had previously been accorded only *de facto* recognition. There was no formal announcement about this. The position, therefore, is that for the past two years Ireland has accorded full recognition to Vietnam.[154]

McCann wrote that the Ambassador took the letter without reading it and said the letter 'disposed of their difficulty in principle on the question of recognition'.[155] McCann's approach to the Vietnamese Ambassador reveals a casual attitude, but Ambassador Luyen did not let the matter rest.

On 13 June 1963, the question of Vietnam appeared once again. Over a month since the government had voted for changes in recognition policy, Sheila Murphy found herself still trying to explain to the Vietnamese authorities why their requests for recognition since 1960 had gone without what they considered a formal reply. A letter sent by Ambassador Ngo Dinh Luyen to Secretary Cremin in January 1963 showed that 'Saigon is not going to be satisfied with the assurance that Vietnam was accorded *de jure* recognition "about two years ago"'.[156] In early 1963, Cremin moved to a new posting in London as Ambassador. He then had to deal directly with Ambassador Luyen and wanted Sheila Murphy's thoughts on how to proceed with the recognition issue. She provided a blow-by-blow falsification.

We feel that we must also offer the Vietnamese some explanation as to why it took us so long to give recognition and why, particularly in view of the *démarches* made in Washington and New York, we did not inform the Vietnamese when *de jure* recognition was accorded. All things considered, we feel that our best course is to plead the 'lost file'. On that basis the explanation to be given by you to the Vietnamese Ambassador would be on the following lines:

As already explained by your predecessor, the reason why we hesitated to accord recognition to Vietnam on its establishment was our apprehension that such a step might have an adverse effect on the Irish missionaries working in the Communist-controlled part of the country. This considera- tion ceased to be relevant after a number of years but, owing to the fact that we had no occasion for official contacts with Vietnam, the change in the situation was not adverted to until the *démarches* referred to above were made in Washington and New York. The position was then fully examined and it was formally decided that there was no longer any justification for withholding *de jure* recognition. At this point the papers were mislaid and in spite of the most exhaustive searches, did not come to light until a couple of weeks ago. When, therefore, the Vietnamese Embassy raised the question of recognition, we were in the very embarrassing position of knowing that *de jure* recognition had been accorded some time in 1960 but of not being able to ascertain the precise date of this decision. The papers have now revealed that the decision was taken on 17th May, 1960. In fact, the last entry on the file is a direction to the Political Section to instruct the Ambassadors at Washington and the United Nations to inform their Vietnamese colleagues that *de jure* recognition had been accorded to Vietnam on that date. Staff changes in the Political Section towards the end of May, 1960, probably account for the fact that the mislaying of the papers was not brought to notice at the time.[157]

Ambassador Cremin met with Luyen on 3 July 1963 to discuss trade terms with South Vietnam. Cremin told the ambassador that the Irish government made the *de jure* recognition official on 17 May 1960.[158] Ambassador Luyan seemed satisfied but introduced another stumbling block. In the initial discussions in 1962, Luyen told Ambassador McCann that 'reciprocity' would be needed to finalize the trade arrangement. Once the recognition issue was settled, Cremin listened while Ambassador Luyan illogically suggested that if the Vietnamese government included Ireland on a 'list of countries enjoying the lower rate' then the government might be accused of approving such a course because 'Ireland is Catholic'.[159] Luyen asked Cremin whether Ireland could send 'one or two persons to teach English' to Vietnam in an effort to counterbalance any criticism. Cremin, surprised by the request, politely suggested that if Vietnam failed to extend the benefit of the lower tariff to Ireland, it would constitute a 'form of discrimination', as the rate already applied to Britain, Australia and New Zealand. Not until the 3 July meeting did Cremin realize a critical element to the Vietnamese demands. Cremin wrote that Ambassador Ngo Dinh Luyen was 'not only a brother of the Archbishop of Vietnam [Ngo Dinh Luc] but also of the President, Ngo-dinh Diem'.[160] In spite of the problem of recognition, Irish exports to South Vietnam began to increase in 1962.[161] After 1963 and the fall of Diem's government, however, trade dropped sharply in 1964.

From 1956 until 1963, the Irish diplomats dealt with a closed circle of Diem's government and seemed to be completely unaware of the Diem family connection between the United Nations, Washington and London. After Nhu's August 1963 purge of the Buddhist community, intelligence about the situation in Vietnam expanded. Sheila Murphy wrote to Ambassador Boland at the United Nations to explain the situation once again. 'When we heard that the Vietnamese treatment of the Buddhist community was coming up in the Assembly, we thought it well that you should be aware that we still have this problem with Vietnam.'[162] Exhibiting an element of hindsight, she complained that 'Saigon kept pressing for the exact date of such recognition and we were eventually forced to pinpoint a date, viz., 14th May, 1960,[163] and to concoct a story to explain why the Vietnamese Government had not been informed at that time.'[164]

On 3 June 1964, Ireland's new ambassador to Great Britain, J.G. Molloy, initiated contact with the new Vietnamese administration in London.[165] On 15 June 1964, the Vietnamese Chargé d'Affaires confirmed receipt of the letter and acknowledged that 'the Irish Government had accorded *de jure* recognition to Vietnam on May 17th 1960 and continue so to recognise Vietnam'. The terms of trade were as follows:

> The Irish Government would be prepared to enter an agreement, by way of exchange of notes, which would ensure to Vietnamese exports to Ireland the treatment not less favourable than that accorded to any country outside the Commonwealth preferential system, in return for the Vietnamese Government's according to exports from Ireland the benefit of the lower Vietnamese tariff as that accorded to Australia, Great Britain and New Zealand.[166]

Perhaps with great relief the Irish government accepted the terms of the Agreement, obviously not volunteering the additional technical information of Ireland's Commonwealth disassociation in 1949.

Over ten years later, in 1974, the London embassy of the Republic of Vietnam requested confirmation (once again) of Ireland's *de jure* recognition in an effort to 'accredit its Ambassador to the Court of St. James as Ambassador to Dublin with residence in London'.[167] Sheila Murphy and F.H. Boland both retired in 1964, and Con Cremin retired three days before receipt of the letter. The file on recognition of Vietnam remained inactive from 1964–74, a period coinciding with US military escalation in Vietnam. Ten years of change saw the replacement of the 'old guard' in Iveagh House, as well as Ireland's integration into the European Economic Community in 1973. The 1974 letter went unanswered. The United States signed a cease-fire agreement with North Vietnam on 27 January 1973, and the government of the Republic of Vietnam collapsed on 29 April 1975.[168] In June 1976, Ireland acted in concert with other members of the EEC in recognizing the reunified state of Vietnam under the direction of Hanoi.

REVISING DIPLOMATIC RECOGNITION POLICY – 1962–63

The issue of *de jure* recognition of Vietnam is marked as the turning point of Irish diplomatic recognition policy. Without the persistence of the Vietnamese Ambassador in London, the Irish practice of ignoring problem recognition issues might not have been called to task. During the summer of 1962, Con Cremin became determined to overhaul recognition policy. Spurred by the problem of Vietnam, Cremin methodically attacked other difficult recognition issues: Cambodia, Jordan, Korea, Laos, Libya, Morocco, Sudan and Tunisia. These states were listed on the DC Circular 6/56 as '*de jure* recognition withheld' and 'recognised *de facto*'.[169]

Cremin noted the inconsistencies in policy toward several of the *de facto* recognized states. For example, he cited the case of Tunisia as being 'particularly anomalous'. The year before, Frank Aiken, Minister for External Affairs, 'formally received President Bourguiba [of Tunisia]' and the President [Eamon de Valera] had asked him to stay with him'. Further, talks between the two governments were held in 1957 on 'a proposal from Tunisia to open a mission in Dublin but had at no time adverted to the absence of *de jure* recognition as an impediment to that course'.[170]

Cremin also suggested to Aiken that the position on Cambodia, Laos and Vietnam be revised. Recognition had been limited in the former Indochina over 'the objections of the Columban Fathers arising from the presence of their missionaries in Communist-controlled countries – a factor which has since entirely disappeared'.[171] Cremin recommended that 'all of the nine countries' be recognized *de jure*, 'with the possible exception of Jordan and Southern Korea'. The mode of recognition was not important, Cremin argued, nor was there a need 'to make any formal announcement in relation to any of them'.[172]

During a meeting with Frank Aiken, Minister for External Affairs, Cremin also raised the question of distinction in practice between *de facto* and *de jure* recognition.

> We also discussed the principle underlying *de jure* and *de facto* recognition and the need to distinguish between recognition of a State and of a Government. The British criteria [the Morrison Statement of 1951] were examined in this connection and we had the feeling that the difference

between the conditions justifying *de jure* as compared with *de facto* recognition is rather tenuous and perhaps lends itself to subjectivity.[173]

The next subject that Cremin and Aiken approached was recognition of Israel. 'After a short discussion of the case the Minister came to the conclusion that it might be best in all the circumstances if we were to accord *de jure* recognition [to Israel]'.[174] The difficulty was that if Ireland accorded full recognition to Israel, 'the grant of *de jure* recognition would almost certainly be followed by a request to us to accept an Israeli Mission'.[175] Aiken advised Cremin to write to the Ambassador at the Holy See to ascertain the Vatican's views on Irish recognition of Israel. The rationale for Israeli recognition included three basic assumptions. First, the development of trade between Ireland and Israel would be beneficial. Second, Ireland in 1962 was 'practically the only Western European country which has not fully recognised Israel'. Third, driving at the heart of non-recognition, Cremin argued: 'it seems unlikely that the situation in relation to the Holy Places will change and even more unlikely that our failing to accord *de jure* recognition will bring about a change'.[176]

Since 1949, when the original policy toward Israel was made, many factors in Irish foreign policy had changed, including what Ireland perceived as its international interests. Only thirteen years had passed, but the expansion, growth and resulting independence of Irish foreign policy was noticeably different. The days of Joseph Walshe exerting his parochial influence on Irish foreign affairs from his ambassadorship at the Holy See were over. Pope Paul VI, whom Keogh has described as 'willing to allow the Catholic Church to make necessary compromises to accommodate itself to a changing world',[177] would soon rectify the lack of conciliatory leadership at Holy See toward Israel.[178] Further, the need for prestige that Walshe sought in most policy decisions disappeared with Ireland's membership in the United Nations and its positive contribution there from 1956 onward, including F.H. Boland's successful presidency during the 15th Assembly in 1960–61 and Ireland's peacekeeping initiative in the Congo between 1960 and 1964.[179] With the establishment of T.K. Whitaker's *Economic Development* and the resulting *First Programme* in 1958, international trade in Ireland under the aegis of the Department of Finance at last expanded beyond Fianna Fáil's long-held protectionism.[180]

The Department of External Affairs was perhaps the most exceptional in the metamorphosis of the Irish government, and by 1962, Ireland prepared its first submission for entrance into the European Economic Community. The application for membership in the EEC symbolized the Department of External Affairs' commitment to an international Irish presence in both politics and economics. In a department file entitled 'Basic Principles of Ireland's Foreign Policy' a newspaper clipping from *Handelsblatt* in Düsseldorf outlined Ireland's participation in the EEC:

It is thus natural that we should wish to participate in the Common Market which embraces the whole range of the national economies and which in agriculture, still the most predominant sector of our economy, offers not merely scope for development but security in marketing arrangements and stability of prices. But we also recognise that the Treaty of Rome represents very much more than an effort to create a common market – that its specific provisions and its political implications will lead to intimate co-operation between the members in all fields and, by bringing the European States closer together, prove to be a powerful factor for the maintenance and the consolidation of peace.[181]

The remaining interest, partition of Ireland, seemed intransigent, but it was clear by 1962 that no outside political force would solve partition as Seán MacBride envisioned in 1949. In March 1963, the situation in Northern Ireland also seemed destined for positive change as the new Prime Minister Terence O'Neill replaced hard-liner Unionist Lord Brookeborough. As Lee has noted, by 1963 'the wider world was changing too'.[182]

With an 'Irish' Catholic in the White House rather conspicuously failing to conform to the stereotype requirement of the Orange psyche, with a Taoiseach [Seán Lemass] in Dublin apparently seeking conciliation, with a Pope in the Vatican acknowledging the humanity of communists, much less Protestants, problems further compounded when Harold Macmillan resigned in October 1963, raising the spectre of an imminent Labour government in Britain, any Northern premier would have had to take increasing cognisance of life beyond Ulster, however he chose to interpret it.[183]

When Cremin and Aiken discussed recognition policy changes in July 1962, the time seemed ripe to consolidate procedural foreign policy in an effort to streamline the growing demands on the Department of External Affairs. Minister Frank Aiken proposed a 'submission to the Government' to reconcile the outstanding recognition issues.[184] In the autumn of 1962, however, Con Cremin received notice that he would be transferred to London to replace Ambassador Hugh McCann in early 1963.[185] McCann would return to Dublin as Secretary.[186] In September 1962, Cremin drafted a 'memorandum for the government' but it did not proceed past the draft stage during his tenure.

Cremin assumed his new post in London during early January 1963. As he recalled later, 'the first significant happening after my arrival was General de Gaulle's veto of British membership of the EEC'. France vetoed the British application on 28 January 1963 in Brussels. In early February, Taoiseach Seán Lemass spoke to Dáil on the outcome of Ireland's application:

In respect of our common desire to join EEC, our expectation that the difficulties are only temporary and that membership will be possible in time, and in respect also of our independent decisions to avoid adopting policies now which would add to the difficulties of negotiating conditions of membership, our policy and that of Britain can be said to be in concert ... As regards the position of our application for EEC membership, we had previously made known to the EEC countries that, although it was not linked to Britain's, as were those of Denmark and Norway, we did not wish to proceed with detailed negotiations on it until the progress of British negotiations had revealed the likelihood of agreement and we had a general indication of its character.[187]

With the flurry of activity surrounding the EEC during the early months of 1963, the overhaul of recognition policy stagnated until the end of March. With Cremin in London, the submission to the government on recognition fell to Seán Ronan. Ronan concluded after reviewing the recognition files:

There is considerable uncertainty... as to where we stand in the matter of *de jure* recognition of states. In general ... it might be useful to survey the field and try to determine once and for all where we are in this connection.[188]

Understandably, Ronan felt frustrated by the mountains of files on diplomatic recognition. However, he successfully narrowed the dilemma to the following statement:

In my investigations of the matter I have come to the conclusion that one of the real problems we face is that we have never really made up our minds as to what acts of ours in the past have amounted to recognition of various states or whether we consider that a formal Government decision is necessary in all cases.[189]

Ronan accurately reasoned that the question of according recognition to states is 'really a matter of intention'. He then dissected a current list of states in the system, derived from a UN membership list, categorically analyzing recognition problems. First, states which were 'independent prior to the Second World War' did not require much consideration, except in pinpointing the dates of recognition and the establishment of diplomatic relations, a task that Ronan found 'impossible'. Second, 'states independent since the beginning of the Second World War' included the list of states from DC Circular 6/56.[190] The only considerable difficulty for this group of states was the problem of China, which Ronan summarized: 'we have continued to recognise the State of China, have accorded *de facto* recognition to the Formosan Government and have not recognised Peking *de facto*'.[191] In the final wording of the 'memorandum for the government', however, the policy changed again.

On 7 May 1963, the final 'memorandum for the government' was submitted and approved on 14 May. The memorandum proposed the following:

1. To confirm that *de jure* recognition is accorded to South Vietnam.
2. To elevate the following States from *de facto* to *de jure* recognition:
   Cambodia, Israel, Jordan, South Korea, Laos, Libya, Morocco, Sudan and Tunisia.
3. To recognize new States *de jure* which came into existence (and/or gained independence) after the Second World War:
   Algeria, Burundi, Cameroun, Central African Republic, Chad, Congo (Brazzaville), Congo (Leopoldville),[192] Cyprus, Dahomey,[193] Gabon, Ghana, Guinea, Ivory Coast, Jamaica, Kuwait, Madagascar, Mali, Mauritania, Niger, Rwanda, Senegal, Sierra Leone, Somalia, Tanganyika,[194] Togo, Trinidad and Tobago, Uganda, Upper Volta[195] and Western Somoa.
4. To recognize the Mongolian People's Republic[196] *de jure* and to recognize the Warsaw Government in Poland *de jure*.[197]
5. To affirm that Ireland recognizes the State of China *de jure* but does not recognize... the Peking Government nor the Formosa (Taiwan) Government is in effective control of the State of China. Rather, Ireland recognizes two governments *de facto* in China, one in control of Mainland China (Peking) and the other in control of Formosa (Taiwan).[198]
6. To continue a policy of non-recognition toward the following States and their governments: German Democratic Republic, Vietnam (North) and Korea (North).
7. To agree that 'a formal announcement should not be made regarding the change of recognition status of any of these states upon which the Government may decide'.

In October 1963, the Department issued DC Circular 2/63 establishing the changes in recognition status. Secretary Hugh McCann provided explanatory notes for the decisions. After seven years in the making, and considerable confusion on recognition policy, the diplomatic corps was presented with a current list of states as recognized by Ireland.

AN ROINN GNÓTHAÍ EACHTRACHA

Confidential

305/149   **D.C. Circular No. 2/63**

RECOGNITION OF STATES

1. As Missions are aware *de jure* recognition has been hitherto withheld or has never been specifically granted in the case of a number of States which are widely recognised by Western European countries. Some of these States have recently had official dealings with us; in the case of others the original factors which led to the withholding of full

recognition have disappeared. In at least one case the failure to grant full recognition may have been disadvantageous to the development of trade. Some of the States listed in this circular might be held, internationally, to have already been fully recognised by official acts on our part e.g. despatch of congratulatory messages, official attendance at independence celebrations, etc. However, no formal decision according *de jure* recognition had been made. Accordingly, the matter was recently submitted to the Government with a view to regularising the present position.

2. The following States have hitherto been regarded as being recognised *de facto* only: Cambodia, Israel, Jordan, Korea (South – Non-member UN), Laos, Libya, Morocco, Sudan, Tunisia, Viet-Nam (South – Non-member UN).

   (i) Cambodia, Korea (South), Laos, and Viet-Nam (South) were not recognised *de jure* in 1949 because of the possibility that the granting of full recognition might have adverse consequences for the Irish missionaries working in the Communist controlled territories in South East Asia; this factor has long ceased to be relevant. It may also be noted that the Vietnamese authorities, with whom efforts are being made to conclude a trade agreement insist that full recognition of Viet-Nam was an essential prerequisite to the negotiation of such an agreement. They had been informed semi-officially that Viet-Nam (i.e. South) was recognised *de jure* 'about two years ago'.

   (ii) Israel was not granted *de jure* recognition because of the dispute over the future of the Holy Places. On this question, we have taken the same view as the Holy See that Jerusalem and the surrounding area should be placed under international supervision with international guarantees on the lines proposed by the United Nations in 1948 and 1950. The Ambassador to the Holy See, on the instructions of the Minister, approached the Vatican authorities in the matter and was informed that there would be no objection to the granting of full recognition to Israel but that the Holy See would be pleased if due care were taken by the Government not to recognise Jerusalem as the capital of Israel. There is little likelihood either that the position regarding the Holy Places will change in the near future or that failure on our part to recognise Israel would help bring a change.

   (iii) Full recognition was not given at the relevant time to the five Arab States, Jordan, Libya, Morocco, Tunisia, and Sudan because of

      (a) uncertainty about the political situation during the period of Arab–Israeli tension, and

(b) Jordan being involved in the dispute concerning the Holy
Places.

3. The following may be regarded as new States having come into
existence since the end of the Second World War and as regards which
there was no good reason why they should not be accorded *de jure*
recognition: Algeria, Burundi, Cameroun, Central African Republic,
Chad, Congo (Brazzaville), Congo (Leopoldville), Cyprus, Dahomey,
Gabon, Ghana, Guinea, Ivory Coast, Jamaica, Kuwait, Madagascar,
Mali, Mauritania, Mongolian People's Republic, Niger, Rwanda,
Senegal, Sierra Leone, Somalia, Tanganyika, Togo, Trinidad and
Tobago, Uganda, Upper Volta, Western Somoa (Non-member UN).

At their meeting on 14th May, 1963, the Government also decided to
accord *de jure* recognition to these thirty States.

4. The Mongolian People's Republic (listed in paragraph 3 above), while
under Soviet influence, has an independent status under a Sino-Soviet
Treaty of 25 August, 1945 and was admitted unanimously to membership of the United Nations in 1961. On the other hand, Byelorussia and
the Ukraine have individual membership of the United Nations but their
existence as sovereign states has never been recognised by Ireland. It
was not recommended that the Government should make any alteration
regarding our non-recognition of these parts of the Soviet Union as
separate States. It is to be noted that *de jure* recognition has long since
been given to the USSR, although incorporation in that country of the
Baltic States of Estonia, Latvia and Lithuania has never been
recognised. Full recognition is also accorded to the following
Communist States and their Governments, viz., Albania, Bulgaria,
Czechoslovakia, Hungary, Romania and Yugoslavia.

5. The Government have never ceased to recognise the State of Poland but
the Polish Government-in-exile was recognised for many years as the
lawful Government of Poland. In this connection it is to be noted that the
Government-in-exile has ceased to maintain any representation in
Dublin. The Government also decided at their meeting on 14th May,
1963, to accord *de jure* recognition to the Government of Poland at
Warsaw.

6. The Government have always recognised the State of China. While
acknowledging that the Peking Government is in effective *de facto*
control of Mainland China and that the Nationalist Government is in
effective *de facto* control of Formosa (Taiwan), the Minister did not
recommend that the Government should take any specific decision in
connection with either Government. Missions may, therefore, continue
the present practice of meeting and corresponding with representatives of

the Formosa Government but should have no contact with representatives of the Peking Government without reference to the Department.

7. It was *not* proposed that the Government should make any decision as regards East Germany, Viet-Nam (North) and Korea (North). For the convenience of Missions a list of the States recognised by Ireland as of this date is attached as Annex I.

8. It should be noted that no formal public announcement is being or should be made of the change of recognition status of any of the States referred to in this circular nor are the changes being formally communicated to any of the Governments of these States. *If* approached on the subject by representatives of any of the Governments concerned, Missions may inform them of the present position, but in no case should the date of *de jure* recognition be given without reference to the Department. The case of Viet-Nam (South) has already been referred to in paragraph 2(i) above.

9. DC Circular No. 6/56, issued on 14th November, 1956, is hereby cancelled.

[signed] Hugh McCann
Runaí

10 Deireadh Fómhair, 1963

ANNEX 1

**List of States Recognised by Ireland
as at 10th October, 1963[199]**

Afghanistan, Albania, Algeria, Argentina, Australia, Austria, Belgium, Bolivia, Brazil, Bulgaria, Burma, Burundi, Cambodia, Cameroun, Canada, Central African Republic, Ceylon, Chad, Chile, China,* Colombia, Congo (Brazzaville), Congo (Leopoldville), Costa Rica, Cuba, Cyprus, Czechoslovakia, Dahomey, Denmark, Dominican Republic, Ecuador, El Salvador, Ethiopia, Federal Republic of Germany, Finland, France, Gabon, Ghana, Great Britain, Greece, Guatemala, Guinea, Haiti, Honduras, Hungary, Iceland, India, Indonesia, Iran, Iraq, Israel, Italy, Ivory Coast, Jamaica, Japan, Jordan, Korea (South), Kuwait, Laos, Lebanon, Liechtenstein, Liberia, Libya, Luxembourg, Madagascar, Malaysia, Mali, Mauritania, Mexico, Monaco, Mongolia (Outer), Morocco, Nepal, Netherlands, New Zealand, Nicaragua, Niger, Nigeria, Norway, Pakistan, Panama, Paraguay, Peru, Philippines, Poland, Portugal, Romania, Rwanda, Saudi Arabia, San Marino, Senegal, Sierra Leone, Somalia, South Africa, Spain, Sudan, Sweden, Switzerland, Syria, Tanganyika, Thailand, Togo, Trinidad and Tobago, Tunisia, Turkey, Uganda, Union of Soviet Socialist Republics, United Arab Republic, United States, Upper Volta, Uruguay,

Vatican City, Viet-Nam (South), Venezuela, Western Somoa, Yemen, Yugoslavia.

*For China, reference is made to paragraph 6 of the Circular.
The following States are listed as Non-members of the UN: Federal Republic of Germany, South Korea, Liechtenstein, Monaco, San Marino, Switzerland, Vatican City, South Viet-Nam, and Western Somoa

CONCLUSION

After the government voted to accept *de jure* recognition *en masse* in May 1963, the next issue of recognition of the states Zanzibar and Kenya appeared in February 1964. A proper 'memorandum for the government' was prepared and voted upon.[200] The department at last seemed to have recognition procedures under control. After providing background information on the former British Colonial territories, the final sentence of the memorandum stated simply: 'The Minister for External Affairs... recommends that the Government accord *de jure* recognition to the new States of Zanzibar and Kenya.' The new procedure of 'submission then vote' streamlined recognition practice, and provided for stability in policy that had been lacking. An obvious respectability in internal organization resulted from clearing up recognition issues, as well as freeing the department of reinventing the wheel each time a recognition issue appeared by distinguishing between recognition of states and recognition of governments. Although no formal policy statement was made, from 1963 onward, Ireland generally has followed the practice initiated in the Estrada doctrine of the Americas and later, the Morrison Statement of Great Britain by discontinuing the practice of recognizing governments, simplifying procedure enormously.[201]

In summary, diplomatic recognition policy in Ireland during the period 1949–63 was influenced by three factors: the effect of individuals upon the underbelly of policy-making, especially Joseph P. Walshe, Michael Rynne and Cornelius (Con) Cremin; the inevitable evolution of the Department of External Affairs administration after 1949, moving from isolation to integration in politics and economics in post-war Europe; and the impact achieving full diplomatic independence in the environment of the Cold War. During the period, Ireland differentiated between 'recognition of states' and 'recognition of governments' based on the changing international political environments, often forcing the abandonment of international legal principles to policy considerations. Ireland's position in limiting recognition and using non-recognition as a tool of foreign policy was not unique, but the pursuance of independent recognition policy in the Cold War environment shows remarkable tenacity and diplomatic confidence.

Although Hersch Lauterpacht argued that manipulating international legal principles to fit particular political needs would have a negative affect on the system of states, it is appropriate to remember that states are meant to reflect the interests of citizens within them. While historical international legal principles serve as guides for the behaviour of states, in rapidly changing and antagonistic situations such as those Europe encountered after the Second World War, the anomalous behaviour of states may lead to new international legal norms and a new international legal order. Ireland's pursuance of independent diplomatic recognition policies from 1949–63 exemplifies a state's ability to pursue self-defined international interests. The administrative procedures devised within the Department of External Affairs did not always keep pace with the changing international political system and some officials would have preferred the status quo inherent in procedural stability, or perhaps the avoidance of recognition issues altogether. However, the blind confidence and related success achieved by the Irish diplomats who were interested in developing recognition policy shows the flexibility of the 'anarchical system of states', and serves as a positive contribution to world order. As Hedley Bull argued in *The Anarchical Society*, 'world order is more fundamental and primordial than international order because the ultimate units of the great society of all mankind are not states ... but individual human beings'.[202] The ability to define interests and act upon them is fundamental to state independence. Overall, Irish diplomatic recognition policy from 1949–63 did not seek to challenge or destroy the order existing within the international legal system. Rather, Irish policy and practice sought accommodation of its own interests within the world system of states. Chapter 6, 'Non-recognition of Israel and the Politics of Prestige' will demonstrate to what lengths the Irish diplomats were willing to pursue what they believed to be indefeasible Irish interests.

NOTES

1   Sir Hersch Lauterpacht, 'Recognition of governments: one of the crucial issues of international law', *The Times* (London), 6 January 1950. This article is found in NAI DFA 305/149 Part 1, NAI DT S14712 and NAI DFA 305/115/1.
2   W. Michael Reisman, 'International law after the cold war', *American Journal of International Law*, 84, 4 (October 1990), p. 860.
3   Robert Ellsworth Elder, *The Policy Machine: The Department of State and American Foreign Policy* (Syracuse, NY, 1960), p. 158.
4   Ibid., pp. 159–60.
5   Lauterpacht, 'Recognition of governments'.
6   John Lewis Gaddis, 'Spheres of influence: the United States and Europe, 1945–1949', in Charles S. Maier, ed., *The Cold War in Europe* (New York, 1991), p. 118.
7   NAI DT S14712, memorandum, 'Possible alternative courses to adopt in regard to the new Czechoslovak government', 23 March 1948.
8   In diplomatic departments, the legal adviser assumes a useful role. 'The legal adviser should tell the political officers whether proposed action conforms to international norms or treaty obligations, how deep an inroad into law and order it would make, whether there is indeed uncertainty or ambiguity and how much, how plausible any available justification would be, how other nations involved are likely to view the law and the justification. He should consider alternatives and suggest where each might lie

in a spectrum of violation. And the wise politician listens, because he knows that violations bring consequences – immediate and eventual, potent and subtle – that may not be worth the advantages to be gained.' Louis Henkin, *How Nations Behave: Law and Foreign Policy*, (New York, 2nd edn, 1979), p. 68.

9   Dermot Keogh, *Ireland and the Vatican: The Politics and Diplomacy of Church–State Relations 1922–1960* (Cork, 1995), p. 236.

10   NAI DT S14712, memorandum, 23 March 1948.

11   This was not the first instance of withholding recognition based on political rationale. Ireland refused to recognize Franco's Nationalist government in Spain until February 1939. Eamon de Valera would not give in to pressure of the Irish Catholic Front, as he considered being in the company of Germany and Italy (and out of favour with the Vatican) much more perverse than the insults from the ICF or Fine Gael. See Keogh, *Ireland and the Vatican*, pp. 127–32.

12   Hersch Lauterpacht in E. Lauterpacht, ed., *International Law: Being the Collected Papers of Hersch Lauterpacht*, Vol. 2 (Cambridge, 1975), p. 168.

13   E. Lauterpacht, *Collected Papers of Hersch Lauterpacht*, p. 169.

14   Reisman, 'International Law after the Cold War', p. 860.

15   On this point see Dermot Keogh, *Jews in Twentieth-century Ireland: Refugees, Anti-Semitism and the Holocaust* (Cork, 1998), p. 229.

16   See Paul Reuter, *Introduction to the Law of Treaties* (trans. José Mico and Peter Haggenmacher) (New York, 1989).

17   Jennings and Watts, eds, *Oppenheim's International Law*, pp. 159–60.

18   J. Frowein, 'Recognition' in 10 *Encyclopedia of Public International Law* 340–47 (1987) quoted in Burns H. Weston *et al.*, *International Law and World Order* (St Paul, MN, 1990), p. 846.

19   Reisman and Suzuki, 'Recognition and Social Change in International Law', p. 411.

20   T. Ryle Dwyer, *De Valera: The Man and The Myths* (Dublin, 1991), p. 33.

21   Maurice Moynihan, ed., *Speeches and Statements by Eamon de Valera 1917–73* (Dublin, 1980), p. 37.

22   Brierly, *The Law of Nations*, pp. 121–2.

23   Carr, *What is History?*, p. 11.

24   Reisman and Suzuki, 'Recognition and Social Change in International Law', p. 414.

25   Dermot Keogh, 'Ireland and "Emergency" Culture, Between Civil War and Normalcy, 1922–61', *Irish Democracy and the Right to Freedom of Information*, a special edition of *Ireland: A Journal of History and Society*, Vol. 1 (Cork, 1995), p. 12.

26   Keogh, 'Ireland and "Emergency" Culture', pp. 12–14.

27   Fanning, *The Irish Department of Finance 1922–58* (Dublin, 1978), pp. 407–8.

28   Gaddis, *Russia, The Soviet Union, and the United States*, p. 190.

29   Ibid.

30   Konrad Adenauer, *Memoirs 1945–53* (trans. Beate Ruhn von Oppen) (London, 1965), p. 142.

31   See Keogh, *Ireland and the Vatican*, pp. 232–49.

32   NAI DT S2309.

33   NAI DT S14712, 'Possible alternative courses to adopt in regard to the new Czechoslovak Government', 23 March 1948.

34   NAI DT S14712.

35   Irish exports to Czechoslovakia fell from £9,083 in 1946 to £2,036 in 1947. Imports from Czechoslovakia grew from £267,202 to £1,426,780. NAI DT S14712. The official trade statistics report imports of £267,203 in 1946 and £1,430,088 in 1947. *Statistical Abstracts of Ireland* (Dublin, various years).

36   NAI DT S14712.

37   *Foreign Relations of the United States* (*FRUS*), Vol. 4, 1948, circular telegram (Washington, 8 March 1948), p. 439.

38   See Michael J. Cohen, *Truman and Israel* (Berkeley, CA, 1990), p. 242.

39   *FRUS*, Vol. 4, 1948, 'United Kingdom/United States Civil Aviation Policy Towards the

Soviet Union and Its Satellites' (London, 7 December 1948), pp. 482–3.

40   Ibid., p. 483.
41   Ibid.
42   NAI DT S14712.
43   See Josef Korbel, *The Communist Subversion of Czechoslovakia 1938–1948: The Failure of Coexistence* (Princeton, NJ, 1959).
44   Ibid., p. 213.
45   *FRUS*, Vol. 4, 1948, memorandum, Steinhardt to Marshall, 30 April 1948, p. 752.
46   Keogh, *Ireland and the Vatican*, p. 236.
47   Ibid., p. 240.
48   NAI DT S14012.
49   Ibid.
50   Ibid. The case, which elicited the British Foreign Office response, was the *Arantzazu Mendi* (1938), a Spanish ship registered at Bilbao. When Franco's forces captured Bilbao, the Republican government requisitioned the ship. The ship was not in Spanish territorial waters at the time, but when it landed at the Surrey commercial docks, the Nationalist government requisitioned it. The managing director of the docks declared that he held the vessel at the disposal of the Nationalist Government. The Republican government issued a writ *in rem* claiming the ship. The Nationalist government moved to set aside the writ on the ground that the action impleaded a foreign sovereign State, the Nationalist government of Spain. The Foreign Office stated that no other government except the Republican government was recognized *de jure* by Britain, but that the Nationalist government exercised *de facto* control over most of Spain, and that the Nationalist government was not a government subordinate to any other government in Spain. The court held that for the purpose of the case, the Nationalist government of Spain was a foreign sovereign state and the writ must be set aside. See British Institute Studies in International and Comparative Law, *British International Law Cases* Vol. 2 (London, 1965), pp. 179–80.
51   NAI DT S14012.
52   Claude, *Swords into Plowshares*, p. 89.
53   Ibid., p. 90.
54   NAI DFA 305/38, 'Weekly review of incoming shortwave broadcasts', 6 January 1950.
55   NAI DFA 305/149 Part 2, memorandum for the government: 'Recognition of the Republic of the United States of Indonesia', 2 January 1950.
56   Ibid.
57   NAI DFA 305/38, letter, Mohammed Hatta to Seán MacBride, 26 January 1950.
58   Lauterpacht, 'Recognition of Governments'.
59   Ibid.
60   Richard Harris, 'Britain and China: coexistence at low pressure', in A. M. Halpern, ed., *Policies Toward China: Views from Six Continents* (New York, 1965), p. 19.
61   Ibid.
62   NAI DFA 305/149 Part 1, letter, Ambassador Boland to Seán Nunan, 28 March 1951. The Morrison Statement was made on 21 March 1951 and may be found at *Parliamentary Debates, House of Commons*, 1950–51, Vol. 485, pp. 1410–11. Britain abolished the practice of recognition of Governments entirely in 1980. See Warbrick, 'The New British Policy'.
63   Percy E. Corbett, *Law in Diplomacy* (Princeton, NJ, 1959), p. 80.
64   NAI DFA 305/149 Part 1.
65   Keogh, *Twentieth-century Ireland*, p. 224.
66   *FRUS*, Vol. 6, 1952–54, memorandum, the Ambassador in France (Bruce) to the Department of State, 11 January 1952.
67   Ibid.
68   Keogh, *Twentieth-century Ireland*, p. 226.
69   Ibid., p. 231.
70   NAI DFA 305/149 Part 1, letter, T.J. Horan to Dr Alfred Kolb, 5 September 1955.

71 NAI DFA 305/149 Part 1, note, 10 November 1955. The letter and note were sent to the following embassies and legations on 15 November 1955: Canberra, Holy See, London, Madrid, Ottawa, Paris, Washington, Berne, Bonn, Brussels, Buenos Aires, The Hague, Lisbon, Rome, Stockholm, Boston, New York, Chicago and San Francisco.
72 For a more complete analysis of the Hallstein Doctrine, see Chapter 4.
73 NAI DFA 305/149 Part 1, working papers, T.J. Horan on Recognition, September 1955.
74 Palestine is listed erroneously.
75 NAI DFA 305/296, telegram, Buenos Aires Legation to Dublin, 24 September 1955.
76 NAI DFA 305/296, note, T.J. Horan, 26 September 1955.
77 Ibid. The government approved the memorandum concerning recognition of Argentina's new government on 7 October 1955.
78 NAI DFA 305/296, letter, Matthew Murphy to Seán Murphy, 16 November 1955.
79 *FRUS*, Vol. 7, 1955–57, editorial note, pp. 384–5.
80 NAI DFA 305/303/1, letter, F.H. Boland to Seán Murphy, 5 January 1956.
81 NAI DFA 305/303/1, memorandum, Eoin MacWhite to Sheila Murphy, 18 January 1956.
82 The issue of recognition of Jordan first appeared in January 1954. See NAI DFA 305/156.
83 NAI DFA 305/303/1, memorandum, 18 January 1956.
84 Ibid.
85 Ibid.
86 Ibid.
87 The following states were admitted to the UN in 1956: Japan, Morocco, Sudan and Tunisia.
88 NAI DFA 305/303/1, handwritten response, Sheila Murphy to Eoin MacWhite, no date.
89 Cremin consistently used the spelling 'recognize' in this letter.
90 Emphasis added.
91 NAI DFA 305/149 Part 1, letter, Con Cremin to Seán Murphy, 7 February 1956.
92 Ibid.
93 Ibid.
94 Ibid.
95 NAI DFA 305/156, memorandum, 'Question of *de jure* recognition of the State of Israel', 21 March 1956.
96 NAI DFA 305/149 Part 1, letter, Ambassador Alfred Rive to Seán Murphy, 15 June 1956.
97 NAI DFA 305/149 Part 1, draft reply, 29 June 1956.
98 Ibid. The Polish government-in-exile had maintained a delegate in Dublin from 1936–54 as Consul General, Wenceslas Dobrzynski. Upon his death, the Vice Consul, Zofia Zaleska took over his responsibilities until 1957. The main dealings with the Polish consulate from 1936-54 were to provide free road tax and driving licences to Dobrzynski and his family. NAI DFA 320/28/27.
99 NAI DFA 305/149 Part 1, memorandum, Sheila Murphy to J. Belton, 19 June 1956.
100 William P. Fay was Legal Adviser in the Department of External Affairs from 1953–54.
101 NAI DFA 305/149 Part 1, DC Circular No. 6/56, 14 November 1956.
102 Ibid.
103 In October 1956 the Soviet Union put a forceful end to calls for the removal of Soviet troops and the neutralization of Hungary by Communist Party Leader and Premier Imre Nagy. In early November Soviet troops invaded Hungary, deposed Nagy and later executed him. For current historiography on this subject, see Terry Cox, ed., *Hungary 1956 – Forty Years On* (Portland, OR, 1997).
104 Rynne's reference is to NAI DT S14712, 'Possible alternative courses to adopt in regard to the new Czechoslovak government', 23 March 1948.
105 NAI DFA 305/149 Part 1, letter, Michael Rynne to Seán Murphy, 27 November 1956.
106 David Engel, *Facing a Holocaust: The Polish Government-in-Exile and the Jews, 1943–45* (Chapel Hill, NC, 1993), p. 169.

107 *FRUS*, Vol. 26, 1955–57, memorandum, 4 March 1957. During this meeting the subject of recognition of Poland was discussed. The West Germans could not 'recognize' Poland due to the *Hallstein Doctrine*, and the United States considered the establishment of diplomatic relations 'premature at the moment' (p. 212). Once again, the terminology used in the word *recognize* could be confusing in this context. The intent was 'to establish a diplomatic relationship'. The United States recognized the government in Warsaw in July 1945 and the state of Poland was a charter member of the United Nations.

108 NAI DT S16270A, letter, August Zaleski to Eamon de Valera, 12 July 1957.

109 NAI DT S16270A, draft letters dated 19 July, 30 July and 23 August 1957.

110 NAI DT S16270A, letter, Eamon de Valera to August Zaleski, 23 August 1957.

111 *Oppenheim's International Law* suggests that governments-in-exile lack the capacity to sue in foreign courts and cannot lawfully print their own currency notes.

112 NAI DFA 305/149 Part 1, report, 'Discussion with a Polish Delegate', Conor Cruise O'Brien, 1 November 1957.

113 Ibid.

114 NAI DFA 305/149 Part 1, memorandum, Con Cremin, 7 July 1962.

115 NAI DFA 305/373, telegram, Michael Rynne to Secretary Con Cremin, 29 July 1958.

116 See Skelly, *Irish Diplomacy at the United Nations*, pp. 68–77.

117 NAI DFA 305/373, note, Eoin MacWhite to Conor Cruise O'Brien, 31 July 1958.

118 NAI DFA 305/373, note, Conor Cruise O'Brien to Eoin MacWhite, 31 July 1958.

119 NAI DFA 305/373, letter, Con Cremin to Michael Rynne, 5 August 1958.

120 Ibid.

121 Ho Chi Minh formed the Vietminh (or League of Independence of Vietnam) in 1941.

122 Jennings and Watts, eds, *Oppenheim's International Law*, p. 141.

123 James Lee Ray, *Global Politics* (Boston, MA, 3rd edn, 1987), p. 57.

124 NAI DFA 305/115/1, confidential report, Washington Embassy, 15 April 1954.

125 See generally, Lloyd C. Gardner and Ted Gittinger, eds, *Vietnam: The Early Decisions* (Austin, TX, 1997).

126 See Frances FitzGerald, *Fire in the Lake: The Vietnamese and the Americans in Vietnam* (Boston, MA, 1972). When Ngo Dinh Diem fled Vietnam in 1950 under Vietminh persecution, his intention was to live with his clerical brother, Ngo Dinh Thuc in Rome. Diem left Rome for the United States, living for two years at the Maryknoll Seminary in New Jersey and in New York until 1954.

127 Joseph G. Morgan, *The Vietnam Lobby: The American Friends of Vietnam, 1955–75* (Chapel Hill, NC, 1997), pp. 62–76.

128 Ibid., p. 63.

129 Spencer C. Tucker, *Vietnam* (London, 1999), p. 95.

130 Ibid.

131 FitzGerald, *Fire in the Lake*, p. 83. FitzGerald argues that the enthusiasm for Diem by Kennedy and Mansfield 'could be explained at least partly by the fact that the early fifties was the height of the McCarthy period. In Washington the Catholic senator from Wisconsin [Mansfield] had attacked as "traitors" those U.S. State Department officials who had recommended that the United States accept as a fact Mao Tse-tung's victory in China.' By 1956, Kennedy supported the 'domino theory' of the Truman and Eisenhower administrations.

132 William Conrad Gibbons, 'Lyndon Johnson and the Legacy of Vietnam', in Gardner and Gittinger, eds, *Vietnam: The Early Decisions*, p. 121.

133 Ibid., p. 122.

134 For example, see various memorandums in *FRUS*, Vol. 1, 1961–63, drafted by the President's Deputy Special Assistant for National Security Affairs, Walt W. Rostow.

135 NAI DFA 305/149 Part 1, letter, W. P. Fay to Seán Murphy, 28 April 1956.

136 NAI DFA 305/108 Part 2, note no. 153, 4 March 1960.

137 NAI DFA 305/108 Part 2, note, unidentifiable author to Conor Cruise O'Brien, 2 July 1960.

138 NAI DFA 305/108 Part 2, letter, 30 July 1960.
139 Morgan, *The Vietnam Lobby*, p. 81.
140 Ngo Dinh Can was tried and executed in a public square in Saigon after Diem's fall in 1963.
141 Diem wanted to elevate Thuc's position to Archbishop of Saigon, but the Vatican refused. Archbishop Thuc was in Rome during the coup. The Vatican later twice excommunicated Thuc for illegal consecrations of bishops. He died in the United States in 1984. Stanley I. Kutler, ed., *Encyclopedia of the Vietnam War* (New York, 1996), p. 360.
142 Ngo Dinh Nhu's open opposition and annihilation of the Buddhists eventually forced the United States to tacitly support the plans for a coup against Nhu and Diem between August and November 1963. Nhu, convinced that the Buddhists were a communist front, ordered a systematic raid on pagodas throughout South Vietnam in August 1963, a decision that appalled the Vietnamese population.
143 Madame Nhu's maiden name was Tran Thi Le Xuan. She has lived in Rome since 1964.
144 See Kutler, *Encyclopedia of the Vietnam War*. Pejoratively known as the 'Dragon Lady', Madame Nhu is not considered 'a sympathetic figure on either side of the Pacific' (p. 359). The US State Department considered Madame Nhu and her husband the pivotal threat to Diem's regime. 'When Secretary [Dean] Rusk suggested that perhaps [Ambassador Henry Cabot] Lodge might bring himself to talk to Diem…and try to separate him from Nhu, Lodge's reply…was peremptory: The prime objective [was] to get the Nhus out. "The best chance of doing it is the generals taking over the government lock, stock and barrel."' Ellen J. Hammer, *A Death in November: America in Vietnam 1963* (New York, 1987), p. 192.
145 Mrs Chuong's name was Than Thi Nam Tran.
146 Their only son, Tran Van Khiem, murdered the Chuongs.
147 NAI DFA 305/149 Part 1, memorandum, Con Cremin, 7 July 1962.
148 Ibid.
149 NAI DFA 348/180/3, letter, Sheila Murphy to F.H. Boland, 13 August 1962. Sheila Murphy was not aware of Mrs Chuong's background.
150 Ibid..
151 NAI DFA 348/180/3, letter 11 August 1962.
152 NAI DFA 305/108 Part 2, letter, Hugh McCann to Sheila Murphy, 17 December 1962.
153 Ibid.
154 NAI DFA 305/108 Part 2, letter, Hugh McCann to Ngo Dinh Luyen, 14 December 1962.
155 NAI DFA 305/108 Part 2, letter, Hugh McCann to Sheila Murphy, 17 December 1962.
156 NAI DFA 348/180/3, letter, Sheila Murphy to Con Cremin, 13 June 1963.
157 Ibid.
158 NAI DFA 305/108 Part 2, letter, Con Cremin to Sheila Murphy, 3 July 1963.
159 Ibid.
160 Ibid.
161 The import trade was negligible with South Vietnam during the years of this study. Exports from Ireland began in 1962 and were IR£339,541. Exports in 1963 were IR£239,260 and in 1964, IR£74,578. *Statistical Abstracts of Ireland*. Sheila Murphy stated in October 1963 that the 'firm mainly interested' in trade with Vietnam was ACEC (Ireland) Ltd, a subsidiary of a British company, 'which [had] been making persistent representations to the Department on the matter for over a year'. Further, the trade figures were not in the Irish statistics, 'no doubt because they go out through Britain'. NAI DFA 348/180/3, letter, Sheila Murphy to F.H. Boland, 14 October 1963.
162 NAI DFA 348/180/3, letter, 14 October 1963.
163 The date given in this letter is incorrect and should read '17 May 1960'.
164 NAI DFA 348/180/3, letter, Sheila Murphy to F.H. Boland, 14 October 1963.
165 NAI DFA 348/180/3, draft letter dated 13 March 1964, noted as sent on 3 June 1964.

166   NAI DFA 348/180/3, letter, Truong Buu Khanh to J.G. Molloy, 15 June 1964.
167   NAI DFA 305/108 Part II, note, Embassy of Vietnam, 10 February 1974.
168   From 1973–76, the Irish Government recognized two states in Vietnam. The file on Recognition of Vietnam continues through 22 June 1976, when *de jure* recognition was extended to the Democratic Republic of Vietnam. 'While Ireland has never recognised the Democratic Republic of Vietnam (North Vietnam) many countries including all those European countries now our partners in the EEC decided to recognise that state after the Paris Peace Agreements in 1972. As the reunited state of Vietnam will be governed from Hanoi, most of our EEC partners will not need to proceed to any new act of recognition... The Minister considers it opportune that Ireland should now also recognise the reunified state'. NAI DFA 305/108 Part 2, memorandum for the government, 'Recognition of Vietnam', 21 June 1976.
169   NAI DFA 305/149 Part 1, memorandum, Con Cremin, 7 July 1962.
170   Ibid.
171   Ibid.
172   Ibid.
173   Ibid.
174   Ibid.
175   Ibid.
176   Ibid.
177   Keogh, *Ireland and the Vatican*, p. 358.
178   For a discussion of Pope Paul VI's policy changes toward Israel, see Chapter 6.
179   For a full record of Ireland's accomplishments at the United Nations, see Skelly, *Irish Diplomacy at the United Nations.*
180   See Fanning, *The Irish Department of Finance*, pp. 461–519.
181   NAI DFA 305/392/1 Part I, 'A New Look At Ireland's Foreign Policy' in *Handelsblatt* (Dusseldorf), 22 October 1962.
182   Lee, *Ireland 1912–1985*, p. 414.
183   Ibid.
184   NAI DFA 305/149 Part 1, memorandum, 7 July 1962.
185   Con Cremin, unpublished memoir. The author wishes to thank Professor Dermot Keogh for access to Ambassador Cremin's memoir.
186   McCann remained Secretary of External Affairs from 1963–73.
187   NAI DT S17246, 'Speech by the Taoiseach on Debate on Motion to adjourn the Dáil', 5 February 1963.
188   NAI DFA 305/149 Part 1, memorandum, 26 March 1963.
189   Ibid.
190   The list reads as follows: Burma, Ceylon, Iceland, India, Indonesia, Israel (*de facto*), Lebanon, Palestine, Philippines and Syria.
191   NAI DFA 305/149 Part 1, memorandum, 26 March 1963.
192   Congo became a one-party State in 1964 with the capital at Brazzaville.
193   Dahomey became Benin in 1975.
194   Tanganyika achieved independence from Britain in 1961 and became a Republic in 1962. In 1964, Tanganyika and Zanzibar became the United Republic of Tanzania.
195   Upper Volta became Burkina Faso in 1984.
196   Name changed to Mongolia in 1991.
197   It is interesting to note that Poland is not categorized in the previous group, which elevated certain states from a *de facto* to *de jure* status. This confirms Ireland's insistence on adhering to separate recognition of states and recognition of governments after 1957. In practice, *de jure* recognition meant that the invitation to enter into diplomatic relations would be considered but would not necessarily be established.
198   The memorandum specified in the case of China that 'the Minister does not recommend that the Government should take any specific decision in the connection with either Government'.
199   The format of this list has been modified. The original was in three columns,

alphabetically listed. See NAI DFA 305/115 Part 2, DC Circular No. 2/63, 10 October 1963.

200　NAI DFA 305/149 Part 1, memorandum for the government, February 1964.

201　One could date the demise of Irish recognition of Governments with de Valera's refusal in 1957 to continue recognizing the Polish government-in-exile.

202　Bull, *The Anarchical Society*, p. 22.

4

Cold War diplomacy in the case of
East Germany

The non-recognition by other nations of a government claiming to be a national personality is usually appropriate evidence that it has not attained the independence and control entitling it by international law to be classified as such. But when recognition *vel non* of a government is by such nations determined by inquiry, not into its *de facto* sovereignty and complete governmental control, but into its illegitimacy or irregularity of origin, their non-recognition loses something of evidential weight on the issue with which those applying the rules of international law are alone concerned.

> CJ William Howard Taft, 'Arbitration between Great Britain and
> Costa Rica', in Burns H. Weston *et al.*, eds,
> *International Law and World Order*[1]

The goal of [the Soviet] policy was crystal clear: to maintain Germany's political and military state of suspense and thus make it impossible for Western Europe to grow together. Without unification and integration Western Europe was bound to crumble and the countries of Western Europe were more or less powerless. Soviet Russia calculated that the United States would lose interest in a crumbling Western Europe and withdraw from the continent. Russia would then draw not only the Federal Republic but also the other countries of Western Europe into its sphere of influence, without any war, and finally be master of all Europe.

> Konrad Adenauer, *Memoirs 1945–53*[2]

INTRODUCTION

This chapter focuses on the factors influencing the Irish government in determining and establishing a policy of non-recognition toward the Soviet-controlled government and territory of East Germany. The primary factors were ancillary to the environment of Cold War politics. First, Ireland's only interest in East Germany as a state was the potential of trade, seen as an addition to normal western European trading relationships. The Department of External

Affairs classified these trade considerations under the general heading of 'trading with the Communists'.[3] Second, during the period of this study, 1949–63, trading potential with East Germany was never so great that it overrode Ireland's primary interest: to firmly position itself economically and ideologically on the side of liberal trade and capitalism. Third, Ireland's relationship with the Federal Republic of Germany was too valuable for Irish foreign policy to turn toward the East Germans in any practical sense. Adenauer's government made certain early in the game, through the Hallstein doctrine (1955), that no state would recognize East Germany as sovereign and continue to enjoy diplomatic relations with the Federal Republic. Clearly, significant trade could have been accomplished with the East Germans during the period of this study if the will had existed on the Irish side. Diplomatic recognition was not fundamental to a trading relationship, but the obstacles to trading with communist bloc countries were too numerous and difficult for any significant trade to develop.

Although the Soviet Union declared East Germany 'sovereign' in 1954, this prerequisite for statehood was interpreted by the Western powers as a 'state less than sovereign'. Without confusing the issue, if four factors are needed to create a state – people, territory, government and sovereignty – then to call a 'state' less than 'sovereign' is logically absurd. This concept of sovereignty, however, is used in an indivisible sense; that is, the powers connected to sovereignty must be singularly held.

Prior to the twentieth century, sovereignty evolved from Bodin's original conception in *De la République* (1577) as an *indivisible* concept. *Oppenheim's International Law* argues that

> after the Westphalian Peace, and the establishment of the United States of America, Switzerland and Germany as federal states with sovereign powers divided between the federal state and the constituent member states, the need to distinguish between absolute and partial sovereignty became widely (although not universally) accepted.[4]

As noted in *Oppenheim's International Law*, the difficulty with the concept of sovereignty in the twentieth century is that, in its original theoretical usage, sovereignty was 'a matter of *internal* constitutional power and authority, conceived as the highest, [non-derived] power within the state with exclusive competence therein'[5] (emphasis added). However, in the twentieth century, practical realities have forced the illogical idea that sovereignty may be divisible.

> Once it is appreciated that it is not so much the possession of sovereignty which determines possession of international personality but rather the possession of rights, duties and powers in international law, it is apparent that a State which possesses some, but not all, of those rights, duties and powers is nevertheless an international person.[6]

Although states may be 'sovereign' in domestic politics, foreign relations in the system of states is characterized by equality, independence and interdependence.[7] In the case of East Germany, proponents of strict international law required the independence factor in order to recognize it as a 'state', an idea that the Federal Republic (FRG) held in abeyance until 1972, when political and economic realities forced acceptance that East Germany (GDR) had, in the legal sense, 'enough' independence to be considered a 'state', although it could not be considered *Ausland*, or a *foreign* state. As a result, the Vienna diplomatic convention only applied on a limited basis to inter-German relations. A separate West German ministry, not foreign affairs, conducted bilateral relations between the FRG and the GDR after the establishment of the Basic Treaty, and the two 'states' could not establish 'regular international relations'.[8]

This case study examines whether the Irish government, in formulating foreign policy after breaking with the Commonwealth in 1949, realized the opportunity to set independent policy regarding recognition of East Germany, or rather, did it follow the lead of the other western states and if so, which ones. The policy tool of withholding recognition from a foreign state or government is a powerful instrument in establishing an independent foreign policy. For Ireland, the East German case was an opportunity for furthering its establishment as a neutral state by basing its non-recognition of the Soviet-controlled zone of Germany on consistent foreign policy rather than appeasing Western democracies, especially the NATO powers and the Federal Republic of Germany. On the issue of the Soviet-controlled zone of Germany, or East Germany, Ireland did not pursue a non-committal policy but actively fought any intimation of recognition either *de facto* or *de jure*.

By examining the archival sources in detail, it is possible to understand what factors led to Ireland's long-term maintenance of the policy of non-recognition of East Germany by studying incremental decisions made by the Department of Foreign Affairs and ultimately, the Department of the Taoiseach. The primary sources used in this chapter for studying the development of policy in East German non-recognition are the comprehensive files in the National Archives in Dublin relating to the Department of External (Foreign) Affairs and East German recognition. These files tell two stories simultaneously. First, since the files contain subordinate material as well as policy statements, the files show the evolution of the concept of non-recognition from 1949–63 in an historical perspective. For example, seemingly irrelevant material (such as newspaper clippings placed in the file as they were published) added to the intelligence reports from the embassies and legations, serving as documents to support or confirm Ireland's policy of non-recognition.

Second, and perhaps more importantly, the files reveal the methodological sense of how the Irish government developed policy concerning the non-recognition issue, given Ireland's status as a newly independent, unarmed neutral state trying to establish trade and diplomatic relations beyond its dependence on the United Kingdom, in the perceived harsh and volatile environment of bipolarity.[9] The professionalism of the Department of External Affairs is strikingly apparent in the files on East Germany.

When one examines archival material in an archaeological sense, noticing what is 'missing' and what remains in the files, the files began to tell a story all their own. Hypothesizing about 'missing' information may be divided into two groups: did the evidence exist, but is absent from the file, or did the evidence never exist at all? For the diplomatic historian, evidence from the archival material is used to support arguments or to trace a progression of events or decisions. What is frequently neglected is viewing the archival material in an administrative sense. That is, in order for the diplomatic or foreign office personnel to make decisions, what information was available for their needs? What information did they rely upon? What information did they simply ignore?

In the archival evidence on East German recognition, one may ask whether there were further intelligence materials that played a role in setting Department of External Affairs' policy, or are the files comprehensive? On the issue of East Germany it is argued that the archival files reveal a complete history of intelligence available to the department.

In a secret memorandum from the Irish legation at Bonn to the Department of External Affairs in Dublin dated 3 April 1954, the diplomatic intelligence was nonchalant:

> Soviet Russia's announcement of sovereignty for East Germany neither surprised nor impressed political circles in Bonn nor indeed elsewhere ... It is inconceivable that the Russians at any time thought that the grant of alleged sovereignty could have any meaning for Western Europe other than the change of name of the territory concerned.[10]

The Soviet announcement, however, initiated changes in the East/West system that had previously been inconceivable. No one foresaw at the Crimea Conference in February 1945 (known as the Yalta Peace Conference), that the decisions of three Western leaders – Roosevelt of the United States, Churchill of the United Kingdom, and Stalin of the Soviet Union – would lead to intractable stalemate over the eastern part of Germany, creating a separate international state and arousing enmity that would become indelible during the course of the Cold War.[11]

The fate of the territory east of the Oder-Neisse line was not decided at Yalta, however. The destiny of the eastern zone of Germany was sealed in increments rather than in a single decision. The idea of spheres of influence in eastern Europe was tacitly established between Stalin and Churchill in May 1944 in the 'notorious percentages agreement' when Churchill suggested to Stalin:

> Let us settle about our affairs in the Balkans. Your armies are in Rumania and Bulgaria. We have interests, missions, and agents there. Don't let us

get at cross-purposes in small ways. So far as Britain and Russia are concerned, how would it do for you to have ninety per cent predominance in Rumania, for us to have ninety per cent of the say in Greece, and go fifty-fifty about Yugoslavia?[12]

Thus began the slippery slope in dividing Europe based on the interests of the victorious Allied Powers. Almost a year after the Churchill–Stalin bargaining, in February 1945 the Yalta Conference further asserted the idea of spheres of influence in eastern Europe when it incorporated Article III, cryptically called the 'Dismemberment of Germany':

The United Kingdom, the United States of America and the Union of Soviet Socialist Republics shall possess supreme authority with respect to Germany. In the exercise of such authority they will take such steps, including the complete disarmament, demilitarization and dismemberment of Germany as they deem requisite for future peace and security.[13]

In 1954, with Roosevelt and Stalin dead and Churchill in his last year of government, the question of limitations on the 'exercise of such authority' in the Soviet sphere was yet to be answered. In the few years after Yalta, the problems concerning East Germany had been numerous, from the forced Berlin Airlift of 1947–48 to the summer riots in Berlin during June 1953. Yet the establishment of East Germany as an 'independent' state in the system inched along, prodded by the continuing bipolarization of the world into communist and anti-communist camps. The post-war reality was determined by the military omnipresence of the United States and the territorial aggrandizement of the Soviet Union, fuelled by US President Harry S. Truman's 'atomic diplomacy'[14] and Stalin's intransigence in maintaining Soviet control of Eastern Europe.

In 1946, Henry A. Wallace, former US Vice President during FDR's last term, summed up the relationship with the Soviets as follows:

[The American] basic distrust of the Russians, which has been greatly intensified in recent months by the playing up of conflict in the press, stems from differences in political and economic organizations. For the first time in history defeatists among us have raised the fear of another system as a successful rival to democracy and free enterprise in other countries and perhaps even our own.[15]

Thus in February 1954, when the Irish representative at Bonn wrote that the Soviet Union's decision to grant 'sovereignty' for East Germany was not a 'surprise', it was based on an attitude developed since the end of the Second World War in which Soviet motives and moves, while not accepted in the ideological sense by Western democracies, developed a logic of their own.

This step was, insofar as one may use such an adjective in such a
connection, a logical sequence of the attitude adopted by the Soviets in
respect of the East Zone before and during the Berlin Conference ... For
the Germans it could of course represent a further step towards the
consolidation of the Oder-Neisse line, but the [West] Germans in present
circumstances see so little hope of restoration of that part of the former
Reich that they did not even ask the Allied High Commission to have the
question put on the Berlin Conference agenda.[16]

The diplomatic position of Ireland was resolute. As a part of the English-
speaking world and an observer in the occupied territory of the former German
Reich, Ireland's foreign policy objective was to maintain a sound diplomatic
relationship with the Federal Republic as a key to developing trade alliances
apart from the United Kingdom.

REMILITARIZATION AND ISOLATION IN EAST GERMANY – 1950–53

In October 1949 the three Allied Powers – the United States, Great Britain and
France – declared that 'the so-called Government of the German Democratic
Republic is the artificial erection of a "popular assembly" which [has] no
mandate for this purpose'.[17] This statement was made in the wake of East
German Minister-President Otto Grotewohl's proposal of a 'politically balanced
"All German Council" – a proposal repeatedly advanced by the Socialist Unity
Party of Germany (SED) until well into the 1960s'.[18] The Allied Powers and the
Federal Republic had no intentions of accepting proposals from East Germany.
One historian of German reunification argued:

> The GDR was not only not taken seriously as a negotiation partner but was
> ignored altogether, since the West German leadership viewed the GDR as
> a Soviet satellite whose international diplomatic recognition — and
> enhanced political status through political contacts – must be prevented
> under all circumstances.[19]

After 1947, the primary concern for the German situation focused on the
integration of West Germany into an Allied-centred Europe, not the reunification
of the two German territories. The rebuilding of Europe, originally financed by
the United States' Marshall Plan[20] in 1947, focused on the establishment of
international organizations that would unify and strengthen western Europe. In
May 1948 an interest in European unity was the basis for the Congress of Europe.
One year later, in response to a resolution adopted at the Congress, the Council of
Europe was established as a supranational organization determined to guide the
debate over the future of Europe through strong leadership from national
governments.[21] West Germany was included in the Council of Europe in 1950.

On 9 May 1950, the French government proposed the Schuman Plan, designed by French integrationist Jean Monnet but named for France's Foreign Minister, Robert Schuman. The Schuman Plan proposed a pooling of coal and steel production under a common supranational authority. Monnet's idea was to put the manufactures used for war in control of a supranational authority, to make the possibility of one state waging war against another more remote. In this instance, the goal was to pacify Franco-German antagonisms and prevent further conflict.

> Under the plan, the whole of Franco-German coal and steel production would be placed under a common High Authority composed of independent persons named by the participating national governments, but acting within an organisation open to participation by other European countries.[22]

The result of the Schuman Plan was the establishment of the European Coal and Steel Community (ECSC), created by the Treaty of Paris in 1951. The ECSC Treaty became effective in July 1952 and included not only the primary states of France and West Germany, but also Belgium, Italy, Luxembourg and the Netherlands. Thus West Germany's industrial growth was not only strengthened but also checked by its participation in the ECSC, the organization that later became the cornerstone of the European Economic Community.

The military security of western Europe fell under the North Atlantic Treaty Organization (NATO) with formal negotiations beginning in December 1948 and concluded with the signing of the treaty on 4 April 1949.[23] West Germany, although established formally as the Federal Republic of Germany in 1949, did not enter NATO until the territorial resolution with France of the Saarland in 1955. Still, by 1952 West Germany had made considerable progress toward integration with western Europe and East Germany was increasingly isolated.

On 10 March 1952, Stalin put forth a Peace Note on Germany. After direct expressions of ideological confrontation with the West – the Berlin blockade in 1947–48, the Czech coup of 1948, and the Korean War (1950–53) – the Soviets now showed a willingness to cooperate with the West but only on their own terms.

> After years of confrontation and stonewalling, the Soviet Union suddenly seemed interested in a settlement. Calling attention to the absence of a peace treaty with Germany, Stalin submitted a draft text to the other three occupying powers... The Peace Note called for a unified, neutral Germany based on free elections, and one that would be allowed to maintain its own armed forces though all foreign troops would have to leave within a year.[24]

The response from the three Western occupying powers was unanimous. They accepted the principle of German reunification but rejected a neutral German state. The West also wanted the right of free assembly and free speech guaranteed for Germany, signposts of democracy that frustrated Stalin's initiatives.[25] Within this political environment, the Irish file on 'Recognition of East Germany' began.

The question of Ireland's granting diplomatic recognition to East Germany initially appears in April 1950 with the receipt of a *pro memoria* from the Dutch government. The document establishes the policy of the Netherlands, along with the governments of France, Great Britain, Belgium, Luxembourg and the United States, for conducting relations with 'the Soviet Zone of Germany'.[26] The avoidance of either *de jure* or *de facto* recognition was the principle aim of relations with East Germany, although economic realities forced the countries concerned to establish trade practices that would be politically ambivalent. Secretary Frederick Boland forwarded the *pro memoria* to Seán Nunan in the Political Section with the attached message:

> Without suggesting that we should bind ourselves to follow an exactly similar policy, it is desirable, I think, that we should keep a sharp eye out for any transaction arising between ourselves and Eastern Germany which might seem to raise the question of *de jure* or *de facto* recognition... It might be well if the Political Section would send a Note to this effect to the other Sections, so as to ensure due coordination of policy in relation to the matter.[27]

The *pro memoria* outlined trade practices as follows:

1. Commercial Relations

> Trade should be conducted solely through the intermediary of private organisations, such as Chambers of Commerce. The fact that such private organisations on the Western side may deal with 'official' organisations on the other is of no significance with regard to recognition.
>
> Insofar as it may be necessary to discuss questions relating to trade agreements with Eastern Germany, it is desirable to maintain the state of affairs existing before the creation of the 'German Democratic Republic', that is to say, to deal with such questions through the intermediary of the Soviet authorities.
>
> Should it prove impossible in some particular and exceptional case to avoid some form of contact with the East German administration, then such dealings as take place should be carried out on as low and 'technical' a level as possible. It should be made clear that such East German administration is considered as acting under the governmental responsibility of the Soviet occupation authorities.

2. Protection of Property and Nationals

It is considered that this protection is incumbent upon the Soviet Government, which is responsible for the acts of the 'German Democratic Republic'.

3. Participation of the East German Government in international organisations

Such participation is considered undesirable.

The Netherlands Government express the hope that the Irish Government will adopt a similar attitude towards these problems and that they will be prepared to exchange with the Netherlands government and other interested Governments information on the difficulties they meet with in their relations with Eastern Germany and, if necessary, to consult with them with a view to maintaining a common attitude.[28]

The Irish policy that resulted was identical in wording to the Dutch memorandum.

The next item in the archival file is an article from the *Manchester Guardian* dated 12 February 1951 discussing the remilitarization of West Germany. The tone of the article is set in a Cold War pitch, showing the Soviet-controlled East Germany as terrified of rearmament in West Germany.

As far as they are concerned he [Konrad Adenauer] is no better than Hitler, and is constantly in touch with the least trustworthy surviving members of the German General Staff. Once he has an army (based on the Ruhr), and the Federal Republic has its sovereignty, there will be every reason, according to the Russians, to expect him to behave as Hitler did in 1941.[29]

The file is silent until 2 December 1952, almost two years later, when an article from *The Times* is inserted that discussed the 'new evidence of build-up' in East German forces. A confidential memorandum by Ambassador F.H. Boland was attached from the Irish Embassy, London to External Affairs in Dublin:

Nobody in London is seriously alarmed about the report of military preparations in the Russian Zone of Germany which was issued by the British Foreign Office on the 2nd December. The report disclosed no important new development... [It] is generally assumed that the primary object of publishing the report at this time was to help Dr. Adenauer in his task of getting the West German Parliament to ratify the Defence Treaties.[30]

Boland noted some caution on the part of the British government with 'persistent reports of air strips being lengthened, railway gauges widened, marshalling yards extended and military training being expanded', but the conservative government opinion in London was 'still proceeding on the basic assumption that Soviet Russia has no intention of launching an aggressive war, and that her policy... will be concentrated on methods of "cold war" designed to embarrass and weaken the Western Powers'.[31]

Only one month later, in January 1953 an article appeared in the *Irish Times* that discussed the impending purge on East German citizens. 'It must be remembered... that the purge is the most common instrument of communist policy. It is used whenever the party-line is about to make an abrupt change, or when an economic crisis is in the air.'[32] In rhetorical Cold War language, the *Irish Times* article predicted:

> There is no doubt that the purge will be accomplished thoroughly and rigorously. A few well-known heads will fall, and many humble comrades will feel the cold chill of apprehension. Another step will have been taken to clasp Eastern Germany even more closely to the Soviet bosom, and to turn the satellite State into the completely trustworthy and predictable garrison which Russia requires on this vital sector of her European front.[33]

In fact, more than a 'few well-known heads' would fall victim to the purges in the Soviet-controlled zone of Germany. Between 1945 and 1950 over 5,000 Social Democrats were sentenced by Soviet and East German courts. The Soviet forces interned at least 122,000 people in the East German zone during this period, executing 736; at least 43,000 died in detention.[34] The last major trial of Social Democrats took place in Prague in 1954.[35]

On 4 August 1953, the Political Section of External Affairs published an internal background paper on the German reunification problem. Comprehensive in its factual description, the paper outlined the June 1953 riots, giving the extracts from Adenauer's speech to the Bundestag on 1 July 1953. Interestingly, but not surprisingly, the Political Section focused on two paragraphs of Adenauer's speech that appeared analogous to the partition of Ireland. Quoting Adenauer:

> We are told that the Soviets with their policy of small concessions want to initiate a genuine easing of tension. Well, Ladies and Gentlemen, there is one thing that could prove their sincerity: let them set free our prisoners, the deportees and political captives, the many hundreds of thousands who for years now have been waiting in Soviet Russia for the day of freedom.
>
> The partition of Germany being a result of the East–West conflict, reunification presupposes an easing of this conflict. German reunification and European unification are necessarily part and parcel of the same policy.[36]

The analogy is somewhat difficult to follow. Perhaps the Political Section authors particularly liked the passionate spirit of the speech and did not analyze the particulars of the situation. However, the editorial comments at the end of the paper were somewhat startling:

> There are factors which favour both sides in the struggle. Psychologically the great mass of the German people must regard Russia as the chief enemy. The memory of the heavy German losses in Russia in the recent war is still fresh in people's minds. The behaviour of the Russian soldiers who invaded Germany must still be revolting to the German people... [After] 12 years of dictatorship the German people find little that is attractive in totalitarian Communism. It is not to be forgotten that the Russians have stripped Germany of her movable capital equipment, while the United States is using surplus wealth to aid German economy: the provisions of cheap food for the people in East Berlin was a noteable recent gesture.[37]

It is not clear what points in Adenauer's declaration are analogous to Irish partition, or what points the Political Section seemed to feel were analogous, apart from *partition* as the common denominator. The memorandum loses credibility, however, when the Political Section proposed this commentary at the end:

> Among the attractions of a pro-Russian policy [for the whole of Germany] may be mentioned one economic argument that may have some force. *A Germany tied to the west and cut off from the east would have to face continuous competition not only from the United States but from British and French industry. In partnership with the Soviets, on the other hand, Germany would have the free run of her traditional markets in central and eastern Europe and even further afield in Communist-controlled countries.* Politically speaking, Western Germany, even a united Germany, would hardly have more than a relatively secondary place to the United States or Britain. Working with the Russians, however, a united Germany would perhaps have the hope of achieving a more dominant position.[38] (emphasis added)

Later that same month, the Political Section issued a memorandum concerning further developments in the German unification issue, analyzing the proposals of the Soviet note of 16 August 1953 to the Allied Powers. Among the proposals was the establishment of an all-German government in which 'representatives of both East and West Germany should participate in relative discussion'. A temporary all-German government should be formed to 'conduct free all-German elections'.[39] Finally, the Soviet note demanded the cessation of reparations payments for all Germany and that occupation costs should be limited to 5 per cent of the German state budget. Chancellor Adenauer 'categorically rejected the ... treaty terms suggested by the Russians'.[40]

The Political Section's analysis concluded by providing the Soviet concessions to Grotewohl's East Germany after the rejection of the Soviet note, among them the cancellation of all reparations payments from June 1954 and the return of several steel mills, chemical and engineering plants to the control of the East German government. Further, the Soviets 'promised to pardon all those German prisoners of war who were sentenced for offences committed during the hostilities "with the exception of those guilty of particularly grave crimes ... who must serve their sentences fully"'.[41]

Further entries for recognition of East Germany appear sporadically until 1955, although no formal requests from the East German government were reported. During the year 1954–55 the long-term division of Germany between the Federal Republic and the German Democratic Republic grew more stable and the prospect for reunification more doubtful. Henry Kissinger argued that the July 1955 Geneva Summit Conference was the 'point of departure' in Soviet foreign policy, resulting in 'Khrushchev crisis initiation' during the years 1956–62.[42] Stephen Ambrose cited a similar point of departure when President Eisenhower, warned beforehand by Secretary of State Dulles not to get into the 'Geneva Spirit' with the Soviets, smiled his 'famous grin' in a photograph with Foreign Minister Bulganin. The photograph was promptly distributed to the Soviet satellite states, spoiling Dulles' plans for 'resistance to Communist rule' in the eastern European states.[43]

During the 1955 Geneva Conference between the United States, the USSR, Britain and France, three primary issues marked the agenda: disarmament; increased cultural and economic ties; and the reunification of Germany. No real progress was achieved on any issue. Ambrose argued that the 'spirit of Geneva' did not mean the end of the Cold War in Germany, as others have asserted and many assumed at the time, but put relations with the Soviets 'on a different basis'.

> The West had admitted that it could not win the Cold War, that a thermonuclear stalemate had developed, and that the status quo in Europe and China (where tensions quickly eased) had to be substantially accepted.[44]

Presumably, Ambrose did not include the feelings of the FRG in his analysis on opinions of 'the West'. The West Germans became very concerned with the diplomatic encroachment of the Soviet Union and fought back with their own proactive policies. The Soviets, too, felt it was time to talk to the West Germans. The West German governments, especially Chancellor Konrad Adenauer, believed that to establish diplomatic relations with the Soviet Union, broken since 1941, 'would also in fact lend [the division of Germany] a certain *de jure* recognition'.[45] The Cold War climate in Western Europe began to solidify. The perception of uncertain motivations on both sides was replaced by a resolute attitude. With hindsight on his side, Kissinger commented on the stalemate over East Germany:

> On the way home from Geneva, Khrushchev stopped in East Berlin to recognize the sovereignty of the East German communist regime. It was a move Stalin had avoided... Since the political values of [East Germany and the FRG] were incompatible and neither state was prepared to commit suicide, unification could have come about by the political collapse of one of them.[46]

The Irish diplomats had seen a slight change of policy occur earlier in 1954. In April, the Irish legation in Stockholm reported talks of the Swedish government and the East German consular division for 'an E. German official being ultimately stationed in Stockholm for the purpose of handling E. German visa business'.[47] On 27 March 1954 the Soviet Union announced that the 'German Democratic Republic' had been granted full sovereignty in internal and external affairs.[48] The reason for the talks was not to facilitate Western trade for the East Germans but to make it possible, based on reciprocity 'for Swedish officials and businessmen travelling to E. Germany, or through E. Germany to Poland, Romania, etc., now that such visas were no longer obtainable from the Russians'.[49] For Ireland, the response of Sweden provided guidance in the neutral position for foreign policy toward East Germany. The Swedish government, however, had no intention of moving toward diplomatic recognition of East Germany. The reciprocal action for visas was meant 'to forestall any more far-reaching proposals from the E. German side'.[50] The proactive Swedish policy proved effective – briefly.

ESTABLISHING IRISH NON-RECOGNITION POLICY – 1954–57

Until 1954, Irish policy decisions concerning the diplomatic recognition of East Germany were made as they arose. In March 1954, in answer to the World Meteorological Organization's (WMO) request for Ireland's opinion on the observer status of several communist states,[51] policy became more formalized. The Irish position in the WMO was to 'object to East Germany's application for membership... on the grounds that having recognized the Bonn Government we are not in a position to recognize any legitimate government in East Germany'.[52] Rather than relying on the question of legitimacy of the East German state, Ireland chose to follow the stern advice of the West German government 'to reject any attempt by East Germany to set up missions in Ireland'.[53] Interestingly, the same memorandum states there to be no 'equally valid reason for opposing membership of the other Communist countries listed' besides East Germany. Upon review, Michael Rynne, the legal adviser in External Affairs, found the logic puzzling but agreed to the policy.

I take you to mean... that we should continue to oppose the admission of East Germany to the WMO but not to object to the other Communist countries on the list, not to the 3 Indochinese 'States'. That means one vote against and about seven abstentions. Clearly this line is not firmly based in logic, but, maybe, it is the inevitable one for us to take in all the circumstances [concerning international organizations].[54]

Between 1948 and 1954, the policy toward 'communist countries' had been based on two considerations. First, private firms in Ireland could trade with 'Communist countries' in any commodity except 'strategic' goods. The only banned commodity under these terms was scrap metal. For private business concerns, 'commercial representatives from communist countries' could enter Ireland if they had established prior relationships with Irish firms, providing there was 'no political objection to them'. Second, Irish governmental agencies were to have no commercial relations with 'communist countries' and 'officials of communist governments [were] not [to have visas granted] to enter Ireland'.[55]

On 28 September 1954 a new policy statement was implemented under the heading 'Trading with countries under communist rule'.[56] With the encouragement of Ambassador Boland in London, Dublin was softening to the possibility of trade with the East Germans. Boland laid the groundwork in March 1954 in response to a request for Irish bloodstock to be sold to the Russian government. He wrote to William P. Fay in External Affairs that 'British and West European businessmen were visiting Moscow every week and Russia has become a large buyer of food'.[57] Earlier, Boland and the Soviet Trade Commissioner in London discussed Ireland's options in the Russian market for butter, meat and pickled herrings. Under the old policy, officials of the Soviet government would not be able to travel to 'examine the goods in the country of origin'. Without explicitly stating his wishes, Boland made it clear that the policy was in need of revision.

The new policy on trading with the Soviet Bloc, as well as the 'other' communist states, relied on the assumption that trade would be established between the Irish government and the countries in question. Three provisions were laid. First, 'such contacts between Irish officials and officials of Communist countries *as may be necessary in the interests of Irish trade* should be permitted' (emphasis added).[58] Second, 'informal arrangements' but not 'formal trade agreements' would be permitted for 'the promotion of Irish exports'. The third provision was explicit:

Subject to necessary security precautions, and on condition that no undue publicity is given thereto, official representatives of Communist Governments should be permitted to enter Ireland in those cases where their presence is essential to the conclusion of an individual commercial transaction.[59]

The Department of External Affairs noted that the Minister for Agriculture, James Dillon, was opposed to the third provision, and that the Minister for Finance, Gerard Sweetman, 'reserved his position as regards the recommendations as a whole'.[60] The rationale for revising the policy was based on the desire 'to remove certain anomalies' for the 'possibility of increased exports to those countries which had been *opened up* in recent times'[61] (emphasis added). Ironically, the new policy initiative had the opposite effect from what the Department of External Affairs had in mind. Exports to East Germany did not change substantially from 1953 to 1954, yet imports from East Germany doubled, from IR£68,747 in 1953 to IR£121,119 in 1954.[62]

By April 1955 an East German government office in Berlin, the equivalent of Posts and Telegraphs, asked that Ireland establish reciprocal telecommunication links.[63] After a heated series of letters with the Irish Department of Posts and Telegraphs, External Affairs agreed to the establishment of the service, provided that the term 'German Democratic Republic' was not used in the agreement.[64] Seán Murphy, Secretary in External Affairs, stated the position tersely:

> We are, of course, not aware of what material advantages are expected to be derived from the proposed telephone service, but however great they may be, they would not in our opinion outweigh the serious consequences that would flow from recognition of the proposed description of the other party to the agreement [the German Democratic Republic]. Accordingly, unless it can be clearly established that the description 'East Zone of Germany' will be accepted by the other party, the Minister for External Affairs very definitely objects to the introduction of the proposed service.[65]

After the dust had settled from the Geneva Summit Conference in July 1955, the Irish Legation in Bonn reported on 'German Federal Government policy in regard to the Pankow regime'. The basis for the document, a conversation between Ambassador T.J. Kiernan[66] and Under Secretary for Foreign Affairs, Walter Hallstein, proved very useful in holding the non-recognition line. Kiernan, before going to Berlin, asked Professor Hallstein 'if there is any objection to diplomats visiting East Berlin'.[67] Hallstein, whose name would come to epitomize non-recognition of East Germany, replied that diplomats were *encouraged* to visit West Berlin. Quoting Hallstein, Kiernan reported that 'a visit to the Soviet sector of Berlin is the best propaganda against Soviet occupation'.[68] Yet any hint of *de facto* recognition of the Pankow regime 'would be misunderstood' by the majority of German citizens who regarded the East German government as a 'puppet authority'. Hallstein reasoned that the highest estimate for Pankow supporters would be 10 per cent and 'it is anywhere between 5 and 10% in the entire Soviet zone'.

Kiernan also reported on the attempt by the mayor of East Berlin, Friedrich Ebert, to meet with West Berlin's mayor 'to discuss the elimination of difficulties arising from the partition of Berlin'. The mayor, Dr Otto Suhr, responded that perhaps it would be possible on a 'technical' level to discuss Ebert's concerns – restoration of uniform telephone, waterway and tramway systems – but not with a 'higher level of representation'. At that point, Ebert terminated the overture.[69]

When the remilitarization of Germany began, and the Paris Treaties for the FRG's entrance into NATO went into effect in May 1955, the East Germans dreaded the move. The counter from the communist side was establishment of the Soviet-controlled Warsaw Pact following the NATO decision.[70] After the summer of 1955 and the Geneva talks, East Germany stood upon the edge of permanent isolation in the international arena. The perception by the international community of its pariah status never entirely disappeared until its demise in 1989. Two months after the Geneva Conference, East Germany's worst fears were confirmed – the Federal Republic of Germany and the USSR established diplomatic relations. The mechanism used to make diplomatic relations possible between the FRG and the Soviets *seemed* to be fortuitous for the East Germans. By signing a treaty[71] recognizing the 'sovereignty' of the German Democratic Republic and terminating the function of the Soviet High Commissioner, the Soviet Union could legally enter into diplomatic relations with the FRG. On the West German side, however, the move was not meant to signify the acceptance of 'two independent sovereign states' in Germany.[72]

For the East Germans, the new relationship meant that the Pankow regime had control over transport and communications in its own territory, but did not have control over military personnel and equipment. The Soviets stipulated that 'control over the movements of military personnel and freight of the armed forces of the United States, Great Britain and France would remain in Russian hands, but only "temporarily until the achievement of a suitable agreement"'.[73] Eventually, the reasoning implied, the military traffic would also be turned over to the East German government.[74]

The development that created the most havoc for the East German Government was not logistical at all. After establishing diplomatic relations with the Soviet Union, the West German government in Bonn intended to guarantee that other governments would follow the lead of the Soviet Union and establish relations with East Germany. On 23 September 1955 the Department of External Affairs received an *aide mémoire* from the West German legation in Dublin, outlining two main features of the Soviet/West German agreement. First, diplomatic recognition was not to include 'recognition of the present state of territorial possessions'. Second, the government in Bonn asserted it claim to be the sole voice for *all* Germans, even those 'outside its factual territorial jurisdiction'.[75]

After the Geneva Conference in July 1955, the Soviet Union shifted its foreign policy to include two Germanys. The most immediate outcome of this shift was the establishment of diplomatic relations with the Federal Republic. Adenauer's government could not give up the possibility of diplomatic channels with the state who held the key to Germany's division, but the appearance of supporting a two-Germany status quo was certainly not its intent. Soviet officials rhetorically stressed the differing societies that were developing between the two Germanys. When Adenauer visited Moscow in late 1955, Khrushchev declared that he was not interested in discussing the two-Germany problem by stating 'the wind is not blowing in our face'.[76] Adenauer's already tentative position of strength seemed to be ebbing away. With hopes of reunification disappearing, the primary concern for the FRG was to stop any further strengthening of the Soviet Union's legitimacy in eastern Europe.

In recognizing the USSR, the Federal Republic made certain that no other state would attempt to recognize East Germany by issuing a unilateral policy. Very quickly the ultimatum became the Hallstein doctrine, named for Under Secretary Walter Hallstein. On 9 December 1955 the West German Foreign Minister, Dr Heinrich von Brentano, proclaimed that any state pursuing diplomatic relations with East Germany would forfeit its relations with the Federal Republic.[77] Five days later, the United Nations approved Ireland's application for membership. Although there is no correlation to the timing of these two events, Ireland's new status as a member of the United Nations created more responsibility for toeing the 'proper' line concerning recognition issues. Not surprisingly, Ambassador T.J. Kiernan sent a timely report to Dublin concerning the duty of neutral states regarding the East German recognition problem. On 13 January 1956 Kiernan began the memorandum with the following remarks:

> Chancellor Adenauer's reserve toward neutralists led him to express himself more forcibly than cautiously to a visiting Maharajah last July. The Maharajah of Patiala came to Germany for the purpose of discussing participation of West German firms in Indian industrialization; and asked to be received by the Chancellor. Dr. Adenauer said to him: 'why does Mr. Nehru travel about so much? Hasn't he got enough to do at home?' The Maharajah answered that Mr. Nehru works for peace and does so by going to all places where he expects success.[78]

Kiernan followed with an excellent analysis of Germany's coolness toward India. He attributed the German attitude to 'negotiation from a position of strength' or 'an attitude of toughness'. In the face of the Hallstein doctrine, the neutral states of Finland and Sweden halted any further diplomatic negotiations with the East Germans, Kiernan reported. Yugoslavia was the one state that held out in defiance until the FRG acknowledged 'the larger part of Yugoslavia's claim for 420 million DM restitution'. Egypt was another problem case, 'following the Tito line of non-entanglement and bargaining between East and West'. Egypt foresaw lucrative trade with the East Germans via the establishment of consular relations but those hopes were soon dashed. The German Foreign Minister, von Brentano, qualified the doctrine by saying that 'economic or consular relations with Pankow would entail a break in relations with the Federal Republic'. The Chinese proceeded at full speed, negotiating a Treaty of Friendship on 25 December 1955 with the East Germans.

India posed a much broader problem, Kiernan wrote. '[Nehru's] fascinating personality is not noticed, nor is it overlooked that German industry may reckon with a major share in India's industrialisation.'[79] The West Germans planned to send the Vice Chancellor to New Delhi to 'find a German key to open the way' first to prevent India from sending a trade mission to East Germany or giving any kind of recognition to the East German government and second, to obtain 'a large share in the new five-year-plan of India's industrialisation'.

In a follow-up report on 26 January 1956 Kiernan wrote that the Kremlin's intent was 'to compel the Federal Republic to recognize the German Democratic Republic, if not *de jure* at least *de facto*'.[80] To meet this objective the Soviets aided East German independence by providing new industrial economic assistance and an army disguised by a 'People's Police'. Kiernan foresaw that the Soviet build-up of the East German *Stasi*[81] was meant not to 'cause fear' in other eastern European states but to form a threat of 'civil war' within Germany. The result would be that the Federal Republic would recognize the legitimacy of the East German state. Kiernan reported that the newspapers in Bonn were filled with headlines that warned of 'fratricidal war', 'an atomic artillery war between brothers' and 'a grotesque and ghastly situation'.

Further, Kiernan described plans for a Soviet-developed and installed nuclear reactor near Dresden in 1957. In short, Kiernan noted, the East Germans were building political and economic institutions 'step by step' to rival the Federal Republic. The purpose of all the activity, in Kiernan's words, was 'to compel Bonn into dealing on a ministerial level with the German Democratic Republic'. The Austrian Ambassador in Bonn told Kiernan the Austrians signed 'virtually a trade agreement' with the East Germans, but in form the agreement was between the Chambers of Commerce. 'This is typical of the breaches being made in the non-recognition principle.'[82]

In 1955 imports from the GDR were IR£39,443, representing a slump from the previous year when imports were IR£121,119. Several arguments could be made on explaining the drop in import trade in 1955 but two central arguments quickly present themselves. One is the Irish preoccupation with UN membership in 1954–55. Ireland was admitted to the United Nations in December 1955, along with the Federal Republic and other states.[83] Certain wariness on disturbing international goodwill by initiating trade with East Germans existed. The second argument involves the return to power of the Fianna Fáil government under Eamon de Valera – 'trading with the communists' was not on de Valera's agenda.

The arguments above explain the import figures with the GDR for years 1954–55 but offer nothing for the jump in import trade the following year. For Ireland, trading with the German Democratic Republic was not considered policy in 1956, the year following the announcement of *Hallstein*. The import figures tell a different story. Imports more than tripled between 1955 and 1956

– IR£39,443 to IR£142,198 from East Germany and continued to rise exponentially in the immediate years thereafter.[84] Yet interestingly, the *Statistical Abstracts* show no export activity in the years 1956–57 – a direct effect of *Hallstein*. Trade occurred but was not reported.

YUGOSLAVIA RECOGNIZES THE GERMAN DEMOCRATIC REPUBLIC – 1957–58

Throughout 1956 no aligned state challenged the Federal Republic by recognizing East Germany. During this period Ireland was careful to refer to 'the Soviet Occupied Zone of Germany' in official correspondence and (most of the time) in intragovernmental documents. The GDR challenged the 'Bern Agreement for the Protection of Works of Literature and Art' of 1886 in the hope that a 'large international agreement would offer a particularly suitable starting-point' for all-round recognition.[85] The year 1956, it will be remembered, also witnessed the CPSU 20th Party Congress (February) in which Stalin was demonized in a secret Khrushchev speech, beginning the 'de-Stalinization' of Soviet foreign policy. Rather than presenting the fatalistic image of lasting bipolarity, Premier Nikita Khrushchev was more hopeful, drawing a 'mellower' picture.[86] This attitude, however, served to weaken the ties between the Soviet Union and the east Europeans.[87] After workers' riots in Poland during June 1956, the Hungarians also attempted to oust the domestic communist regime and leave the communist bloc in October. While the United Nations and major powers were entangled in the Suez Crisis, the Soviet Union invaded Hungary and crushed the rebellion.

In November 1956 the Central Statistics Office (CSO) in Dublin received a request to send information for the 'Statistical Yearbook of the German Democratic Republic'. The CSO sent to letter of request to External Affairs, which approved the entry but carefully reiterated its position of non-recognition.

> As . . . Ireland does not recognize the East German regime, I am to request you to ensure that the terms of your reply to the enquiry are in keeping with this attitude of non-recognition. In particular no reference should be made to the 'German Democratic Republic'. It might be best to transmit the data with a brief covering note addressed simply . . . as if the enquiry were a personal one.[88]

Another development in 1957 caused Ireland to hold fast to the *Hallstein* principles and western Europe to hold its breath. Until 1957 the Federal Republic and Tito's Yugoslavia enjoyed diplomatic relations. Yugoslavia owed the West Germans 200 million marks in post-war commercial debts. In March 1956 the two states agreed to exchange one debt for another and to establish settlement for damages during the Second World War. After eighteen months of negotiation, the Federal Republic agreed to provide payments and credits to the

Yugoslavian government for almost 400 millions marks.[89] But after Khrushchev's de-Stalinization speech and efforts at reconciliation, relations between the Soviets and the Yugoslavs began to develop. David Childs (1969) argued that Tito had been impressed by the 'national and liberal posture' of the Polish leader, Gomulka, and was persuaded by him to recognize the GDR.[90]

At the opposite end of the spectrum were the Canadians who were fiercely against recognition of the GDR.[91] By December 1957 Ambassador T.J. Kiernan, formerly of the Bonn legation, headed the mission in Ottawa and continued to report on the East German situation. The intelligence from the Canadians proved helpful for Kiernan to connect Yugoslavian motives to recognition. Seen as 'a matter of consistency in principle' of European principle, Yugoslavia intended to hold an 'independent position enabling it to talk to both of the German governments'.[92] Kiernan emphasized that Yugoslavia had a specific agenda for foreign trade. Trade policy did not include either a close relationship with only the communist bloc or a 'Common Market' or 'Free Trade Area' for Europe. (The Treaty of Rome establishing the European Economic Community was signed in 1957.) Breaching *Hallstein* was not critical for the Yugoslavian government, Kiernan reported, yet they were trying to 'heal' relations with the FRG. Overall, the Canadians saw the move by Yugoslavia as a 'good' one because they could be 'an honest broker' between the communist and non-communist parts of Europe.

The Irish diplomatic recognition files for 1958 are sparse. That year Khrushchev set out to settle the Berlin problem and various files appear elsewhere on developments in the GDR. Khrushchev's campaign reached a climax in August 1961 with the Berlin Wall in establishing the status quo. In this respect, the Cuban Missile Crisis and the Berlin issue was the denouement. For recognition, all was quiet apart from an occasional request by the World Meteorological Organization (WMO) to vote for the inclusion of non-member states at the next conference in April 1959.[93] Ireland consistently abstained in these votes.[94] The East Germans did manage to make headway in joining an international organization that included western European states in the International Union of Geodesy and Geophysics (IUGG) at their 11th Assembly meeting.[95] The IUGG voted for a resolution that would allow the term 'Germany' to be used to connote the five academies of science in the territory of the two Germanys.[96]

In 1958 Secretary Con Cremin of the Department of External Affairs explained in a memorandum that the Irish government had no intention of backing down on non-recognition policy in light of pressure received from the WMO and the IUGG ruling. Speaking of the WMO, he wrote:

> I took the opportunity of the German Minister's [Dr. Felician Prill] call this morning in connection with the discussion in Bonn for the renewal of the Trade Agreement, to speak to him about the recent approach from Mr. Briest, Counsellor of the Legation, concerning the proposed invitation

from WMO to non-members to attend the forthcoming [meeting]. I told him that Mr. Belton had formed the impression when he handed Mr. Briest our *Aide Mémoire* that the letter seemed to think that this was the first occasion on which Eastern Germany had been included in the list of non-Members ... and I wished to dispel this impression ... I went on to tell him of the attitude we had taken up in 1954 and that we had taken a precisely similar attitude this year. He could thus, I stated, see that the answer we had given to the recent approach did not represent any change whatever as compared with our earlier position ... and did not connote an evolution in our thinking on the matter of Eastern Germany which, I assured him, the Government is quite firm in refusing to recognize.[97]

The West German legation in Dublin sent an *aide-mémoire* the next month to reiterate its argument that such invitations for non-members were 'the wish of the Soviet bloc to see the Soviet occupied zone of Germany invited' to have both Germanies present and to ask Ireland to vote against such admission.[98] Secretary Cremin wrote to the WMO five days later, explaining Ireland's position. Ireland's abstention, Cremin said, 'should not be interpreted as meaning that Ireland is in favour of these countries being invited ... however [we are in favour] of individual specialists ... in those countries being invited to attend *ad personam*'.[99] In the end, several non-member states were included in the WMO meeting but the GDR was not on the list.

EAST GERMANY'S CAMPAIGN FOR RECOGNITION – 1959–61

During 1959, rumblings of recognition of the GDR by Egypt and India were heard in the press and in Germany through the Irish legation in Bonn. The situation with Egypt was delicate. West Germans formed the largest group of foreigners in Egyptian territory. Unknown to many until 1964, the West Germans had been selling military equipment to the Israelis since 1956.[100] The West German parliament agreed to pay reparations to Israel in 1953 and relations had been improving since then. But there were also developing relations with the East Germans, especially after the 1955 Bandung Conference of Non-Aligned States. In 1959 the East German Prime Minister, Otto Grotewohl, travelled to Cairo and gave the Egyptians 87.5 million marks credit.[101] Neither the financial credit nor the visit persuaded General Nasser to supply reciprocal diplomatic recognition. Fear of further developments led the FRG to cease selling military equipment to the Israelis but grant Israel full diplomatic recognition. At that point, ten Arab states (including Egypt) responded by breaking relations with Bonn. 'Nasser retained the *ultimate* sanction of recognizing East Berlin as a reserve weapon' (original emphasis).[102]

Although Egypt was the first African state to consider recognition for East Germany, in March 1960 Guinea became the first African state to follow through, although the Touré government later denied that recognition had been extended. Immediately the intelligence reports filtered into Dublin concerning the seriousness of the Guinea recognition. An official from the German embassy in Dublin, Counsellor Wever, paid a 'courtesy call' to Secretary of External Affairs, Con Cremin on 9 March. Secretary Cremin's note expressed the implication of recognition by Guinea:

> If it is true that Guinea has recognized East Germany, the matter is serious. There is a risk that other African States may do likewise (and immediately Ghana)...Mr. Wever regards it as difficult...for Germany to abandon the Hallstein Doctrine. It has clear disadvantages, but if it ceases to apply, in his view recognition of East Germany by other States would snowball.[103]

The next month William Warnock, Ambassador to Bonn, provided an assessment of Guinea's position.

> [The] ambassador of Conakry was summoned home to report. In an interview with M. Touré before he left, [the Ambassador] failed to get a clear answer to his question whether Guinea had, or had not, extended formal diplomatic recognition to the Pankow administration...If Dr. von Etzdorf [of the FRG's foreign office] succeeds in drawing a definite statement from M. Touré to the effect that his government has not extended diplomatic recognition to the East German régime – and I understand from the Foreign Office that it is hoped that he may be able to do so – that will be an important point for Bonn. East Berlin has remained very quiet about the whole thing.[104]

Later in the month, Ambassador Warnock reported 'the Minister for Foreign Affairs stated in the Bundestag...that he was satisfied from assurances given by M. Sekou Touré...that Guinea has not extended diplomatic recognition to the East German administration'.[105]

In the meantime, Ambassador Fred Boland at the United Nations answered an inquiry from Secretary Cremin to determine the correct story on the Guinea recognition decision. Boland's letter arrived on 11 April 1960 and provided the following explanation:

> I asked...the African expert in the UN Secretariat what was the true explanation of the recent misunderstanding about the accreditation of an Ambassador of Guinea to Eastern Germany. [He] told me that, incredible as it might sound, the Ambassador of Guinea in Moscow had presented a forged letter of credence to the East German Government. Sekou Touré had said that the signature on the letter was not his and that the letter of credence had been presented without his knowledge or authority.[106]

Boland's informant reasoned that the 'forged letter' was the result of 'continual conspiracies and intrigues engineered by Sekou Touré's unscrupulous and ambitious half-brother, Ismail Touré' who 'is definitely a Communist and is steadily gaining political power and influence'.[107] The conspiracy turned out to be false, as Cremin later wrote to Boland.

The panic inspired by the near miss of the Guinea decision caused the Department of External Affairs to be more vigilant in not implying tacit recognition to the East German government. When the East Germans tried to gain a place at the International Folk Music Council (IFMC) to be held in neutral Vienna during July 1960, Ireland's representative to the Council was instructed to vote against any resolution admitting the 'so-called German People's Republic'.[108] Another meeting of the International Union of Geodesy and Geophysics (IUGG) prompted an *aide-mémoire* from the West German embassy in Dublin.

[It] would be very much appreciated if the Irish Government could find a way to make the Irish Union of Geodesy and Geophysics see the dangers involved and thus support the common effort to make impossible any progress of the German communist régime in the international field.[109]

Other requests for non-recognition of East Germany in international organizations followed. The International Council for the Exploration of the Sea (ICES) in Moscow during September 1960, as well as the General Assembly for Measures and Weights in October 1960, were also possibilities for East German participation. The Department of External Affairs reaffirmed its policy of voting against participation by the East Germans.

By October 1960 the department was inundated with requests from the West German embassy in Dublin to oppose the participation of East Germany at many international conferences. A one-page note in the file by P.J.G. Keating stated tersely:

It would appear to me in the present case the Bonn Government are perhaps over delicate in their apprehension and I would feel that if good and adequate technical reasons exist for admitting E. German experts on a similar 'ad personam' basis we should not be inhibited by the *small degree of indirect recognition* involved by the approval . . . It seems to me that in this case the Federal Government is damaging a valid case by an excessive zeal based on quibbles.[110] (emphasis added)

Keating's note did not prompt an immediate change in the policy. But at the end of December 1960, when the Dublin embassy of the FRG continued with its anti-recognition campaign (this time aimed at East Germany's application to join the European and Mediterranean Plant Protection Organization [EMPPO] in Paris), the reply from Secretary Con Cremin in the Department of External Affairs revealed an unambiguous attitude.[111]

I am directed by the Minister for Agriculture to state that this country considers that future applications for full membership should be considered only from countries which are either covered by Article III.a.1 of the Convention for the establishment of the Organisation or are members of the United Nations or of any of its Specialised Agencies. We would, however, have no objection to individual specialists from East Germany being invited *ad personam* to attend meetings of the Organisation.[112]

Cremin restated an attitude he had expressed in 1958, and again in 1959, for the World Meteorological Organization concerning *ad personam* representation by the East Germans (as well as other non-recognized states) in international organizations:

I should be glad if you would be so good as to note that the intimation therein conveyed in respect of China (People's Republic), Germany (Democratic Republic), Korea (People's Republic), Mongolia (People's Republic) and Viet Nam (Democratic Republic) should not be interpreted as meaning that Ireland is in favour of these countries being invited to send official observers to the Congress. We are, however, in favour of individual specialists from the corresponding Meteorological Services in those countries being invited to attend *ad personam*.[113]

Ireland's policy of non-recognition toward the East German government remained firm, yet the policy for individuals was softening. In the following years, economics, not politics, set the tone for Ireland's non-recognition policy toward East Germany.

COLD WAR SILENCE – 1961–63

By early 1961, rumblings in Germany's own Bundestag brought the issue of recognition of East Germany into sharp focus. A former member of Konrad Adenauer's coalition government in 1949, Dr. Thomas Dehler of the Free Democratic Party (FDP) became Vice President of the Bundestag in 1961. A report from Ambassador Warnock in Bonn described Dehler's actions:

Dr. Dehler is known as an eloquent speaker. He is very Anti-Adenauer and anti-clerical. While he supports NATO, he is not satisfied with the present policy of the Government towards the countries in Eastern Europe . . . [He has stated] there is no point in denying that there are now two German states . . . even though the East German administration might not be legitimately constituted, there was still no denying its existence.[114]

At this point the archival files on diplomatic recognition of East Germany jump from early 1961 to February 1962, a lapse notable in this case due to the erection of the Berlin Wall in 1961. In early 1962, the Tripartite Allied Travel Board in West Berlin considered issuing travel documents for the East German hockey team. The team requested permission to go the world championships in Colorado Springs and was 'finally refused'.[115] Then, on 7 February 1962, a headline in *The Guardian* read: 'Cold War puts end to world ski contests'. The article announced that the International Ski Federation Championship in Chamonix, France, had cancelled the event because the French would not allow the East Germans to participate. The NATO decision was supported by the French authorities 'as a retaliation against the Berlin Wall'.[116]

The issue of travel from East Berlin in general grew tense. The archival files reveal editorials suggesting travel arrangements from East to West for private citizens. The real issue was the demilitarization of West Berlin. A *New York Times* article in March 1962 stated:

> Walter Ulbricht, leader of East Germany, made public... a proposal for an international authority to arbitrate disputes over access to West Berlin... Dean Rusk, United States Secretary of State ... has rejected the Ulbricht proposal... The western powers have insisted on their right to maintain their occupation of West Berlin until German unity is achieved. They have also insisted upon retaining unrestricted access to the city.[117]

As diplomatic historian Walter LaFeber described, the beginnings of the Cuban missile crisis of October 1962 occurred earlier in 1962. LaFeber argued that the 'root of the crisis' stemmed from Khrushchev's ICBM-oriented foreign policies after 1957 and 'his intense concern with removing NATO power from West Berlin'.[118] From early 1962 until January 1963, the archival files on diplomatic recognition for East Germany are silent. In the tense environment of US/Soviet relations, recognition of the East German regime was not considered by the Department of External Affairs.

However, on 14 January 1963 the file became active once more. An *aide-mémoire* from the West German embassy in Dublin described the decision for the break of diplomatic relations with Cuba. In line with *Hallstein*, once the government of Fidel Castro recognized East Germany, the Federal Republic severed relations with Cuba.[119] The French government assumed the interests of West Germany in Cuba. Although Ireland had no intention of recognizing the East German government in January 1963, especially in light of its application to the European Economic Community, the lure of trade possibilities initiated an exchange with East German officials during the spring of that year.[120]

EPILOGUE

During 1963 the Comhlucht Siúicre Éireann Teoranta, the national sugar producer for Ireland, engaged in negotiations with the East German government for the importation of potash.[121] As a gesture of goodwill, the East German authorities purchased butter from Ireland beginning in 1963.[122] An article in the *Irish Times* proved more telling of the softening Irish attitude to attract East German business:

> [The] need to bring Irish protected industries up to the international mark; the need to seek wider markets abroad; the need to make harder bargains with Britain on agricultural exports; and above all the need to redress the imbalance of trade with all our commercial partners, whether east or west of the arbitrary curtain [are reasons to trade with the East Germans]. We have sent a Córas Tráchtála delegation to Russia and Poland; we have had talks with the Czechs . . . But it is perhaps, with East Germany – a State that is not even recognized by our Government – that we have made the most significant progress towards balancing imports and exports. In the case of this Communist country, private enterprise and State bodies here have combined to prove that it is not impossible to deal with the East on a purely commercial basis without involving ideologies and with considerable benefit to Irish exports.[123]

In spirit, the article was true. However, the official import and export figures for the years 1962–63 reveal another side. Imports indeed continued to grow from East Germany, and by 1962 they were IR£888,138. Although reported exports to East Germany grew significantly from 1960 to 1963 – IR£11,079 to IR£214,518 – they did not create an official balance of trade.[124]

Diplomat Henry Kissinger argued that after the Berlin Wall was built in 1961, the issue of German unification gradually receded from East–West talks and the 'German quest for unity' was put on hold.[125] President Charles de Gaulle of France explored the possibility of negotiating with Moscow by creating a policy of 'détente, entente, and cooperation' with eastern Europe.[126] The initiative failed with the USSR's 1968 invasion of Czechoslovakia, but it opened the way for the new West German leader, Willy Brandt, to establish a policy of *Ostpolitik* with the East. Brandt's proposals included three actions: recognize East Germany, accept the border with Poland (the Oder-Neisse Line), and improve relations with the Soviet Union.[127] Brandt reasoned that East–West *rapprochement* might convince the Soviets to be less rigid on unification. Author Karl Kaiser, writing in 1968, appraised the situation more frankly:

> West Germany's attempt at adapting to protracted partition is therefore not a matter of choice but of necessity. As we have seen, the trend is clearly in the direction of accepting East Germany *de facto* as a second German state. But how far recognition of the division can proceed remains uncertain. German policy-makers have drawn a line beyond which recognition of East Germany is not supposed to go: the GDR

cannot be regarded or treated as *Ausland*.[128] But even such a concept is more a declaration of faith in eventual German unity than a guide to practical action. West German leaders are unwilling to recognize the GDR *de jure* as a separate German state and to extend to it the formal paraphernalia of official relations between nations such as the exchange of ambassadors.[129]

When the government of Iraq decided to give *de jure* recognition to East Germany in 1969 (the first Arab state to do so), the West German government described it as 'an unfriendly act' and severed relations under *Hallstein*. As much as Brandt's government was willing to entertain the notion of two Germanys, the practical application of the idea was still quite distant. A flurry of recognition by smaller and periphery states followed the Iraqi lead. The rapprochement with West Germany brought a 'wave' of international diplomatic recognition.[130] From May 1969 through August 1970, East Germany welcomed recognition from Cambodia (Kampuchea) (*de jure* – 8 May 1969), Sudan (*de jure* – 27 May 1969), Syria (*de jure* – 4 June 1969), Egypt (*de jure* – 9 July 1969), Algeria (*de jure* – 20 May 1970), Ceylon (Sri Lanka) (*de jure* – 16 June 1970) and India (consulate only – 3 August 1970).[131]

In May 1971, new leadership came to East Germany under Erich Honecker. His predecessor, Walter Ulbricht, was resistant to Brandt's *Ostpolitik*, and retired under pressure from the Soviet Union. Honecker seemed to recognize that improved relations with the FRG could consolidate East Germany's identity and economic system.[132] International recognition of East Germany, Honecker believed, would follow. One source shows that by December 1972, at the end of negotiations for the Basic Treaty, fifty-three states accorded some degree of recognition to the GDR.[133] Ratified in 1973, the new relationship paved the way for the acceptance of both states into the United Nations on 18 September 1973. In Europe, Switzerland was the first state to accord *de jure* recognition to the German Democratic Republic (20 December 1972), followed shortly by Sweden and Austria (21 December 1972) and Australia (22 December 1972). Belgium was the first NATO state on 27 December 1972. By January 1973, the Netherlands, Luxembourg, Finland, Spain, Iceland, Denmark, Norway and Italy had accorded full recognition.

The sources are not clear as to the date of Ireland's recognition and the archival material is not available at this date.[134] As a new member of the European Economic Community as of 1 January 1973, Britain accorded *de jure* recognition on 9 February 1973. France also gave recognition *de jure* on 9 February 1973. After lengthy negotiations, the United States followed in September 1974. Canada recognized the FRG *de jure* in 1975.[135] Although the scope of this study ends in May 1963 with the Department of External Affairs' 'memorandum for the government' setting out uniform recognition policy, the history of relations between Ireland and East Germany continued in an atmosphere of non-recognition throughout the 1960s.

NOTES

1   CJ William Howard Taft, sole arbitrator, Arbitration Between Great Britain and Costa
     Rica (Tinoco Case), p. 852.
2   Adenauer, Memoirs 1945–53, p. 367.
3   NAI DFA 305/129/1 Part IB, memorandum, 5 November 1954.
4   Jennings and Watts, eds, Oppenheim's International Law, p. 124. Oppenheim's cites the
     defenders of indivisible sovereignty as Rousseau in Le contract social (1762), and
     Calhoun, A Disquisition on Government (1851).
5   Jennings and Watts, eds, Oppenheim's International Law, p. 125.
6   Ibid., p. 123.
7   Ibid., p. 125.
8   Treaty over the Basis of Relations between the Federal Republic of Germany and the
     German Democratic Republic. Eric G. Frey, Division and Détente: The Germanies and
     Their Alliances (New York, 1987), pp. 18–19.
9   One might imagine, by the appearance of the files on this subject, when a policy issue
     arose concerning recognition of East Germany, the first response would be to examine
     the 'file' and therein one would find the supporting newspaper articles and summaries,
     which reinforced the policy of non-recognition. More than any files examined for this
     research, the diplomatic recognition files seem 'complete' in themselves on the issue
     concerned; in other words, the existence of any other material on this subject in the
     Department of External Affairs archival records is doubtful that would have served as
     decision-making factors at the time.
10   NAI DFA 305/129/1 Part 1, memorandum, 3 April 1954.
11   The origins of the Cold War, as well as an official beginning and ending, are still under
     considerable debate by diplomatic historians and political scientists alike. The purpose
     of this chapter is to define the concept of recognition under international law in the case
     of East Germany, not to enter the argument for dating the Cold War. The period
     1945–89 is generally known to be the Cold War period. For this study, the Cold War
     assumes the years inclusive between the Yalta Conference of February 1945 and the
     autumn of 1989, culminating with the 'fall' of the Berlin Wall on 9 November 1989.
12   Thomas Paterson, Major Problems in American Foreign Policy: Documents and
     Essays (Lexington, MA, 3rd edn, 1989), p. 238.
13   Ibid., p. 242.
14   See Gar Alperovitz, 'More on atomic diplomacy', in David Carlton and Herbert M.
     Levine, The Cold War Debated (New York, 1988), pp. 27–34.
15   'Henry A. Wallace Questions the "Get Tough" Policy, 1946', in Paterson, Major
     Problems in American Foreign Policy, p. 294.
16   NAI DFA 305/129/1 Part 1, memorandum, 3 April 1954.
17   Statement issued by the three Allied High Commissioners on 10 October 1949, quoted
     from Keesing's Contemporary Archives (15–22 October 1949), p. 10284A and found in
     David Childs, The GDR: Moscow's German Ally (London, 1983), p. 299.
18   Johannes L. Kuppe, 'West German policy toward East Germany: a motor of
     unification?', in M. Donald Hancock and Helga A. Welsh, eds, German Unification:
     Process and Outcomes (Boulder, CO, 1994), p. 37.
19   Kuppe, 'West German policy toward East Germany', p. 37.
20   Ireland's participation in the Marshall Plan, subsequently known as European
     Recovery Programme, is discussed in Chapter 2.
21   The founding states were Denmark, Sweden, Great Britain, Norway, Ireland, Italy,
     Luxembourg, France, the Netherlands, Belgium and Greece. For a comprehensive view
     of Ireland's involvement in the Council of Europe, see Hederman (O'Brien), The Road
     to Europe, pp. 21–42.
22   George A. Berman, et al., eds, Cases and Materials on European Community Law (St
     Paul, MN, 1993), p. 5. The Treaty of Paris of 18 April 1951 established the European

Coal and Steel Community (ECSC) and was signed by the three Benelux countries, France, Germany and Italy. Jean Monnet became the High Authority's first President.

23   The original members of NATO were Belgium, France, Luxembourg, the Netherlands and Great Britain, the original signatories to the Treaty of Brussels, signed in March 1948. The Treaty of Brussels also was the basis for the Western European Union.

24   Henry Kissinger, *Diplomacy* (New York, 1994), p. 497. The source of the peace note is from 'Note from the Soviet Union to the United States Transmitting a Soviet Draft of a Peace Treaty with Germany, 10 March 1952' in US Department of State, *Documents on Germany 1944–1985* (Washington, DC, undated), Department of State Publication #9446, pp. 361–4.

25   See Kissinger, *Diplomacy*, pp. 498–9. The text for the 'Note from the United States to the Soviet Union Proposing Creation of a Freely-Elected All-German Government Prior to Negotiation of a Peace Treaty, 25 March 1952' in US Department of State Publication #9446, as above.

26   NAI DFA 305/129/1 Part 1, *pro memoria*, Netherlands legation in Dublin, 6 April 1950.

27   NAI DFA 305/129 Part 1, memorandum, F.H. Boland to Seán Nunan, 25 April 1950.

28   NAI DFA 305/129/1.

29   NAI DFA 305/129/1 Part 1, 'Soviet Policy in Germany: A Change in Direction', *Manchester Guardian*, 12 February 1951.

30   NAI DFA 305/129/1 Part 1, memorandum, 4 December 1952.

31   NAI DFA 305/129/1 Part 1.

32   NAI DFA 305/129/1 Part 1, *Irish Times*, 7 January 1953.

33   NAI DFA 305/129/1 Part 1, Political Section memorandum, 4 August 1953.

34   Karel Bartošek, 'Central and Southeastern Europe', in Stéphane Courtois, ed., *The Black Book of Communism: Crimes, Terror, Repression* (Cambridge, MA, 1999), p. 400.

35   Ibid., p. 408.

36   NAI DFA 305/129/1 Part 1, Political Section memorandum, 4 August 1953.

37   Ibid.

38   NAI DFA 305/129/1 Part 1, Political Section memorandum, 7 August 1953.

39   NAI DFA 305/129/1 Part 1, memorandum, 29 August 1953.

40   Ibid.

41   Ibid.

42   See Henry Kissinger, *Diplomacy*, pp. 520–1.

43   Stephen E. Ambrose, *Rise to Globalism: American Foreign Policy Since 1938* (New York, 6th rev. edn, 1991), p. 152.

44   Ibid.

45   Wolfram F. Hanreider, 'German reunification, 1949–63', in Roy C. Macridis, ed., *Foreign Policy in World Politics: States and Regions* (Englewood Cliffs, NJ, 7th edn, 1989), p. 122.

46   Kissinger, *Diplomacy*, pp. 520–1.

47   NAI DFA 305/129/ Part 1B, memorandum, 12 April 1954.

48   NAI DFA 305/129/1 Part 1B, background paper, 'Reunification of Germany', 1 June 1954.

49   NAI DFA 305/129/1 Part 1B, memorandum, 12 April 1954.

50   Ibid. The list of States included: Albania, 'Chinese People's Republic', East Germany, North Korea, 'Mongolian People's Republic'.

51   NAI DFA 305/129/1 Part 1B, memorandum, 30 April 1954.

52   Ibid.

53   Ibid.

54   NAI DFA 305/129/1 Part 1B, note, 12 May 1954.

55   NAI DFA 305/129/1 Part 1B, memorandum, 5 November 1954.

56   Ibid.

57   NAI DFA 348/44/3, letter, F.H. Boland to William P. Fay, 24 March 1954.

58   NAI DFA 305/129/1 Part 1B, memorandum, 5 November 1954.

59   Ibid.

60   Ibid.
61   Ibid.
62   Compiled by the author from the *Statistical Abstracts of Ireland*, various years. Exports
      to East Germany from Ireland were a mere IR£434 in 1953 and IR£400 in 1954.
      Exports did not increase substantially until 1958 (IR£20,090). By 1964, exports were
      relatively large – IR£377,044 – but declined in the following years. In 1973, the year
      after the Federal Republic recognized East Germany, exports were only IR£38,817.
63   NAI DFA 305/129/1 Part I, letter, 'Republique Democratique Allemande Ministere des
      Postes et Telecommunication' to 'M. le Secretaire de l'administation des postes et des
      telegraphes Irlande', April 1955.
64   NAI DFA 305/129/1 Part I, letter, Seán Murphy to Secretary, Department of Post and
      Telegraphs, 27 June 1955.
65   Ibid.
66   Kiernan's personal title was 'Ambassador' although the position was 'Minister
      Plenipotentiary'.
67   NAI DFA 305/129/1 Part 1B, memorandum, 28 July 1955.
68   Ibid.
69   Ibid.
70   The GDR was accepted into the Warsaw Pact on 24 May 1955.
71   The treaty was negotiated in April 1954.
72   Thomas E. Hachey, *The Problem of Partition: Peril to World Peace* (Chicago, IL,
      1972), p. 101.
73   Ibid.
74   As a personal footnote, the military traffic of the Allied powers was not turned over to
      the GDR, but remained in the hands of the Soviets until German reunification on 3
      October 1990. As US Air Force personnel, we travelled on 'flag orders' to Berlin in
      April 1990, through Checkpoints Alpha, Bravo and ultimately, Charlie into East Berlin.
      The Soviets were present in the watchtowers at every stop.
75   NAI DFA 305/129/1 Part 1B, *aide-mémoire*, 23 September 1955.
76   Wolfram Hanrieder, 'German Reunification', p. 122.
77   Childs, *The GDR*, p. 299.
78   NAI DFA 305/129/1, memorandum, 13 January 1956.
79   NAI DFA 305/129/1 Part 1B, memorandum, 13 January 1956.
80   NAI DFA 305/129/1 Part 1B, memorandum, 26 January 1956.
81   *Ministerium für Staatssicherheit.*
82   NAI DFA 305/129/1 Part 1B, memorandum, 26 January 1956.
83   See Chapter 2.
84   The exception is the 1958–59 period when imports fell from IR£714,112 to
      IR£484,244, recovering to IR£510,891 in 1960. Beginning in the 1958–59 period,
      exports appeared on the books once more – IR£20,090 in 1958 and IR£77,149 in 1959.
      Exports dropped after 1959 until 'the end of the Adenauer era' and the streamlining of
      Irish recognition policy in 1963. By 1964 imports from the GDR were IR£1,379,411.
      Exports were IR£377,044. There was never a balance of trade during the period
      1949–63, with East German imports predominating the trade.
85   NAI DFA 305/129/1 Part I, memorandum, 6 March 1956.
86   See Vernon V. Aspaturian, 'Soviet foreign policy', in Roy C. Macridis, ed., *Foreign
      Policy in World Politics*, pp. 201–2. In Khrushchev's speech, the perception of
      'capitalist encirclement' was officially terminated in security policy. He also
      emphasized a third dimension in the world system that included 'anti-imperialist but
      non-socialist powers . . . carved out of decaying colonial empires' that had separated
      from capitalism but were not communist. Stalin's 'fatal inevitability of wars' was
      denounced, as it 'tended to render the Soviet peace campaign hypocritical'.
      Khrushchev's speech indicated his belief that Soviet policy could move beyond
      'capitalist encirclement' to 'socialist encirclement' as a prelude to the 'final victory of
      Communism'.

87   See Ray, *Global Politics*, p. 59.
88   NAI DFA 305/129/1 Part 1B, letter, External Affairs to Central Statistics Office, 9 January 1957.
89   David Childs, *East Germany* (New York, 1969), p. 249.
90   Ibid.
91   The Canadian government did not officially recognize the East German government until 1975.
92   NAI DFA 305/129/1 Part 1B, report, 9 December 1957.
93   NAI DFA305/129/1 Part 1B, letter, WMO to members of the organization, 27 August 1958.
94   See Chapter 2.
95   NAI DFA 305/129/1, report on 11th Assembly of the International Union of Geodesy and Geophysics, undated. Although this report is not dated, the insertion by the Department of External Affairs of this item into the diplomatic recognition files points to a date of 1958.
96   NAI DFA 305/129/1/, report of the IUGG, undated. The resolution read in part: 'Considering that it is the desire of the German Academies of Science to adhere as a common group to the IUGG under the name "Germany", agreed to accept the common adherence...and recommends that the interested academies work out such arrangements as to permit the implementation of the above resolution.'
97   NAI DFA 305/129/1 Part 1B, memorandum, 28 October 1958.
98   NAI DFA 305/129/1 Part 1B, *aide mémoire*, 13 November 1958.
99   NAI DFA 305/129/1 Part 1B, letter, Cremin to WMO, 18 November 1958.
100 Childs, *East Germany*, p. 252.
101 Ibid., p. 253.
102 Ibid.
103 NAI DFA 305/129/1 Part 1B, note, 10 March 1960.
104 NAI DFA 305/129/1 Part 1B, confidential note, 4 April 1960.
105 NAI DFA 305/129/1 Part 1B, follow-up note, 14 April 1960.
106 NAI DFA 305/129/1 Part 1B, letter, Boland to Cremin, 5 April 1960.
107 Ibid.
108 NAI DFA 305/129/1 Part 1B, note, T.J. Horan, 21 June 1960.
109 NAI DFA 305/129/1 Part 1B, *aide-mémoire*, 29 Jun 1960.
110 NAI DFA 305/129/1 Part 1B, note, 9 October 1960.
111 NAI DFA 305/129/1 Part 1B, *aide-mémoire*, 23 December 1960.
112 NAI DFA 305/129/1 Part 1B, draft letter, Cremin to the Director-General of the EMPPO, presumably early January 1961.
113 NAI DFA 305/129/1 Part 1B, letter, Cremin to WMO, 18 November 1958. Another letter was sent on 21 September 1959.
114 NAI DFA 305/129/1 Part 1B, letter, Warnock to Cremin, 18 January 1961.
115 NAI DFA 305/129/1 Part 1B, *The Guardian*, 1 February 1962.
116 NAI DFA 305/129/1 Part 1B, *The Guardian*, 7 February 1962.
117 NAI DFA 305/129/1 Part 1B, *New York Times*, 27 March 1962.
118 Walter LaFeber, *America, Russia, and the Cold War 1945–1992* (New York, 7th edn, 1993), p. 224.
119 The Allende regime in Chile was the second American/Caribbean State to recognize the GDR in March 1971. See Childs, *The GDR*, p. 311.
120 On Ircland's first application to the EEC, see Chapter 2.
121 NAI DFA 305/129/1 Part 1B, Foreign Trade Committee minutes, 2 May 1963.
122 NAI DFA 305/129/1 Part 1B, Foreign Trade Committee minutes, 7 May 1963.
123 NAI DFA 305/129/1 Part 1B, *Irish Times*, 4 December 1963.
124 See *Statistical Abstracts of Ireland*, various years.
125 Kissinger, *Diplomacy*, pp. 734–5.
126 Ibid., p. 734.
127 Ibid., p. 735.

128   Meaning 'a foreign state'.
129   Karl Kaiser, *German Foreign Policy in Transition* (London, 1968), pp. 137–8.
130   Laurence H. McFalls, *Coomunism's Collapse, Democracy's Demise? The Cultural Context and Consequences of the East German Revolution* (Basingstoke, 1995), p. 36.
131   See Eleanor Lansing Dulles, *One Germany or Two: The Struggle at the Heart of Europe* (Stanford, CA, 1970) for a list of states that granted *de jure* recognition before the negotiation of the Basic Law. Dulles' list, compiled from US State Department intelligence, includes the early consular activities of Indonesia, Yemen and Burma (Myanmar). The Soviet bloc countries in Eastern Europe (USSR, Bulgaria, Hungary, Czechoslovakia, Romania, Poland and Albania) recognized East Germany in 1949. China and North Korea gave *de jure* recognition to the GDR in October and November 1949 respectively. North Vietnam announced *de jure* recognition in 1954. Zanzibar (Tanzania) followed in 1964.
132   McFalls, *Communism's Collapse*, p. 35.
133   The listing of the states according recognition is problematic. The best source appears to be Eberhard Schulz, ed., *Drei Jahrzehnte Aussenpolitik der DDR* (Munich, 1979), pp. 857–9. Unable to locate the original text, the list for this work is compiled from two sources: Henry Krisch, *The German Democratic Republic: The Search for Identity* (Boulder, CO, 1985), p. 55 and the English translation of Eberhard Schulz's *Drei Jahrzehnte Aussenpolitik der DDR*. See Eberhard Schulz et al., eds, *GDR Foreign Policy*, (trans. Michel Vale) (New York, 1982).
134   An exhaustive search by this author through periodicals has failed to produce a date for Ireland's *de jure* recognition. Both the *Washington Post* and the *New York Times* ran comprehensive stories on 10 February 1973, citing the states according recognition. Ireland was not mentioned.
135   Childs, *The GDR: Moscow's German Ally*, p. 312.

5

Diplomacy before and after UN membership:
Non-recognition of China, 1949–63

The cold war was rearmament and alliances and ultimatums and crises and confrontations; it was trade controls and military assistance and competitive economic aid; it was espionage and subversion and propaganda; and it was a way of acting and reacting – a way of looking at things, a frame of mind, a manner of speaking, a tone of voice. In a sense the cold war was an experiment in conflict without war; all elements of national power, influence, and prestige were brought into confrontation – and all save the military element were brought into direct use.

Thomas W. Wilson, Jr.
The Great Weapons Heresy[1]

INTRODUCTION

In Irish diplomatic recognition policy during the years 1949–63, the case of China stands in sharp relief to Ireland's *de facto* recognition of Israel, East Germany and Vietnam. Compared to an interest based on principle or consistent policy in other non-recognition cases, the Chinese recognition problem had a real human interest, a 'romantic sympathy', concerning the safety of the Catholic missionaries in the new People's Republic of China.[2] Yet Ireland's policy toward China in the early Cold War years did not actively involve measures to protect remaining missionaries on the Chinese mainland, nor did the policy reflect a circumspect analysis of the situation in China. The lack of information about events in China did not result from indifference toward the situation there. Had more information been available on the plight of the missionaries, perhaps the Irish government's stance toward China would have been less open-and-shut. Ireland, sitting as a newly independent, neutral state in 1949, could not afford to waffle on its views toward the menacing Chinese threat. The Department of External Affairs immediately twinned its policy with that of the United States: no recognition for Mao's government. This policy did not mean automatic endorsement of Chiang Kai-shek's

Nationalist government on Formosa, or Taiwan. In 1949, Ireland had no economic or geopolitical ties to south Asia, nor any aspirations of developing relationships in the region. Asian relations, apart from occasional correspondence from foreign diplomats in India, remained very remote in the existence of Ireland.

Author William C. Kirby argued that the alliances between the Soviet Union and China's new communist regime, paired with the United States' support of the Nationalist government, created the foundation of Chinese diplomacy throughout the 1950s.

> Divided between Communist and Nationalist rule, China became incorporated into not one but two contending international systems. The 'two Chinas' and the two superpowers entered into bilateral military, political, economic, and cultural relationships of greater depth and complexity than any of modern China's foreign relationships before or since. The New People's Republic of China (PRC) took the Soviet Union as its political and economic model; on Taiwan, Sino-American cooperation flourished as it had never done under the Republic of China on the mainland.[3]

The interesting element in the Chinese recognition files concerns Foreign Minister Frank Aiken's foray into China policy during the period 1957–59 at the United Nations. At a time when Ireland was looking to increase its prestige at the United Nations, it is ironic that years of non-recognition policy toward China should lead to Ireland's pursuance of measures to counter the moratorium on the 'Chinarep' problem. Aiken's idea was for Ireland to support a resolution to allow the open discussion of the Chinese representation problem in the General Assembly which had been held under moratorium since the beginning of the Korean War. As will be shown later in this chapter, Aiken's plan very nearly backfired with serious consequences.

Ireland's involvement on the China issue at the United Nations is yet one more example of the malleable nature of recognition policy during the Cold War. How could it be that Ireland would support a resolution to benefit a state that it did not recognize, or in harsher terms, that it openly opposed? Policies that were set based on international legal principles could be cast aside by states at a moment's notice to further prestige or security. With the security stakes so high for small nations, national interests were destined to be redefined when significant change in the international political environment occurred. Importantly, the perception of change was relative to the state's overall prestige, power or capability within the international system. Small waves in the international environment that would be virtually unfelt by larger states would hit Irish foreign policy-makers with great force simply because they did not have the intelligence-gathering machinery to predict the impact of such changes on Ireland. The pursuit of prestige became the most effective means of increasing perceived power vis-à-*vis* the larger states.

Intelligence-gathering on issues concerning China was more difficult than from any other non-recognized state during this period. Between 1949 and 1955, Irish diplomats found it difficult to gather intelligence on faraway states due to a lack of consular or embassy contacts. The Department of External Affairs expanded Ireland's diplomatic posts during the period but not into Asia. When the Chinese mainland fell to Mao Zedong's Chinese Communist Party in October 1949, there was no hesitation in setting Irish policy to reflect the anticommunist leanings of the department. Until Ireland's membership in the United Nations almost six years later, there was very little first-hand information. In spite of the predicament of the Irish missionaries before and after the outbreak of the Chinese Civil War, the Irish government did not formally become involved in aiding the Irish missionaries after Mao Zedong's communists were victorious in October 1949. In fact, upon reviewing the diplomatic files, there is an abundance of press clippings from 1949–54 but relatively few policy materials such as memoranda and statements compared to the other recognition cases described in this text.

As noted above, the most logical explanation for the paucity of material on Chinese recognition issues in the Department of External Affairs files is a lack of substantial intelligence from which to make policy. Not being 'in the loop' on decision-making prior to its entry into the United Nations, most Irish intelligence from Asia came second-hand and was not considered reliable. Ireland's intelligence-gathering operations were dependent upon connections with other states, especially information obtained from Irish diplomats abroad. There were no Irish diplomats in China, or anywhere near Asia. The closest embassy in 1949 was in Australia, opened only three years earlier in 1946.

The gathering of intelligence from British diplomatic channels in the area was possible but did not become a reality until Frederick H. Boland became Ambassador to Great Britain in 1950. When Freddie Boland became Secretary of the Department in 1946, he had made a conscientious effort to insist that the newly created Political Section would collect 'international opinions and ideas for distribution' to other diplomats within External Affairs.[4] This method of keeping issues fresh by circulating information to diplomats and requesting their observations on international policy was an anathema to the department under Joseph P. Walshe, especially in an administrative area such as diplomatic recognition. As historian Michael Kennedy stated in his analysis of the Irish diplomatic service during the period, diplomatic recognition fell into an area of policy 'where Walshe would have relied solely on his own opinion'.[5]

As Ambassador in London, Boland passed on British intelligence to the Irish government when he was able to obtain it. In the recognition files of China, the first intelligence from the British Foreign Office came in August 1951, over a year into the Korean War. The memorandum briefly provided a history of the 'toleration of Christian missions' under the Maoist regime from 1949–51. This important piece of intelligence for the Irish government, considering the presence of Irish missionaries still in the PRC, provided an explanation for the sudden Chinese hostility toward the Catholic missions.

At the end of December 1950 an ordinance was issued by the Peking Government providing that religious bodies might only continue their existence if maintained by home support without any foreign subsidies. While it is not inherently impossible for Protestant Churches to continue to exist without any connexion with, or subsidy from, foreign bodies, this is clearly impossible for the Catholic Church, and a protracted struggle between the Church and authorities developed.[6]

The argument that the structure of the Catholic Church invited intolerance from the Chinese authorities was not a new one, and not unique to the Communist Chinese government. Mary Horton Stuart, an American Presbyterian missionary to China from 1874–1925, mentioned in a letter home in 1876 that although the Chinese categorized all foreigners into the single category of 'foreign devils', she believed Catholics 'invited' violence by their hierarchical structure and loyalty to Rome.[7] Intelligence that provided rationale for policy rather than new information is not uncommon in the recognition files on China.

Another explanation for the lack of policy analysis on the China recognition issue is the disorganization of the Department of External Affairs once secretaries Joseph Walshe and Freddie Boland moved on to postings as ambassadors in 1946 and 1950, respectively. As Michael Kennedy noted on the overall state of affairs in the Department after 1950:

> After twenty-four years under the direction of Walshe and sixteen under the political control of de Valera, it may be that the changes of the decade from 1946 to 1956, with three changes of secretary and four of minister, combined to create a situation where despite the many developments in the department over these ten years, the department eventually lacked overall cohesion, perhaps even direction.[8]

The problems in China were remote, and from the beginning of Mao's government, the Irish government declared its anticommunist position in alignment with the United States' hardened stance toward the PRC. The other important recognition issues of the time were in status quo mode after 1949. Camps were already divided on the Israeli issue between the British and Americans, and the Irish would not recognize Israel until 1963. For the moment, the status of East Germany was in limbo and was not a pressing issue. The Korean War (1950–53) required intelligence-gathering from available sources (such as newspapers and diplomatic reports from Washington), and Chinese recognition issues were subsumed under other requirements.

The third and most obvious explanation for the lack of policy decision-making on China prior to 1955 concerns the necessity of the Irish government not to contradict the policy of the Holy See, leaving the protection of Irish missionaries to the purview of the Church. Conveniently in the case of China, the Irish could look to both the United States and the Vatican for justification to firmly oppose the PRC. In this way the Irish decision parallels the approach of non-recognition toward Israel. When Ireland finally entered the United Nations in 1955, the approach to the 'China problem' suddenly shifted, yet research shows that Ireland's political or economic interests in China remained minimal from 1949–63. When Ireland began participating in General Assembly issues in 1956, with Frank Aiken serving as Minister of External Affairs and Freddie Boland as Permanent Secretary, the 'China problem' became a proxy to jettison Ireland's prestige at the United Nations.

TREATMENT OF CATHOLIC MISSIONARIES IN CHINA, 1949[9]

The year 1949 is the watershed in China's entry into international affairs. When the communist revolutionaries successfully gained control of mainland China in October 1949, the international community was not surprised that Mao Zedong's foreign policy became characterized as 'theoretical proletarian internationalism' with the 'natural and complete solidarity of interests of China with other Communist powers, especially the Soviet Union, against the non-Communist world as a whole, especially the United States'.[10] Mao termed this foreign policy 'lean to one side', stating that 'one either leans to the side of imperialism or the side of socialism. Neutrality is a camouflage and a third road does not exist.'[11]

In 1949, the relatively few Catholic and Protestant missionaries who were still on mainland China knew that communism and Christianity ultimately could not exist within the same governmental command, so there was great surprise and confusion when the Chinese Communist Party's Common Programme declaration in September 1949 guaranteed religious freedom. Oi Ki Ling (1999) argued that the Catholic missionaries knew it was simply a matter of time before communist persecution drove them out of China.

> It seems that Catholic missionaries and Chinese Catholics, more than the Protestants, were able to form a realistic assessment of the Communist policy towards religion in New China. The Catholics, who had a good deal of experience with persecution in the Communist-controlled territories before the changeover, had less doubt that freedom to oppose religion was, in fact, the dominant feature of Communist policy.[12]

Late in October 1949, Dr Fergus Murphy, Superior at St Columban's Mission in Shanghai, wrote a letter to his sister Sheila. 'Have you any idea what the Irish Government's policy will be as regards recognizing the new Government in China?'[13] Miss Murphy was in a position to know. A veteran member of the Department of External Affairs, Sheila Murphy began her Irish diplomatic career at the age of 23, working in the Publicity Department of the first Dáil Éireann in 1921. In 1926 she became private secretary to Secretary of the Department, Joseph P. Walshe. Upon Walshe's posting as Ambassador to the Holy See in 1946, Murphy became Second Secretary in the Political and Treaty Relations Section of the Department of External Affairs.[14] Promoted to First Secretary in 1948, Sheila Murphy's career revealed a steady increase in responsibility and authority within the department. The files of the Department of External Affairs are replete with questions that were received and answered by Sheila Murphy. The question at hand, however, had personal consequences. A letter from brother to sister, sent through diplomatic channels, expressed the growing concern of all Christian missionaries in China.

> It may affect our situation out here considerably – as regards getting permission for men to return to China – internal travel and general treatment. If Britain recognizes it and Ireland does not – I can see all those with Irish passports getting turned down in any requests they make.[15]

Father Murphy's initial concern did not anticipate fully the severe consequences of communist Chinese rule upon all the Catholic priests and nuns of St Columban's and other missions. When Mao Zedong officially declared victory on 1 October 1949, over 4,000 Protestant and Catholic missionaries were resident on mainland China but many of the missionaries began to leave as early as 1948.[16] Until 1948, there were 152 Columban Fathers in China, yet by July 1952, only twenty-two remained at their posts.[17] Many of the priests stayed in Asia, going to Korea, Japan, Burma, the Philippines and the Fiji Islands after the Chinese Communist Party victory. The publication of the St Columban's Foreign Mission Society, the *Far East*, reported in July 1952 that of the 1,121 Protestant and Catholic priests remaining in China, at least 75 per cent of them were 'under arrest, either in communist jails or in their own homes'.[18] St Columban's, established in 1920 by Father (later Bishop) Edward Galvin of Crookstown, Co. Cork and John Blowick of Belcarra, Co. Mayo, had over 700 members in China, Japan, Korea, Burma and the Philippines in February 1949. By 1953 there was only one remaining Columban priest at liberty in Shanghai, Father Edward McElroy.

The previous thirty-three years of St Columban's Mission Society in China had been riddled with what Father Murphy characterized as times of 'trial and anxiety'.[19] Although the British Treaty Port System reached its peak of influence in the 1920s, granting the missionaries the right to travel, acquire real property and proselytize through China,[20] in 1927 the Chinese Revolutionary Army 'swept up the South' under Chiang Kai-shek[21] with a left-wing headquarters in Hankow just across the river from the St Columban's headquarters in Hanyang.[22] J.A.G. Roberts (1996) wrote that Tang Liangli, a Guomindang politician who railed against the influence of Christian missionaries since China's signing of the Treaty of Tianjin in 1860 (ending the Second Opium War, providing Treaty Ports to Britain and forcing the Chinese government to protect the Christian missionaries), complained in 1927 that no group of foreigners had done greater harm to China than foreign missionaries, whose activities had served to denationalize hundreds of thousands of Chinese converts and whose misrepresentations had led to China being grievously misunderstood in the West.[23]

Jonathan D. Spence (1990) provided a more complex picture of the Guomindang's relationship to the missionaries in the 1920s. Most of the missionaries in China in the 1920s were Protestant (6,636 Protestants compared to 5,000 Catholics), with over half the Protestants being from American missions scattered across mainland China. Spence argued that American influence spread in China due to the Chiangs' friendships with individual Protestant missions.

> Once Chiang Kai-shek started his determined attempt to destroy the Jiangxi Soviet, the missionary influence grew, for Chiang and his wife made their summer home in the cool, breezy hills of Kuling (near Jiujiang), which had long been the chosen summer resort for the foreign community. The house the Chiangs rented belonged to the Nanchang Methodist Mission, and Madame Chiang in particular became a close friend of their landlord, William Johnson, a Methodist from Illinois who had been in China since 1910 and was especially interested in rural reconstruction... Chiang had lengthy discussions with many of the American missionaries. Later he was to draw more heavily on some of them, especially the Congregationalist missionary George Shepherd, a New Zealand-born naturalized citizen who was described as 'the one trusted American' in Chiang's 'innermost circle'.[24]

At the end of the Second World War, the United States decidedly turned toward Chiang Kai-shek's Nationalist government, while ambitiously hoping that some accommodation could be reached with Mao's CCP in the event it prevailed in a future civil war. The missionaries relied on the strength of the American presence in China. Yet the American-backed Guomindang (GMD) quickly lost domestic standing within China after 1945. The Chinese reacted to the 'wide-spread corruption' and 'runaway inflation in the Nationalist-controlled areas'.[25] Chiang Kai-shek's status as China's 'wartime national leader' suffered under the strength of the growing CCP. The American policy grew increasingly ambivalent toward the GMD while exploring the possibilities with the CCP; and as the GMD and CCP moved closer toward civil war, the status of foreign civilians in China became perilous. Protestant and Catholic missionary societies were not the only groups of foreigners at risk.

Nancy Bernkopf Tucker (2001) explored the growing concern of diplomats and missionaries in a comprehensive oral history project.[26] The response to Tucker's questions concerning evacuation of foreign citizens from China in 1948 demonstrates the conflicted feelings toward staying in an untenable situation by the diplomats and missionaries who had spent much of their lives studying and living in Chinese culture.

Tucker: *The military situation for the GMD deteriorated sharply in the last months of 1948, as the battle for Manchuria turned against them. That was followed closely by disastrous losses in Central China. At what point did the US embassy and consulate officers decide to evacuate Americans?*

John Melby, Political Officer, US Embassy, Chongqing/Nanjing, 1945–48: We had a lot of trouble in Shanghai. The mobs got out of control. We evacuated people. We were under a lot of pressure from the GIMO [Chiang Kai-shek]. 'Please don't evacuate! Don't do it because it will just give the advantage to the Communists!' Finally, it got to the point, in October 1948, where I just had to make the decision, 'Look, I'm sorry, but we've got to do it.' We warned Americans, private citizens to get out. Which meant mostly missionaries. Most of the business community had left. As usual, missionaries didn't do it. They never want to go. And then they get into trouble, and start yelling because the embassy doesn't get them out of trouble.[27]

Jerome Holloway, Officer, Consulate General, Shanghai, 1949–50: You have to distinguish in the missionary movement between the head-quarters groups, let's say, in Shanghai, and the missionaries out in the field. They were two different breeds of cats. The missionaries in Shanghai, the headquarters, were pretty sophisticated, politically astute people, who were well aware of the power they had behind them in Washington. The missionaries in the field tended to be good-hearted, somewhat naïve, but certainly men of good will. I talked to a lot of them when they came into Shanghai, after they lost their churches and the Chinese had turned on them.[28]

The story of the Catholic missionaries in China primarily centred on those 'out in the field'. Although the presence of Jesuit missionaries in China dated back to the late Ming period (1368–1644) with the work of Matteo Ricci beginning in 1555, the relationship between Catholics and the Chinese authorities was always an uneasy one. The Chinese found the bureaucracy of the Catholic Church to be in direct competition with their own stratified government. The Protestant missions were not criticized in the same way as the Catholic societies due to the relatively informal structure and the substantial authority of the Protestant minister within his local mission and church. In addition, the presence of missionaries in China was, from Matteo Ricci's time, the providence of the emperor exclusively and considered to be a subject of 'foreign' relations. During the Qing dynasty of the eighteenth century, Jonathan Spence (1990) found that:

European missionary contact with China was supervised mainly by the imperial household, an autonomous bureaucratic institution in Peking. This agency managed a wide range of the emperor's affairs... It was most commonly the bondservants in the imperial household – often men of considerable power – who dealt directly with the missionaries and escorted papal embassies. Their general role in missionary business underlined the prevailing view that this dimension of foreign affairs was an aspect of the court's prestige rather than of national policy. The Jesuits especially found their role much constricted by this arrangement and tried to emphasize their independence in letters back to European colleagues. Some of the Jesuits, along with other Catholic missionaries and Chinese priests, worked secretly inside China, sheltered by their converts. All faced serious punishment if caught by the authorities.[29]

By the early twentieth century, the subsequent Chinese governments – from Sun Yat-sen's new Republic of China in 1911 – saw the missionaries as a thorny presence. With the formation of the CCP in 1921, the treatment of Catholic missionaries became especially brutal – both at the hands of the Communists and the Guomindang. In 1928 the Communists were driven out of Hankow by the Nationalists to the southwestern borders of the Hanyang diocese into an area called Red Lake. Bishop Galvin, along with six Columban sisters and four priests were captured on Easter Monday in 1930 at Shien Tao Chen. Galvin, the sisters and two of the priests escaped but two others were held prisoner for nine months.[30] Fergus Murphy was not present at Shien Tao Chen during the crisis. A brief mention of this case appeared in the Seanad Éireann debates in December 1930.[31]

After Easter, 1930, Father Fergus Murphy and Father Gerry O'Collins returned to Shien Tao Chen. Calamities began to mount for the Columban Fathers. In 1931 an enormous flood devastated the valley of the Changjiang (Yangtse) River. 'Two thirds of the Hanyang vicarate was under water, 12,000 Chinese drowned, 23 million were destitute and 50 million people suffered serious loss.'[32] Between 1932 and 1937, years that included the Japanese attack on Shanghai and the beginning of the Sino-Japanese War, Murphy, O'Collins and their colleagues performed 30,000 baptisms in Hanyang and its sister mission in Nancheng. There was also a third mission in Huchow. From 1939 until 1941, the missions were under Japanese occupation. In April 1942, with the Japanese determined to capture the main Chinese airfields, a successful bombing campaign set in motion an army advance from Hangchow and Nanchang.[33] The Japanese were unable to hold their gains due to Chinese counterattacks that were aided by the newly arrived US forces. In their retreat southward, however, the Japanese systematically destroyed the occupied cities.

At Nancheng, aside from the Roman Catholic Mission, there were only about 12 houses left standing. Irish priests had had a hard time. The hospital was deliberately burned, radios taken, machinery deliberately smashed, money torn up, spectacles taken from priests. All villages on the line of retreat were reported to have been systematically burned, with all bedding, agricultural implements and harvested crops. All iron was removed from the district. All instruments and serums were taken from the Catholic hospital.[34]

At the end of 1945, Father Murphy, as newly appointed director of St Columban missions in China, reported that 'work started in full swing again'.[35]

By Christmas 1947, the communists broke into the Hanyang area from the north. In recently captured sections the communists were tolerant of the missions, but religion was to be 'wiped out' in conquered districts.[36] Nancy Tucker (1983) concluded 'the official attitude toward the missionaries between January 1948 and June 1950 drew notice for its restraint and tolerance'.[37] Yet as we have seen, the situation on the ground was somewhat confusing. Oi Ki Ling (1999) has argued that the toleration policy offered protection to the Protestants but not Catholics:

> Even when the policy of toleration had brought some relief to foreign missionaries in the period from late 1948 to early 1950, the pressure on Chinese Catholic priests did not cease... Many authors have observed that the Catholic missionaries' intransigence and the hostile stance of the Vatican towards Communism hardened Communist policy toward Catholic missionaries and Chinese Catholics... More Catholic than Protestant churches, seminaries, and mission properties were occupied by the authorities. A Catholic seminary was turned into a factory and elsewhere mission buildings became a jail. In some places Chinese clergy were expelled from mission stations and were obliged to take up residence with Catholic families. Although both Protestant and Catholic missionaries complained about the heavy taxation imposed on mission property, only Catholic priests were jailed for their failure to pay taxes.[38]

In April 1949 Archbishop Richard J. Cushing of Boston exaggerated the missionary presence in China in stating 'there are more Catholics in China than there are in Ireland'.[39] Archbishop Cushing, praising the work of the Columban Fathers, noted that the policy of the missionaries was 'to remain in their parishes even though these are in Communist-held territory'.[40] Not until the outbreak of the conflict in Korea in June 1950 did the CCP policy against missionaries become clear, although 'Catholic reports indicated that Catholic missionaries and Chinese believers had felt the iron hand of Communist policy against the Catholic Church long before the outbreak of the Korean War'.[41] Ling argued that the backlash against Catholic missions was due to the Vatican's 'tight control' of the Catholic Church in China.

The Department of External Affairs learned of events unfolding in communist China in various ways. The primary source was the British press, followed by embassy reports from Irish diplomats abroad. Since there was no reliable communication from the interior of China from the missionaries themselves, many aspects of the missionary situation in 1949–50 became evident after the fact. In the early Cold War environment, the Department of External Affairs also followed other incidents of 'religious persecution' from 1945 onward, including Stalinist eastern Europe, the Middle East, the Indian subcontinent, southeast Asia and South Africa.[42] However, the China files are the most voluminous.

Not long after he wrote to his sister at the Department of External Affairs, Father Fergus Murphy became ill and returned to America from Shanghai. By the autumn of 1950 Murphy had recovered and was sent to South America where he once again became ill. He died on 16 February 1951, aged 47, and was buried in Lima, Peru. Bishop Galvin, who co-founded the society in 1920 and arrived in China in 1926, was one of the last Catholic missionaries to be expelled to Hong Kong on 19 September 1952. He was 70 years old and his articles in the *Far East* detail the ordeal of his final days on mainland China. Suffering from leukemia that was diagnosed once he entered Hong Kong in September 1952, he travelled to Los Angeles where his diagnosis was confirmed. The bishop journeyed throughout the United States in 1953, gathering signatures on a petition for Rome to have St Columban's name added to the Universal Calendar of the Church.[43] Between visits to hospital for treatment, Bishop Galvin continued to speak of his long-term work in China. Bishop Galvin eventually returned to Ireland in May 1954 and died there on 23 February 1956 at the age of 73, forty years since he first went to China.[44]

Throughout the years of persecution of the St Columban Fathers, and other missionaries in China, and especially after 1949, the Irish government did not become formally involved with the plight of the missionaries. When the Korean War began in the summer of 1950, the Department of External Affairs produced a crude map outlining the approximate position of Catholic missionary societies remaining on mainland China. There were six orders, the largest being the Society of St Columban located in Hanyang, Shanghai, Nanchang and Huchon. The Sisters of St Columban were also present, as were the Vincentian Fathers, the Franciscans and the Church Missionary Society.[45] From 1950–53, the files on 'Recognition of China' become mysteriously lacking in material apart from newspaper clippings, most of which deal with the imprisonment of priests. The issue of the 'two-China problem' between the years of 1950–53 does not appear to have been troublesome for the Department of External Affairs. Virtually all the archival material related to China during this period is specific to the Korean War. Clearly the Irish government in early 1950 placed its trust in the foreign policy of the United States, and continued to support the US policy toward China throughout the Korean War. Trade with China – both the mainland and Formosa (Taiwan) was minimal during the years 1950–53. The imports from China ranged from IR£577,624 in 1950 to IR£283,724 in 1953. Exports to

China ceased altogether between 1950 and 1952, and were only IR£11,133 in 1953. Despite the lack of trade with China, and a relatively weak interest in aiding the Catholic missionaries left in China between 1949–52, the files of the Department of External Affairs still tell an intriguing story of Irish policy formation during the early Cold War years.

RECOGNITION OF THE PEOPLE'S REPUBLIC OF CHINA, 1949

The communist takeover in autumn 1949 did not produce political movements for widespread revolt in mainland China. On the contrary, the change in government initially motivated the Chinese toward increased economic productivity, progress in health and sanitation measures, relative political stability and effective military and political control in Beijing.[46] Yet Western policy analysts believed that Chinese domestic and foreign policy relied on the establishment of full-scale communist internationalism, supported by its Soviet neighbour. One Cold War scholar (writing in 1963) described the 1949 period as one of Sino-Soviet coordination in expansionist policy, writing in phrases that inflated both Chinese intent and capacity.

> By the summer of 1949, Russian leaders began to stress the importance of the Chinese example for Communist movements in Southeast Asia and allowed the Chinese Communists to take the lead in co-ordinating or guiding them. Flushed with revolutionary fervor and emboldened by their smashing victory over the Nationslists against overwhelming odds, the Chinese Communists accepted without hesitation their new role of leadership in Asian affairs.[47]

With the benefit of hindsight, the historian Martin Walker wrote in 1993 that although many analysts expected a sudden push of communism in Asia after Mao's victory, analysts with experience could see cracks in Sino-Soviet designs for internationalism. Dean Rusk, working on Far East policy at the State Department in 1949, considered the 'relentless global challenge by Soviet-led Communism' to be less sinister than most Western analysts predicted.[48] When Chairman Mao began attempts to move closer to the Soviet Union in December 1949, Chinese ambitions set the Western governments on edge.

On 16 December Mao had his first meeting with Joseph Stalin. Uneasy about Mao's motives, Stalin questioned him about China's negotiation expectations. Mao's interpreter later recalled that Mao answered Stalin by saying he wanted to 'bring about something that not only looked nice but also tasted delicious', an inference to the establishment of a new Sino-Soviet Treaty to replace the 1945 Treaty with the GMD.[49] After three weeks of stonewalling the Chinese in negotiation, Stalin compromised. A new treaty was signed on 14 February 1950 that allowed the Soviets to maintain military advantage in northern China. The

Chinese were to receive increased military support from the Soviets, as well as air-defence in coastal areas of mainland China.[50] However, the terms of the 1950 Sino-Soviet Treaty 'were significantly modest' and only required reciprocal military aid should one or the other fall prey to Japanese aggression.[51]

The newspapers in Britain and Ireland in early 1950 were filled with speculation on whether Europe and the United States would recognize communist China. The recognition problem became 'a regular feature' of US–British diplomatic discussions on the developments in China.[52] Nancy Tucker (1983) suggested that the British decision to recognize the People's Republic in January 1950 resulted from 'the impetus toward recognition of the Chinese Communists' rather than 'the desire to accommodate American policy'.[53] The US State Department hoped that non-recognition by Western powers would force moderation in international behaviour by the Chinese communists. Until the British announced recognition of the PRC in January 1950, the British and Americans seemed to be taking a parallel course in policy. 'As late as September 1949 Ernest Bevin pledged [to the US] that Britain would avoid appearing eager to establish diplomatic relations with the CCP.'[54] Yet Bevin's department previously had prepared a position paper in December 1948 that outlined the British interests in the event that communist China gained control of the mainland. The British intent was to recognize communist control, should it come, *de facto*. However, US intelligence analysts wrote in November 1949 that 'Britain is no longer debating the issue of recognition; the case has been made to the satisfaction of interested opinion in the country. It is the reluctance of other countries ... to come along that is responsible for British caution.'[55]

Three months later, the British Secretary of State for Foreign Affairs, Ernest Bevin, caved into British interests at the expense of American relations. At midnight on 5 January 1950, Britain formally withdrew diplomatic recognition from the Guomindang's nationalist government, renouncing the Moscow Declaration of December 1945 in which the United States, the Soviet Union and Great Britain pledged non-interference in China and recognized Chiang Kai-shek's regime in Nanjing as the *de jure* government. With the benefit of hindsight, Bevin's reversal of policy was inevitable.

First, the perception in London in 1948 was that the Americans had discarded Japan 'as a threat to security but as a potential help in its Cold War confrontation with the Russians'.[56] The British believed Japan, if left unchecked by Allied control, could become a potential threat to Australia and New Zealand. Second, if the communists were to gain control of all China, Hong Kong's existence as a British colony might 'depend on whether the Communists found the presence of a well-administered British port convenient for their foreign trade'. In that event, the colony could 'continue its life, but would be living on the edge of a volcano'.[57] The third interest was far-reaching. Communist domination of China would move 'militant communism' closer to Malaya's northern border. The newly independent republics in French Indochina and Thailand would be 'poor buffers'. Communist activity could infiltrate Malaya, with reports that communists had already reached Singapore. Increased communist influence 'in Burma, Tibet, Nepal, and Bhutan would generate pressures on India and Pakistan'. The French and Dutch positions in Indochina and Indonesia, respectively, 'might well become untenable'.[58] In a letter to *The Times* (London) on 12 January 1950, Lord Russell succinctly provided the crux of the British position, the most convincing of the British policy rationales:

> British trading interests in China are worth many millions of pounds and could not lightly be sacrificed... It is to be hoped that the recognition of the Peking Government will hasten this resumption of normal relationships between China and her traditional markets.[59]

The British could not understand the American preoccupation with China. Although the British presence was significant, 'the bulk of British opinion, especially of the younger generation, was sympathetic to Asian countries setting out to rule themselves and to develop their own economic life'.[60] But the British decision ran into difficulties. The Chinese government wanted to negotiate the terms of diplomatic relations on two key points. First, the Chinese wanted British assurance that the new government would have the 'seat' on the Security Council of the United Nations. Second, the Chinese had several claims on property in Hong Kong that would have to be settled before the opening of diplomatic relations. Notes flew back and forth until Britain formally asked whether the Chinese were willing to exchange ambassadors. After the war in Korea began in the summer of 1950, the British received no more replies to their notes. Still willing to negotiate with the Chinese, the British 'did vote for Peking's admission to the UN General Assembly in September 1950, before the Chinese intervened in the Korean War. After the Chinese intervention, attitudes naturally changed again.'[61] The British continued to negotiate with Beijing throughout the Korean War, even though British troops were fighting with UN forces.[62]

International relations scholar Edward R. Drachman wrote that President Truman's decision not to extend diplomatic recognition to China had numerous consequences in US Cold War policy. Apart from breaking with its traditional ally, Britain, the United States faced the dilemma of a 'two-China policy'.[63] In explaining President Truman's decision, Drachman highlighted the effect of the developing confrontations with the Soviets in Europe in 1948 – the Soviet-engineered coup in Czechoslovakia and the Berlin Blockade – that propelled Truman's policy toward the Chinese. 'With the formal establishment of the PRC in October 1949, Truman worried more about the global and monolithic nature of the communist threat. The conclusion of the Sino-Soviet alliance in February 1950 further strengthened the president's view.'[64] In April 1950, upon Truman's insistence, National Security Council document 68 (NSC 68) on containment was drafted. Just as fascism had been the main threat during the 1930s and 1940s, Truman saw communism as the dominant threat in the 1950s. 'The

Soviet Union was hesitant to engage the West in a general war, but it would find ways to spread communism through proxies.'[65]

While the Department of External Affairs in Ireland did not present a position paper on China policy, the members of the Department gravitated toward the American policy. There is no record in the Department's files that drafts or papers existed to express ambivalence or hesitation in policy alignment with the United States. Ireland had no strategic interests in China, no significant trade in the Far East, and no desire in preventing the crumbling of colonial empires in Asia. However, the Irish government did have an ideological interest in standing against communist aggression.

Today it is difficult to understand an international system where the interests of states are not connected or interdependent. In early 1950, however, Ireland had few practical interests in China yet its ideological interests were large. The stated interest of the Irish government in China was limited to the many Catholic nuns and priests residing there. Even though the missionaries were in a perilous position after 1949, the primary concern for the Irish government was to avoid giving any tacit recognition to Mao's Chinese Communist Party. Members of the Department of External Affairs, and especially former secretary Joseph P. Walshe (who in 1949 was Ambassador to the Vatican), squashed any idea that Ireland was sympathetic to communist China. Concerning Asian policy, the Department of External Affairs had moved very quickly in granting *de jure* recognition to the new Republic of the United States of Indonesia in January 1950 after the transfer of sovereignty by the Netherlands in December 1949.[66] In the 'memorandum for the government' for Indonesian recognition, the wording was clear: granting recognition to Indonesia was part of a policy of 'the particularly friendly and sympathetic attitude which [Ireland] would generally be expected to adopt towards a new State created in vindication of the principles of national independence and self-determination'.[67]

Although the United States had not made its position toward China clear in the autumn of 1949, when word came of the British decision to recognize China *de jure*, the Irish immediately made it clear to the US government that Ireland had not been consulted in the British decision. In addition, Irish recognition policy was firmly aligned with the Americans. Once Britain decided to recognize the CCP *de jure*, the Department of External Affairs drafted a memorandum for the US State Department.

MEMORANDUM

1.   The Government of Ireland has not hitherto accorded recognition to the Government set up in the communist dominated area of China. This might be of merely academic importance were it not for the fact that throughout the whole of communist dominated China there are very numerous and far-flung Irish missionary priests and nuns engaged in educational and medical work. Their position under the communist

regime in China is very precarious and is a cause of grave concern to the Irish government.

2.   The Government of Ireland was not consulted by the British Government or by the other Governments who recognised the new Chinese Communist Government prior to that decision being taken by them.

3.   The issue of the recognition of the Chinese Communist Government by the Irish Government has not, so far, arisen as a vital factor in relations to the safety of the Irish missionaries referred to in China, and it is possible that it may not so arise for some considerable time. However, the more Governments accord recognition to the Chinese communist administration, the more isolated and precarious will become the position of citizens of States which do not accord such recognition.

4.   The Government of Ireland has no wish or intention to accord recognition to the Government set up in the communist area of China but is nevertheless anxious not to add [to] the very grave hardships and dangers to which Irish missionaries are already exposed.

5.   For these reasons, but without wishing in any way to influence the policy of the Government of the United States in relation to its attitude towards the Chinese Communist Government, the Minister for External Affairs would be grateful to the Secretary of State if he could, informally, acquaint the Minister for External Affairs should at any time in the future a change be contemplated by the Government of the United States in its attitude towards the Chinese communist administration.[68]

First Secretary Con Cremin noted on 4 February 1950 that the memorandum was delivered to the US Chargé d'Affaires in Dublin. The affirmative US response was to treat 'the matter as very confidential having regard to the delicacy...of the question at issue'.[69] Secretary Freddie Boland noted that Minister Seán MacBride should be informed of the US response.[70] The formal reply from the US government came almost a month later from the American legation in Dublin. The Department of State would be 'glad to inform the Irish Government of changes in the position of the United States Government regarding recognition of the Communist regime in China'.[71] During the period under discussion here, the US position did not change. One might assume that this fact would be the end of the story for Ireland's non-recognition of China. However, the decision for non-recognition created a new set of policy headaches for the Department of External Affairs. As with the decisions for non-recognition of Israel, East Germany and Vietnam, the maintenance of the policy of non-recognition required considerable effort on the part of the staff of the department.

THE MAINTENANCE OF NON-RECOGNITION POLICY TOWARD CHINA, 1950–63

With the Irish policy toward China dovetailing with US non-recognition in

1950, there was little for the Department of External Affairs to do but to maintain the present course. Especially on the China question, Irish foreign policy seemed to be pro-American, much as Australian foreign policy has been described for the same time period.

> With ready access to American thinking on the course of international events, the Australian defense and intelligence community made that thinking its own, and Australian views eventually became scarcely distinguishable from those of the USA.[72]

Apart from Ireland's decision concerning Israel, non-recognition policy did follow the American line. It should be remembered that between 1949 and 1951, Seán MacBride occupied the position of Minister for External Affairs. Noted in other Irish diplomatic histories, and in Chapter 3 of this book, MacBride's preoccupation was bringing an end to partition and using acquiescence to US policy in order to gain favour with the US Congress over the partition issue. Yet Ireland did not look to the Americans for security in the international environment. Rather, the Irish foreign policy-makers looked to Britain and the Commonwealth states to act as proxies in areas where Ireland had no diplomatic representation.

At the outbreak of the Korean War, Seán MacBride sent a letter to the High Commissioner for India in Great Britain, Krishna Menon (Vengalil Krishnan), asking 'if Your Excellency would be good enough to enquire...in the absence of any Irish diplomatic or consular representatives in China, [whether] the government of India would be willing to undertake responsibility for the protection of Irish interests in that country'.[73] Almost a year later, T.J. Kiernan, serving as Ambassador to Australia, seemed oblivious to the Irish position when he approached the new Secretary in the Department of External Affairs, Seán Nunan, with an idea for Ireland to make a diplomatic approach to the Chinese:

> The great danger from the Chinese Peiping Government is that through fear and suspicion of the western nations and the U.S.A., they will turn completely toward the power-expansionist policies of the Soviet [sic]... [Sir Douglas] Copland [a former Australian diplomat] suggests that an approach from Ireland would to the Chinese be less open to suspicion and that we ought to consider taking an active part which would bring us forward as being a possible bridgehead for negotiation and pacific settlements; that we are in a uniquely strong moral position to act as peacemakers or at least as peace-seekers. All the countries of Asia would look well on an Irish initiative. There should be support from Britain, Belgium, [and] Holland...We are known in China through our Missionaries; and they are the only missionaries who have never carried a flag with the Gospel.[74]

The theme of Ireland rushing to the negotiating table at the last minute to save the day recurs in Irish foreign policy during the period 1949–63, but in this instance, Ambassador Kiernan seemed to be oblivious to the realties. Ireland was not yet a member of the United Nations, did not recognize China diplomatically, and was actively pursuing a policy of non-recognition. The idea was scurried away without notice into the diplomatic recognition files.

The real action occurring on the China problem was in departments other than External Affairs. The Department of Posts and Telegraphs faced the perennial problem of which China to recognize in the Universal Postal Union. Ireland abstained in the conference proceedings, relying on Canada to state its position 'should the net question of admitting the Beijing administration in place of the Taipei administration come to a vote'.[75] Canada would later pursue a strategy for an independent China policy of its own, but in 1951, the Canadians were following the line of the British Commonwealth nations.[76] A telegram received from the Taipei Director General of Posts dated 23 March 1951 requesting Irish participation in the vote received no reply. The following year Ambassador to the US John J. Hearne requested clarification on the issue from the Department of Posts and Telegraphs, as he had been approached by the Republic of China's Ambassador to support the continuation of the policy to not admit the PRC to the Universal Postal Union. Sheila Murphy typed a lengthy background memorandum on the issue, presenting it in Cold War terms:

> Russia takes every opportunity at international conferences of proposing that Taipeh should be unseated in favour of Peking and the U.S.A. invariably makes a counter proposal that no decision be taken on the Russian resolution or that consideration of the matter be postponed. The U.S. proposal is always carried, being supported even by some of the western European States which have recognised Communist China. These latter are, of course, influenced by the fact that China is at war with them in Korea. Peking, however, got a pretty good vote in the U.P.U. referendum, no doubt because it is somewhat illogical to keep out of the Union the administration which controls all Chinese post offices except those on the island of Formosa.[77]

The Department of Posts and Telegraphs responded to Ambassador Hearne in Washington: 'Our line has been not to participate in the controversy.'[78]

In July 1952, the persecution of Irish priests persisted. Four St Columban's priests were arrested by the Chinese government, although one long-term prisoner, Father Maurice Kavanagh, was released.[79] All department intelligence on the fate of the priests came from newspaper clippings, including a lengthy story in the *Cork Examiner* concerning the persecution and imprisonment of Father Kavanagh and Father Daniel Fitzgerald. Father Fitzgerald related in the story that 'we Irish priests out there had a quiet laugh at Irishmen being labelled as of all things, imperialists'.[80] Just a week after the *Cork Examiner* story,

Bishop Galvin of the Maynooth mission was expelled. This provoked a declaration from the Cork Corporation of its protest:

> Meeting of the Cork Corporation held on 23rd September 1952. The Right Honourable the Lord Mayor, Alderman P. McGrath in the Chair. It was proposed by Councillor P. J. O'Brien seconded by Councillor S. D. Barrett and passed unanimously, 'That this Corporation requests the Minister for External Affairs to forward to the Government of China a strong protest against the expulsion from China of His Lordship Bishop Galvin and other Missionary Priests'.[81]

By 1952, Fianna Fáil had returned to power, with Eamon de Valera as Taoiseach and Frank Aiken as Minister of External Affairs. William P. Fay, who later had a distinguished ambassadorial career, was Assistant Secretary and Legal Adviser under Aiken from 1951–54, and was charged with providing the Irish government's reply to the Cork Corporation resolution. Sheila Murphy, First Secretary of the Department, passed on the resolution to Fay with the following notation: 'Mr. Fay, This is for your side! pressure.'[82] Secretary Fay replied with a terse message that found its way into the *Irish Press* a few weeks later.[83]

> While the Minister naturally finds himself in complete sympathy with the intention of the resolution, he has asked me to request you to be good enough to inform the Lord Mayor and Corporation of Cork that he feels it would be unwise for him to take the action requested.
>
> In the first place, it is difficult to see to whom such a protest should be directed, since the Irish Government do not recognise the Central Peoples Government in Peking as being the Government of China, either *de jure* or *de facto*. A second and, in the Minister's view, a more important consideration, is the fact that it has been conveyed to him by missionaries just returned from China that it would be better for those of them who remain in China that the Irish Government should not intervene actively on their behalf. This is because one of the principal accusations brought against them by the Communists is that they are agents of foreign powers; and intervention on their behalf by such powers only gives their persecutors an opportunity of re-inforcing their unjust charge. The Minister fears therefore that an official protest in relation to the expulsion of Bishop Galvin would be calculated to intensify the persecution at present being suffered by our missionaries in China.[84]

Although the letter and resolution from the Cork Corporation concerning the fate of missionaries in China did not produce any shift in Irish policy, it did stir up department intelligence-gathering on the missionary presence on mainland China. The word was sent out to Joseph P. Walshe, Ambassador at the Vatican, and he replied with two letters. The first, dated 18 October 1952, provided a numerical listing of Catholic missionaries still in China, presumably provided by a source at the Holy See.

> My dear Secretary,
>   According to a statement made in the Gregorian University by the Archb. Of Kaifeng, Monsignor Pollio, on thursday 16th October, the following summary represents the results of the persecution of the Church in China: "Out of 143 Archbishops, Bishops and Prefects Apostolic, who were in China, 42 have been expelled, 20 are in Prison, 8 are dead, and the others are maintained in such conditions that it is absolutely impossible for them to exercise their ministry.
>   "Of 2500 Missionaries only 900 remain in China; of 2500 Sisters only 300, and not one of them all is allowed to engage in missionary activity." See "Osservatore Romano" 18 october page N.2.
>   Mons. Pollio is an Italian aged 41 years.
>   Yours sincerely,
>   J.P. Walshe[85]

Walshe's letter was followed by another on 21 October 1952, sent with the heading 'Persecution in China'.

> My dear Secretary,
>   The QUOTIDIANO, in its number of today publishes the following, from Hong Kong:
>   "Missionaries, fugitives from China, have described the tragic and sacriligious [sic] transformation of the Catholic Churches in Communist China. The example of St Michael's Church in Peking holds for all the others. One of the most frequented in China, it had hundreds of communicants every Sunday. Now, it is administered by so-called Progressive priests, the altars are draped with the hammer and sickle, and a huge red star hangs behind the Crucifix. The names of Mao and Stalin have taken the place of those of Jesus, Mary and Joseph, and the arches and pillars are covered with Propaganda posters. The Church of St Michael is still frequented by Catholics, but their number is in constant diminution, and those who go to Communion are few indeed."
>   Yours sincerely,
>   J.P. Walshe[86]

Walshe's commentary, always on the inflammatory side in matters concerning communism, expressed an apprehension of Chinese aggression that was apparent in October 1952. While talks were continuing on a Korean ceasefire, the Chinese forces launched heavy offensive attacks against UN forces early in October. The Royal Thai Expeditionary Force halted the aggressive attacks, concluding with the struggle for Pork Chop Hill.[87] During the autumn of 1952 the US presidential elections centred on Republican candidate General Dwight D. Eisenhower and Democrat candidate Adlai Stevenson. Eisenhower was the quintessential military hero and Stevenson was the diplomat. At the opening session of the United Nations on 24 October, Secretary of State for the US, Dean Acheson, appealed for an agreement between China and Korea on the repatriation of prisoners of war. The resulting resolution, offered by India, carried in the General Assembly by 54 votes to five. However, in the Security Council, the USSR used its veto power and the proposal was lost. Eisenhower had described Korea as 'Truman's War', calling the Korean peninsula 'the burial ground for twenty thousand American dead'. Clearly, the anti-communist mood of the West was at an all-time high. The British announced in February 1952 that they possessed an atom bomb, and on 6 November of that year the United States exploded the first hydrogen bomb at Eniwetok Island in the Pacific.[88]

In this environment, the only hold the Irish had on China policy was to reiterate the position concerning Catholic missionaries still residing on the mainland. In a lengthy report from the Washington embassy in December 1952, Ambassador John J. Hearne wrote of a meeting he attended with Ambassador Wellington Koo of the Republic of China (ROC) (Formosa, or Taiwan). The issue of representation on several international bodies was the subject of Dr Koo's discussion with Ambassador Hearne. From the Universal Postal Congress to the International Telecommunications Union, the ROC asked for Ireland's positive vote rather than abstentions. Ambassador Hearne carefully explained the Irish position, that nothing would be done to 'bring further suffering to those Irish missionaries who still carried on their work in China'.[89] In April 1953 an internal memorandum from the Department of External Affairs concerned Ireland's representation at the International Labour Organization (ILO), and whether to participate in the vote on the 'two China' problem. During the previous year's conference (1952), Ireland had voted in favour of 'allowing a China vote' at the ILO. This was seen as a mistake, and instructions were given to abstain on any vote concerning China at the ILO conference to be held in June 1953.

> The settled policy as regards the recurring question of the representation of China at international conferences is that Ireland should abstain from voting. The reason is, of course, mainly to avoid taking any steps which might jeopardise the interests of such Irish missionaries.[90]

A statement in the Department of External Affairs files on 'President Eisenhower on China Situation' bolstered the Irish government's hardened position toward communist China. The question of a 'two China' solution was asked at an early press conference for the new President Eisenhower.

> When asked at his press conference on May 14 whether he would be prepared to accept the British thesis that China should be admitted to the

United Nations after the Korean War had been settled, the President said in a lengthy reply... that the British and American differences on China were not as serious as they seemed on the surface. Newspaper reports state that the reply was on the lines that ever since the time of Woodrow Wilson the policy of recognition had always implied for the United States at least tacit approval of the foreign government concerned while other countries like Great Britain followed another tradition and were ready to recognise a government if it had a *de facto* control and authority over the country it ruled.

The President concluded his answer on China, after again stressing that the complicated and turbulent problems of the Far East would produce a variety of interpretations in the free world, by remarking that he would not say at that moment that China's admission to the United Nations should necessarily follow an armistice in Korea.[91]

In his memoir written ten years later, President Eisenhower recalled the reasoning of his decision:

Though the British had recognized Communist China early in 1950, I explained that I would ignore the claim of Communist China that it should be received into the United Nations or at a conference table, until it had established its right to be treated as a respectable member of the family of nations. Among the requirements were withdrawal from Korea, cessation of support for the Communist faction in Indochina, adoption of a decent deportment in its contacts in the Western World, and a commitment to abandon its military threat against Formosa.[92]

Eisenhower asked the National Security Council (NSC) to draw up a plan for Taiwan. The resulting NSC document 146/2 incorporated Taiwan into the western Pacific defense perimeter. The current perimeter, as outlined by President Truman in NSC 48/5 of May 1951, included Japan, South Korea, the Philippines, Australia and New Zealand. Taiwan and Indochina (Cambodia, Laos and Vietnam) were not included in the perimeter but were considered of military and strategic interest. The policy, approved by Eisenhower on 6 November 1953, laid the basis for the US–ROC defense treaty of 1954 which had three main tenets: deter the People's Republic in military action against Japan; encourage *de facto* separation acceptance by Beijing; and allow the US to use Taiwan's military bases.[93]

Throughout the last six months of 1953, the recognition files on China are filled with the growing concern over the question of admitting China into United Nations membership. A rather lengthy position paper on US policy was drafted by the Department of External Affairs Political Section, based on a critique of Secretary of State John Foster Dulles' book, *War or Peace* (1950). The international political environment shifted slightly in the spring of 1953 with the death of Joseph Stalin, and the Irish report noted the easing of Cold War tensions.

> The development of the Russian peace moves following upon the death of Stalin brought closer to the public mind the possibility of an early peace in Korea and the question of what might happen in regard to the admission of Communist China to the United Nations was more actively canvassed in political circles in the United States. The Administration probably intended to keep their policy flexible for as long as possible.[94]

With the opening of the Geneva Conference in April 1954, the settlement of the Korean War seemed at hand. Also on the agenda of the conference were the continuing difficulties in Indochina and the 'two China' problem. Irish intelligence on the Geneva Conference consisted of an eight-page paper based on newspaper reports taken primarily from the *New York Times* and *The Times* (London). Also included in the report was a statement from Ambassador John J. Hearne in Washington outlining the US position on Indochina dated 15 April 1954. Marked with an 'X' in Hearne's paper was the following paragraph:

> The prospects before the Geneva Conference are not bright. A strong impression, in corps circles here, is that the Soviet Union will use every possible endeavour to get the French to turn away from EDC [European Defence Community], and to secure the entry of Red China into UNO. Republican party leaders have, however, warned Mr. Dulles that the Administration's support for a proposal to bring Red China into UNO would spell political disaster for the Party in November. It is unlikely, therefore, that the United States will agree at Geneva either to recognise Red China or support her entry into the United Nations.[95]

The momentum for bringing the 'two China' question to the Geneva Conference was primarily sponsored by Britain. Winston Churchill, who had already proposed that the United States and Britain take part in Anglo-Soviet summit diplomacy, was also pushing for a settlement to the Chinese recognition problem. Foreign Secretary Anthony Eden was not convinced that President Eisenhower was interested in summit diplomacy, and he knew with certainty that Secretary of State John Foster Dulles was against it.[96] The recognition of Mao's China would encounter similar obstacles – namely the unwillingness of Eisenhower and the US public to welcome 'red China' into the fellowship of nations less than a year since the cessation of conflict in Korea.

Churchill's proposals did not get far. Eisenhower responded to the knowledge of Churchill's correspondence with the Soviets with a scathing letter: 'You did not let any grass grow under your feet. When you left here [Washington], I had thought, obviously erroneously, that you were in an undecided mood about this matter.'[97] This was Eisenhower's frame of mind as he contemplated diplomacy at the Geneva Conference. Although scholars of international law argued that recognition of 'two Chinas' would not involve moral approval, and that the question of seating Chinese Communist delegates in the United Nations is distinct from recognizing specific governments, the Eisenhower White House was firm in its resolve to support the Republic of China on Formosa.[98]

At some point during the Geneva Conference period, from April 1954 onward, there is a noticeable shift of attitude within the Department of External Affairs toward the Chinese recognition problem. Ambassador Freddie Boland in London sent two reports on the divergence between British and US policy on the China question. These reports are the beginning of thoughtful analyses on the China problem from the Irish point of view. Until July 1954, there is nothing in the files to suggest Boland's serious contemplation of Ireland's role in the question.

> I hope to send a further report at an early date about the serious foreign policy differences which now exist between the British and the United States Governments. In the meantime, however, I understand from a normally reliable Foreign Office source, that the British Government, regarding the American policy towards the admission of Communist China to the United Nations, as being based, not on practical consideration but on emotional and political factors, have definitely made up their mind not to pursue the matter further in present circumstances. My informant told me that it was realized that it might take as much as two years for American public opinion to straighten itself out on the issue but there was reasonable confidence in the Foreign Office that it would come around to a more realistic view in the end. It is freely rumoured here that Mr. Dulles regards the Formosan policy as absurd and would not be opposed personally to the admission of Communist China to U.N.O. It is appreciated, however, that neither he nor President Eisenhower can do anything with American public opinion as it is.[99]

In August 1954, Boland sent a follow-up that noted the beginnings of a Sino-Soviet rift:

> The British Government are apparently satisfied...that the Kremlin has nothing like the same control over the Chinese government that it has over the governments of Russia's European satellites...The British used the conclusion they have reached on this point as an additional argument in favour of the admission of communist China to the United Nations. In their view the primary aim of allied policy in the Far East should be to drive a wedge between Russia and China. They consider that there are enough potential sources of friction between Russian and Chinese interests in the area to promise such a policy of [*sic*] reasonable hope of success...In the British view, however, such a policy cannot be exploited to the full unless

Communist China is admitted to the United Nations and closer contacts between the Peking government and the governments of the free world thereby made easier.[100]

Since the beginning of the Korean War in 1950 there had been a moratorium on discussing the Chinese representation problem at the United Nations. In these early reports from Boland lies the genesis for an Irish plan to open the question to discussion once again.

MOVING TOWARD UN MEMBERSHIP, 1954

When examining the files of the Department of External Affairs, one cannot but notice the significant improvement in intelligence gathering and reporting from 1954 onward. Several explanations may account for this change – increasing technology, growing experience – yet the most likely cause is that the seasoned diplomats were now 'out in the field' rather than in Iveagh House. Although the Fianna Fáil government lost control in June 1954, the members of the department who had been significant in developing policy in the 1940s were now of ambassadorial rank and were reporting regularly on various issues. John J. Hearne continued to give substantial reports on the Chinese recognition question from Washington.[101] Séan Murphy reported just as eloquently on Canadian foreign policy from Ottawa.[102] Michael Rynne, long-time Legal Adviser in the Department since 1932, was in 1954 at the top of his game. Rynne continued to guide recognition policy on the technical points, enforcing Ireland's abstention policy toward the China issue in international organization voting. A mistaken vote in alliance with US policy toward 'Nationalist China' prompted the following response from Rynne:

> In the event that the subject should be raised by the Chinese Embassy – but only in that event – you might explain that through an oversight the Irish Delegation recently voted in the Finance Committee of the ILO [International Labour Organisation] against affording voting rights to Nationalist China while in arrears with her contributions. This vote was a blunder on the part of the Delegation which had overlooked its specific instructions to abstain from voting. The incident gave rise to representations by the American Ambassador here. The mistake was immediately brought to the attention of the Delegation who were instructed to abstain from voting when the issue was subsequently raised at a Plenary Session of the ILO Conference.[103]

Con Cremin, Ambassador at the Holy See, also crafted well-written reports on Vatican policy. In a statement dated 18 November 1954, Cremin reported on the attitude of the Vatican toward Formosa:

In the general context of the attitude of the Vatican towards non-Christian countries, my Portuguese Colleague called my attention to a curious reticence on the part of the *Osservatore Romano* to carry quite a lot of publicity about the event: it is generally reported very prominently on the front page, and there is generally too a photograph with a biographical note about the new representative on the inside page... The Chinese Minister was apparently struck by the contrast between the treatment he received from the *Osservatore Romano* and that normally accorded to newly-accredited representatives and he spoke about this to our Portuguese Colleague. The latter interprets it to mean that the Vatican is inclined to 'soft-pedal' the presence here of a Chinese Minister representing the Formosa Government.[104]

As the date approached for a vote on Ireland's entry into the United Nations (as the result of a Canadian initiative supported by the Soviets in September 1955), the Department of External Affairs coincidentally received a letter from Alfred Kolb of the Legation of the Federal Republic of Germany in Dublin. T.J. Horan of the Department provided a list for Dr Kolb of the states that Ireland did not recognize as of September 1955. The list included 'the German Democratic Republic, North Vietnam, South Vietnam, Laos, Cambodia, Nationalist China, Red China, North Korea, South Korea, and Poland'.[105] In a follow-up note dated 10 November 1955 was the correction on Irish recognition policy:

The position with regard to China and Poland as set out in the attached letter of 5th September, 1955, is not quite accurate. A distinction must be drawn between the recognition of States and the recognition of Governments.

Ireland fully recognizes the States of China and Poland but in the case of China Ireland recognizes neither the Peking nor the Formosa regime and in the case of Poland it recognizes the Polish Government-in-exile.[106]

The Irish position, then, in September 1955 was that Ireland recognized the State of China but neither the government of the People's Republic nor the Republic of China. The second inter-party government was in power in 1955, with John A. Costello as Taoiseach and Liam Cosgrave as Minister for External Affairs. With the old hands out of the department and serving abroad – Freddie Boland, Con Cremin, William P. Fay, William Warnock and Michael Rynne (who had become Ambassador to Spain) – there was no one to stop the re-examination of recognition policy toward China once it began in early 1956. The problem of the missionaries was still very fresh on the minds of diplomats yet there was only one Irishman, Father Aidan McGrath of St Columban's Mission, still attempting to do his work – not on mainland China but in Formosa.[107] Irish interests in China were minimal. Yet the positive vote for Ireland's membership to the United Nations on 14 December 1955 pushed the problems of recognition to the forefront within the department.

Sheila Murphy, whose brother had been a priest in St Columban's and is mentioned above, received a telephone call from Father Aidan McGrath in April 1956 while he was at home on leave from his post in Taipei. McGrath was asked by the Chinese Nationalist Government (Mr Loo in the Foreign Office) to inquire whether Ireland recognized the successor government on Formosa as 'legitimate'. Sheila Murphy typed a memo to Eoin MacWhite, a long-term diplomat who acted as Legal Adviser after Michael Rynne, in which she asked MacWhite to determine whether the Chinese Nationalist Government had directly approached Ireland at the end of the Second World War for diplomatic recognition.[108] MacWhite's answer stressed that recognition of Chiang Kai-shek's regime in China was never withdrawn and was therefore 'tacitly assumed'. This statement of policy clearly contradicted prior attitudes of the Department.

Miss Murphy,

(1) We have failed to trace any communication from the Formosa Foreign Office despite a close search. It is possible that the impression of Mr. Loo that we do not recognize the Formosa Government is due to our non-reply to this communication which we either never received or which was received and lost.

(2) I have examined all the library press clippings relating to China for 1949 and 1951 and the World Diplomatic Directory for 1950 and 1951 and I have not found any case of re-recognition by any state of the Chiang Kai-Shek [sic] regime in Formosa. Around June 1949 most countries withdrew their Ambassadors or Ministers from Nanking, the Nationalist capital, 'for consultations'. The Central Government of the Chinese People's Republic was proclaimed on October 1st, 1949. In these cases of countries then recognizing the Communist regime including the USSR the procedure was first to withdraw recognition from the 'Knomintang [sic] Government' by so informing the local Chinese Ambassador and then announce recognition of the Pekin [sic] regime. The time difference between these two acts may have been only a matter of minutes but it shows that up to the act of withdrawal of recognition on October 2nd the Soviet Government considered that it was still legally recognizing Chiang's regime. The British went through the same procedure on January 6th, 1950 (and Egypt the other day).

Although a number of countries continue to recognize the Nationalist Chinese Ambassador or Minister accredited to their capitals, as far as can be ascertained here comparatively few have special missions in Formosa. Of those listed in the World Diplomatic Directories most are new appointments so the question of re-recognition does not arise. Indeed, in the case of the present Apostolic Internuncio the 1956 editor of the *Annuncio Pontifico* gives the name of Archbishop Ribera [sic], the address of the office in 'Formosa-China' and notes the date of presentation of letters, 6th July, 1946.

From this it is clear that no act of re-recognition is called for and, indeed, an act of de-recognition is required before according recognition to Pekin [*sic*]!

(3)   File 305/115/1 throws some interesting side lights on the question of our recognition of Chiang Kai-Shek's [*sic*] regime. We have abstained consistently on the Chinese recognition question in UPU, ITU, ILO and WHO[109] not on the issue of recognition but because we wished 'to avoid taking any steps which might jeopardise the interests of such Irish Missionaries as are still endeavouring to pursue their work on the Chinese mainland'. On 9/10/1952 the Ambassador at Washington was told that he 'may frankly inform' Mr. [Wellington] Koo the (Nationalist) Chinese Ambassador of our reasons for abstaining on this issue in the ITU. On December 12th, 1952, the Ambassador reported that he had done so and in this report there is no sign on Mr. Koo's part that he was under the impression that we did not recognize his Government; this was tacitly assumed.

On November 27th, 1953, the Ambassador at Washington reported an informal approach from Mr. Koo asking whether the Irish Government would consider opening diplomatic relations with the Formosa Government. It was suggested to Mr. [John J.] Hearne that he inform Mr. Koo that we could not contemplate the opening of new diplomatic missions for budgetary reasons. Again our recognition was assumed and unquestioned.

On December 20th, 1955 the Ambassador at Washington reported that he had again been approached by Mr. Koo who asked if, in view of our membership of the UN, we might reconsider our attitude to establishing diplomatic relations with Formosa. On 25th January, 1956 Mr. Hearne was instructed that there was no change on this question since 1953 and that 'there is no likelihood of any change in the foreseeable future'.

(4)   If we wish to correct any misapprehensions that may exist in Formosa we could (i) instruct Mr. Hearne to ask Mr. Koo to inform his Government that we have never withdrawn recognition from the Nationalist Government or (ii) tell Father MacGrath the position and have him suggest that if they wish to have this confirmed they could make enquiries through, say, their Ambassador in Washington.
19th May, 1956.

                                        Eoin MacWhite

Fortunately for MacWhite, his position required giving advice, not serving as the arbiter of truth. However, MacWhite's interpretation of the Chinese recognition problem did stir up trouble within the department and in the diplomatic posts abroad. After a diplomatic circular note was sent to the Irish missions on 10 November 1955, Ambassador Con Cremin requested clarification of the policy, as well as an explanation of the distinction between recognition of a state and of a government. Cremin completed his letter with the following statement: 'While these points may seem to be largely of an academic nature they may perhaps have taken on a certain practical aspect now that we are in the United Nations.'[110] In November 1956, another circular ignited the ire of former Legal Adviser Michael Rynne, now Ambassador to Spain. Complaining that all Irish recognition policy was in complete disarray, Rynne specifically addressed the Chinese recognition problem.

> Our reasons for declining to commit ourselves to recognizing any of the above [States] used to be (a) that they were either Communist or potentially so and (b) that, owing to some Irish missionaries still remaining in the Far East, the better course seemed to be to take no positive action which might prejudice them in communist eyes.
>
> Even if that position no longer pertains, I wonder if it is correct to say, concerning China, that 'recognition has not been withdrawn' from the Formosan Government which 'we continue to recognise'.
>
> My recollection is that we firmly declined, during World War 2, to give any recognition to Chang-Kay-Chek [sic], whom we regarded as an ex-bandit thrown up by the fortunes of war to become a ruling puppet of the Western Allies with the financial backing of the notorious 'China Lobby' in Washington...
>
> In this connection, I note that the Minister [Liam Cosgrave] suggested at UNO that it might not be possible to withhold recognition from Communist China indefinitely, although he considered that this was not an appropriate moment (in view of the Hungarian crisis) to welcome the Peking Government into UNO.[111]

Michael Rynne's frustrations echoed the mood of the period. The year 1956 brought renewed Cold War tensions. Nikita Khrushchev revealed the atrocities of Stalin to his Twentieth Congress of the Communist Party of the Soviet Union in a 'secret' speech on 25 February 1956. Pakistan was created on 29 February 1956. France recognized Morocco as an independent state on 2 March 1956. The British were bogged down in Cyprus. The British–French–Israeli Suez Crisis prompted the ill-timed bombing of Egyptian airfields by the French and British on 31 October, angrily provoking the United States to call for a UN Security Council resolution which was then vetoed by the British. The events in Suez overshadowed a more menacing threat in Hungary by the aggression of the Soviet Union against attempts at democratic reforms.[112] With Ireland's membership to the UN in December 1955, the Irish at last had a civilized playing field for foreign affairs, yet the Cold War negated any attempts for traditional diplomacy – especially at the United Nations.

POLICY MAYHEM AT THE UNITED NATIONS, 1957–59

Although Ireland was admitted to the United Nations in December 1955, representatives were sent to New York early in 1956. During the eleventh General Assembly Session beginning in September 1956, Freddie Boland headed the new permanent mission for Ireland at the United Nations. Boland was active in discussions on the Hungarian crisis and the Suez during the 1956 session. From the beginning, Boland committed to following principled policy at the UN. As Dermot Keogh recorded in *Twentieth Century Ireland*, the Irish delegation drafted principles of policy which were announced to the Dáil in July 1956.[113] The three principles were: to be faithful to the obligation of the Charter of the United Nations; to avoid associations with political blocs; and to contribute to the preservation of Christian civilization through UN membership. Early on, Freddie Boland had his eye on the presidency of the General Assembly (GA), an elected position with a term of one year. The presidency of the GA, according to diplomat Conor Cruise O'Brien, was 'not attainable by anyone but a discreet but understanding supporter of American policy on all important matters'.[114]

Dermot Keogh, Joseph Morrison Skelly and Conor Cruise O'Brien have each written at length on the early years of Ireland at the United Nations.[115] Boland spent considerable time in 1956–57 fostering a relationship with his US counterpart, Henry Cabot Lodge. When Foreign Minister Frank Aiken arrived on the scene during the summer of 1957, Boland was slightly uneasy with Aiken's drive for independent policy at the UN – especially his attitude toward US policy. As Keogh noted, 'Aiken was never reflexively pro-American'.[116] Examining the China representation problem at the United Nations allows a closer look at the interplay between large power states and the smaller powers during the Cold War. In spite of ideals, there are hard political realities. What seemed to be the perfect power play for Ireland almost cost Boland his bid for the presidency.

Frank Aiken told Conor Cruise O'Brien during the summer of 1957 that 'Ireland's position in the previous session of the General Assembly had been too subservient to the position of the United States'.[117] In an effort to counter the 'mindless servitude to policies framed and enforced by the United States', Conor Cruise O'Brien suggested to Aiken:

> I told the Minister that if any delegation at the General Assembly wished to be accepted as following an independent line, the test was the annual vote on the question of representation of China…I knew that this decision, if Aiken could sustain it, would make a big change in my life.[118]

Freddie Boland and his second-in-command, Eamon Kennedy, were firmly against Aiken's plan to break the moratorium. Boland reminded Aiken that 'there were indeed some anomalies there, but the anomalies could be left for the Americans to sort out for themselves in the fullness of time without any need for new initiatives on our part'.[119]

Con Cremin, who returned to Ireland in 1958 to become Secretary of the

Department of External Affairs, recalled Frank Aiken's motivation some years later in his unpublished memoirs:

> Mr. Aiken's thesis was that the U.N. should be free to discuss every important question but entirely without prejudice to the decision on the substance of the question and he voted for discussion by contrast with the attitude taken by Mr. Cosgrave... As far as Ireland was concerned the question came up first in 1956 shortly after we had entry into the United Nations... In 1956 the Delegation voted against acceptance of the item. Between then and the following Regular Session of the Assembly there was a change of Government and the new Minister of External Affairs Mr. Frank Aiken indicated he would vote in favor of the item being discussed.[120]

Aiken perhaps had seen a report from John J. Hearne in Washington earlier in the summer of 1957. In an analysis of US policy toward communist China, Hearne sent the following assessments:

1. The US could try to bring 'force to bear' on China. This thesis was not given much credence because it would provoke war with the Soviets.
2. The second alternative was to 'accept the fact of Communist China's strength, and make adjustments'. This course was also ignored because 'it conflicted with the deep sentiment of the American people'.
3. The final alternative was to 'deal with the problem' on an 'ad hoc basis' and to approach a solution 'step by step, and over a long period of time'.[121]

The wording of Hearne's letter that might have grabbed Aiken's attention was the perception for some movement in US policy. Hearne concluded that 'with regard to membership in the UNO, it is generally felt here that... the United States would find it extremely difficult, on a show-down in the Assembly, to keep Red China out of the organization'.[122] Conor Cruise O'Brien had also been part of a discussion with the Formosa representative at the United Nations during the summer of 1957. The diplomat from Taipei made a stop in Ireland on his way from Iceland to Austria. Repeating similar attempts at establishing relations through John J. Hearne in Washington, the diplomat suggested that even if Ireland did not wish to pursue a legation in Taipei, an ROC legation could be opened in Dublin. The members of the department present stressed that unilateral relations were out of the question, and due to budgetary constraints, Ireland was not in a position to open a legation in Taipei.

India submitted the resolution to call for a vote on the moratorium question on Chinese representation on 23 September 1957. It is interesting to note that India's recognition policy toward China mimicked the British decision of 1950, yet as the decade passed, India became the most independent voice for the Chinese representation question to be answered at the United Nations.[123] K.P. Misra, in a comprehensive text on Irish recognition policy, argued that the

Indian and British decisions were based on pragmatism rather than ideology.[124] Beginning in 1956, India pushed for an end to the moratorium on the Chinese representation issue. By 1959, when China threateningly invaded the Indian border near Tibet, India still clung to the pragmatism of bringing China into the United Nations rather than opposing it.

The 1957 Indian resolution itself was worded in the negative, stating that the General Assembly 'decides not to consider... any proposal to exclude the representatives of the Government of the Republic of China or to seat representatives of the Central People's Republic Government of the People's Republic of China'.[125] The Department of State noted in a diplomatic circular on 10 October 1957 that Ireland had changed its vote from 1956, voting against the resolution in the 1957 session. Ireland was not in entirely anticommunist company in the vote: Afghanistan, Albania, Bulgaria, Burma, Byelorussia, Ceylon, Czechoslovakia, Denmark, Egypt, Finland, Ghana, Hungary, India, Indonesia, Morocco, Nepal, Norway Poland, Romania, Sudan, Syria, Syria, Sweden, Ukraine, USSR, Yemen and Yugoslavia also voted against the resolution.

The reaction from Washington was expected. In the White House staff notes of 1 October 1957, the last point on the agenda was entitled 'Proposed US–Irish Talks'.[126] 'We are urgently requesting a top-level US–Irish exchange of views because of our concern over recent Irish behaviour in the UN.' It is not clear whether a meeting took place. By 23 October 1957 Frank Aiken was back in Ireland. The reaction at home was unexpected. A heated exchange occurred in the Dáil on 23 October 1957 in which Aiken was taken to task for the Irish vote.

> **Mr J.A. Costello** [Leader of the Opposition] asked the Minister for External Affairs if he will state whether the policy advocated by him at the U.N.O. with reference to... the proposal to discuss the representation of China in the U.N.O. continues to represent Government policy having regard to the adverse international reactions caused by it.
>
> **Minister for External Affairs (Mr Aiken):** ... The proposal in relation to China for which I voted was that an item entitled "The representation of China in U.N.O." should be placed on the agenda for discussion. As there has been no improvement in the situation in ... the Far East, and as the risk of a suicidal war has rather been intensified, I see no reason why our attitude to either of these questions should be changed.
>
> **General Mulcahy:** Would the Minister say whether that continues to represent Government policy?
>
> **Mr Aiken:** I have answered that question. We are not a Coalition Government.
>
> **Mr Blowick:** You must be a very queer Government with the Minister saying one thing in America and his colleagues saying other things at home.

Mr T.F. O'Higgins: Is the Minister aware that his speeches on these... matters have occasioned adverse international reactions?

Mr Aiken: Some people objected to them and a lot more approved.

A Deputy: I am sure China approved.

Mr M.J. O'Higgins: Is the Minister in a position to state whether or not the speeches he delivered in the United Nations Assembly were discussed with his colleagues in the Cabinet before he went to America?

Mr Aiken: I have already answered that; this is not a Coalition.

Mr Dillon: Will the Minister state whether it has caused him or the Government any concern to note that his observations elicited strong approval from Communist sources and deep resentment in countries which have hitherto been our friends, to wit the United States of America, and in the light of that can he reassure the House as to whether any steps could be taken... by the Government to reassure our friends in the United States of America that the attitude adopted by the Minister was not an indication that the Government of Ireland has ceased to regard America as our friend and has ceased to reject contemptuously the offer of friendship from Moscow and the U.S.S.R.?

Mr Aiken: ... There is nobody in this House, or outside it, who has as much admiration and respect for the American people as I have, but I do not believe it would serve either the interests of Ireland or be in keeping with the traditions of those who fought for Ireland during the years, to stand silent and not offer our opinion truthfully and honestly on certain matters that come before the United Nations for discussion. We went to the United Nations to represent the views of this country and it may be very valuable...

General Mulcahy: That is the point.

Mr Aiken: ... to countries that bear the real burden to have an independent nation which is prepared to make proposals and suggestions in the present disastrous world situation.

Mr M.J. O'Higgins: Would the Minister consider adopting a procedure whereby he would consult with, or at least notify, the Leader of the Opposition before he makes any further such speeches?

An Ceann Comhairle: That is a separate matter.

Mr Aiken: On that matter I would very gladly consult with the Leader of the Opposition before he makes statements condemning the Government attitude without knowing what it is.

Mr O'Sullivan: Nobody knows what it is. It is a mystery.[127]

Throughout the autumn of 1957 and into 1958, the Formosan government relentlessly pursued the question of establishing diplomatic relations with Ireland. The ROC Minister to the Holy See even approached Taoiseach Eamon de Valera in Rome. The Taoiseach listened to the sales pitch but politely replied that Ireland 'simply could not afford' to establish missions with all countries.[128] Secretary Con Cremin became the voice for establishing policy on non-recognition of the Formosa Government once he returned to Dublin in 1958. In New York, Freddie Boland continued to listen for changes in US policy toward recognition of the PRC. On 9 May 1958 Boland sent a lengthy report to Con Cremin about a recent dinner with Eustace Seligman, a partner in Secretary of State Dulles' former law firm. Mr Seligman testified before the Foreign Relations Committee of the US Senate 'in favor of Communist China's admission to the United Nations'.[129] Cremin read Boland's seven-page report, making notations in the margins concerning Seligman's ideas of how the United States could recognize the PRC without 'losing face' in Asia. Then the report was sent to the Taoiseach's office. Little happened concerning the non-recognition of the 'two Chinas' in Irish foreign policy from May until September 1958. Then, with the opening of the Thirteenth General Assembly, Foreign Minister Frank Aiken decided to bring the moratorium issue to the United Nations once more. The political climate, however, had substantially shifted between 1957 and 1958.

The 'hot' issue in early 1958 was called the 'Taiwan Straits Crisis' and involved the small offshore islands of Jinmen (Quemoy) and Mazu (Matsu) near mainland China and inhabited by Nationalist Chinese from Formosa. The offshore islands had been a source of tension since 1949 when Chiang Kai-Shek sent Nationalist troops to Jinmen. In 1954 the Chinese began shelling these islands periodically. The Nationalists kept the garrisons on the islands supplied with arms, largely provided by the United States. If the islands were forced to surrender to the Chinese communists, the US foreign policy analysts predicted that their loss would have a devastating effect on the Nationalist government in Formosa.[130] On 23 August 1958 the Chinese communists began shelling the islands. The United States began escorting Nationalist vessels through the straits in order to rearm the islands. A more direct US intervention on behalf of the Nationalist government appeared to be within the realms of possibility. In a letter to Prime Minister Harold Macmillan of Britain, US Secretary of State John Foster Dulles spelled out the significance of the crisis.

> We have had a very careful study of the situation made by our intelligence community, by the State Department officials, by the Joint Chiefs of Staff, and they are unanimous to the effect that if Quemoy were lost either through assault or surrender, this would have a serious impact upon the authority and military capacity of the present government on Formosa; that it would be exposed to subversive and military action which would probably bring about a government which would eventually advocate

union with Communist China; that if this occurred it would seriously jeopardize the anti-Communist barrier, including Japan, the Republic of Korea, the Republic of China, the Republic of the Philippines, Thailand, and Vietnam; that other governments in Southeast Asia such as those of Indonesia, Malaya, Cambodia, Laos and Burma would probably come fully under Communist influence; that Japan with its great industrial potential would probably fall within the Sino-Soviet orbit, and Australia and New Zealand would become strategically isolated ... confidence in the United States would be shaken, the entire psychological alignment in Asia would alter in favor of Communism, and Peiping's prestige would reach new heights.[131]

With such domino-theory thinking, any attempt to cause a rise in Beijing's prestige in 1957–58 would have been met with great disapproval by the Americans. Dulles' policy toward Taiwan ended with a communiqué on 23 October 1958 relating overall US support for the Chinese Nationalists, but not for their retaking of the mainland by force. From the date of the communiqué onward, the Nationalists knew that the United States was backing their political rather than military policies to regain mainland China. This subtle shift in US policy brought a wider opening for talk about the Chinese representative issue in the United Nations. Yet the United States was not prepared for the tactics of Frank Aiken, who was guided by a drive to enhance Irish prestige at the United Nations and who decided (again) to oppose the US by supporting the Indian initiative to end to the moratorium on the China representation problem.

Britain, the United States and the Soviet Union all expected a difficult vote on the moratorium question in 1958. Britain favoured the approach of allowing Mao's China into the United Nations in order to make it 'more controllable'.[132] Nikita Khrushchev of the Soviet Union sent a scathing letter to President Eisenhower on 7 September 1958 in which he stressed that US policy toward China 'extends beyond the framework of purely internal affairs of the United States'.[133] In the same letter Khrushchev stated that any US attack on China would be regarded as an attack on the Soviet Union.

Within this political environment, Frank Aiken addressed the General Assembly on the Chinese representation question on 22 September 1958. In explaining the Irish position, a statement was prepared for the General Assembly.

Mr. President, like many others here we have no sympathy whatever with the Ideology of the Peking Government. We condemn its aggressive policies in China itself and its conduct in North Korea. No Country has a greater horror of despotism, aggression and Religious persecution than Ireland has. On all these grounds we reprobate the record of the Peking regime.

If merely by refusing to discuss the question of the representation of China in the United Nations we could do anything to improve the situation in China and Korea we would vote without hesitation in favour of that course. We are not, however, convinced that refusal to discuss the question can now serve such a purpose.

Our aim should be to win acceptance for the Principles of the Charter in China and to secure self-determination for the People of Korea. The belief of my Delegation is that in present circumstances progress can best be made to these ends by having a full and open discussion of the question of the Representation of China in this assembly. We are voting, therefore, in favour of the Amendment proposed by the Delegation of India.[134]

This incident produced no White House staff notes demanding a high-level meeting with the Irish government. The Irish vote was expected. However, US diplomats were thinking strategically about Ireland's position within the United Nations.

THE US DEPARTMENT OF STATE, TIBET AND BOLAND'S CANDIDACY, 1959

By January 1959, it was clear that Freddie Boland would be running for the presidency of the General Assembly in its fourteenth session to begin in September 1960. Frank Aiken's position on the China representation question had caused enough trouble for the United States to rethink its support of Boland's candidacy. In the meantime, Ireland was trying to follow principled diplomacy in the area of recognition. The Department produced a comprehensive statement on Irish recognition policy toward communist governments in January 1959.[135] The Irish policy still showed a strict avoidance of any affirmative recognition of the PRC or the ROC. The memo suggests that there was a question whether Ireland could say it recognized the PRC *de facto*, but concluded that 'there is no record of any State at present according only *de facto* recognition of the Chinese People's Republic as a definite act of policy'.

In April 1959, a question arose whether the new president of the GA would come from Latin America or Europe. A State Department telegram to the US mission at the UN confirmed the apprehension: 'we assume West European would be logical choice, but US could not possibly support Boland without modification Irish position on Chinese representation'.[136] If the presidency were to go to the Europeans, 'US will probably wish discuss directly with Irish Government problem of Irish policy on Chinese representation'.[137] The UN mission replied in a telegram on 24 June 1959: 'Whenever European President is discussed here, Boland's name almost invariably heads list. He is a first-class parliamentarian.'[138]

In early 1959 an ancillary issue to the Chinese representation question became prominent in UN discussions. Since being smuggled out of Tibet in March 1959, the Dalai Lama had sought asylum in the Indian town of

Mussoorie. The Chinese communists invaded the region of Tibet in 1950 under the pretence of uniting China's 'five races'. Throughout the 1950s the Chinese squeezed Tibet, destroying any attempts at continued national identity for the Tibetans. Once the Chinese forces became increasingly aggressive in 1959, the Dalia Lama escaped to India. The Chinese set up their own 'Panchen Lama' and began expropriating the lands of the Tibetan monasteries. Over 13,000 Tibetans fled into India. Although, in 1954, the Indian government negotiated a commercial treaty with the PRC in relation to Tibet, the border questions of the north-east frontier were never fully settled. Also, the independence of the ancient kingdoms of Bhutan and Sikkim increased the tension between India and China. China wanted the two kingdoms to fall under Chinese influence, while India insisted that it would militarily defend any encroachment into Bhutan or Sikkim. On the surface, the Americans and British were ambivalent to the issues in the north-east frontier in 1959, although the CIA had been training Tibetan guerillas since 1956.[139] Author Peter Calvocoressi argued that the United States and Britain 'periodically expressed sympathy with Tibet so long as they were on poor terms with the Chinese but both gave the Dalai Lama the brush-off when they became engaged in improving relations with Beijing'.[140]

When persecution of the Tibetan Buddhists by Chinese forces resumed in the spring of 1959, the Dalai Lama declared that he was indeed the government-in-exile of Tibet. This pronouncement did not sit well with India nor with most members of the United Nations who wanted to avoid any disputes with China. Yet the United Nations had voted 1959–60 as the 'year of the refugee' and Western opinion sided with the Tibetans. The public US policy was non-committal on the Tibetan drive for independence and preferred to view the issue as one of human rights, although by 1958 both the State Department and the Defense Department gave 'full-scale commitment to support the Tibetan resistance'.[141] Boland, on the verge of the GA presidency, decided that the fiasco on the issue of the Chinese representation vote could be balanced by Ireland's support for a Tibetan initiative. Only in the Cold War environment could such a dichotomy of policy make any sense.

Joseph Morrison Skelly wrote at length on the Tibet initiative presented by Ireland at the fourteenth General Assembly Session at the UN in October 1959.[142] Skelly argued:

There is absolutely no question that Boland's concern for the rights of small nations and his unwavering devotion to the rule of law in international affairs engendered this commendable recommendation. Yet he also hoped to provoke an Irish censure of China to temper the negative reaction in the west to the delegation's China vote. That is why he stressed that Aiken should deliver the message. If the spokesman of Ireland's China policy condemned the invasion of Tibet it would send an unmistakable signal to the west as to where Ireland really stood.[143]

From April until the Tibet initiative entered the GA in October 1959, the Irish diplomats spun the issue of Tibet both in Ireland and at the United Nations. Early on in the process, the US delegation made it clear that they would not oppose such an initiative from Ireland. Once Boland thought about an Irish initiative on Tibet, he was not as convinced of its success. 'So far as my enquiries go, the feeling here against bringing the Tibetan question before the U.N. in any formal way remains as strong as before.'[144] To complicate Boland's dilemma, Henry Cabot Lodge, Permanent Representative for the United States, still had reservations about the Irish at the United Nations. In a telegram to Secretary of State Herter in July, Lodge said that the

> US should not be in position of stimulating Boland candidacy until clear he preferred choice West Europeans and clear satisfactory assurance re Chi Rep can be obtained. US should also avoid formal commitment this matter . . . in order not establish awkward precedent.'[145]

Later, the US would openly encourage the Irish to proceed with the resolution on Tibet, offering support from behind the scenes.

Boland knew the stakes were high. If the Tibetan initiative was a success, with US backing he knew he could count on a shot at the GA presidency in the coming year. On 20 October 1959 the assembly agreed to 'take up' the measure offered by Ireland and Malaysia on Tibet.[146] The Americans were impressed with the Irish performance on the initiative. Lodge telegraphed Herter on 26 October 1959:

> Now that Tibet question is completed with Irish having played major role with skill and distinction, I believe time has come for me to talk to Aiken (Ireland) about possibility Boland running for Presidency 15th GA.
>
>   My instructions on this subject (Deptel 27, Jul 14) do not seem to me to meet situation which now faces US.
>
>   . . . Western Europeans, I think, are generally favorable to Boland but we cannot expect this favorable sentiment to crystallize until Boland becomes active candidate and he will not do this until he gets green light from US.[147]

Lodge then requested new instructions from Herter to talk to Aiken with the following proposals:

> (1)   That we are anxious support Boland's candidacy if he decides run. Only thing that worries us is our disagreement with Ireland over ChiRep issue but we are confident Boland would not use his position to influence 15th GA's action this question and I should talk to him about it so that we may be satisfied on that point.
> (2)   That we assume Aiken understands danger to Boland's candidacy

posed by Nosek's (Czechoslovakia) prior entry into field and vital necessity that Boland openly enter race immediately or withdraw his name conclusively.

I can well understand that Dept might feel Boland not best possible Western European for Presidency. But as practical matter Boland has first refusal... I believe Boland is determined to run and has Aiken's full support... I do not think Boland would use his position as GA Pres against US. There is no doubt Nosek would.[148]

The Department of State agreed with Lodge's proposals, and Boland's candidacy for the UN GA presidency was launched. On 9 November 1959 the Irish Cabinet agreed to Boland's candidacy as well. From 1959 onward, Ireland's approach to the Chinese recognition problem took a more decidedly anticommunist stance. When Séan Lemass became Taoiseach in June 1959 upon Eamon de Valera's retirement from the position, he was determined to distance himself

from an aspect of de Valera's and Aiken's independent policy he found disconcerting, establishing a basis for voting against communist China should the substantive question ever arise... a successful public relations exercise designed to calm the domestic furor aroused by Ireland's policy.[149]

Taoiseach Lemass's mood came from his own ideological convictions, but the tension of the Cold War in early 1960 reflected the growing divergence between the policies of the People's Republic of China and the Soviet Union, the emergence of the Sino-Soviet split. While many could see that the policies of the two States were never successfully integrated, in 1959 the Eisenhower–Khrushchev talks at Camp David resulted in Khrushchev conveying to Mao that 'we on our part must do all that we can to exclude war as a means of settling disputes'.[150] The Chinese were not in agreement. After the failure of the Great Leap Forward in 1958 and the resulting famine, Mao Zedong was more concerned with internal security than international prestige. Early in 1960 Mao advised Ho Chi Minh of Vietnam to discontinue his aggression against South Vietnam, to take a more 'flexible approach' while 'waiting for the right opportunities'.[151] Mao's attitude toward Vietnam would change in 1962, but faced with a short-lived détente between Washington and Moscow, Mao had no interest in shifting foreign policy. The good relations between Eisenhower and Khrushchev disintegrated quickly in the aftermath of the U-2 incident in May 1960 in which Captain Gary Powers was shot down and sentenced to ten years' imprisonment by a Soviet military court. At the end of 1960, Boland having been elected president of the GA in September by a large majority, Ireland voted once more for the proposal to bring the question of China's representation at the United Nations. Boland's first day on the job also resulted in the admission of eleven new African States. Ireland's day in the sun had at last come.

CHINESE RECOGNITION ISSUES, 1960–63

In September 1959 Bishop James A. Walsh of the Maryknoll (USA) Mission was arrested in China. Bishop Walsh was 68 years old and had been on mainland China since 1918. Walsh would spend twelve years in a Chinese prison. The Department of External Affairs, with the help of Freddie Boland at the United Nations, produced a statement of protest to the Walsh imprisonment.

> The sentence passed by a Communist Chinese Court on the Most Reverend Dr. Kung Pin-Mei, Bishop of Shanghai, and the Most Reverend Dr. Walsh, Titular Bishop of Sata, cannot but evoke feelings of abhorrence in the minds of all those throughout the world who regard freedom to worship God in the manner that He Himself has ordained as the inalienable right of man, respect for which is essential to the preservation of peace among nations. This sentiment is felt particularly in Ireland which has always stood for freedom of worship and has never failed to rally to its defence when denied or threatened elsewhere.
>
> The Irish people are convinced that these two prelates and the Chinese branch of the Irish Legion of Mary are being persecuted not for plotting with foreign powers against the regime in Peiping, but for their efforts to uphold the rights of the Chinese people to religious and personal liberty.
>
> We pray that the example and sufferings of these noble men will help the Chinese people to secure recognition for the fundamental human rights which are gradually being accorded to all peoples throughout the world.[152]

Conor Cruise O'Brien, who made a notation on Boland's letter to Secretary Con Cremin, expressed disbelief that the Irish government would forward the governmental statement to Cardinal Spellman of New York and Cardinal Cushing of Boston.

> Am I alone in feeling that there is something excessive in sending such statements to these cardinals? We carry oral statements, after all, in our Bulletin which goes to both of them. To draw their attention especially to it might be taken as indicating a nervous desire to placate and retrieve past 'errors'. No?

Both Spellman and Cushing had criticized the members of the Irish delegation, and especially Frank Aiken, in their handling of the Chinese representation question of 1957.

The department also sent copies of the statement to all Irish missions, including thirty copies for New York, twenty-eight copies for Washington, and two copies for Rome. Cardinal Cushing of Boston replied on 24 March, thanking Boland for the 'magnificent statement' and adding: 'Happy to know of the leadership that the Irish Delegate at the UN has assumed in recent times.'[153]

In 1961, the General Assembly addressed the Chinese representation question in a slightly different manner than in years past. In the sixteenth assembly, New Zealand asked that the 'Question of the Representation of China in the United Nations' to be placed on the agenda. The next day, the Soviet Union asked for an item, entitled 'Restoration of the Lawful Rights of the People's Republic of China in the United Nations', to be placed on the agenda as well. The General Committee recommended the placement of the two items on the agenda. Due to the presence of several new member states added during Boland's term as president, both items became part of the sixteenth Session. Ireland voted for the New Zealand resolution and against the Soviet resolution.

The recognition issue of the People's Republic of China versus the Republic of China momentarily settled. The Department of External Affairs undertook a review of all recognition policy beginning in July 1962. The general agreement in the department was to recognize the state of China *de jure* and the government of the PRC and the ROC *de facto*. This was Ireland's own interpretation of the international law, and although entirely politically motivated, it proved to be an effective mechanism – at least until 1964 when the recognition problem opened once again upon France's recognition of the PRC.

Leading up to a Memorandum for the Government issued in May 1963, overhauling and clarifying recognition issues that have been described in other chapters of this book, one frustrated diplomat in the Department of External Affairs summarized what he found to be an exhaustive search of the Chinese recognition issue:

> One of the problems here is that I can find no record of a clear and responsible decision regarding our recognition position of the two China Governments. Mr. Kennedy's note of 30/9/55 on this side of file states "in the case of the two Chinas we recognise neither Government". Mr. Horan's circular to missions of 10/10/55 states that "Ireland recognizes neither Peking nor the Formosa regime". Dr. MacWhite's note of 18/1/56 indicates that we do not recognise Formosa. Miss Murphy's note of 7/11/56 states that D. C. Circular 6/56 corrects the statement in the note circulated to missions on 10/10/55 that we no longer recognise the Nationalist Government of China. The circular referred to said that "we continue to recognise that Government (Formosa) as the Government of the Republic of China". I am unable to trace a Governmental or Ministerial decision to back up that statement in the circular. In fact Dr. Rynne in his minute of 27/10/56 on this file says "my recollection is that we <u>firmly</u> declined, during the Second World War, to give any recognition to Chiang Kai-Shek [sic]...The position has been that we have had correspondence from representatives of

the Formosa Government which we have acknowledged and replied to but we have always resisted their approaches to (a) establish diplomatic relations and (b) to conclude a trade agreement with them. On the other hand, we have never acknowledged any communications from Peking... Therefore, my interpretation is that to date we have continued to recognise the State of China, have accorded *de facto* recognition to the Formosan Government and have not recognised Peking *de facto*.[154]

The resulting Memorandum for the Government emphasized recognition of the state of China *de jure* and *de facto* recognition for both Beijing and Taipei.

During the ensuing years, Irish diplomats were involved in several initiatives concerning China, most notably Frank Aiken's 'Two China Plan' at the United Nations in 1964. Ireland followed the policies of the United States closely during the 1960s and 1970s, recognizing Beijing as the sole government of China in 1979. The history of the protracted process which followed is the subject of a current study.

Table 5.1
Countries which recognized the People's Republic of China between 1949–64

Country	Recognition	Diplomatic relations
USSR	2 Oct 1949	3 Oct 1949
Bulgaria	3 Oct 1949	4 Oct 1949
Romania	3 Oct 1949	5 Oct 1949
Hungary	4 Oct 1949	6 Oct 1949
Czechoslovakia	5 Oct 1949	6 Oct 1949
North Korea[1]	5 Oct 1949	6 Oct 1949
Poland	5 Oct 1949	7 Oct 1949
Yugoslavia	5 Oct 1949	10 Jan 1955
Mongolia	6 Oct 1949	16 Oct 1949
East Germany[2]	27 Oct 1949	27 Oct 1949
Albania	21 Nov 1949	23 Nov 1949
Burma	16 Dec 1949	8 Jun 1950
India	30 Dec 1949	1 Apr 1950
Pakistan	5 Jan 1950	21 May 1951
United Kingdom	6 Jan 1950	17 Jun 1954
Ceylon[3]	7 Jan 1950	17 Feb 1957
Norway	7 Jan 1950	5 Oct 1954
Denmark	9 Jan 1950	11 May 1950
Israel[4]	9 Jan 1950	Jan–Feb 1992
Afghanistan	12 Jan 1950	20 Jan 1955
Finland	13 Jan 1950	28 Oct 1950
Sweden	14 Jan 1950	9 May 1950
North Vietnam[5]	15 Jan 1950	18 Jan 1950

Country	Recognition	Diplomatic relations
Switzerland	17 Jan 1950	14 Sep 1954
Netherlands	27 Mar 1950	19 Nov 1954
Indonesia	13 Apr 1950	9 Jun 1950
Nepal	1 Aug 1955	1 Aug 1955
United Arab Republic[6]	16 May 1956	30 May 1956
Syria	3 Jul 1956	10 Aug 1956
Yemen	21 Aug 1956	24 Sep 1956
Cambodia	18 Jul 1958	23 Jul 1958
Iraq	18 Jul 1958	25 Aug 1958
Morocco	31 Oct 1949	1 Nov 1958
Sudan	29 Nov 1958	1 Dec 1958
Guinea[7]	4 Oct 1959	4 Oct 1959
Ghana	5 Jul 1960	5 Jul 1960
Cuba	2 Sep 1960	28 Sep 1960
Somalia	14 Dec 1960	16 Dec 1960
Senegal[8]	14 Mar 1961	–
Tanzania[9]	9 Dec 1961	–
Laos	28 Jun 1962	28 Jun 1962
Algeria	3 Jul 1962	3 Jul 1962
Uganda	18 Oct 1962	18 Oct 1962
Kenya	14 Dec 1963	14 Dec 1963
Burundi	23 Dec 1963	23 Dec 1963
Tunisia	10 Jan 1964	10 Jan 1964
France	27 Jan 1964	27 Jan 1964
Congo (Brazzaville)[10]	18 Feb 1964	22 Feb 1964
Central African Republic	27 Sep 1964	29 Sep 1964
Zambia	25 Oct 1964	29 Oct 1964
Dahomey[11]	12 Nov 1964	12 Nov 1964

1   Democratic People's Republic of Korea.
2   German Democratic Republic.
3   Present-day Sri Lanka.
4   Although Israel recognized the PRC as a state in 1950, diplomatic relations were not established until 1992. During the same period (1993), Israel established relations with India, Mongolia, Vietnam, Cambodia and Laos.
5   Democratic Republic of Vietnam.
6   The United Arab Republic (UAR) was a state that existed as a union between the republics of Egypt and Syria between 1958 and 1961. Egypt continued to be known as the UAR until 1970.
7   Present-day Equatorial Guinea
8   In 2005, the Republic of China (Taiwan) had formal diplomatic relations with 25 states. Senegal and Tanzania are among this group and do not have diplomatic relations with the PRC.
9   See note 8 above.
10 Present-day Republic of the Congo.
11 Present-day Benin.

Source: adapted from A.M. Halpern, ed., *Policies Towards China* (New York, NY: McGraw-Hill, 1965).

NOTES

1   Thomas W. Wilson, Jr. *The Great Weapons Heresy* (Boston, Houghton Mifflin, 1970), p. 50.

2   Robert A. Divine, Professor Emeritus of History at the University of Texas at Austin, described the American involvement in China as 'a romantic sympathy' in his foreword to Warren Cohen's text, *America's Response to China: An Interpretative History of Sino-American Relations* (New York, 1971), p. vii. 'Ever since Columbus sailed westward searching for a shortcut to Cathay, China has loomed large in the American experience ... But we soon developed an ambivalent attitude toward China. On the one hand, missionaries and merchants saw the American role as redemptive, remaking an ancient civilization along modern lines, but in the United States the Chinese immigrant met with ridicule and hatred, culminating in his exclusion in 1882 ... Although Americans frequently expressed a romantic sympathy for China, they rarely acted on it ... The ultimate act of rejection came in the Cold War years when the United States reacted to the triumph of the Communists by refusing to recognize Mao's regime and by aligning itself instead with the defeated and discredited Nationalists on Formosa.'

3   William C. Kirby, 'The two Chinas in the global setting: Sino-Soviet and Sino-American Cooperation in the 1950s', in Robert S. Ross and Jiang Changbin, eds, *Re-examining the Cold War: U.S.-China Diplomacy, 1954-1973* (Cambridge, MA, 2001), pp. 25–6.

4   See Michael Kennedy, 'The challenge of multilateralism: the Marshall Plan and the expansion of the Irish diplomatic service', in Till Geiger and Michael Kennedy, eds. *Ireland, Europe and the Marshall Plan* (Dublin, 2004), p. 110.

5   Ibid.

6   NAI DFA 410/132, memorandum, FC 1783/13 (CHI/7/51), 'The Treatment of Christian Institutions under the Present Regime in China', Foreign Office [London], Research Department, 29 August 1951.

7   See Wayne Flynt and Gerald W. Berkley, *Taking Christianity to China: Alabama Missionaries in the Middle Kingdom 1850–1950* (Tuscaloosa, AL, 1997), p. 297. Mary Horton Stuart was the mother of Leighton Stuart, a scholar and diplomat who lived in China most of his life, becoming president of Yengching University, and later serving as US Ambassador to China from 1946–52. Mao later called Leighton Stuart a 'loyal agent of US cultural imperialism in China upon Stuart's departure' (p. 327). A more recent argument concerning the conflict between the Catholic hierarchy and the Chinese government suggests: 'Precisely because it claimed for itself a quasi-religious status, the Maoist regime could not tolerate an independent Chinese Catholic Church'. See Richard Madsen, *China's Catholics: Tragedy and Hope in an Emerging Civil Society* (Berkeley, CA, 1998), p. 34.

8   Kennedy, 'The Marshall Plan and the expansion of the Irish diplomatic service', p. 127.

9   The Chinese proper names, places and terms used in this text follow the *pīnyīn* system, developed in China in 1958. However, in quotations containing primary sources, the spellings remain true to the original document. The spellings within the documents vary due to the evolution of the Romanization of the Chinese language, beginning in 1859 with Sir Thomas Wade's early system. In 1912, Herbert Giles produced a dictionary based on transcriptions of Wade's earlier work. The resulting spelling for Chinese words was known as the Wade-Giles system of Romanization. For many years, the Department of External Affairs relied on the Wade–Giles system. In 1928, the Chinese government officially adopted the National Romanization system based on Wade-Giles but written to distinguish the four tones of the Chinese language. This system was known as *Guóyu cídiãn*. In 1931, the China Inland Mission in Shanghai published R.H. Mathews' *Chinese–English Dictionary* that was often used by English-speaking writers until the 1970s. Some of the Chinese terms in department correspondence reflect the changes. In 1945 the United States War Department issued the anonymous *Dictionary of Spoken*

Chinese that contained both Chinese–English and English–Chinese sections. The distinguishing feature of the post-war dictionary was the use of monosyllabic and polysyllabic words rather than single characters to aide in colloquial pronunciation. The War Department dictionary was not widely used but served as the predecessor to a publication by the Institute of Far Eastern Language at Yale University entitled *Dictionary of Spoken Chinese* (1966). Currently Chinese writers use the newest edition of the *New China Dictionary* of *Xînhuá zìdiǎn* (first published in 1953 and primarily a dictionary of Chinese characters based on the old *Guóyu cídiǎn* system from 1928). In 1978 a more comprehensive *Dictionary of Modern Chinese* (or *Xiàndài hànyu cídiǎn*) entered circulation, and is now viewed as 'an outstanding example of lexicography'. See Jerry Norman, ed, *Chinese* (Cambridge, 1988), p. 180. See also San Duanmu, *The Phonology of Standard Chinese* (Oxford, 2000) and Hua Lin, *A Grammar of Mandarin Chinese* (Munich, 2001).

10   Coral Bell, 'China and the international order', in Hedley Bull and Adam Watson, eds, *The Expansion of International Society* (Oxford, 1984), p. 256.

11   Ibid.

12   Oi Ki Ling, *The Changing Role of the British Protestant Missionaries in China, 1945–1952* (Cranbury, NJ, 1999), p. 126.

13   NAI DFA 305/115/1, letter, Dr Fergus Murphy to Sheila Murphy, 28 October 1949.

14   See Kennedy, 'The challenge of multilateralism', p. 109.

15   NAI DFA 305/115/1, letter, Dr Fergus Murphy to Sheila Murphy, 28 October 1949.

16   Nancy Bernkopf Tucker, *Patterns in the Dust: Chinese–American Relations and the Recognition Controversy, 1949–1950* (New York, 1983), p. 101.

17   *Far East,* July 1952, p. 7.

18   *Far East,* July 1952, p. 6.

19   *Far East,* March 1949.

20   Gerrit W. Gong, 'China's entry into international society', in Hedley Bull and Adam Watson, eds, *The Expansion of International Society* (Oxford, 1984), p. 178.

21   In most all literature I have consulted on Chinese history of this period, Chiang Kai-shek's name is not given in the *pīnyīn* spelling, or Jiang Jieshi. A notable exception is found in Chen Jian, *Mao's China and the Cold War* (Chapel Hill, NC, 2001).

22   *Far East,* March 1949.

23   J.A.G. Roberts, *The Complete History of China* (Stroud, 2003), p. 312.

24   Jonathan D. Spence, *The Search for Modern China* (New York, 1990), pp. 385–6.

25   Jian, *Mao's China and the Cold War,* p. 22.

26   Nancy Bernkopf Tucker, ed., *China Confidential: American Diplomats and Sino-American Relations, 1945–1966* (New York, 2001), p. 36.

27   In *China Confidential*, Nancy Tucker provided a substantial note on the missionary situation in China in 1948. 'The American missionary community in China constituted the largest and wealthiest portion of the foreign missionary presence, numbering some 62 per cent of the Protestant missionaries. They ran 236 schools, 248 hospitals, 13 colleges, and 50 theological institutes, and operated activities related to the Young Men's Christian Association in 40 urban areas. American Protestant property in China was value at $70 million in 1949. The American share of Catholic holdings in China was also large.' Tucker, *China Confidential,* p. 36.

28   Tucker, *China Confidential,* p. 36.

29   Spence, *The Search for Modern China,* p. 118.

30   *Far East,* March 1949. The priests who escaped capture were Fathers Gerry O'Collins and Billy Walsh. The two others, Fathers Laffan and Linehan, were held for nine months by the Chinese revolutionaries.

31   Seanad Éireann – Volume 14 – 3 December 1930. Private business – safety of Irish missionaries in China.historical-debates.oireachtas.ie/S/0014/5.0014.19301200004.html.

32   Diarmuid Linehan, 'Bishop Galvin of Cork – Missionary' at Killmurry Parish Website. homepage.tinet.oe/~kilmurryonline/history/bishop-galvin/bishop-galvin.html.

Retrieved 8 October 2003. For other works on this period in St Columban missionary activities, see Thomas F. Ryan, *China Through Catholic Eyes* (Hong Kong, 1942); Edward Fischer, *Maybe a Second Spring: The Story of the Missionary Sisters of St Columban in China* (New York, 1983).
33 Note there are two distinct place names of Nanchang and Nancheng. Nanchang was the larger of the two and was occupied by the Japanese. Nancheng was the location of the Columban mission and was located southwest of Nanchang.
34 Charles H. Corbett, 'Conditions in Chekiang and Kiangsi', *Far Eastern Survey*, 12, 10 (17 May 1943), p. 96.
35 *Far East*, March 1949.
36 *Far East*, April 1949.
37 Tucker, *Patterns in the Dust*, p. 101.
38 Ling, *The Changing Role of the British Protestant Missionaries in China, 1945–1952*, p. 126.
39 *Far East*, April 1949.
40 Ibid.
41 Ling, *The Changing Role of the British Protestant Missionaries in China*, p. 127.
42 A copy of 'Files of Religious Persecution' may be found in NAI DFA 410/132, the China file. Other files include 'Religious Persecution in Yugoslavia – Resolution of Protest against Trial and Sentence of Archbishop Stepinac' in NAI DFA 410/37 and 'Persecution of the Church in Hungary – Arrest and Trial of Cardinal Mindszenty – Primate of Hungary' in NAI DFA 410/68.
43 *Far East*, May 1956, p. 17.
44 *Far East,* April 1956.
45 NAI DFA 305/115/1, map, 26 June 1950.
46 Quincy Wright, 'The Chinese Recognition Problem', *American Journal of International Law*, 49, 320 (1955), p. 321.
47 Tang Tsou, *America's Failure in China 1941–50* (Chicago, IL, 1963), p. 563.
48 Martin Walker, *The Cold War: A History* (New York, 1993), p. 63.
49 Jian, *Mao's China and the Cold War*, p. 52.
50 Ibid.
51 Walker, *The Cold War*, p. 63.
52 Tucker, *Patterns in the Dust*, p. 24.
53 Ibid.
54 Tucker, *Patterns in the Dust,* p. 24. Tucker notes that one US Senator, William Knowland (R, CA) advocated discontinuing the Marshall Plan aid if Britain recognized Beijing.
55 Tucker, *Patterns in the Dust*, p. 25.
56 Qiang Zhai, *The Dragon, the Lion, and the Eagle: Chinese–British–American Relations, 1949–1958* (Kent, OH, 1994), p. 33.
57 Quoted in Ibid. The statement originated in Bevin's position paper to the Cabinet, 'Recent Developments in the Civil War in China', 9 December 1948, CAB 129/31, C.P. (48) 299.
58 Ibid.
59 *The Times*, London, 12 January 1950.
60 Richard Harris, 'Britain and China: Coexistence at Low Pressure' in Abraham Meyer Halpern, ed., *Policies Toward China: Views from Six Continents* (New York, 1965), p. 17.
61 Ibid., p. 19.
62 After the Korean armistice in 1953, the British–Chinese relationship entered a new phase. At the 1954 Geneva Conference on Indochina, Anthony Eden, the Foreign Secretary, approached Zhou Enlai directly, chiding him for not having a Chargé d'Affaires in London. Beijing at last made a formal reply to the British notes, and Chargé d'Affaires were exchanged.
63 Edward R. Drachman, *Presidents and Foreign Policy: Countdown to Ten Controversial Decisions* (Albany, NY, 1997), p. 14.

64   Ibid., p. 35.
65   Ibid., p. 34.
66   *Memorandum for the Government*, 'Recognition of the Republic of the United States of Indonesia', NAI DFA 305/149 Part I, 2 January 1950.
67   Ibid.
68   NAI DFA 305/115/1, memorandum, Department of External Affairs to US State Department, 30 January 1950.
69   NAI DFA 305/115/1, Cremin to Boland, 4 February 1950.
70   NAI DFA 305/115/1, handwritten note in file by Boland, 6 February 1950.
71   NAI DFA 305/115/1, memorandum, US legation, Dublin to External Affairs, 23 February 1950.
72   Stewart Firth, *Australia in International Politics* (St. Leonard's, NSW, 1999), p. 13.
73   NAI DFA 305/115/1, letter, Seán MacBride to Krishna Menon, 26 June 1950. A personal letter followed this official one, spelling out the Irish missionary commitments. The number of Irish missionaries residing in China at that time was estimated to be 200 by the department.
74   NAI DFA 305/115/1, letter, T.J. Kiernan to Seán Nunan, 19 April 1951.
75   NAI DFA 305/115/1, extract of letter, C.J. Acton of Canada to T. O'Doherty, 11 September 1951. See also NAI DFA 408/114/5, letter, W.B. Butler to Secretary, Posts and Telegraphs, 8 June 1951.
76   For Canadian recognition policy toward the PRC, see John W. Holmes, 'Canada and China: the dilemmas of a middle power', in Abraham Myer Halpern, ed., *Policies toward China: Views from Six Continents* (New York, 1965), pp. 103–22.
77   NAI DFA 305/115/1, memorandum, Sheila Murphy to D.R. McDonald, 2 May 1952.
78   NAI DFA 305/115/1, letter, D.R. McDonald to John J. Hearne, 10 May 1952.
79   The priests were all from St Columban's including Patrick Roman of Kilkenny, John Casey of Galway, Owen O'Kane of Antrim and Patrick O'Reilly of Meath. Father Kavanagh had been the Superior of the Vincentian mission in Beijing.
80   NAI DFA 410/132, *Cork Examiner,* 'Cork Priest Tells of Red Terror in China, 16 September 1952.
81   NAI DFA 410/132, declaration, Cork Corporation, 23 September 1952.
82   NAI DFA 410/132, letter, Philip Monahan to Secretary, Department of External Affairs, 24 September 1952.
83   NAI DFA 410/132, article, *Irish Press*, 'Minister's reason for no protest to China', 15 October 1952.
84   NAI DFA 410/132, letter, W.P. Fay to Philip Monahan, 30 September 1952.
85   NAI DFA 410/132, letter, Joseph P. Walshe to William P. Fay, 18 October 1952.
86   NAI DFA 410/132, letter, Joseph P. Walshe to William P. Fay, 21 October 1952.
87   See Martin Gilbert, *A History of the Twentieth Century: Volume 3 1952–1999* (New York, 2000), pp. 24–5.
88   Ibid., p. 25.
89   NAI DFA 305/115/1, letter, John J. Hearne to Secretary, Department of External Affairs, 12 December 1952. Copies of this letter were sent to several different files.
90   NAI DFA 305/115/1, memorandum, 14 April 1953. Original found at NAI DFA 325/6/42.
91   NAI DFA 305/115/1, Department of External Affairs statement with no source, 14 May 1953.
92   Dwight D. Eisenhower, *Mandate for Change: 1953–56* (New York, 1963), pp. 248–9. President Eisenhower gave this explanation to Prime Minister Winston Churchill and Premier Laniel of France at the Bermuda Conference, 4–8 December 1953.
93   See John W. Garver, *The Sino-American Alliance: Nationalist China and American Cold War Strategy in Asia* (New York, 1997), pp. 53–4.
94   NAI DFA 305/115/1, internal memorandum, 'Attitude of the U.S.A. towards the admission of Communist China to the United Nations Organization', 1 August 1953.
95   NAI DFA 305/115/1, memorandum, 'Situation in Indochina', 15 April 1954.

96   See Klaus Larres, *Churchill's Cold War: The Politics of Personal Diplomacy* (New Haven, CT, 2002), pp. 341–55.
97   Ibid., p. 346.
98   See, for example, Philip C. Jessup, 'The two Chinas and US recognition', in *The Reporter* (6 July 1954), pp. 21–4. This article is found in NAI DFA 305/115/1.
99   NAI DFA 305/115/1, report, Frederick H. Boland to Department of External Affairs, 15 July 1954.
100   NAI DFA 305/115/1, report, Frederick H. Boland to Department of External Affairs, 18 August 1954.
101   See NAI DFA 305/115/1, confidential report, John H. Hearne to Secretary, Department of External Affairs, 2 March 1954.
102   See NAI DFA 305/115/1, confidential report, Séan Murphy to Secretary, Department of External Affairs, 26 March 1954.
103   NAI DFA 410/132, confidential letter, Michael Rynne to Ambassador, Madrid, 23 June 1954.
104   NAI DFA 305/115/1, report, Con Cremin to Department of External Affairs, 18 November 1954.
105   NAI DFA 305/149 Part I, letter, T.J. Horan to Dr Alfred Kolb, 5 September 1955.
106   NAI DFA 305/149 Part I, internal note, Department of External Affairs, 10 November 1955. A copy of the original letter to Kolb had been sent to all Irish legations and embassies, presumably as a statement of policy. This note also was sent to all diplomatic posts.
107   NAI DFA 410/132, letter, Con Cremin to Secretary, Department of External Affairs, 22 December 1955.
108   NAI DFA 305/149 Part I, memo and note, Sheila Murphy to Eoin MacWhite, 4 April 1956.
109   The United Postal Union, the International Trade Union, the International Labour Organization, and the World Health Organization.
110   NAI DFA 305/149 Part I, letter, Con Cremin to Secretary, Department of External Affairs, 7 February 1956.
111   NAI DFA 305/115/2, letter, Michael Rynne to Secretary, Department of External Affairs, 27 November 1956.
112   For an excellent account of Ireland's measures to integrate five hundred Hungarian refugees after the crisis of 1956, see Eunan O'Halpin, *Defending Ireland* (Oxford, 1999). pp. 295–6.
113   Keogh, *Twentieth-Century Ireland: Nation and State*, pp. 234–8.
114   Conor Cruise O'Brien, *Memoir: My Life and Themes* (New York, 1988), p. 181.
115   See Skelly, *Irish Diplomacy at the United Nations 1945–1965*.
116   Keogh, *Twentieth-Century Ireland*, p. 235.
117   O'Brien, *Memoir*, p. 185.
118   Ibid., p. 189.
119   Ibid., p. 190.
120   Cornelius C. Cremin, unpublished memoirs, p. 91. The author wishes to thank Professor Dermot Keogh for access and use of these memoirs.
121   NAI DFA 305/115/2, confidential letter, John J. Hearne to Secretary, Department of External Affairs, 13 June 1957.
122   Ibid.
123   It is interesting that India's policies toward China very often were similar to Britain. Cabinet minutes from 1950 reveal that the British government thought 'political considerations' might make it difficult for the United States to accept policies toward China. India 'would be useful' in aiding British policy decisions. Perhaps Indian policy was not as independent as perceived at the time. See H.J. Yasamee and K.A. Hamilton, eds, *Documents on British Policy Overseas,* Series 2, Vol. 4 (London, 1991).
124   K.P. Misra, *India's Policy of Recognition of States and Governments* (Bombay, 1966).
125   *FRUS 1955–1957* Vol. 11, pp. 506–7. Instruction from the Department of State to

Certain Diplomatic Missions, 10 October 1957.

126 White House Confidential Staff Notes, 1 October 1957. Found at galenet.galegroup.com on 7 October 2003, reproduced in *Declassified Documents Reference System* (Farmington Hills, MI, 2003).

127 *Dáil Éireann*, Vol. 164, 23 October 1957, Ceisteanna – Questions. Oral Answers. Government Policy at the UNO.

128 NAI DFA 305/115/2, letter, Leo T. McCauley to Secretary, Department of External Affairs, 26 October 1957.

129 NAI DFA 313/36A, confidential letter, Frederick H. Boland to Con Cremin, 9 May 1958.

130 *FRUS* 1958-60 Vol. 19, China, p. 137. Letter from Secretary of State Dulles to Prime Minister Macmillan of Britain.

131 Ibid.

132 *FRUS* 1958–60 Vol. 19, China, p. 165. Letter from Foreign Secretary Lloyd to Secretary of State Dulles, undated.

133 *FRUS* 1958–60 Vol. 19, p. 151. Telegram 547 from Moscow with text of letter dated 7 September 1958, Soviet Council of Ministers Chairman Nikita Khrushchev to President Eisenhower.

134 NAI DFA 305/115/2, statement, Frank Aiken to UN, 22 September 1958.

135 NAI DFA 305/149 Part I, note, January 1959.

136 *FRUS* 1958–60 Vol. 2, United Nations and General International Matters, p. 130. Telegram, Department of State to Mission at the United Nations, 17 April 1959.

137 Ibid.

138 *FRUS* 1958-60 Vol. 2, United Nations and General International Matters, p. 135. Telegram, Mission at the United Nations to the Department of State, 24 June 1959.

139 See John Kenneth Knaus, *Orphans of the Cold War: America and the Tibetan Struggle for Survival* (New York, NY, Public Affairs, 1999).

140 Peter Calvocoressi, *World Politics Since 1945* (London, 6th edn, 1991), p. 404.

141 Knaus, *Orphans of the Cold War*, p. 155.

142 See Skelly, *Irish Diplomacy at the United Nations 1945-1965*, pp. 171–87.

143 Ibid., p. 173.

144 NAI DFA 313/36B, confidential letter and position paper on Tibet, Frederick H. Boland to Con Cremin, 22 June 1959.

145 *FRUS* 1958–60 Vol. 2, United Nations and General International Matters, p. 142. Telegram, Department of State to Mission at the United Nations, 14 July 1959.

146 Skelly, *Irish Diplomacy at the United Nations 1945–1965*, p. 183.

147 *FRUS* 1958–60 Vol. 2, United Nations and General International Matters, p. 190. Telegram, Mission at the United Nations to the Department of State, 26 October 1959.

148 Ibid.

149 Skelly, *Irish Diplomacy at the United Nations 1945–1965*, p. 227.

150 Gilbert, *A History of the Twentieth Century, Volume Three*, p. 221.

151 Jian, *Mao's China and the Cold War*, p. 206.

152 NAI DFA 410/132, statement for the press, 19 March 1960.

153 NAI DFA 410/132, letter, Cardinal Richard Spellman to Frederick H. Boland, 24 March 1960.

154 NAI DFA 305/149 Part I, draft memo, 5 April 1963.

6

Non-recognition of Israel and the politics of prestige, 1948–63

Maintaining relations with other governments is normal behaviour within the international system, but there is no legal obligation to maintain diplomatic relations with another government. Some governments refrain from maintaining relations with particular governments because they see no need for such relations, or find it too costly; some because they wish to show their disapproval of those governments.

Louis Henkin, *International Law: Politics and Values*[1]

Recognition, in its various aspects, is neither a contractual arrangement nor a political concession. It is a declaration of the existence of certain facts. This being so, it is improper to make it subject to conditions other than the existence – including the continued existence – of the requirements which qualify a community for recognition as an independent state, a government, or a belligerent in a civil war.

Robert Jennings and Arthur Watts, eds, *Oppenheim's International Law*[2]

INTRODUCTION

Upon its declaration of independence on 14 May 1948, the Provisional Government of Israel immediately sought diplomatic recognition from countries around the world, including Ireland. *De jure* recognition for the State of Israel was declared by a small number of states but recognition of the provisional government was limited to as *de facto*. Recognition by the United States toward Israel has often been referred to as a *precipitate recognition*[3] as it occurred within eleven minutes of the Israeli declaration of independence.[4] Many governments hesitated in according *de facto* recognition to Israel, as did the Irish government. Ireland's approach to Israel's request was clearly encapsulated in a Department of External Affairs memorandum recommending that Ireland grant 'the virtual minimum of recognition' toward the new state that it was 'possible to concede'.[5] This policy ignored the concept of *de jure* recognition of the state and focused on recognizing the government *de facto*. There was no commitment to exchange diplomatic representatives or establish relations. The aim of Ireland's long-term policy of *de facto* recognition was meant to be *non-recognition*. The policy persisted until 1963 when, in a streamlined effort to establish more consistent recognition policy, Ireland recognized Israel *de jure*.

Several factors make Ireland's policy toward Israel unique. First, *de facto* recognition was maintained from 1949 to 1963 by a small number of Irish government officials whose justifications for the policy, although not anti-Semitic, stemmed from normative reasoning that viewed Israel as anti-Christian. Second, non-recognition endured as a policy in deference to the diplomatic wishes of the Holy See, in spite of the opportunity for independent Irish initiatives toward Israel. Third, even considering the ambiguities that arise when international recognition law is translated into foreign policy practice, Ireland's position was legally and politically untenable. As the years passed, many officials within various government departments, but especially External Affairs, knew that the policy was untenable, yet were reluctant to change it. On the surface, the rationale for *de facto* rather than *de jure* recognition is easily explainable: Ireland insisted on guarantees from the Israeli Government for protection of the Holy Places in and near Jerusalem.[6] Upon examination of the diplomatic recognition files, however, the Holy Places thesis becomes transparent and another rationale emerges: the refusal to recognize Israel *de jure* from its independence in 1948 to 1963 reflected a desire to delay Israeli diplomatic representation in Dublin, a political manoeuvre motivated by the fear of rising 'Jewish influence' in Ireland.

BIRTH OF THE STATE OF ISRAEL

No example of state creation in the twentieth century is more emotionally charged than the case of Israel. Chaim Weizmann's statement to the Peel Commission in 1936 – 'Have we the right to live?' – highlighted the plight of European Jews trying to immigrate to Palestine before the Second World War.[7] Although Theodor Herzl and others demanded a Jewish state during the First World Zionist Congress in 1897, the imperative gained critical mass only after 1945 as a means of assuaging the collective guilt of Western civilization for the atrocities of the Holocaust. During the years 1945–47, the majority of the remaining Jewish population in Europe migrated to Palestine, the United States or to other states. The indigenous population of these countries, especially in western Europe, often feared the influx of the Jews. Likewise, in Ireland hostile attitudes towards Jews were prevalent but hushed during the post-war period.[8]

Between 1920 and 1936 almost 165,000 Jews were admitted into the British-controlled mandate of Palestine.[9] The 1922 census in Palestine estimated there were 83,790 Jews living there among 598,177 Moslems and 71,464 Christians. By 1924, the harsh Johnson Act in the United States reduced the quota of new immigrants admitted to the United States. Over 37,000 European Jews had been admitted to Palestine since 1919. This figure swelled to 70,000 Jewish immigrants between 1924 and 1928. By 1935, after the rise to power of Adolph Hitler in Germany, there were over 320,000 Jews in Palestine, compared to the overwhelming majority of Muslims numbering 826,457.[10]

Many of the new Jewish settlers took up residence in the vicinity outside the walled city of Old Jerusalem in an area called the New City, or West Jerusalem. Their presence was a persistent threat to the Arab-controlled Old Jerusalem (East Jerusalem) and riots often erupted between Arabs and Jews. The British, claiming Palestine from Turkey as a result of the First World War, attempted to preserve the status quo arrangements for rights of ownership and administration of the Holy Places in Jerusalem, regulated by an 1852 statute of the Ottoman Sultanate.[11] The British commissioned several studies of the problem, the last being the Peel Commission in 1936–37. After hearing evidence predominantly provided by the Jews in Palestine, the Peel Commission concluded that the problem between the Arabs and Jews in Jerusalem, and in other parts of Palestine, was intractable.[12] The 'practicable' solution was a partitioned state.

To no one's surprise, the indigenous Arabs did not accept partition as a solution, denouncing the concept of a national home for the Jews. The proposed solution of the Peel Report (1938) included 'Trans-Jordan and a Jewish state in those areas of Palestine where the Jews already made up a clear majority of the population'.[13] In addition there would be a 'Jerusalem enclave' to include the holy city, to be administered by an international authority. The Zionist leaders, Chaim Weizmann and David Ben-Gurion, were willing to accept a partitioned Palestine, knowing that force was more useful than negotiation in setting territorial limits.[14]

Finding themselves a target of continued hatred by both the Arabs and the Jews during the term of the League of Nations mandate, the British instead issued a White Paper in 1939 that ignored calls for a partitioned Palestine as outlined by the Peel Commission, declaring Britain would 'set up one independent Palestinian state in ten years in which Arabs and Jews [would] share in government in such a way as to ensure that the essential interests of each community are safeguarded'.[15] Further, in order to preserve the proportion of Arabs to Jews, the British enforced limitations on Jewish immigration to 75,000 over the next five years. After 1944, it was proposed, 'no further Jewish immigration [would] be permitted unless the Arabs of Palestine [were] prepared to acquiesce to it'.[16]

The intervening war years changed the attitude of the British toward Palestine. As one author describes, the British were 'shattered by Arab resentment, international condemnation, growing terrorist attacks from Jewish extremists, and the cost of maintaining a 100,000-man peace-keeping army in Palestine'.[17] After the Potsdam Conference in July 1945, President Truman informed the US press that he had asked the British 'to allow into Palestine as many Jews as possible'.[18] By October 1945, Foreign Secretary Ernest Bevin retorted by proposing an Anglo-American committee to 'involve the Americans responsibly' in the problem of Palestine and the immigration of 'displaced persons'.[19] Although considerable objections were mounted in the United States, including a scathing letter from Eleanor Roosevelt to Truman[20] on the subject, President Truman accepted Bevin's proposal. The resulting committee presented its report on 20 April 1946, providing ten recommendations, including the resettlement of 100,000 Jewish 'displaced persons' into Palestine by the end of 1946.[21]

By May 1946 the figure of 100,000 was, as Cohen describes it, 'an anachronism', for the refugees from pogroms in Poland now totalled over 250,000. In the following months, the British proposed a new scheme, 'whereby Palestine would be given a federal government in which there would be semiautonomous Jewish and Arab provinces'.[22] The Americans jumped on the scheme, soon to be called the 'Morrison-Grady scheme for provincial autonomy'. But the Zionists were convinced that the new plan attempted to perpetuate the British mandate, and the White House was 'flooded with telegrams and letters demanding that the President repudiate it'.[23]

Under severe political pressure from Jewish organizations and fearing a loss of Democratic votes in the upcoming Congressional elections, on 4 October 1946, the eve of the Jewish holiday Yom Kippur, President Truman issued the following statement:

> The British Government presented to the [London] Conference the so-called Morrison Plan for provincial autonomy and stated that the Conference was open to other proposals. Meanwhile, the Jewish Agency proposed a solution of the Palestine problem by means of the creation of a viable Jewish state in control of its own immigration and economic policies in an adequate area of Palestine instead of the whole of Palestine. It proposed, furthermore the immediate assurance of certificates for 100,000 Jewish immigrants ... it is my belief that a solution along these lines would command the support of public opinion in the United States. I cannot believe that the gap between the proposals which have been put forward is too great to be bridged by men of reason and goodwill. To such a solution our Government could give its support.[24]

From the date of the Yom Kippur statement in October 1946, President Truman's policy clearly advocated a 'national home' for the Jews. By February 1947, the British had relinquished the problem of Palestine to the United Nations. George W. Ball, the American diplomat, described the dilemma of the resulting United Nations Special Committee on Palestine (UNSCOP) in 1947:

> Britain's decision to leave put the burden on the United Nations and the other leading powers to determine who should govern Palestine after the British departed. There were two practical solutions: either to partition the mandate and thereby create two nations; or to maintain the unity of the

land, which, under democratic rules, meant giving control to the Arab majority. It was far from an easy choice. When the British had offered partition in 1937 [after the Peel Commission report], the Arabs had indignantly rejected it; when the British backtracked and favored a unitary state in 1939 [found in the White Paper proposal], the Zionists cannonaded them with abuse.[25]

On 31 August 1947 UNSCOP submitted its recommendation: partition Palestine into two separate states, linked in economic union. The report suggested that Jerusalem be 'internationalized'. During the autumn, the General Assembly debated the issue. The Arab states and Britain obstinately refused the partition compromise. The United States in principle supported the recommendations of UNSCOP, yet the top-ranking diplomats, George F. Kennan of the State Department's Policy Planning Staff and Secretary of State George C. Marshall, were opposed to partition. President Truman remained undecided until he received a letter of appeal from his long-time friend and former business partner, Eddie Jacobson. On 5 October 1947, Truman instructed Secretary of State George Marshall 'to make public American support for partition'.[26]

During a secret lunchtime meeting on 19 November, Truman met with Chaim Weizmann to discuss the territorial partition, including the Negev region. Weizmann convinced Truman that the Negev desert, which some thought more useful to 'Arab herdsmen... than use by Jewish colonies', would be made fertile and would provide an alternate route to the Suez Canal.[27] The Negev objections foreshadowed a miserably flawed territorial settlement. On 29 November 1947, the United Nations General Assembly adopted Resolution 181(II), partitioning Palestine and awarding 56.47 per cent of territory to the Jewish state.[28] George Ball summarized the territorial imbalance that was prejudicial to the Palestinians:

> Both Arabs and Jews agreed that the boundaries as drawn were unworkable. As delineated by UNSCOP, these boundaries would have given the Jews access to their properties along the Jordan Valley only through a tiny passageway southwest of Nazareth, while the Arabs would hold equally tiny corridors connecting their holdings in West Galilee or Gaza with the West Bank. The city of Jaffa would become an Arab enclave in the middle of the Jewish coastal plain; Jerusalem would remain a pocket of Jewish settlers completely surrounded by Arabs in an internationalized city.[29]

Although Ireland was not a member of the United Nations in 1947, and played no role in the UN resolution, by December reports were sent to Iveagh House from the Irish diplomats in Ottawa and Washington concerning the viability of the solution.[30] The difficulties inherent in a forced territorial settlement between the Jews and the Arabs in Palestine were compared to Ireland's own imposed partition dilemma.

ATTITUDES FORESHADOWING IRISH POLICY ON ISRAEL

At the beginning of the Palestine crisis, the Irish government's attention focused on guarding against the implications that rising Jewish nationalism in Palestine might have for Irish citizens at home. On 17 October 1946, writing from his new post at the Holy See, Ambassador Joseph P. Walshe, former Secretary to the Department of External Affairs in Dublin, sent the following letter to Frederick H. Boland, his successor in Iveagh House:

> My dear Secretary,
> It is always interesting to know the reactions of our people when they travel abroad, and to see how these reactions affect their attitude towards Ireland. In recent weeks, as you know, I have met a large number of Irish priests and nuns visiting Rome for the purpose of their Orders, in most cases to elect a new Superior General. All of them without exception spoke in terms of the highest praise of the Taoiseach and the Government, and of the manner in which difficulties were being surmounted and real progress achieved. Indeed, if the religious orders are a good indication of the mind of the Church in Ireland, the Government has its complete confidence.
> Speaking of the difficulties facing the Government, they were unanimous in thinking that something ought to be done to prevent the jews buying property and starting or acquiring businesses in Ireland. There was a general conviction that the jewish influence is in the last analysis anti-Christian and anti-national, and consequently detrimental to the revival of an Irish cultural and religious civilization. Some of them say that jewish materialism encourages communism (not an unusual view here). They were also generally perturbed by the influx of British subjects who are purchasing Irish property.
> These comments were made with the full recognition that there was a real problem which had to be solved somehow, and not in any way through lack of loyalty or sympathy. I am sure the Taoiseach would wish me to pass on these views of Irish men and women holding the highest positions in their respective orders. Although my natural reaction to sympathetic critics is to ask them to formulate a precise plan, I could not but be struck by the fact that, in their view, our only serious problem was the jewish infiltration. It is one of the problems in all other Western European countries, where it is very much graver than in Ireland, but all these countries have infinitely graver tasks before them.
>
> Yours sincerely,
>
> [signed] J.P. Walshe[31]

The letter was received in Dublin one week later and marked 'copy for Taoiseach', most likely by one of Boland's assistants. Walshe assumed that

Boland would 'pass on' the views of the visiting clergy to Eamon de Valera. Instead, a further notation on the letter read: 'copy not sent to Taoiseach on recommendation by secretary'. Walshe's fear of 'jewish infiltration' was thus contained by Boland's better judgement. Clearly, Walshe's concern was not the growing immigration of European Jews to Palestine, but rather the influx of Jewish refugees into Ireland. As will be seen, Walshe was influential in setting the initial policy toward Israel in 1948–49.

Although official governmental policy allowed for the immigration of 10,000 refugees into Ireland beginning in early 1946, other attitudes toward Jewish refugees within the Irish government echoed Walshe's concerns.[32] The wording of a draft memorandum from the Department of Justice was doctored from the blatant 'restrict the immigration of Jews' to a more subdued tack: 'immigration of Jews is generally discouraged'.[33] Eamon de Valera's 'liberal and generous'[34] immigration policy was not well received by all departments within the Irish government, which may explain Boland's tactful handling of Walshe's letter.

The uneasiness of Ireland's ultimate position concerning Israel (refusing to recognize Israel as a state *de jure* until long after it was legitimately established) stems from the ironic absence of a sympathetic echo supporting self-determination – either for the Jews or the displaced Palestinians. But if proponents of Irish foreign policy failed to notice the similarities inherent in the diaspora of both nations, as well as the effects of imposed partition upon the Palestinian Arabs, neither the Jews nor the Palestinians were oblivious to the parallels.[35] Yitzak Shamir recalled in his memoirs that he chose 'Michael' as his *nom-de-guerre* in the underground organization *Lehi* (the force formed by Abraham Stern in 1940 and known pejoratively as the Stern Gang) because he 'was stirred in some special manner by what [he] had read about Michael Collins, the Irish leader'.[36] Chaim Herzog, who spent much of his childhood in Dublin, remembered that his father 'was an open partisan of the Irish cause' and that the Herzog name 'is still associated with those who fought for liberty'.[37]

The parallels in rhetoric were apparent. In the post-war, Cold War atmosphere after 1946, however, the drafters of Irish foreign policy could not contemplate taking an independent position based on self-determination ideology. Ireland had no voice in the United Nations since it did not become a member until 1955, nor was it on the best of terms with the United States or Great Britain.[38] The Irish thus were not direct participants in solving the international puzzle of Palestine. They did, however, receive intelligence reports, as mentioned earlier, from Washington and Ottawa throughout 1947 that were placed into a file entitled 'The UNO and Palestine', which forms the core working file concerning the diplomatic recognition of Israel.[39]

Dáil records reveal one reference to the Palestine question in 1947, found under the topic 'Jewish immigration to Palestine'. The debate showed the limited extent to which Ireland had a stake in the problem, namely, the supposed embarrassment caused by the TD Robert Briscoe, who was accused by the ever-virulent TD Oliver Flanagan of advocating a homeland for Jewish refugees.[40]

Eamon de Valera dismissed the allegation that Briscoe had personally been involved in negotiations between the United States and Britain during the Morrison-Grady talks concerning the immigration of 100,000 Jews to Palestine in 1946. For de Valera, however, the issue of Jews in Palestine had strong emotional connotations due to his personal relationship with Briscoe and the former Chief Rabbi of Ireland, Isaac Herzog. Chaim Herzog, the latter's son, described the relationship of the three men in his memoir:

> My father was an open partisan of the Irish cause. When Irish prisoners went on a hunger strike, he pleaded with them to cease endangering their lives...The outstanding Jewish leader in the revolution was Robert Briscoe, later a member of the Irish Parliament (the Dáil) and lord mayor of Dublin (his son, Ben Briscoe, also became lord mayor). The Jewish community as a whole gave a lot of help to the Irish. After the establishment of the Irish Free State, when Eamon de Valera was in the opposition, he would come to visit, usually with Robert Briscoe, and unburden his heart to my father. He obviously never forgot these sessions, because in 1950, after the State of Israel was established, de Valera was one of the first foreign statesmen to visit. He dined with Ben-Gurion and Bobby Briscoe at my parents' home in Jerusalem.[41]

In the years immediately following the Second World War, de Valera did not concentrate on Palestine. The majority of the archival material concerns the Jewish refugee situation in Europe and its implications for Ireland. Dermot Keogh, whose research examined the interplay of the Departments of Justice and External Affairs in refugee policy, concluded that de Valera's government 'failed to respond generously' to the post-war problem of refugees.[42] In fact, when Rabbi Herzog requested assistance from de Valera after the war, the responses wired to Herzog suggested 'doing everything possible', while the reality was 'no action is fine'.[43] The position of the Irish government toward refugees foreshadowed its lack of responsiveness toward a national home for the Jews. The rhetoric masked an attitude of fear and uncertainty toward Jews within Ireland and unwillingness to enter into any diplomatic relationship with Jews in Palestine.

Although Ireland had no interest in participating in the politics of Palestine, Joseph Walshe knew that standing behind Vatican policy would gain prestige for Ireland. After twenty-four years at Iveagh House, Walshe accepted the ambassadorship to the Holy See as a farewell assignment. Walshe was exceedingly prepared for the post by his skill at procedural diplomacy, yet his worldview was somewhat limited by his dedication to, and duration at, Iveagh House. During the latter stage of his career, his analyses were riveted with personal, often parochial judgements. His personal opinions concerning Israel were eventually incorporated into Irish foreign policy with little questioning.

Aside from Joseph Walshe's vociferous campaign against anything Semitic at the Holy See, to complicate matters, three months before the end of the British mandate, Eamon de Valera's government fell. In February 1948 Fianna Fáil was replaced by an eclectic grouping of five parties referred to as the first inter-party government, which was led by the new Taoiseach, John A. Costello of Fine Gael. As many authors of Irish domestic politics have written, the new government was not elected on any platform except one to shake Fianna Fáil out of power. The implications of the change in government for the Department of External Affairs were significant. For the first time since Patrick McGilligan's tenure as Minister of External Affairs ended in 1932, someone other than Eamon de Valera was in control of Irish foreign policy. The leader of the Clann na Poblachta Party, Seán MacBride, who became Minister for External Affairs and approached the difficulties in Palestine with ambivalence, replaced De Valera. Foreign policy decision-making in the new Irish government did not attract the scrutiny of other states, and, as a result, recognition policy went unnoticed. For the government, rhetoric championing the protection of the Holy Places in Palestine camouflaged a policy of aloofness toward Israel.

THE QUESTION OF THE HOLY PLACES – 1948

In the months leading to the establishment of Israel in May 1948 the task of implementing the partition plan became extremely difficult. The commission sent to implement and supervise partition could not begin operations in Palestine for two reasons. First, Britain would not transfer authority until the official end of the mandate on 14 May 1948. Second, the partition decision was a catalyst for what the commission identified as 'virtual civil war' in Palestine.[44] Critical to the partition issue was the status of Jerusalem. The United Nations Resolution 181(II) called for the internationalization of Jerusalem and the protection of the Holy Places. In other words, Jerusalem would be a *corpus separatum* under the supervision of the Trusteeship Council of the United Nations. The initial response of the international Christian community to the developing crisis in Palestine, led by the Vatican and including Ireland, was to ensure the safety of the Holy Places in the region.[45] Chaim Weizmann, elected the first President of Israel in 1948, described the confusion associated with the term Holy Places, remarking that 'although the Vatican had never formulated any claims in Palestine, it had a recognised interest in the Holy Places. But then practically all of Palestine could be regarded as a Holy Place.'[46]

The UN resolution created considerable uncertainties for most states in developing recognition policy toward the new Jewish state. When the British flag was lowered on 14 May 1948 and David Ben-Gurion announced the independence of the State of Israel later that same day, as mentioned above, the United States immediately granted 'full recognition' of the State of Israel and recognized the 'Government of Israel' *de facto*. Several states followed with *de facto* recognition, including the Soviet Union three days later. Poland,

Czechoslovakia, Uruguay and Nicaragua were among the other forerunners in recognizing Israel. Czechoslovakia, which participated in gunrunning for the Israelis, announced *de jure* recognition on 19 May. The Catholic countries of South America, including Venezuela, Paraguay and El Salvador, granted *de facto* recognition in the first few months after Israel's declaration of independence. Canada granted *de facto* recognition in December 1948. The western European states, especially those with Catholic populations, were much slower to address the issue. Britain, due to its sensitive relations with the Arab states, faced a particularly difficult challenge and withheld *de facto* recognition until January 1949.

On 28 May 1948 Ireland received a telegram sent the previous day from Moshe Shertok (later, Sharett), the Foreign Secretary of the Israeli provisional government, asking that 'Eire may grant official recognition to [the] state of Israel and its provisional government'.[47] On 4 June the Irish government discussed the cable's contents. In a memorandum circulated to his cabinet colleagues the previous day, Seán MacBride proposed 'that no action be taken on the telegram apart from the appropriate acknowledgement', meaning that only confirmation of its receipt should be forwarded to Israel.[48] The cabinet duly approved MacBride's recommendation.[49] Throughout the summer neither the Department of External Affairs nor the Taoiseach's office reconsidered the issue of recognizing Israel. However, significant intelligence gathering continued within the department.

William Warnock, a seasoned diplomat who had been stationed in Germany during the Second World War, reported on the Israeli situation from his post as Chargé d'Affaires in Stockholm. On 29 May 1948 the UN Security Council adopted a resolution calling for a four-week truce between the warring Arabs and Israelis, appointing a mediator to oversee the maintenance of the cease-fire as well as to make recommendations for a permanent solution. Count Folke Bernadotte, a well-respected Swedish diplomat, was appointed to the post. Warnock wrote to Dublin that 'Bernadotte considers his chance of success is about one percent'.[50]

The Security Council resolution also called for a cessation of all military shipments to the area.[51] The Israeli army took advantage of the lull in fighting, which lasted from 11 June to 9 July, 'to replenish [its] equipment with weapons procured from diverse sources around the world'.[52] In Iveagh House there was confusion on whether the Security Council resolution applied to Ireland, since it was not a member of the United Nations. While the truce was in effect, a member of the United States legation in Dublin, Edward McLaughlin, visited the department on 17 June to determine whether or not Ireland was complying with the arms embargo.[53] McLaughlin's primary interest was to monitor illegal flights travelling through Irish airports. External Affairs replied that it had received no official communiqué from the United Nations, but the government would, nevertheless, abide by the terms of the Security Council resolution.[54]

Less than a month later McLaughlin became specifically interested in flights

from Miami to Israel.[55] His memorandum to External Affairs reported that three
B-17 'Flying Fortresses' had left Miami without proper clearance and were
believed to be intended for use as bombers for the transport of munitions within
the Middle East. Reports in the *New York Times* traced the bombers up the
eastern coast of the United States, after which they disappeared.[56] In reality there
were four bombers, American-made but purchased in Mexico to be sent to
Israel. One B-17 was intercepted at Halifax, Nova Scotia. The three remaining
unauthorized planes flew to Czechoslovakia where they were armed with
bombs. Given their intermediate destination, it is possible the planes flew the
southern transatlantic route, through the Azores instead of Shannon. However,
that explanation is doubtful since the planes were flown to Canada first. By the
evening of 15 July they had bombed Cairo on their way to Israel.[57]

In McLaughlin's haste to find the 'Flying Fortresses', he missed transactions
taking place right under his nose. In the summer of 1948 Aer Lingus was eager
to sell several spare Vickers 'Vikings'.[58] A shortage of spare parts for the reliable
DC-3 caused Aer Lingus to purchase seven 'Vikings'. The 'Viking' was
developed from the Wellington bomber and proved very expensive to operate.
In 1948 Aer Lingus solved the DC-3 problems and accepted bids for the sale of
the 'Vikings'. In the midst of a second UN truce, which lasted from 18 July to
15 October 1948, two of the planes were sold to an 'Egyptian air company'. On
30 August Con Cremin, an Assistant Secretary in Iveagh House, recorded his
uneasiness with the transaction:

> On Friday afternoon 20 August Mr. Devlin telephoned from [the London
> embassy] to say that...he had approached the British authorities for
> permission for two Vikings, which were being ferried to Egypt to be taken
> over by an Egyptian air company which had bought them, to land in
> Tripoli and Libya, but that he had been told that such permission would not
> be granted...as Britain, in common with other members of the United
> Nations, was bound by a resolution of the United Nations which imposed
> an embargo on the transport of arms and equipment, including civil
> aircraft, to the Arab states and Palestine...On Saturday morning 21 August
> Mr. Shanagher [from Industry and Commerce] telephoned to say that Aer
> Lingus and the Department of Industry and Commerce were rather worried
> about the news from London as the proposal [by Egypt] to buy the aircraft
> was the only reasonable [offer] received.[59]

The next few lines of Cremin's note illustrate Ireland's ability to exploit
ambiguities in international law during this period, a pattern repeated
throughout its policy of non-recognition of Israel:

> [Mr. Shanagher] wondered whether, in the circumstances, there would be
> any objection to sending the planes via Spain and Italy, neither of which is
> a member of the UN. I informed him that I had, in the meantime,

ascertained that we had received communication of the UN resolution concerned and the government had contemplated observing it, but that no definite action had been taken.[60]

In the final action, Minister Seán MacBride approved the departure of the planes to Egypt, 'provided there was no suggestion that the government had approved their course'. Secretary Boland advised 'that it was essential to avoid any publicity whatever'. The files do not show whether the planes were diverted through Spain or Italy, but a history of Egypt Air (Misr Air) shows that ten Vickers 'Vikings' were put into service in 1949.[61]

Cremin's note concerning sale the planes is remarkable in several ways. First, it shows a lack of coordination between the Department of External Affairs, the Department of Industry and Commerce and Aer Lingus. Second, during this period Israel was scrambling for arms and equipment, but the airplanes were sold clandestinely to Egypt. Third, Cremin wrote the note one week after the diversion of the planes occurred. It is possible that he was contemplating whether to make an entry in the files at all. Fourth, although Iveagh House assured Edward McLaughlin that Ireland would comply with the terms of the truce, Cremin noted that 'the government had contemplated observing it, but that no definite action had been taken'. Finally, it is evident that McLaughlin did not know of the Aer Lingus transaction. On 28 August he sent a memorandum to the Department of External Affairs requesting the Irish government's help in surveillance, inspection of cargo and personnel in 'clandestine air operations of American planes by American citizens between points outside the United States'.[62] McLaughlin, intent on solving the puzzle of the 'Flying Fortresses', missed the sale of the 'Vikings' completely.

THE VATICAN AND ISRAEL – 1948

By September 1948 Israel's government was stable and its position as a sovereign state was in less doubt. Count Bernadotte worked throughout the summer on a plan for Jerusalem and the Holy Places, submitting his report to the United Nations on 16 September. His plan included a new partitioning of Palestine and the repatriation of 360,000 Arabs. The plan was very unpopular with the Lehi, however. Coming only four months after Israeli independence, the underground forces saw it as a certain threat and assassinated Bernadotte on 17 September.[63] Yitzak Shamir recalled the incident in his memoirs, bluntly writing:

> The *Yishuv* [Jewish population] were appalled [by Bernadotte's plan]; somewhere, it was thought, the British – with whom Bernadotte had close connections – were pulling the strings. At all events, Lehi believed it was imperative for the plan to be shelved and Bernadotte removed from the

arena... he was warned... But Bernadotte was sure that with this Plan he was entering history and he paid no heed. On 17 September 1948, he was shot and killed in Jerusalem... Lehi took no responsibility for the deed... Our opinion was asked and we offered no opposition.[64]

Although David Ben-Gurion's provisional government detained members of Lehi and disbanded the Irgun, another paramilitary organization, the murder provoked considerable outrage against Israel within the international community.

Bernadotte's assassination certainly did not make it any easier for other states to recognize Israel. The number of states doing so had continued to rise throughout 1948, but Britain, France, the Netherlands, Denmark, Norway, Sweden, Switzerland, Italy, Spain, Greece and many Central and South American countries still hesitated. The Irish diplomats abroad were faced with routine procedural questions about Israel and its membership on international organizations. The Irish legation in Switzerland, for example, questioned Ireland's position on Israel's application to the Universal Postal Convention. Sheila Murphy prepared a memorandum for Secretary Boland on the subject.[65] Miss Murphy, without the assistance of the legal adviser, Michael Rynne, suggested that Ireland follow the position of France, Italy and others in withholding a decision on the application. Her rationale was that Ireland 'should not wish to express disapproval and we could hardly be the only non-recognising state to approve'. Sheila Murphy's instinctual reaction was reinforced by the published position of Pope Pius XII (Eugenio Pacelli).[66] In his Encyclical Letter, '*In Multiplicibus*' dated 24 October 1948, the Pope expressed his continued concern for the safety of the Holy Places: 'It would be necessary to assure, with international guarantees, both free access to Holy Places scattered throughout Palestine, and the freedom of worship in respect of customs and religious traditions.'[67] Although unknown to Sheila Murphy and others in the department at the time, the Holy See's statement of October 1948 pre-empted any alternative Irish foreign policy initiative toward Israel until 1963. American diplomats in Rome summed up the Vatican's position in a telegram to the State Department:

[Monsignor Domenico] Tardini,[68] Vatican Acting Secretary of State received me this morning to give me in strict confidence Pope's views on Jerusalem. He said:
1. Vatican in view position taken respectively by Arabs and Jews in Palestine considers internationalization Jerusalem and outskirts most appropriate solution in present circumstances to ensure peace, order, tranquility in Palestine.
2. Vatican maintains rights traditionally enjoyed by Catholics in Palestine must be fully respected and protected, especially with regard to holy places.
3. Vatican has no particular preference with regard any specific manner

whereby Jerusalem and environs would be placed under international control provided such control would effectively protect Catholic interests ...

Tardini emphasized his opinion not only Latin America but Christendom at large would heartily welcome placing Jerusalem and environs under international control and likewise, with international guarantees giving free access to holy places throughout Palestine.[69]

Not only was the Holy See cementing its position toward Israel, but also the Arab countries were confronting the reality that the State of Israel was not going to disappear. In a report from the Irish legation in Spain, one diplomat relayed the disheartened comments of an Egyptian diplomat returning to Cairo:

The Chargé d'Affaires saw no hope of any permanent settlement being made between the Arabs and Jews. He said that Egypt was quite convinced that the Jews meant to take not only all of Palestine, but to advance in every other direction as far as they could. There were no bounds to their ambitions to territorial aggrandisement ... As things were, all the Arab League could do was to make all possible appeals to UNO ... but more particularly to the USA and the Western European Powers to impress on them the future menace what a powerful rampant Israel could mean. He had no confidence that these appeals would bear fruit, due to the powerful influence of the Jews in so many countries. All he felt that Egypt would ever have, at some not too distant date, would be the melancholy consolation of saying 'I told you so'.[70]

In the last months of 1948, after a year of upheaval in Palestine, the issues of Israeli statehood, protection of the Holy Places and diplomatic recognition were more complicated than when the partition resolution was presented to the United Nations in 1947. Israeli triumphalism countered Arab dissolution. The United States and the Soviet Union eyed Israel as a proving ground for Cold War policy. At the same time, Britain and the other European countries knew that a decision on recognition was required in order to stabilize relations with both the Arabs and Israelis. The Vatican, meanwhile, maintained its uncompromising position: no recognition of Israel until it guaranteed the internationalization of Jerusalem and the protection of, and free access to, the Holy Places throughout Palestine.

IRELAND GRANTS *DE FACTO* RECOGNITION – 1949

For Ireland the issues of Israeli statehood, protection of the Holy Places, the status of Jerusalem and diplomatic recognition remained unsolved. Ireland could have chosen any argument concerning Israel, including the Arab position that the partitioning of Palestine was illegitimate, as were the resulting territorial conquests by Israel. Partition rhetoric was abundant in Seán MacBride's department in 1948–49. Conversely, the drafters of Irish foreign policy could have capitalized on the diaspora argument and championed a national homeland for the Jews. Instead, Ireland chose the position of the Holy See as a basis for its policy toward Israel. Not only did the Holy Places argument win prestige for Ireland from the Holy See, but also the placing of such a condition on recognition meant that Ireland would not be entering into diplomatic relations with Israel in the immediate future. One may even argue that the unspoken aim of the policy was to prevent 'Jewish infiltration' into Ireland by prohibiting diplomatic relations.

Until January 1949 the Department of External Affairs played a waiting game with the issue of Israel. Then Joseph Walshe began to wrestle his own demons. Toward the end of the month, with Britain's *de facto* recognition of Israel imminent, he sent a series of letters to Secretary Boland. On 20 January he advised against joining a proposed Catholic-nations *démarche* on Jerusalem, since the Vatican Secretary of State, Monsignor Domenico Tardini, had told him that Ireland 'would be more influential on its own'.[71] Walshe was convinced that by working in this singular capacity Ireland could exert pressure on other states to follow the 'thesis' of the Vatican on internationalization and he provided Boland with a list of rationalizations to prove his point:

> Our position *vis-à-vis* America and Australia enables us to exercise persuasive influence on the two governments to accept the thesis of the Holy See that Jerusalem should be ruled internationally and Catholic nations given an important place on the ruling body... [which] would not necessarily be composed exclusively of [United Nations] members. Indeed, I gather... that the [Holy See] would like to see us on it and probably Spain.[72]

Walshe felt compelled to remind Boland that the crux of the problem for the Holy See was 'at the very least they regard [Israel] as anti-Roman Catholic', thus echoing the irresponsible comments he made in his 1946 letter ('the jewish influence is, in the last analysis, anti-Christian and anti-national and, consequently, detrimental to the revival of an Irish cultural and religious civilization'). Walshe also commented on what steps he felt should be taken to reconcile Ireland's position toward Israel.

> I see from the Jewish press that some of the [Israeli Government] ministries [have] already been transferred to Jerusalem from Tel Aviv, and there does [not] seem to be any doubt that it is [the] intention of the Jews, while the going is good, to establish the capital in the Holy City at the first possible opportunity... It seems the prospect of an international regime is getting darker every hour, and it may be better for the Holy See to take half a loaf. Certainly there is little prospect of securing the adhesion of the

American and British governments for an international regime. The powerful Jewish propaganda has become too strong for both of them, and they couldn't stand up to the accusation of trying to deprive the Jews of their ancient capital... One has the feeling that we have to [go] slowly just now rather than walk into a morass, with or without bad company.[73]

On 22 January Walshe sent Iveagh House another letter. The urgency for Walshe, and the sense of haste in his letters, stemmed from his notion that the Department of External Affairs should not follow Britain's lead without prior counsel from the Vatican. Walshe suggested that the 'form of the British declaration will provide us with some guide... whether Jerusalem is being regarded by the [Americans] and [British] as an integral part of the [Israeli] state'.[74] Following Britain's formal announcement, Walshe promised to 'ascertain from the Vatican and inform you by cable what their attitude would be in face of the taking over of the whole of Palestine, including Jerusalem, by the Jews'.[75]

The British decision to grant the minimal *de facto* recognition ignored the status of the Negev in the southern-most region of partitioned Palestine. President Truman acceded to Chaim Weizmann's arguments for the Negev in October 1947. But in September 1948, Israel reassured Britain that the Negev would be transferred to the Arabs under the 16 September plan of Count Bernadotte's mediation mission. The Negev would go the Arabs, and in return, Israel would receive Galilee. Jerusalem, under the plan, would remain under UN control. This bundle of conditions did not take into account Israeli intentions in the Negev, or the Arab hold on Galilee. Foreign Secretary Ernest Bevin reluctantly supported the plan. From the British viewpoint it formalized partition and served to 'burn His Majesty's Government's boats with the Arabs'.[76] The British asked the United States to formally support Bernadotte's plan as well. The Americans agreed in principle, apart from a strip of land in the northern Negev where many Jewish settlements were located. President Truman's position, however, was that the Israelis should not have territorial settlements dictated to them. Truman, in a post-election euphoric mood, wrote to Chaim Weizmann in November 1948:

I remember well our conversation about the Negev, to which you referred in your letter [5 November 1948]. I agree fully with your estimate of the importance of that area to Israel, and I deplore any attempt to take it away from Israel. I had thought my position would have been clear to all the world... Since your letter was written, we have announced in the General Assembly our firm intention to oppose any territorial changes in the November 29th [1947] Resolution which are not acceptable to the State of Israel.[77]

The British considered the Negev to be of vital strategic interest to them, as it contained the important land bridge between two colonial allies, Egypt and

Transjordan. Ronald Campbell, the British Ambassador to Egypt, considered a policy of unilateral action to drive the Israelis out of the Negev. He commented:

> If the Jews are permitted to seize and hold the whole of the [Negev] not only will our strategic position in the whole region be hamstrung but politically we shall be pretty well bankrupt in this part of the world.[78]

Despite the intentions of Britain and the United States, in a series of campaigns in October and December 1948, the Israeli military conquered the Negev. Michael Cohen argues that the British were not capable of coming to terms with the new Israeli state and could not 'brush aside the mutual suspicions nurtured so intensively'.[79] Beginning in January 1949 the British tried one final diplomatic initiative to persuade the United States to adopt the British point of view on the strategic importance of the Negev. From 12–29 January the British met with US officials in Washington to identify common interests in the Middle East, but the process become merely symbolic. President Truman knew as early as November 1948 that the United States would extend *de jure* recognition after Israeli elections to be held in early 1949. Truman wrote to President Weizmann that the United States would use the Israeli election date of 25 January as 'a definite target date for extending de jure recognition'.[80] Bevin addressed the House of Commons on 18 January, bringing *de facto* recognition one step closer with a reference to 'the Government of Israel'.[81] In an effort to solidify Britain's position, Bevin sought an American public statement declaring that Britain and the United States had a common policy toward the Middle East. On 24 January, Truman approved a draft announcing that the objectives of the two governments were similar.[82]

Britain and the United States planned a simultaneous recognition plan for Israel – the United States granting recognition *de jure* and Britain offering limited *de facto* recognition. On 29 January 1949 Britain granted *de facto* recognition to Israel. The United States followed on 31 January, granting *de jure* recognition to both Israel and Transjordan.[83] In January and February, several other states also granted varying degrees of recognition.[84] By February 1949, it was clear that Ireland would have to make a decision as well.

On 27 January Secretary Boland received Count Ostroróg, the French Ambassador, at Iveagh House. The French envoy explained that his government faced a considerable challenge in Palestine – trying to maintain functional relationships with the Palestinian Arabs while protecting the French Catholic religious and educational establishments in Israel – and so the French, like the British, decided to grant *de facto* recognition to the government of Israel. The Count mentioned that the French viewed the United Nations as 'the appropriate body to assume the responsibility' of internationalizing Jerusalem.[85] When Ostroróg asked Boland what Ireland planned to do, Boland replied that the matter was 'under consideration' but for Ireland, 'the question was now less one of substance than of timing'. Boland's methodical approach to the issue was in sharp contrast to the over-zealousness of Walshe. On 28 January Boland sent Walshe a report of the meeting with Ostroróg.[86] The next day Britain granted *de facto* recognition to Israel.

Interestingly, the internationalization of Jerusalem and the Holy Places was not presented to the Irish public as a rationale for non-recognition of Israel. The Irish press reported on the appointment of a new Chief Rabbi of Ireland, Immanuel Jakobovits, with headlines such as 'Recognition of Israel: Irish attitude surprises Rabbi' and 'Chief Rabbi hopes Eire will recognise Israel'.[87] The rationale that Jakobovits had assumed drove the government's policy played well with the Irish public: 'I expect the reason [for not granting recognition toward Israel] is that Ireland, being a partitioned country, is rather slow to recognise a state that is based on partition.'[88] Jakobovits' assertion, however, was inaccurate: Ireland's official policy toward Israel still hung on the internationalization of Jerusalem.

In the meantime, on 5 February, after the *fait accompli* of British recognition, Walshe wrote to Boland offering a new, bizarre justification for the continuing non-recognition of Israel:

> On the question of doctrine, you know that the Arabs have always believed and advocated the immaculate conception of our Lady, whereas the Jews have always adopted the most insulting attitude towards this doctrine. That is one of the strongest reasons why the Holy See hates to have any truck with the Jews.[89]

Walshe again asked Boland to reconcile any decision on Israel with the wishes of the Holy See, and said that if Ireland did grant *de facto* recognition to Israel it should be conditional on 'the rights of Catholics to approach the Holy Places and to celebrate the Sacred Mysteries'.[90]

As Walshe put pressure on Boland to make a decision compatible with the Vatican's policy, Boland did research on his own. He asked Michael Rynne, the Department of External Affairs' legal adviser, for his opinion. Rynne, not unaccustomed to providing advice in the area of international law, reasoned that *de facto* recognition was the 'virtual minimum' and that the idea of 'conditional recognition' would be 'improper' under international law.[91] (See Appendix 1.) He suggested that if Ireland 'were to attach... a condition about the preservation of the Holy Places we should... be going too far below the minimum prescribed by commonsense and normal practice'. Rynne clarified the point:

> Commonsense indicates that since *de facto* recognition is recognition of a state of fact, no extra conditions or proviso would ever be relevant in the context. A condition, or string, to the government's recognition ought therefore not to be announced in the actual instrument whereby its recognition is accorded to the Israeli Government.[92]

Rynne also advised that if questions should arise in the Oireachtas concerning the Holy Places, reference should be made to the Israeli government's promise 'to safeguard the sanctity and inviolability of the shrines and Holy Places' given in Shertok's original telegram in May 1948. To bolster the government's position, Rynne suggested that an official press release should explain 'why full recognition of Israel is not yet being granted'.

Rynne addressed one final issue that turned the problem of recognition on its head. He stated that it was 'not easy to defend mere *de facto* recognition of the Israeli Government at this advanced stage'. He was convinced that if Britain were to later grant *de jure* recognition Ireland would be 'bound' to withdraw or complete its own recognition. If the Irish government was not prepared to either provide *de jure* recognition at some later date or withdraw recognition altogether, then the 'onus [would] immediately rest upon [the Department of External Affairs] to show why we are going thus far, but no farther just now'.[93] Rynne was aware that only *de jure* recognition would eliminate considerable legal difficulties in the future. A citizen of a non-recognized state would have no standing in Irish courts. Irish citizens doing business with Israel would encounter considerable risk in establishing trade relationships with a non-recognized state, since they would not have access to Irish courts.[94]

Boland concurred with Rynne's commonsense conclusions. After considering the legal adviser's submission, he sent his own memorandum to Seán MacBride on 11 February proposing that the Irish government:

> decide to recognise *de facto* the state of Israel. It is suggested that the decision should be announced by the Taoiseach tomorrow night at the dinner for the new Chief Rabbi of Ireland [Jakobovits], and that a telegram should be despatched to Mr. Shertok, the Israeli Foreign Minister, tomorrow.[95]

Boland explained that recognition should be limited to *de facto* status, even though the United States had announced *de jure* recognition of Israel on 31 January, since France and Britain had 'not yet accorded' full recognition due to the internationalization issue. He reasoned that 'as public opinion here would probably expect this country to be not less zealous in endeavouring to secure proper provision for the future of the Holy Places', granting *de jure* recognition 'might possibly invite attack and criticism'. The cabinet met on 11 February 1949 and granted *de facto* recognition to the state of Israel.[96] The decision was announced to the public the following day.[97]

Joseph Walshe hoped that any form of recognition toward Israel would be delayed as long as possible. Walshe thus was concerned when he received a telegram from Iveagh House stating that *de facto* recognition had been accorded. In a letter dated 24 February the Ambassador asked Secretary Boland for an explanation, emphatically urging that the Government withhold *de jure* recognition 'until the guarantees are defined and are accepted by the HOLY SEE'.[98] Walshe's primary concern was the possible loss of prestige in the Vatican. Walshe was convinced that Ireland should continue to support the internationalization issue and would gain prestige only if *de jure* recognition were delayed. In his familiar tone of rationalization, he assured Boland that the question of the Holy Places has 'in it all the elements which make it an ideal case for championing by our Minister'.[99]

Boland also sent a letter to Walshe on 24 February, their letters crossing in the post. The Secretary explained that 'everything that could reasonably be done' was carried out before the decision was made, including requesting assurances on the protection of the Holy Places from the Israeli government through diplomatic channels in Washington and London.[100] To placate Walshe's vanity, Boland suggested that Ireland could 'exert an indirect pressure by withholding the *de jure* recognition which the Israeli Foreign Minister [had] already solicited'. Interestingly, the files suggest that Walshe began to lose interest in 'championing' the Holy Places issue once the *de facto* decision was made. By the end of September 1949, Walshe had dropped the initiative entirely.

STATUS QUO FOR THE HOLY PLACES – 1949

The situation in the Middle East appeared to stabilize in the spring of 1949. Israel was admitted to the United Nations on 11 May 1949. Schoenbaum argues that the internationalization of Jerusalem was subsumed under Israel's growing strength:

> By the spring of 1949, the situation had seemingly crystallized for years to come. First was the question of Jerusalem. Its division looked solid enough. On the other hand, internationalization seemed ever more remote. Historical associations aside, wartime experiences had settled the question for both sides. 'No government in Israel which agreed to [internationalization] would last five minutes', John H. Hilldring informed Dean Acheson. It remained for both Israel and Jordan to struggle for their respective shares.[101]

When the Spanish and Italians once again proposed unified action by the four Catholic European countries (Spain, Italy, Portugal and Ireland) during the spring of 1949, Walshe was skeptical. He reported to Dublin that a meeting that had been arranged between the four was not productive:

> We had one meeting, at which the Italian Ambassador did not turn up. It was declared by the Portuguese and Spanish Ambassadors to be a private conversation, a definition to which I could oppose no objection. Before the arrival of the Spaniard, the Portuguese told me that the Italian wasn't coming because he didn't want to be mixed up in talks with the Spaniard.[102]

Apart from the political infighting, Walshe and the Spanish Ambassador, Count Tovar, exchanged views on the Vatican's continued course toward the internationalization of Jerusalem, despite the 'repercussions on the part of the Jews against Catholicism'.[103] The talk did not lead to a more hopeful solution than before. Walshe attached a note to the letter that provided a suggestion to Iveagh House:

> For the moment I think we should wait until we are asked for *de jure* recognition by Israel and then, if the Minister agrees, I could say to them 'What exactly would you like us to say to the Israel Govt.?...' I wish I could feel absolutely certain that they were not trying to use other States and individuals only in such a way as to be able, in the end, to secure all the KUDOS for the Holy See itself.[104]

In Dublin, other forces were at work. Archbishop McQuaid made an appeal to Chief Rabbi Jakobovits to provide a 'firm and authentic guarantee' from the Israeli government toward internationalization of Jerusalem, which would 'allay our fears'.[105] Throughout the summer, the correspondence between Walshe and Iveagh House continued on the Holy Places issue. Referring to the stalled Catholic initiative, Walshe admitted, 'We shall no doubt see better counsels prevail in the Vatican when someone plucks up the courage to talk frankly to the HOLY FATHER, and then all those countries like Spain which are so whole hog, in private especially, will find themselves let down with a bang.'[106]

The files suggest that Joseph Walshe lost interest in the Holy Places initiative after September 1949. But just before Walshe abandoned the issue, one further development added a new argument, confusing the problem.

LINKING RECOGNITION OF ISRAEL TO PARTITION

Not surprisingly, MacBride inserted a well-worn argument that reflected his foreign policy theme as Minister of External Affairs: the linkage of Ireland's own partition problem to negotiations concerning Israel. But it should be remembered; during 1949 MacBride linked partition to almost all Ireland's diplomatic efforts.[107]

In a recent study, Ronan Fanning remarked that the foreign policies of the First Inter-Party Government (1948–51) contained 'surrealist simplicities' that included MacBride's persistent linkage of partition to Ireland's cooperative activities with other states.[108] Freddie Boland, as Secretary of External Affairs from 1946–50, managed to keep the policy scales in balance, even during the unsettling period of the Costello/MacBride government. But it might be argued that in spirit, MacBride's attempts at linkage, making 'deals' that would cross over normal issue boundaries, were efforts that might have propelled Ireland into interdependent relationships with other states, had they been successful. More often that not, however, MacBride's attempts, whether in a public forum like the Council of Europe, or in secret negotiations with officials of other states, were detrimental to Ireland's prestige in the system. Fanning cites MacBride's linkage of NATO membership with partition. Another example is in recognition of Israel, in which MacBride, spurred on by the input of Conor Cruise O'Brien in Washington, saw an opening for a lobby in the United States on partition. The formula seemed simple enough: recognize Israel and have the Jewish lobby on Ireland's side in the partition issue.[109]

During the summer of 1949, the archival files show that Irish diplomats in Washington pursued the American Jewish lobby, and to a limited extent, they were successful at highlighting the parallels between Irish partition and Israeli statehood. On 13 July 1949, Seán MacBride delivered a carefully worded speech for domestic consumption in the Dáil concerning the Holy Places, delivered on the same day as the 'Vatican Decree on Communism'.[110] The Irish embassy in London sent a copy of MacBride's speech to the legation of Israel.[111] The following week, on 21 July 1949, Congressman Arthur Klein of New York addressed the US House of Representatives:

> Mr. Speaker, it is not new or startling for me to restate the often-noted parallel between the history of the Jewish Nation and Ireland. Nevertheless, the parallel is so striking that it can bear repeating. Both nations have suffered under the heavy hand of the British Empire. Both nations, under the extremes of adversity, have kept alive the eternal flame of independence and liberty. Both nations, in spite of the broken promises of England and with the sympathy of world opinion, have achieved their dream of freedom. Yet both nations still find the dreams made rough by the arrogant antagonism of Great Britain, even though England has lost the imperial effort to block nation aspirations completely.[112]

The bases of Congressman Klein's remarks were two Department of External Affairs bulletins on the subject of 'what Britain has taken from the Irish nation by partition'. Conor Cruise O'Brien sent Klein's remarks to Iveagh House, suggesting to both Boland and MacBride that the parallel between Ireland and Israel 'raises a propaganda angle which we have, perhaps, insufficiently exploited'.[113] MacBride seemed confident with the approach, yet Secretary Boland was not so eager, advising Conor Cruise O'Brien:

> I would feel bound to advise [MacBride] against the making of any open gesture of friendship to Israel as long as the problem of the Holy Places – to which the Pope has devoted three allocutions and one encyclical within the space of 10 months – has reached some kind of solution.[114]

Conor Cruise O'Brien then spoke with Seán MacBride. Immediately following the meeting, MacBride composed a letter to Joseph Walshe at the Holy See on the proposition of linking recognition to partition:

My dear Joe,

Following upon the speech I made in the Dáil on my Estimate, relating to Palestine and the Holy Places, I have been approached by a number of prominent jewish people here who are anxious to know if they could assist in any way. I have also recently been approached with a view to granting De Jure recognition to Israeli. [sic]

In the course of various discussions particularly with Mr. Sayers[115] I urged the advisability of reaching a settlement with the Holy See in regard to the Holy Places and indicated that I would gladly do anything I could to bring about a settlement. To-day Mr. Sayers came to see me and informed me that he had been in direct contact with the Israeli Government and was authorized to say that the Israeli Government would welcome direct negotiations with the Holy See concerning the Holy Places, and would be glad if I could ascertain what the Holy See's reactions would be in the matter.

All this was verbal and Mr. Sayers has no written authorization. He offered, without any request from me, to obtain a written communication from the Israeli Government. I did not encourage this suggestion as I felt that it would be wiser first to find out the reactions of the Holy See to such a suggestion. In the meanwhile I thought it better to leave the matter completely informal. I feel, however, that Mr. Sayers was in a position to speak with a degree of authority on behalf of the Israeli Government.

Could you ascertain from the Secretariat what the reactions would be to the opening of direct negotiations concerning the Holy Places between the Holy See and the Israeli Government...It may well be that I am walking where angels fear to tread and that all this ground has been gone over before and been rejected by the Holy See for some good reason...It would be, of course, of tremendous importance if we were in a position directly or indirectly to bring about negotiations and an ultimate solution of this question. In addition to our direct interest in the Holy Places from a prestige point of view if would be of great importance.[116]

At the end of the letter, Minister MacBride addressed the issue that was foremost in his mind, although he tried to minimize the urgency:

From another angle we have also a considerable interest in bringing about a settlement of this question between the Holy See and the Israeli Government. With the development of the Anti-Partition campaign in the United States it would be a help if we were in a position to accord De Jure recognition to the Israeli State. I feel that pending the settlement of the issue concerning the Holy Places that [sic] I would be faced with some difficulty in granting De Jure recognition. The settlement of this question and the granting of De Jure recognition would be very important factors aligning the Jewish population and influence in the United States with the Irish American movement. Were it not for the difficulty concerning the Holy Places they would be our natural allies in the United States as they are violently opposed to Britain and are a powerful influence in the Democratic Party.[117]

MacBride's rapprochement with Israel stemmed from the same diplomatic conundrum that President Franklin Roosevelt faced in allying with the Soviet Union in 1941. For MacBride, to negotiate the coup of ending partition with the help of the Jewish lobby in Washington, he might have agreed with Roosevelt: 'to cross this bridge I would hold hands with the Devil'.[118] But in August 1949, the international efforts for a *corpus separatum* in Jerusalem were losing ground for two reasons. First, the Vatican did not want to accept the proposal of the Palestine Conciliation Commission (PCC), specifically a provision that would have given the Arabs and Israelis 'limited sovereignty' in their respective zones in Jerusalem. The view from the Vatican, expressed by Acting Secretary of State Monsignor Tardini, insisted upon an international regime and not simply international control by the United Nations.[119] Second, by 14 September, the US State Department concluded that 'the establishment of a Jerusalem regime in the nature of a *corpus separatum* under the United Nations is entirely impracticable' due to the financial burden on the United Nations and the fact that Israel would find the solution 'unacceptable'.[120] Without the support of the United Nations, the United States or Israel, a *corpus separatum* would prove impossible.

Walshe replied to MacBride that within the Vatican there existed division on the solution for the Holy Places, and that the 'very radical statements' of Pope Pius XII did not represent the views of Mgr Tardini, and especially not Mgr Montini.[121] For almost a year Walshe had championed the cause of a *corpus separatum* for Jerusalem, setting a deferential foreign policy on Israel to win prestige at the Holy See. Sensing the waning importance of the Holy Places issue in September 1949, Walshe's final paragraph to MacBride illustrated his sense of fatalism in the secular environment of the Cold War:

> One thing is quite clear to me, that the French, Spanish and Italians will never see eye to eye on the Holy Places issue. Each of them will try to win for itself some kind of influence through interfering in religious matters, which the British and Americans can acquire by simple power pressure.[122]

Ironically, Ireland held out longer than any of the other Catholic countries, including Spain, Italy and Portugal, in refusing to recognize Israel. From September 1949 to May 1963, the challenge in Irish diplomacy was to maximize non-diplomatic relationships with the Israelis, specifically trade, while adhering to the non-recognition rhetoric of Joseph Walshe.

IRISH NON-RECOGNITION AND TRADE WITH ISRAEL

Many variations of *de facto* recognition existed in the case of Israel. For example, France established diplomatic relations with Israel after granting only *de facto* recognition.[123] In legal matters, the case of *Luther* v. *Sagor* (1921) established the principle that no distinction should be made in legal consequences of a government, whether recognized *de facto* or *de jure*.[124] Because the *Luther* v. *Sagor* principle was not tested in Ireland during the period 1949–63, whether the principle would have been applied to Israel is difficult to establish. The importance of *de facto* recognition and trade in the Irish/Israeli non-recognition period is due to the zeal of Irish diplomats in avoiding the appearance of *de jure* recognition, or what they interpreted in that period as *implied* recognition. Unlike other states who merely hesitated on *de facto* recognition, the Irish made a strict non-recognition policy within the Department of External Affairs.[125] Convincing the Department of Finance that care should be taken in avoiding the appearance of *de jure* recognition required Iveagh House's diligence in the early years of non-recognition.

Although Ireland limited recognition of Israel to *de facto* status in February 1949, the diplomatic straightjacket did not seriously impact trade between the two states. The Foreign Trade Committee, beginning in the summer of 1949, was lured by the prospect of trade with Israel. As early as December 1948, an Israeli delegation headed by Joseph Fisch, Trade Commissioner for Israel in Britain and A.S. Cohen of the Tel Aviv Chamber of Commerce, arrived at the Irish Department of Agriculture discussing the export of kosher meat.[126] The Israeli delegation was specifically interested in canned meat and frozen meat, as well as condensed milk and ware potatoes. Trade was to be based on barter, as the Israelis were short of sterling and dollars. Generally, the Irish government discouraged barter trade, but the Israelis were told that private traders could arrange two-way trade, which 'would balance'.

> It was pointed out to Dr. Fisch that there should be no difficulty from the point of view of his Government since they could secure ample sterling by the sale of oranges and fruit here and then utilise the sterling so acquired for the purchase of tinned meat, potatoes or other goods. A list of Irish goods available for export was handed to Dr. Fisch.[127]

But thoughts of trade became difficult in light of Ireland's trade agreement with Britain. 'Licences to export canned Kosher stewed steak from this country will not ordinarily be granted but special consideration will be given to the issue of an export licence... in any case in which 100% payment in USA dollars is forthcoming.'[128]

A newspaper article appearing in an Israeli newspaper March 1949, one month after Ireland's *de facto* announcement suggested that Iceland, Ireland and Israel could participate in the exporting of iced fish and export meat.[129] But when the Israelis offered to buy seed potatoes, they were refused due to the export quotas to Britain and Europe.[130] In June 1949, however, meetings conducted between Fisch and the Department of Agriculture produced a tentative export list for goods to be sent to Israel:

Frozen Kosher Beef – not more than 500 tons on the condition that payment is made 100% in US dollars.

Potatoes – 2,500 tons of seed potatoes – payable in sterling.

Dried milk – 500 tons of full-cream milk powder. Prices in sterling FOB Cork or Rosslare – Dungarvan Creamery Co., Waterford, and Ballyclough Creamery, Mallow.

After submitting the financial terms to the Department of External Affairs, on 27 August 1949 an agreement was reached to sell '500 tons of frozen Kosher carcase beef and 1000 head of [Kerry] cattle to be exported either alive or as frozen'.[131] During these trade negotiations, Dr Fisch stated that Philip Sayers was fully authorized to act on his behalf and on behalf of the Israeli government. 'He requested that accordingly any further dealings in the matter between your Department and his Office should be made with Mr. Sayers.'[132] Iveagh House's acceptance of Philip Sayers to negotiate between Dublin and Israel proved to be problematic but provided comic relief to the Foreign Trade Committee minutes for almost two years.

THE FOREIGN TRADE COMMITTEE AND ISRAEL

Throughout the autumn of 1949, the United Nations General Assembly discussed the question of Palestine, specifically addressing relief for refugees, the internationalization of Jerusalem, and the protection of the Holy Places.[133] The discussions led to General Assembly Resolution 303 (IV), a vote to establish Jerusalem as a *corpus separatum* led by Latin American and other Catholic member states of the United Nations. Upon hearing the results of the vote, a rousing 39 to 14 with 7 abstentions, David Ben-Gurion and the Israeli cabinet defied the resolution by moving the seat of the Israeli government to Jerusalem. Conor Cruise O'Brien explained the relevance of the move:

In taking this stand, Ben-Gurion was certainly influenced by the fact in totally rejecting internationalization, he spoke, not merely for the Jews, but for the ruler of the rest of Palestine [King Abdullah ibn Hussein of Transjordan]. The Muslim king, who now controlled most of the Holy Places, could not give them up to some international body without an unbearable loss of prestige, to himself and to his dynasty. It was in Britain's interest to avert that: consequently, it was in the interest of the British Government – though little to its taste – to let Israel get away with it. So in this case, exceptionally, the British Foreign Office would tell the State Department substantially the same thing as the Israeli delegation at the UN would tell the US delegation: let the General Assembly resolution of December 9, 1949, quietly wither away, which it duly did.[134]

Although the Irish Government had a fair amount of trade with Israel in 1949, including the sale of 'a quantity of aircraft and overhaul maintenance equipment',[135] the possibility of a trade agreement with Israel did not appear until February 1950. Philip Sayers, a private Cork businessman, instigated the talks with the Department of Agriculture, and was interested primarily in the export of beef to Israel.[136] The Irish government was reluctant to take advantage of Sayers' eagerness to act as intermediary between Ireland and Israel. Throughout 1950, Sayers approached various departments in Dublin with trade agreements that the Israeli government eventually termed 'the Sayers schemes'.[137] Sayers also actively approached the Irish Embassy in London, but by March 1951, when efforts were being made to open talks between the Foreign Trade Department of Israel and Dublin, the Embassy suggested 'that it would be preferable if [Sayers] did not try to muscle in on any official discussions that might be arranged'.[138]

The difficulty with establishing trade agreements with Israel, however, did not stem from the activities of Philip Sayers. Rather, during the course of negotiations it was learned that the Israelis lacked sufficient funds in sterling to pay for exports, as the British had frozen their sterling balances.[139] The Israelis, through Sayers, proposed the following financial arrangements:

> [F]or the next two or three years payments for Irish exports to Israel would have to be made half in Irish currency, which would be collected by the Jewish Community in Ireland, and the other half not paid for immediately but held as a credit for Ireland until such time not longer than two to three years when Israel would be free from the present payment difficulties imposed by the British... They seem to be approaching the question of a trade agreement in present circumstances altogether from the point of view of securing some help for Israel which they think should be forthcoming having regard to the good relations which have always existed between the Irish and the Jews.[140]

The Department of External Affairs quickly vetoed the idea, citing the fact that the 'Jewish colony' in Ireland was able to raise only IR£8,000 for Jewish refugees in Palestine and that the balance of funds would have to come from the 'Jewish population in Britain'.[141] The Department of Finance countered, saying that they 'wished to examine the proposals for payment carefully'. Finally, the Department of Agriculture advised that Israel 'was a potential market for some years to come and in view of the present surplus supplies of milk it might be a good outlet for dried milk'.

The Foreign Trade Committee considered that trading under the financial arrangements of the Sayers proposal would be tantamount to 'further unblocking of Israeli sterling assets' but the Department of Finance should determine whether to be bound by the British decision, 'taken without consultation with us'.[142] The following week, Con Cremin of the Department of External Affairs, suggested that the 'proposal might be an attempt by the Israeli government to use [Ireland] as a means of putting pressure on the British to unblock further sterling' but in consideration of the potential volume of trade, the Irish government 'should be prepared . . . to do something to help them make payment'.[143] The representative from Agriculture agreed, saying 'nothing should be done which would prevent such a trade'. The committee agreed that the representations so far concerning Israel might be 'kite flying' by Mr Sayers and a formal invitation for talks should be extended to the Israeli High Commissioner in London.

By April 1950, the Israelis provided a shopping list that included frozen kosher meat, canned kosher stewed meat, and cured herring, cheese and dried milk spray.[144] The potential of trade seemed imminent, but the Department of External Affairs became nervous when, in the next round of discussions with Sayers, he presented a letter from the Director-General of Trade in Israel that suggested the idea of a permanent Israeli trade representative in Ireland.[145] The question of Irish recognition of Israel arose only two days later, when Britain announced that it would extend *de jure* recognition as of 27 April 1950.[146] Between the British decision and the lure of Israeli trade, the lack of *de jure* recognition dominated the Foreign Trade Committee discussions concerning Israel.

On 5 May 1950, John Belton of External Affairs warned that were an official invitation given to the Israeli High Commissioner in London to come to Dublin for trade negotiations, the Israelis would 'without doubt regard this as *de jure* recognition'.[147] As a way out, the committee decided to send an Irish delegation to London instead. By 12 May, the Department of External Affairs approved the decision to send an Irish trade delegation to meet the Israeli High Commissioner, but two weeks later, the decision to hold talks in Dublin was also approved. Also, External Affairs suggested that Philip Sayers not be included in the negotiations, as he was 'an Irish citizen and not an accredited representative of the Israeli Government'.[148] Possibly not knowing the situation concerning the status of Philip Sayers, Conor Cruise O'Brien once again tried to establish the link between Israel and Ireland upon hearing of the trade delegation meeting. He wrote to Pete Barnicle in the Irish Consulate General in New York:

> We are to have here shortly a Trade Delegation from Israel. We do not yet know who will be participating but it occurs to us that it might be a useful change for you to get Irish–Jewish publicity. I shall send you out material and photographs as soon as possible. Perhaps you would think of getting Elliseva Sayers to do a feature. I think her father, Philip Sayers, has been partly instrumental in getting the delegation over.[149]

The Foreign Trade Committee held its ground and refused to negotiate with Sayers in Israeli trade talks.[150] Sayers was not disheartened by the reception he received in Dublin, but went to London and approached the Irish embassy there. A telegram from London on 26 May read:

> Re Trade with Israel. Sayers has been trying to see me since Wednesday
> but I have avoided seeing him on one pretext or another. When he rang this
> morning he was told I was not here and he then asked for the Trade Officer.
> Slevin spoke to him. Sayers merely said to him that he would like Slevin
> to tell the Dublin authorities that he Sayers would be going to Dublin in
> the next few days and would like to have an interview on the subject of
> Irish-Israel trade. Slevin was noncommittal in his reply.[151]

Although Sayers was never formally declared *persona non grata*, the personnel
in both London and Dublin did not regard him as an official representative of
the Israeli Government, and resented the familiarity of his approaches.

THE DEPARTMENT OF EXTERNAL AFFAIRS AND RECOGNITION POLICY

Before the trade negotiations were to begin in the summer of 1950, Seán
MacBride broached the subject of *de jure* recognition toward Israel. His private
secretary, Valentin Iremonger, prepared a substantial memorandum on states
that had extended recognition to Israel.[152] MacBride also wrote an ingratiating
letter to Moshe Sharett, Foreign Minister of Israel:

> Ireland and Israel are both ancient nations and at the same time new States
> that have achieved freedom after a long and hard struggle. In the case of
> Ireland, that freedom is still imperfect for six of our counties are still under
> British occupation and, to that extent our efforts towards international co-
> operation have been impeded. None the less, maimed as our country is, we
> have striven to our utmost to help on this great work and will continue to
> do so.[153]

MacBride discussed the possibility of trade with Sharett's envoy, Major Michael
Comay during a series of congenial trade talks in the middle of June. Comay
played to the Dublin press on the question of the Holy Places, stating that cutting
Jerusalem out of Israel would be as 'impracticable as the cutting of Dublin out of
Ireland'.[154] The official trade delegation from Israel did not materialize during the
summer of 1950. The on-going conversations between the Israeli High
Commissioner in London and John Molloy of the London Embassy concerning
trade hit an impasse when the Israelis provided an ultimatum, reported in the
Foreign Trade Committee minutes on 25 August 1950:

> The Department of External Affairs representative reported that Mr.
> Molloy in London had had conversations with Dr. Shinnar. It now
> appeared that the conclusion of a trade agreement with Israel would
> depend on whether this country would be prepared to give Israel a loan of
> from IR£1.5–2 million to finance the import of food stuffs from here. This

would be a credit rather than a loan. Such loans had already been given Israel by France and Switzerland. The loan would be repayable in dollars. The Israeli Government assumed that Irish exporters would be paid through banks in Ireland but if the Irish Government did not wish to bring the banks into the matter arrangements could be made for payment through a private Jewish group in Dublin.[155]

The proposal of supplying a credit to Israel caught Dublin by surprise. Immediately, the Department of External Affairs contacted the Irish Legation in France to find out about Israeli–French financial arrangements. Con Cremin, newly appointed Ambassador to France, responded that France had not made a loan to Israel *per se*. The semi-state Assurance Credit d'État simply backed credits granted by French exporters concerning goods exported to Israel.[156] Cremin added:

> Gibert [French Director of Commercial Agreements] expressed himself as sceptical as to the soundness of the particular arrangement made with Israel. He gave me to understand in strict confidence that it flowed from a personal undertaking given by Mr. Petsche, Minister of Finance, to the Israeli Minister. In Gibert's opinion, Israel is not, on present information, a very sound risk, and he offered the personal advice that we should approach any similar proposition made to us with extreme caution.[157]

At the next meeting of the Foreign Trade Committee, the decision was made to tell the Israelis that the 'Irish Government was not prepared to grant a loan or credit' but would entertain the original proposition of Israel's buying 'with payment from sterling funds in the hands of the Jewish community in Britain and Ireland'.[158]

Meanwhile, Seán MacBride continued to push the theme of partition and Ireland's relationship with the Jews, peppering a speech to the Jewish Discussion Club in Dublin with the words 'sectarianism and intolerance'.[159] MacBride's former private secretary, Valentin Iremonger, also wrote a lengthy memorandum on the subject of recognizing Israel *de jure* in October 1950. In 1950, Iremonger echoed the MacBride theme in rationalizing the necessity of granting *de jure* recognition:

> It is likely that discussions over the actual form of internationalization [of Jerusalem] will go on for quite a long time to come but I do not think that the details of such internationalization should prevent us according *de jure* recognition. It is likely that the granting of full recognition by us would be of immense benefit to us in other fields. Our relations with the Government of Israel would be improved immensely and it is probable that full recognition would tend to help our Anti-Partition campaign in the United States by winning for us the sympathy of the Jewish population

there and, as the Vatican considerations which entered into our decision almost two years ago are not now, to my mind, of the same importance, I submit that the question of our extending full recognition should be decided as soon as possible.[160]

The initiative begun by Iremonger continued throughout the autumn and winter, leading to a 'memorandum for the government' in April 1951. The memorandum repeated Iremonger's rationale:

It is probable that discussion and negotiation over the form that the internationalization is to take will go on for a considerable time to come. In view of this fact, the Minister for External Affairs [Seán MacBride] is of the opinion that the acceptance by the Israeli Government of the principle of the internationalization satisfies [our] requirements in regard to the Holy Places.[161]

Michael Rynne, appointed legal adviser in 1950, had no legal objections to *de jure* recognition for Israel, nor did it appear that such a decision would impinge on any interests in Iveagh House or Dublin. However, one person had much to lose. Joseph Walshe, 'out of the loop' as Ambassador at the Holy See, received word of the memorandum for the government on 23 April. Walshe's first words were: 'I should like to emphasize once more the importance of sending letters of the slightest importance by Air Mail, more especially when time is an essential factor.'[162] Annoyed with the new Secretary in External Affairs, Seán Nunan, for not consulting him earlier, Walshe seemed to miss the even-handed days with Fred Boland as Secretary. But Boland was promoted as Ambassador to London in 1950, and apparently Walshe felt he was losing control of the Israel policy. Obviously enraged, Walshe wrote:

My task was not made easier by the minute and draft memorandum, since neither gives cogent reason for de jure recognition here and now. We have never accepted the 'International Law' of the text books in any great moral issue and it would be extreme naïveté to put such arguments before the Holy See. Most of our own propaganda quite rightly regards the international law devised by the great powers as an instrument to serve their own exclusive interests. We cant [*sic*] have it both ways.[163]

Walshe, convinced that *de jure* recognition would lead to the opening of diplomatic relations with Israel, was adamant that Ireland should not change its 'moral stand'. In the letter to Nunan he provided several reasons why *de jure* recognition should not be granted. First, Walshe felt the question was a matter of principle, not of political expediency. '[It] is because we base our International behaviour... on fundamental principles that we enjoy such a high reputation in the world.' Second, in spite of the benefits that might be gained from *de jure* recognition, specifically anti-partition support from Jews in the United States and the promise of trade, Mgr Tardini of the Vatican 'regarded our intended recognition as a breech in the front, and as a probable cause of scandal in the theological sense'. Third, Walshe argued that *de jure* recognition was more than a routine decision: 'It is a question of changing a fundamental attitude.' He also sensed a 'hardening of the Holy See position'.[164]

Although Walshe openly spoke of Pope Pius XII's attitude as 'excessively rigid', that same rigidity was a part of Walshe's character. The Ambassador's view of Israel and the Jewish influence in Ireland created intransigence in policy that was not beneficial to Ireland but offered Walshe the opportunity for self-interested prestige. The matter of *de jure* recognition was dropped (once again) at Iveagh House in deference to Walshe. When the issue of establishing a formal trade agreement arose once more in the summer of 1951, Michael Rynne commented on the legality of an agreement with Israel and the policy position:

> I agree with Miss Murphy – and Mr. Fay – that we can make a Trade Agreement with Israel without committing ourselves to recognising it *de jure*. But in view our [*sic*] keen desire (inspired largely by Ambassador, Holy See) to avoid doing anything at all ambiguous in this regard, I think we should inform the Israeli delegates, before starting trade or air agreement talks, that in our understanding the conclusion of a trade or air agreement with them will not affect the recognition.[165]

Once again, a prospective policy change on recognizing and establishing diplomatic relations with Israel was 'dead in the water' due to Joseph Walshe's influence at the Holy See. However, the temptation of trade was an equally powerful force. Over the next twelve years, in spite of the diplomatic barbed wire, Iveagh House found a way to establish trade with Israel.

A NEW TRADE INITIATIVE – 1950–51

Although not considered welcome in governmental trade negotiations, Philip Sayers and his ideas did not disappear. Chastised by the Department of Agriculture, and especially by the Irish embassy in London, Sayers had a new plan by October 1950. Rather than involving himself with the difficulties of Israel's lack of import financing, Sayers was 'prepared to pay cash for Irish meat and other agricultural products for Israel', inquiring whether the Department of Agriculture 'had any objection to the proposal'.[166] The Foreign Trade Committee determined there was no objection to Mr Sayers, as a private citizen and not an agent for the Israeli government, acting as a buyer 'provided appropriate payment arrangements were made'. The Committee insisted that Sayers 'would have to give full information as to the origin of the funds to be used'.

The following week, while the committee entertained a new round of discussions on a trade agreement with the Israeli High Commissioner in London, Frank Biggar suggested that if 'the Sayer's deal' went through, there would be no need for a trade agreement.[167] The committee agreed.

A new economic counsellor replaced Dr Shinnar at the Israeli legation in London in autumn 1950. The new counsellor, J.A. Brin, reviewed the files on trade negotiations with Ireland, commenting that talks that 'had been dragging on in a desultory way for many months seemed to have got nowhere'.[168] The Irish representative, M.J. Barry in London, commented that 'this was not correct', explaining the negotiations with Sayers and the difficulty in making financial arrangements. Brin could not understand why Ireland would not provide a credit for the Israeli government. Barry reported: '[Brin] said this did not mean a loan by the Irish Government to the Government of Israel but rather payment by a group of Jews in Ireland or in England', the same story the Irish negotiators heard from Sayers and Shinnar. Barry summed up the situation:

> I pointed out to him that in a general way we felt that since there was a ready market for most of the foodstuffs we produced, we could not see any advantage in exporting under such unorthodox payments arrangement as Israel proposed.[169]

By April 1950, Brin, Sayers and Silverstone of the Anglo-Palestine Bank Ltd met with the Departments of Finance and Agriculture in Dublin. The purpose of the meeting was to finalize credit arrangements with the Irish government. Agricultural products were secondary to the financial terms. The delegation approached the Bank of Ireland to negotiate a credit of IR£2,000,000, but were told by the bank that its period of lending was limited to six months and were turned away.[170] Mr Brin also questioned Ireland's *de facto* recognition of Israel. William P. Fay, upon hearing the report in the Foreign Trade Committee, remarked that the delegation's visit produced 'one good result'.

> Mr Fay thought that the visit of the delegation had produced one good result in demonstrating to them that Mr. Philip Sayers was not a person who could be entirely relied upon. His failure to obtain the loan from the Bank of Ireland must have lowered his stock considerably.[171]

At the end of negotiations, trade with Israel never got off the ground. The prospect of trade created slight movement, but in 1951, when *de jure* recognition was questioned in the April trade talks and then refused in May, trade suffered as a consequence. In 1949, exports to Israel were IR£46,860, rising to IR£141,930 in 1950. By 1951, exports were only IR£68,657 and continued to drop throughout the 1950s. Imports faced the same decline, from IR£269,257 in 1949 to IR£143,413 in 1952 and slowly moving to IR£401,998 in 1960.[172]

MAINTENANCE OF NON-RECOGNITION – 1951–55

When the dust settled from the failed trade talks in April 1951, the Department of External Affairs compiled a memorandum on the 'question of *de jure* recognition of the state of Israel' on 11 September 1951.[173] The memorandum reiterated Walshe's position expressed earlier that spring from the Holy See. The policy remained in place throughout the winter, but when Walshe came to Dublin in May 1952, Sheila Murphy and Michael Rynne discussed the subject. A hastily penned note by Michael Rynne reaffirmed Walshe's hold on the policy:

> Miss Murphy and I discussed with the Ambassador, Holy See (who is at home on leave) the question of according Irish *de jure* recognition to Israel. The Ambassador was strongly of opinion that we should not recommend that such recognition be given until we hear from him that the Holy Father is satisfied with the policy of Israel in respect of the Holy Places. Meanwhile, it is clear that unless the Government are subjected to renewed pressure of an almost irresistible character... the Dept. need take no initiative, pending Mr. Walshe's 'all clear'.[174]

The policy toward Israel, firmly adhering to the legal methods of non-recognition yet entertaining a trade relationship, stabilized in summer 1951. Not coincidentally, in June 1951, Eamon de Valera's Fianna Fáil government replaced the First Inter-Party Government. At age sixty-eight de Valera became Taoiseach once more. His eyesight failing, de Valera assigned the Department of Foreign Affairs portfolio to Frank Aiken rather than taking on the additional duty himself. The Department continued to grow, but de Valera's sense of 'rigidity in principle and flexibility in practice' was not rejuvenated.[175] Under Aiken's leadership, the Department of External Affairs became a fully functioning bureaucratic machine. As Keogh commented in *Ireland and the Vatican*, Aiken 'was far less in awe of the Holy See than his immediate predecessor [Seán MacBride]'.[176] The finesse and idealism that de Valera could have provided as Minister of External Affairs in the Israel issue never materialized. But one cannot place the blame in one particular area – not de Valera's *sub silencio* relationship with Israel through the Herzog family, nor Frank Aiken's approach to foreign policy issues, nor the Cold War clientele personality that Israel acquired vis-à-vis the United States and USSR in the early 1950s. From every viewpoint, the status quo policy approach seemed the best course of action for the Irish government toward Israel.

In November 1952, upon the death of President Chaim Weizmann, the Department of External Affairs was faced with the dilemma of acknowledging Weizmann's death without deviating from a policy of non-recognition. The department succeeded quite well in matters of protocol. In sending a message of sympathy, the Department decided that 'since we have not given *de jure* recognition to the state of Israel it would be inappropriate for the President to send a message' but that in light of Dr Weizmann's 'international reputation' a message would be sent by Frank Aiken, Minister of External Affairs to the Foreign Minister of Israel.[177] Eamon de Valera was in Utrecht for eye surgery at the time, and sent a personal note to Isaac Herzog, the Chief Rabbi of Israel, his old friend from Dublin.[178] Robert Briscoe, TD, represented the Minister for External Affairs at the memorial service held in the Adelaide Road Synagogue on 16 November. The question of lowering the flags on government buildings became moot when it was learned the ceremony would be held on a Sunday.[179]

Although one premise for continuing *de facto* recognition of Israel was the effect it might have on relations with other Arab countries in the region, Israel was Ireland's largest trading partner in the Middle East. The trade was miniscule, but much greater than trade with Iraq, Turkey, Lebanon, Jordan, Saudi Arabia or Iran. In the recognition files, a singular report on trade stands out for the year 1953. The year 1954 saw the retirement of Ambassador Joseph Walshe at the Holy See, replaced by Con Cremin.[180] After June 1954, the second inter-party government took office, with John A. Costello as Taoiseach and Liam Cosgrave as Minister for External Affairs. Under Costello's government, foreign policy took a more realist approach, and in December 1955 Ireland was admitted to the United Nations.[181] The recognition files were inactive until 1955 when Professor Leonard Abrahamson of Dublin wrote to John Costello questioning Ireland's non-recognition policy:

> I am writing because I understood from Seán MacBride when we had the pleasure of your company and his, that in his term of office, the matter had not been concluded simply because of neglect and not for any special reason. As there would, I believe, be economic advantage in full diplomatic relations between the two countries, I now venture to raise the matter with you.[182]

The files do not contain a reply to Professor Abrahamson's letter, but on 16 September 1955, Ambassador Con Cremin reported from his post at the Holy See on the status of Jerusalem and the Holy Places. The question of *de jure* recognition once again seemed ripe, but no new initiatives were taken in External Affairs. In February 1956, Dr Eoin MacWhite, now legal adviser, also questioned the policy. The next month, with political tensions escalating in the Middle East due to Egypt's Aswan Dam project, Chief Rabbi Jakobovits wrote to Seán Murphy, Secretary of the Department of External Affairs.[183] During the course of Ireland's *de facto* stance concerning Israel, ranging from February 1949 to March 1956 (the date of Jakobovits' letter) no serious international legal consequences arose. (See Appendix 2 for Irish policy toward Israel in March 1956.) The new issue of Irish nationals in a hostile Middle East awakened serious concerns within the department.

THE HUMAN FACE OF NON-RECOGNITION POLICY

On 27 March 1956, Seán Murphy, Secretary of External Affairs, received a letter from Chief Rabbi Jakobovits of Dublin. The Rabbi expressed concern for the safety of members of the Jewish community in Ireland who were living in Israel as Irish nationals. Jakobovits' request was straightforward:

> I would indeed be most grateful if your Department could make arrangements whereby Irish citizens would, in the event of an emergency, be entitled to the same protection and privileges as are enjoyed by other non-Israeli nationals at present in that country.[184]

In the summer of 1954, as the British prepared to disengage from the Suez Canal zone, Israel became considerably more vulnerable to Egypt. When Ben-Gurion returned to power in 1955 after 'retiring' in December 1953, he was convinced that Gamal Abdel Nasser, the 'first genuinely independent ruler of Egypt', was Israel's most dangerous enemy.[185] Upon the departure of the British, the attacks on Israeli territory by Arab infiltrators, the *fayadeen* raids, were now originating from the Egyptian border. The United States, in order to deflect Soviet aggression in the region, included Iraq in its defence arrangements for Greece, Turkey and Iran in 1954, but had limited its aid to Egypt by provisionally approving a World Bank loan to finance the Aswan Dam Project. Meanwhile, to counter Egyptian influence in other parts of the Arab world, Iraq and Turkey signed a defence treaty in 1955, the seedling of the Baghdad Pact. Conor Cruise O'Brien wrote of Israel's reaction to the defence arrangement:

> From the viewpoint of Israel, the Baghdad Pact appeared most menacing, especially if Jordan were to be included in it, as seemed likely at first, granted Britain's continuing authority there. It looked as if Israel's Arab enemies were about to be armed by Israel's cooling friend [the United States], while Israel itself was locked in growing isolation. The arms were intended by the donors for defense against Russians, but Israel feared that they were much more likely to be used for new attacks against Israel.[186]

In this atmosphere, the perceived isolation and encirclement of Israel, Rabbi Jakobovits wrote to the Department of External Affairs in an attempt to provide a diplomatic refuge for Irish nationals residing in Israel in the event of increased tensions. The original list provided the names of eight families for a total of twenty-seven people. One person on the list provided details of the situation in a letter dated 31 March 1956:

> As the political situation in this part of the world grows more tense, the question of protection of Irish nationals has arisen. On enquiring at the British Embassy in Tel Aviv, I was informed that they were not authorised

to act on behalf of the Irish Govt. & that they were accepting registrations of British subjects only. I wonder, therefore, whether it would be possible for some arrangement to be made by which Irish nationals could feel more secure in the event of the situation worsening. I think there are quite a number, especially Irish University graduates, who, while participating in educational and humanitarian work here, never forget their loyalty to, & affection for, Ireland.[187]

By July, the author of the letter, J.S. Steinberg, travelled to the Irish embassy in London. Steinberg repeated the difficulty of being the national of a state that did not have any diplomatic ties to Israel. He emphasized that there was 'no neighbouring country in which they could find refuge', that 'all the surrounding countries were hostile and in the event they had to leave Israel, they would have to face starting back to Ireland'.[188] Assured that Ireland was 'to have some plan put into operation without delay', Mr Steinberg left, promising to call again before his return to Israel in September.

In Iveagh House, the situation raised the alarm once again on the question of *de jure* recognition. Frank Biggar discussed the issue with Freddie Boland, Ambassador in London. Boland questioned the soundness of granting recognition, but passed the decision back to Seán Murphy, Secretary of External Affairs. Eoin MacWhite, the legal adviser, argued that the purpose of *de facto* recognition was to enable diplomacy through third parties – in this case, the British Embassy in Tel Aviv – and that *de jure* recognition was not necessary to make contingency plans for the Irish nationals in Israel.[189]

Seán Murphy, upon reading the reports from London and the legal adviser, entered a rather sardonic comment in the file:

I think that we are making too much fuss about this recognition question. If we can make a practical arrangement for the evacuation of <u>Irish Citizens</u> the fact that Israel can claim it as *de jure* recognition would not keep anyone awake.[190]

As a result of the Secretary's attitude, Frank Biggar in London was instructed by MacWhite to approach the British 'immediately' and 'should we come up against the "recognition" question we shall deal with it when it arises'.[191]

Four days later, Biggar met with the British officials who stated that in principle, 'the British Government were always prepared to take on the protection of [Irish] citizens whenever we requested it' and would contact the embassy in Tel Aviv to confirm the position.[192] Iveagh House considered the most critical element to the evacuation plans was to have a 'register' of the Irish citizens involved, perhaps putting an advertisement in an Israeli newspaper. But given the tensions involved in the Suez Canal crisis, which in July had been nationalized by Nasser, Biggar advised against an advertisement as 'contributing to the tension' in Israel.[193]

The resulting contingency plans, incorporating performance by the British consuls, centred on the following points:

> The first stage at which developments are tending towards a deteriorating situation and aliens are leaving or being advised to leave the country. At this stage we should like the consulates to make the usual repatriation facilities available to our citizens and their wives and children, who want to return to Ireland and who arc unable to meet the expense of returning in whole or in part... We should appreciate in connection with persons who are able to pay their way home, if the consulates would... given any assistance possible in regard to securing transport, travel reservations etc....
>
> The next or second stage, which we visualize as the critical one preceding an outbreak of hostilities, will be the stage at which emergency measures such as the evacuation of their nationals will be put in train by foreign consulates... We should be much appreciative if the British authorities would as far as possible allow our citizens... to participate in any evacuation measures... for British subjects.[194]

By 7 September the plan for repatriating the Irish nationals from Israel was in place. The Department of External Affairs estimated that fifty persons were involved in the plan, including twenty adult males, fifteen adult females, and fifteen dependent children. The total cost of airline transportation was estimated at IR£3,400 for the group, and a somewhat smaller figure of IR£2,000 was provided for sea travel and 'a small amount for subsistence'.[195] The 'rules' for repatriation expenses were three:

(a) that only those who find they are unable to pay their own fares will be assisted;
(b) that any expenditure incurred will be subject to repayment within the shortest time possible, an undertaking to repay and the address of destination being obtained in each case; and
(c) that every effort will be made to keep expenditure as low as possible.[196]

When the Suez crisis was initiated on 29 October with the Israeli attack on the Sinai, the Irish contingency plans were in place. Although the plans were never used, as the fighting ended on 6 November, the episode illustrates two important facets of Irish diplomacy toward Israel. First, *de facto* recognition was a permanent position and would not be dismantled even during an impending crisis. Second, the Department of External Affairs initiated an appropriate and effective response in meeting the demands of its citizens in a hostile environment. The department clearly was not practicing *ad hoc* diplomacy in matters that affected the lives of individual citizens.

But the Irish government proved its ambivalence in choosing sides in the crisis when in November 1956, Liam Cosgrave, Minister of External Affairs, visited the US State Department. During a conversation with the Acting Secretary Hoover and Ambassador John Hearne in Washington, Cosgrave was told the American view was that 'the British and French action in Egypt had the unfortunate effect [of inviting] Soviet penetration of the area and [of serving] to build up Nasser's prestige. Cosgrave said that the Irish Government was in complete agreement with the United States on this issue and felt that the British and French action had been most unwise.'[197] Diplomatic lip service was never in short supply during the Cold War.

DE JURE RECOGNITION AND AIKEN'S MIDDLE EAST PEACE PROPOSAL – 1958

In *The Passionate Attachment*, George and Douglas Ball termed the 1956 crisis 'the Suez adventure', a phrase reeking of American perspective. The attitude of US foreign policy leaders toward the crisis was expressed in the ultimatum President Eisenhower gave to David Ben-Gurion in February 1957, based on a plan by John Foster Dulles. After the fighting ceased on 6 November 1956, the Israeli forces refused to withdraw from the Sinai Desert. Provoked by the increased tension with the USSR in the region, Eisenhower demanded that Israeli forces pull back from the Sinai to their border. He also instructed Secretary of State John Foster Dulles to 'make provisions to cut off the flow of aid to Israel'.[198] Eisenhower planned to terminate all forms of military assistance, as well as cancelling export licences for shipment of military goods and munitions. Finally, in an attempt to pressure Ben-Gurion through the American Jewish lobby, Eisenhower ordered his Secretary of the Treasury 'to draft a change in US tax regulations so that the Jewish American organization benefactors would no longer be entitled to a federal income tax deduction for contributions that benefited Israel'.[199] Israel did not cave in, nor did the United States. But Israel began to run out of funds early in March 1957 and Ben-Gurion capitulated. 'On March 16, Israel withdrew from almost all the territory it had occupied in the Suez offensive.'[200]

In 1958, during the last year of John Foster Dulles' life and his foreign policy partnership with Eisenhower, another crisis erupted in the Middle East, this time in Lebanon. Pro-Nasser Lebanese nationalists rebelled against the conservative government when it announced it would stay in office beyond its term. In a 'state of panic' the Lebanese and Jordanian governments urged British–American intervention, fearing the intervention of Iraq or Syria or both.[201] The Americans responded by placing 14,300 troops in Lebanon and the British sent more than 3,000 troops to Jordan. To resolve the crisis, the Lebanese government stepped down and was replaced by another government. Two American scholars have argued that at this point, 'the hatred of the United States was increased, and the Arab left was driven closer to the Russians'.[202] Another US author remarked: 'If the commitment to use force, backed up by enough military power to make it credible, did not work, then force was used where the interests involved dictated it'.[203]

Within this antagonistic framework, Frank Aiken set out to establish a proposal for peace in the Middle East, confident that the Irish delegation at the United Nations could make an impact. Aiken's confidence stemmed from the perception that Irish foreign policy celebrated something of a honeymoon period in the late 1950s. Ireland's ability to maintain neutrality as a foreign policy in the face of the Cold War throughout the decade provided Aiken with an idealistic vision of creating 'world peace'.

Indeed, the new Irish cabinet was immensely experienced in foreign policy. With de Valera as Taoiseach, Seán Lemass as Tanaiste and Minister of Industry and Commerce, and Frank Aiken as Minister of External Affairs – a position he would hold until 1968 – the voice of Irish foreign policy was the voice of experience. At the same time, Frederick Boland, former Secretary of the Department and Ambassador to Britain, was entering his distinguished career as Permanent Representative at the United Nations, a tenure that included the Presidency of the General Assembly in 1960–61. Con Cremin, following the ambassadorship at the Holy See and then London, guided the Department of External Affairs as Secretary from December 1957. John J. Hearne was in his ninth year as Ambassador to Washington, and on his last posting before retirement in 1960. J.E.W. Morrissey had been William P. Fay's assistant legal adviser until 1956, when he replaced Fay. Eoin MacWhite, at the age of thirty-five in 1958, had already proved himself in international legal matters. In short, Minister Frank Aiken and his foreign policy team were in the best possible position to introduce his vision for world peace at the United Nations in August 1958.

Conor Cruise O'Brien had asked Freddie Boland to review Aiken's plan. Tactfully but assuredly, Boland agreed with many of Aiken's points. Yet an important element in Aiken's initial plan was to confirm the borders of Israel, as they stood, problematic for Ireland's recognition policy.[204]

> Last, Boland raised a technical issue in his report to [Cruise] O'Brien. If Aiken explicitly recognized the borders of Israel in his speech he would compromise Ireland's official policy of not establishing *de jure* [recognition] with Israel until it acceded to the internationalization of the Holy Places in Jerusalem.[205]

When Aiken delivered the speech on 14 August at a special session of the UN General Assembly, to avoid the embarrassment of the press pointing out Ireland's lack of *de jure* recognition, he inserted the following paragraph:

> If [the problem of Arab refugees] is put on the way to settlement it would greatly facilitate the attainment of satisfactory solutions for the remaining problems which must be faced if a general settlement is to be attained. The improvement in Arab–Israeli relations which ought to be ushered in by

progress on the refugee problem should, in particular, help bring about a just solution of the problem of the Holy Places, under an international regime which would be responsible for their preservation and accessibility. This problem also, in the inflamed atmosphere of the past years, has made no progress towards solution. Surely, however, if the general atmosphere can be improved this organisation [the UN] can achieve what, throughout the world, Christian, Jew and Moslem so profoundly desire: the effective protection of the Holy Places in Palestine.[206]

Skelly has argued that Aiken's proposal 'was flawed in certain respects'.[207] The resulting resolution, sponsored by the Arab nations, 'ignored many aspects' of Aiken's plan.

The resolution referred to neither the neutralization nor the denuclearization of the entire region, nor the internationalization of the Holy Places. It made no reference to the Palestinian refugees, nor suggested a new approach to this intractable issue. Unsurprisingly, since the Arab nations sponsored it, the resolution did not recognize Israel. It foresaw no major role for the UN in the Middle East.[208]

Overall, the Aiken plan for the Middle East was 'over-ambitious' and 'unrealistic'. Aiken miscalculated the ability of the United Nations to undertake the practical arrangement of such a plan, as well as the determination of the 'great powers' to refrain from disengagement in the area.

What makes Aiken's proposal more compelling, however, is to ponder his motives for trying to solve such an 'intractable' problem as the Middle East in the first place. Skelly attributed Aiken's actions to 'championing the needs of the refugees'.[209] However, one could argue that Aiken's behaviour was a psychological compensation for the inability to solve the intractable problem at home – partition. Fanning has suggested that 'Aiken... placed Ireland's UN policies firmly in the context of her struggle to escape from British domination', and one could argue that the Middle East proposal, had it proved successful, would have provided the incentive for UN participation in the Irish problem.[210] Although the days of trying to bring the partition issue to an international forum were well over, such as Seán MacBride's attempts at the Council of Europe before Ireland's admission to the United Nations, perhaps Aiken subconsciously thought his idealism concerning the Middle East would bring political rewards at home. In 1958 Ireland's policy toward Israel still rested upon Walshe's initial decision.

THE SLOW DEMISE OF *DE FACTO* RECOGNITION POLICY TOWARD ISRAEL – 1958–63

The role of the Vatican in the internationalization of Jerusalem was modified in 1958 with a change in papal leadership. In the autumn of 1958, Pope Pius XII was seriously ill. From 1953 onward the Pope had 'an unspecified combination of complaints'.[211] On Monday, 6 October 1958, he 'took to his bed', and by Thursday he was dead. Cardinal Tisserant, the *Camerlengo* of the Holy Roman Church, arranged the details of his funeral and burial. Tisserant did not necessarily admire Pius XII and had voted against the Pope in the conclave of 1939, 'convinced that he was the wrong choice'.[212] Only a month after the Pope's death, Ambassador Leo McCauley visited Tisserant at the Vatican on 7 November and was surprised to review the Cardinal's 'particular plan' for the Holy Places.'[213] McCauley's report revealed the rift at the Vatican on the issue, bringing Tisserant further to the right than even Pius XII on the issue:

His Eminence did not like the proposed trusteeship by the United Nations because about one-third of the troops required to police the area would be drawn from countries behind the Iron Curtain. He estimated that the perimeter to be patrolled would be in the neighbourhood of 120 kilometres, for which duty would be required 3,000 troops including reserves and maintenance units. His Eminence disapproved of a plan which would keep some thousand Communists stationed permanently in garrison at Jerusalem. He admitted that His Holiness Pope Pius XII would have accepted the United Nations' solution in spite of this drawback but His Eminence differed from the late Holy Father on this point.[214]

Tisserant's quirky plan included the establishment of Jerusalem as a sovereign state, 'something like Liechtenstein' but governed by a council composed of various national groups. McCauley's report, as well as a question in the Dáil on 26 November 1958, brought the question of *de jure* recognition of Israel once more to the forefront of Irish foreign policy. As had been done on numerous occasions before, the department prepared a memorandum on the history of the issue, mentioned more often in the files than in this study, with one great difference: the deference shown to Pope Pius XII and the Vatican could be questioned by the Irish government with the accession of Pope John XXIII (Angelo Guiseppe Roncalli). The memorandum read in part:

As far as Deputy [Noel] Browne's question is concerned, the answer should be quite simple and on the following lines: 'Ireland has not yet accorded de jure recognition to the State of Israel. Accordingly, the question of establishing formal diplomatic relations with that State does not arise.' There may be a supplementary question as to when de jure recognition may be accorded. It will be quite adequate... to say that the matter was under consideration... On the attached file there are a number of memoranda resuming the position and various developments from time to time. The main point is that the late Holy Father was adamant in his views that nothing less than an international regime would be acceptable. The present Holy Father [John XXIII] may have other views on the matter

but until such time as his view become known, the question of Ireland's de
jure recognition of Israel will hardly be considered.[215]

Clearly, Ireland would have to wait to determine Pope John XXIII's views on
the Holy Places. Cremin was probably the most informed at the Department on
the issue. He was Assistant Secretary when Seán MacBride, Joe Walshe and
Freddie Boland established the policy in 1949. Then, serving as ambassador to
the Holy See from 1954–56, he gained a first-hand perspective of the Vatican.
Now, in 1958, he was Secretary of the department. The depth of his academic
knowledge on the subject of recognition had improved considerably since 1949,
along with his practical experience in maintaining the posture of non-
recognition toward Israel. Cremin's main concern in changing the policy in late
1958 stemmed from Ireland's desire to maintain cordial relations with the Arab
states. In this way Cremin was showing respect for both Boland and Aiken at
the United Nations.

> [I] think that such a step in respect of Israel at the present moment might
> lead to wrong interpretations on the part of the Arab States and might thus
> compromise whatever beneficial action we may be able to take in the
> United Nations towards solving the Arab–Israeli problem.[216]

The Irish government did not have to wait long to determine the new Pope's
attitude. The ambassador at Brussels, D.R. McDonald, reported in March 1959
that 'Israel's relations with the Holy See have taken on a new turn since the
accession of the present Pope'.[217] As a result of secret talks, the Holy See
appointed a Vicar Apostolic to Israel. McDonald reported that 'the Israel
authorities are overjoyed at the change and promise it affords of the
normalisation of their relations with the Holy See'. McDonald's source was
Gideon Rafael, the Israeli Ambassador in Brussels, who saw the movement as
an opportunity to press McDonald for a response on full recognition for Israel.

Both Con Cremin and Conor Cruise O'Brien answered McDonald's inquiry
as to Ireland's position, Cremin noting that 'the development mentioned ... is of
considerable interest'.[218] Cremin also noted a softening in position in that 'the
present Holy Father deleted some of the prayers at Easter the reference to
"perfidious" Jews ... on the ground ... that this adjective ... has come to have a
much more pejorative meaning'.[219] Regardless of the changing climate at the
Vatican, Cruise O'Brien was more pragmatic. 'It is doubtful whether there is
anything to be gained from recognising Israel.'[220] He believed that by sustaining
the *de facto* recognition against Israel, relations with both the Arabs and Israelis
would remain 'excellent'. For Cruise O'Brien, the Holy Places issue was only
the first stumbling block to diplomatic relations with the Israelis. There were
'many other aspects to be considered'. He asked MacWhite to submit a report
of what states recognized Israel and to what degree. MacWhite's comprehensive
report added the following caveat:

A factor which should be recalled is that if we do recognize we will be subjected to insistent demands for an Israeli mission here which, even if based in Europe, would mean that we would be subjected to demarches of only the non-Arab interests in the Middle East and which might result in the Jewish community here attempting to exercise some pressure on the formation of our Middle East policies.[221]

Yet the provincial attitude of MacWhite toward an Israeli mission would soon be displaced by a more powerful set of interests operating within Iveagh House. De Valera resigned the office of Taoiseach in June 1959, leaving his protégé, Seán Lemass, in control of the Fianna Fáil government. Lemass had vast experience in Irish foreign trade, holding the Industry and Commerce portfolio exclusively for almost seven years in the 1950s. Lemass and T.K. Whitaker had jointly outlined the first 'Programme for Economic Expansion' in May 1958, and implementing the programme was Lemass' primary objective when he succeeded de Valera in June 1959. Lemass viewed increased foreign trade as the only way to relieve the economic 'malaise' of Ireland.[222] From the Lemass perspective, Israel could not be ignored.[223]

In anticipation of determining the viewpoint of the Holy See toward a renewed Irish interest in *de jure* recognition for Israel, Con Cremin drafted a letter to send to Ambassador McCauley. The files imply that Cremin never sent the letter, but, for self-edification, he narrated the possibilities:

You will recall that the late Joe Walshe was accustomed to maintain strongly that the rigidity of the Vatican attitude in the late forties and early fifties was particularly due to the personal outlook of Pope Pius XII and that, while this attitude was rather unrealistic, there were no prospects of a change during the late Pope's lifetime... The reason I raise the question now is because Mr. William Norton, TD, has spoken to me about the possibility of our according de jure recognition ... He tells me that when he saw the Pope [John XXIII]... His Holiness spoke in very warm terms of [Israel]... Mr. Norton is personally convinced that the Pope does not take the view that formal recognition of Israel by us would constitute an act to which the Holy See could take exception... One can... easily conceive Cardinal Tardini making a case in this sense.[224]

Cremin stated later that he never sent the letter, but it provided a sound policy assessment of the situation.[225]

The role of William Norton, to whom Cremin refers, is not insignificant in provoking a reassessment of the department's position on Israel. Norton, twice Tanaiste in the inter-party governments of 1948–51 and 1954–57, served as director of an import–export organization operating in Israel called the Irish and Allied Trading Corporation Ltd. In January 1960 Norton's firm accomplished what no other Irish concern had in relation to Israel. The trading company entered into an agreement with the Israel Export and Trust Company (ISRAT), a state-owned enterprise operating in Tel Aviv.[226] The resulting agreement, although the terms were pro-Israeli, provided for IR£500,000 total trade between the two firms over a four-year period. The import list for Ireland included 'food stuffs' such as bananas, brandy, tinned tomatoes and groundnuts as well as general goods (for example, nylon stockings, plywood, cotton yarns, marble, potash, pharmaceuticals, fertilizers, 'frigidares', cement mixers, tyres and tubes). In return, the Irish firm would export the following items: live bulls, cows, sheep and horses; 'drink' and tobacco; herrings and fish; hay and straw; food waste and prepared animal feed; coke and coal; glass and glassware; iron ore, lead ore, scrap iron zinc ore; brass and copper; agricultural machinery and vehicle spare parts. The Department of External Affairs approved the agreement, but stressed that the nature of Norton's firm was private and not state-sponsored.

In March 1960, the Irish government was lured by the possibility of increased trade with Israel. Con Cremin met with the Economic Counsellor of the Israeli Embassy in London, Dr Gilat, and discussed the possibility of an astronomical amount of trade. The figure of $5 million had been presented to Industry and Commerce as well.[227] Gilat questioned Cremin on trade status for Israel, and was reassured that 'there [was] really no problem whatever on m.f.n. [most-favoured nation] treatment as Israeli imports...have enjoyed such treatments from the beginning'. Cremin explained the *de facto* status of Israel to Gilat:

> I explained that the fact that we have not accorded *de jure* recognition to Israel does not connote an attitude of hostility or any lack of friendly feelings on our part, either for Jews generally or for the State of Israel. I expressed the view that if there should be a change in this matter, the Government would probably like to make it by a direct decision and not by implication, such as might be involved in an exchange of notes or a formal trade agreement.[228]

But other voices in the department thought otherwise. Conor Cruise O'Brien of External Affairs, sensing that the days of 'excellent relations' with both the Arabs and Israelis were numbered, argued that perhaps *de jure* recognition of Israel could be accomplished with least offence to the Arab states by implying recognition through a bilateral trade agreement.[229] Cremin, hearing the pros and cons from every side, next did what came so naturally to many Irish diplomats: he contacted Freddie Boland at the United Nations for a reasoned approach to the problem. Boland, in the middle of a campaign for the presidency of the United Nations, came through for Cremin.

> I rather wonder if the time hasn't come when we should take another look at our attitude on the question of the *de jure* recognition of Israel. When we first took the decision...the situation in Palestine was still in a state of flux and the ultimate outcome had yet to be seen. We were therefore justified in

> hoping at that moment that the international regime for the City of
> Jerusalem which had been recommended by [the Palestine Conciliation
> Commission]...would eventually become a reality...A lot of water has
> flowed under the bridges since then...To continue to make our *de jure*
> recognition of Israel dependent on the realisation of the plans...is tanta-
> mount to withholding recognition from Israel until the Greek Kalends
> [forever].[230]

Boland felt that the best possible course of action, if the decision were made to
recognize Israel *de jure*, would be 'via the indirect legal consequences of some
act such as the conclusion of a trade agreement rather than by...a formal
government announcement'. At the United Nations, Boland had been approached
by Israeli delegates on the issue and knew that 'the Israelis [would] attach some
importance' to Ireland's recognition, but there was no need to 'excite
controversy'. During a subsequent exchange of letters, Cremin pointed out that a
further obstacle to a change in policy would be the almost certain negative
reaction from the Arab states.[231] Fred Boland, showing uncharacteristic self-
interest and the rare use of an exclamation mark, responded: 'From the point of
view of timing...the present moment is not a good one – particularly having
regard to the forthcoming election for the Presidency of the Assembly!'[232]

As had happened so many times in the past eleven years, the initiative to
change the policy toward Israel lost steam during the summer of 1960. The issue
would not become pertinent until Con Cremin decided in 1962 to clarify many
unresolved recognition issues in Irish foreign policy. Additionally, the issue of
the Holy Places had reached a certain status quo under the papacy of John
XXIII. Although a basic premise of this case study is that Ireland used the issue
of the Holy Places as an excuse to delay Israeli representation in Dublin, the
perception held by most in Iveagh House included the internationalization of
Jerusalem as the *ultima ratio* of recognition policy toward Israel.

AD KALENDAS GRAECAS – THE END OF NON-RECOGNITION – 1963

The impetus in 1962 that caused a shift in policy toward Israel emanated from
an unusual source. In July of that year Secretary Con Cremin considered the
possibility of Ireland entering into a trading relationship with South Vietnam.
The South Vietnamese government had not received any formal notice that the
Irish government recognized the state *de jure* and insisted that the Irish
government provide evidence of recognition.[233] During a discussion in Iveagh
House concerning South Vietnam, the question of Israel arose:

> After a short discussion...the Minister [Frank Aiken] came to the
> conclusion that it might be best in all circumstances if we were to
> accord *de jure* recognition, [which] would almost certainly be followed

by a request to us to accept an Israeli mission. The Minister would prefer if such a move could be postponed for some years, but feels that this matter can be dealt with independently of the grant of *de jure* recognition.[234]

What was unstated for so many years finally found its voice in Frank Aiken's explanation of why *de jure* recognition had been delayed: if Ireland were to recognize Israel *de jure*, a diplomatic mission in Ireland would be Israel's next request.

In the 'memorandum for the government' of 7 May 1963 discussed at length in Chapter 3, many outstanding recognition issues were settled. In drafting a circular to send to diplomatic missions concerning the changes in overall recognition policy, Israel once more presented a challenge. The Irish did not want excessive publicity concerning the decision. Even the Israelis did not necessarily want the decision announced 'in a demonstrative or spectacular manner'. As result, the decision was made to 'communicate the decision' to Israel's Foreign Minister, Golda Meir, 'with an indication that [the Government] did not wish any publicity be given to the matter'.[235] The fear of Iveagh House was that with the issuance of the diplomatic circular, 'the news will gradually percolate back to the Israeli Foreign Office' and in that case, 'the decision would be much more likely to receive publicity'. The ploy worked. Mrs Meir was notified and the decision was not made public by the international press until January 1964 upon Pope Paul VI's historic visit to the 'Holy Land'.[236]

CONCLUSION

Although the historical narrative of the establishment of diplomatic relations between Ireland and Israel has yet to be researched in the National Archives, as it extends beyond the present thirty-year period of record release, Keogh summarized the progression of Irish–Israeli diplomatic relations after 1963:

> [In December 1974], Ireland and Israel agreed to an exchange of diplomatic representatives. This was to be initially on a non-residential basis. At first, Ireland's representative in Switzerland was accredited to Israel... that was changed in 1979 when it was decided that the Irish ambassador to Greece would be accredited to Israel. The Irish Government gave approval for the establishment of an Israeli embassy in Dublin in 1993; Zvi Gabay presented his credentials on 22 July. An Israeli embassy was opened in Dublin in 1996.[237]

On 30 December 1993 the Vatican and Israel announced the establishment of diplomatic relations. The provisions for Jerusalem have yet to be determined.

In March 2000 the late Pope John Paul II visited Jerusalem in an effort to formalize an agreement not only with Israel, but also with the emerging Palestinian state.

In Ireland's unique policy of *de facto* recognition of Israel during the years 1949–63, virtual *non-recognition* of the State of Israel, three major themes are apparent in studying the diplomatic files. First, the policy of *de facto* recognition was closely held, made by a small number of individuals in Iveagh House, influenced by Ambassador Joseph Walshe at the Holy See. The justification for *de facto* recognition policy stemmed from two sources: the protection of the Holy Places and the desire to prevent 'Jewish infiltration' in Ireland.

The second argument concerns the maintenance of *de facto* recognition toward Israel for over fourteen years. The influence of the Holy See in Irish foreign policy dominated any impetus for change in the policy and was not necessarily in Ireland's long-term best interests. Ireland continued to limit diplomatic and economic initiatives with Israel, foregoing vital Irish foreign policy interests concerning trade, at first in deference to the wishes of Ambassador Walshe, and later out of fear of negative reactions from the Arab states. Throughout the period of *de facto* recognition, several times officials at Iveagh House questioned the policy and considered it untenable under international law, yet the policy endured.

The final argument concerns the status of *de facto* recognition in international law. Ireland's practice in the case of Israel illustrates the substantially political nature of diplomatic recognition in the latter half of the twentieth century. Although the decision was unique, Irish foreign policy did not violate international law in continuing *de facto* recognition for a protracted period. A posture of non-recognition is the prerogative of the sovereign state initiating the policy, although non-recognition does not change certain facts on the international plane nor does it affect 'the continued existence of the state itself'.[238] Ireland's practice in diplomatic recognition displays the primary instinct of a small state within the international system: survival. In order to maximize its interests, Ireland aligned with a more powerful entity on the subject of Israel, the Vatican, until its confidence grew and led to independent policy. The contradictions in the Irish policy toward Israel were not as numerous as one might expect. Once the decision for non-recognition was made, Iveagh House consistently operated within the confines of that policy. The case of Israel is unique not only in Irish foreign policy but also in terms of international law. The recognition of Israel presented a true opportunity for independence in policy-making by determining policy on the emergence of a *new* state, and in navigating recognition between the limited *de facto* status and full *de jure* recognition. The case of East Germany, in the period 1949–63, could not offer the same flexibility in policy. Nevertheless, Irish foreign policy adjusted and thrived in the hostile environment of the Cold War.

NOTES

1   Louis Henkin, *International Law: Politics and Values* (Dordrecht, 1995), p. 16.
2   Jennings and Watts, eds, *Oppenheim's International Law*, p. 175.
3   Some international legal scholars refer to this form of recognition as *premature* rather than *precipitate*. See von Glahn, *Law Among Nations*, pp. 88–9. It may be argued that *de facto* recognition of the State of Israel was not precipitate at all, since inherent in precipitate recognition is the idea of succession of a new state from an existing state. Britain's relinquishing the mandate for Palestine changes the nature of state succession in the case of Israel. *Oppenheim's* argues that 'precipitate recognition is more than a violation of the dignity of the parent state. It is an unlawful act, and it is frequently maintained that such untimely recognition amounts to intervention.' Jennings and Watts, eds, *Oppenheim's International Law*, p. 143. The United States, by granting *de facto* recognition did not infringe upon any rights of a *parent* state. No *parent state* existed.
4   Martin Gilbert, *Israel: A History* (New York, 1998), p. 189. *Oppenheim's* suggests that the United States granted *full recognition* to the State of Israel and recognized the government *de facto* on 14 May 1948. The argument for immediate *state* recognition stems from the fact that Great Britain relinquished its mandate over Israel, and there was no parent state. Later, the US elevated government recognition to *de jure* status on 27 May 1948. Jennings and Watts, eds, *Oppenheim's International Law*, p. 144–5. See also, Michael J. Cohen, *Truman and Israel* (Berkeley, CA, 1990), pp. 226–8.
5   NAI DFA 305/81/1, memorandum, Michael Rynne to Frederick H. Boland, 10 February 1949.
6   Since the conquest of Jerusalem by Khalif Omar in 637 AD, the holy places have been the subject of international interest for the three monotheist world religions. After the Ottoman Turks seized power under Selim I in 1517, a period of stabilization occurred, continuing through the capitulation of Louis XV of France to the Ottoman Sultan Mahmoud I in 1740, allowing Catholic pilgrims free access to the sites. In 1757 Osman II, ensuring the status quo principle, made similar guarantees. With the end of the Ottoman Empire in 1917, and the acceptance of the League of Nations mandate for Palestine by Britain, there was to be no essential change in the status of the holy places. See George Emile Irani, *The Papacy and the Middle East: The Role of the Holy See in the Arab–Israeli Conflict, 1962–84* (Notre Dame, IN, 1986).
7   Quoted in Conor Cruise O'Brien, *The Siege: The Saga of Israel and Zionism* (New York, 1986), p. 196.
8   See Keogh, *Jews in Twentieth-century Ireland.*
9   Richard H. Pfaff, 'Jerusalem', in John Norton Moore, ed., *The Arab–Israeli Conflict* (Princeton, NJ, 1977), p. 255. The term *Palestine* was a Roman word 'which fell into local disuse until the arrival of the British. To most Jews it meant nothing. They knew the country as the Land of Israel, Erez-Israel'. David Vital, *The Origins of Zionism* (Oxford, 1975), p. xvi. The spelling Eretz-Israel is also widely used.
10   Donald Neff, *Warriors for Jerusalem: The Six Days That Changed the Middle East* (Brattleboro, VT, 1988), pp. 21–2. Neff's figures reveal 103,371 Christians in Palestine in 1935 as well.
11   Irani, *The Papacy and the Middle East.*
12   See Cruise O'Brien, *The Siege*, pp. 224–6.
13   Pfaff, 'Jerusalem', p. 256.
14   Conor Cruise O'Brien argues that both Weizmann and Ben-Gurion were intent on the aggrandizement of a territorial settlement given to the Jews. See Cruise O'Brien, *The Siege*, p. 230.
15   Neff, *Warriors for Jerusalem*, p. 22.
16   Ibid.
17   Ibid., p. 23.
18   Cohen, *Truman and Israel*, p. 122. Secretary of State Dean Acheson remarked on

President Harry Truman's championing the cause of a Jewish state: 'Almost immediately upon becoming President, Mr. Truman with the best will in the world tackled that immensely difficult international puzzle – a homeland in Palestine for the Jews. Inevitably I was sucked in after him. The fate of the Jewish victims of Hitlerism was a "matter of deep personal concern" to him and as President he "undertook to do something about it". The Balfour Declaration, promising the Jews the opportunity to re-establish a homeland in Palestine, had always seemed to him "to go hand in hand with the noble policies of Woodrow Wilson, especially the principle of self-determination". For many years of talk with him I know that this represented a deep conviction, in large part implanted by his close friend and former partner, Eddie Jacobson, a passionate Zionist.' Dean Acheson, *Present at the Creation: My Years at the State Department* (New York, 1969), p. 169.

19   Cohen, *Truman and Israel*, p. 123.

20   Eleanor Roosevelt wrote to President Harry Truman on 20 November 1945: 'I am very much distressed that Great Britain has made us take a share in another investigation of the need of the few Jews remaining in Europe. If they are not to be allowed to enter Palestine, then certainly they could have been apportioned among the different United Nations and we would not have to continue to have on our consciences the death of at least fifty of these poor creatures daily... Great Britain is always anxious to have someone pull her chestnuts out of the fire... I object very much to being used by them.' Cohen, *Truman and Israel*, p. 125.

21   Cohen, *Truman and Israel*, p. 127.

22   Ibid., p. 131.

23   Ibid., p. 132.

24   Ibid., p. 144.

25   George W. Ball and Douglas B. Ball, *The Passionate Attachment: America's Involvement with Israel, 1947 to the Present* (New York, 1992), p. 20.

26   Cohen, *Truman and Israel*, p. 157.

27   Ibid., p. 158.

28   Neff, *Warriors for Jerusalem*, p. 23. The United Nations resolution that provided for partition of Palestine and a *corpus separatum* for Jerusalem is cited as GA Res. 181 (II), 2 UN GAOR, Resolutions Sept. 16–Nov. 29, 1947, at 131–2, UN Doc. A/519 (8 January, 1948).

29   Ball and Ball, *The Passionate Attachment*, p. 21.

30   NAI DFA 305/62/1.

31   NAI DFA 313/6, letter, Joseph P. Walshe to F. H. Boland, 17 October 1946.

32   Keogh, *Jews in Twentieth-century Ireland*, p. 206.

33   Ibid., p. 203.

34   Ibid., p. 206.

35   Although widely used by historians of modern Irish history in reference to the flight of emigrants from Ireland, the word *diaspora* is of Greek origin describing the Jews who were exiled after the Babylonian captivity in 586 BC. The basis of the concept is Biblical and found in Deuteronomy 28:25.

36   Yitzak Shamir, *Summing Up: An Autobiography* (London, 1994), p. 8.

37   Chaim Herzog, *Living History: A Memoir* (New York, 1996), p. 12.

38   Ireland refused to participate in the American initiative concerning the North Atlantic Treaty Organization (NATO) and also severed all colonial ties with Britain in 1949 by declaring Ireland a republic, repealing the External Relations Act of 1936, and 'disassociating' from the Commonwealth.

39   NAI DFA 305/62/1.

40   *Dáil Deb.*, 104, 1473, 27 February 1947. Flanagan's anti-Semitic remarks are described at length in Keogh, *Jews in Twentieth-Century Ireland*, pp. 172–3 and 187.

41   Herzog, *Living History*, p. 12.

42   Keogh, *Jews in Twentieth-century Ireland*, p. 224.

43   Ibid., p. 191.

44   Richard H. Pfaff, *Jerusalem: Keystone of an Arab–Israeli Settlement* (Washington, DC, 1969), p. 23.
45   The holy places include the Basilica of the Holy Sepulchre, Bethany, Cenacle, Church of St Anne, Church of St James the Great, Church of St Mark, Tomb of the Virgin, House of Caiphas and Prison of Christ, Sanctuary of the Ascension, Pool of Bethesda, Birthplace of John the Baptist, Basilica of the Nativity, Milk Grotto, Shepherd's Field and the Nine Stations of the Cross, collectively known as the Via Dolorosa.
46   Chaim Weizmann, *Trial and Error: The Autobiography of Chaim Weizmann* (London, 1949), p. 240.
47   NAI DT S14330, telegram, 27 May 1948.
48   NAI DT S14330, 'Memorandum for the government', 3 June 1948.
49   NAI DT CAB 5/18, 4 June 1948.
50   NAI DFA 305/62/1, letter, William Warnock to F.H. Boland, 27 May 1948.
51   United Nations General Assembly Resolution 187 (5-2). A copy of this Security Council initiative appears in the *UNO Bulletin*, 15 June 1948 and is found at NAI DFA 305/62/1.
52   Ball and Ball, *The Passionate Attachment*, p. 26.
53   NAI DFA 305/62/1, internal memorandum, 17 June 1948.
54   NAI DFA 305/62/1, internal memorandum, Michael Rynne to F.H. Boland, 8 July 1948.
55   NAI DFA 305/62/1, memorandum from the American legation, 13 July 1948.
56   Martin Gilbert has written that B-17s were flown to Israel from 'an American base in the Atlantic' as early as 18 May 1948. See his *Israel: A History*, pp. 200–1.
57   These reports are confirmed in David Ben-Gurion, *Israel: A Personal History* (New York, 1971), p. 218.
58   See the Aer Lingus history at www.aerlingus.ie.
59   NAI DFA 305/62/1, note, Con Cremin, 30 August 1948.
60   Ibid.
61   See 'Egypt Air – Brief History' at www.egyptguide.net, May 1999.
62   NAI DFA 305/62/1, memorandum, McLaughlin to the Department of External Affairs, 26 August 1948.
63   Shamir, *Summing Up*, p. 75.
64   Ibid.
65   NAI DFA 305/149 Part I, memorandum, Sheila Murphy to F.H. Boland, 26 October 1948.
66   John Cornwell's description of Pope Pius XII is colourful: 'Some spoke of a "feline" sensibility, others of an occasional tendency to "feminine" vanity. Before a camera there was a hint of narcissism. And yet he impressed most who met him with a sense of chaste, youthful innocence, like an eternal seminarian or monastic novice. He was at home with children, and they felt drawn to him... His eyes froze, harelike, when felt assailed by overfamiliarity or a coarse phrase. He was alone – in a quite extraordinary and exalted sense.' John Cornwell, *Hitler's Pope: The Secret history of Pius XII* (New York, 1999), p. 2.
67   The text of the Encyclical Letter is found in NAI DFA 305/62/1, translated and printed in *The Tablet*, 30 October 1948.
68   Tardini was deputy for foreign relations. Cornwell's description of Tardini is in sharp contrast to the more reticent Giovanni Montini (Pope Paul VI). '[Tardini] gave any money that came his way to an orphanage. He had no love for Fascists or the Nazis, and dubbed Hitler "a motorized Attila". Tardini spoke bluntly and was to emerge as a popular refreshing figure among the intriguing diplomats of the wartime Vatican. His corresponding deputy... was Giovanni Montini, the future Paul VI... Montini was a man of sweet and yielding disposition, assailed by scruples, contemplating each problem from all points of view, weighed down by the burdens of history... Pacelli [Pope Pius XII] loved him and was to favor him until, in the post-war years, he showed signs of sailing close to socialism.' Cornwell, *Hitler's Pope*, pp. 221–2.

69   *FRUS*, Vol. 5, 1948, telegram, Gowan to Acting Secretary of State, 12 November 1948, pp. 1572–3.
70   NAI DFA 305/62/1, letter J. Belton to F.H. Boland, 26 November 1948.
71   NAI DFA 305/62/1, letter, Joseph Walshe to F.H. Boland, 20 January 1949.
72   Ibid.
73   Ibid.
74   NAI DFA 305/62/1, letter, Walshe to Boland, 22 January 1949.
75   Ibid.
76   Cohen, *Truman and Israel*, pp. 237–8.
77   Weizmann Archives, Rehovot. Letter, Harry S. Truman to Chaim Weizmann, 29 November 1948. Original document printed in Aaron S. Klieman, ed., 'Recognition of Israel: An End and a New Beginning', in Aaron S. Klieman and Adrian L. Klieman, eds, *American Zionism: A Documentary History,* Vol. 13 (New York, 1991), pp. 466–7.
78   Cohen, *Truman and Israel*, p. 270.
79   Cohen, *Truman and Israel*, p. 268.
80   Weizmann Archives, Rehovot. Letter, President Truman to Chaim Weizmann, 29 November 1948. Original document printed in Klieman, 'Recognition of Israel', p. 467.
81   *FRUS*, Vol. 6, 1949, p. 680.
82   *Ibid.*, p. 273.
83   The British-American negotiations are documented in *FRUS*, Vol. 6, 1949, pp. 658–81.
84   Among the States were Belgium, the Netherlands, Luxembourg, Australia, New Zealand, Switzerland, Ecuador, Colombia, Denmark, Norway, Brazil, Italy, Iceland, Argentina and Bolivia. In March 1949 Turkey was the first Islamic state to recognize Israel *de facto*; *de jure* followed in July 1950.
85   NAI DFA 305/81/1, note, F.H. Boland, 27 January 1949.
86   NAI DFA305/81/1, letter, F.H. Boland to Joseph Walshe, 28 January 1949.
87   NAI DT S14330, various reports from the *Irish Times*, *Irish Independent* and *Irish Press*, 1 February 1949.
88   NAI DT S14330, *Irish Independent*, 1 February 1949.
89   NAI DFA 305/62/1, letter, Joseph Walshe to F.H. Boland, 5 February 1949.
90   Keogh commented on Walshe's letter-writing style: 'The Holy See was a posting Walshe greatly desired. He was sixty, single and he enjoyed moderately good health. He was committed to the service of his country and his church. As a former secretary of the Department of External Affairs for over twenty years, Walshe exhibited none of the inhibitions of a new envoy in the field when writing to a superior. Psychologically he never quite relinquished his position as *secretary* of the department. As ambassador, Walshe continued his practice of using *back channels* to his minister by writing *personal* letters. Fortunately for the historian, Frederick Boland believed in keeping a comprehensive file.' Keogh, *Ireland and the Vatican*, p. 197.
91   NAI DFA 305/81/1, memorandum, Michael Rynne to F.H. Boland, 10 February 1949.
92   Ibid.
93   Ibid.
94   In contract law declaring a court of jurisdiction in the original contract (i.e. Israel) often averts this difficulty.
95   NAI DFA 305/81/1, memorandum, F.H. Boland to Seán MacBride, 11 February 1949.
96   NAI DT S14330, cabinet minutes, 11 February 1949.
97   NAI DFA 305/81 Part 1, press release, 12 February 1949.
98   NAI DFA 305/81 Part 1, extract of secret report, Walshe to Boland, 24 February 1949.
99   Ibid.
100 NAI DFA 305/81 Part 1, letter, F.H. Boland to Joseph Walshe, 24 February 1949.
101 David Schoenbaum, *The United States and the State of Israel* (New York, 1993), p. 70.
102 NAI DFA 305/62/1, letter, J.P. Walshe to F.H. Boland, 14 June 1949.
103 Ibid.
104 Ibid.

105   NAI DFA 305/62/1, letter, John Charles McQuaid to Immanuel Jakobovits, 26 May
      1949. McQuaid also states in a rather celestial manner, that should the Israeli govern-
      ment issue a declaration, not only would it allay the fears of the Irish government, the
      statement 'will be carefully noted wherever Irishmen are found, that is, throughout the
      universe, and especially, in the United States of America'. In an interview with the
      author in June 1998, Gerald Goldberg of Cork emphasized that the Jewish community
      interpreted McQuaid's letter to mean that unless the holy places were secured,
      McQuaid could not be responsible for the safety of Jewish persons in Ireland.
106   NAI DFA 305/62/1, letter, J.P. Walshe to F.H. Boland, 8 August 1949.
107   Miriam Hederman summed up Seán MacBride's foreign policy efforts at the Council of
      Europe in autumn 1949 with a quote by Conor Cruise O'Brien: 'Our Parliamentary
      delegates to the Council of Europe seemed to devote their time to making speeches about
      partition; speeches which were designed to be read at home, but which unfortunately had
      to be listened to abroad.' Hederman, *The Road to Europe*, p. 32.
108   Ronan Fanning, 'Raison d'Etat and the evolution of Irish foreign policy', in Michael
      Kennedy and Joseph Morrison Skelly, eds, *Irish Foreign Policy 1919–66: From
      Independence to Internationalism* (Dublin, 2000), p. 321.
109   Seyom Brown noted that linkage in a bipolar organization of state power is quite
      different from a system in which numerous participants agree that 'we will support you
      on this issue, if you support us on that issue'. When two states have comparable foreign
      policy objectives, and the comparable ability to meet those objectives, then linkage is
      simply a trade-off. But in the case of Ireland during 1949, whose capability for meeting
      foreign policy objectives against the interests of larger states was minimal, linkage was
      a wholly ineffectual measure. As Fanning noted when MacBride attempted linkage
      with NATO and partition, the representatives of the state department simply said, 'it's
      been nice knowing you'. Fanning, 'Raison d'Etat and the evolution of Irish foreign
      policy', p. 321. See also Seyom Brown, 'The changing essence of power', in Ray
      Maghroori and Bennett Ramberg, eds, *Globalism versus Realism: International
      Relations' Third Debate* (Boulder, CO, 1982), p. 26.
110   NAI DFA 305/62/1, 'Statement regarding the Holy Places in Palestine, on Introduction
      of the Estimates for the Department of External Affairs', Seán MacBride, 13 July 1949.
      'The Vatican Decree on Communism', in Margaret Carlyle, *Documents on
      International Affairs 1949–1950* (Oxford, 1953), pp. 406–7.
111   NAI DFA 305/62/1, letter, Legation of Israel to John W. Dulanty, 25 July 1949.
112   *Congressional Record*. 80th Congress, 3rd session, 1949. A4914 (21 July 1949).
      Statement by Arthur G. Klein.
113   NAI DFA 305/81/1, memorandum, Conor Cruise O'Brien to F.H. Boland and Seán
      MacBride, 16 August 1949.
114   NAI DFA 305/81/1, handwritten memorandum, F.H. Boland to Conor Cruise O'Brien,
      19 August 1949. It is interesting to note that the file NAI DFA 348/117/1 is entitled
      'Suggested gestures of friendship to Israel', echoing Boland's terminology.
115   Philip Sayers of Cork. Sayers played a prominent role in trying to negotiate trade
      agreements between Israel and Ireland during 1949–50. Gerald Goldberg described
      Sayers as 'having traveled all over the world, wealthy, a Zionist, and Lithuanian'.
      Interview with Gerald Goldberg, June 1998.
116   NAI DFA 305/62/1, letter, Seán MacBride to Joseph Walshe, 22 August 1949.
117   Ibid.
118   Keith David Eagles, 'Ambassador Joseph E. Davies and American-Soviet Relations'
      (Ph.D. dissertation, University of Washington, 1966), p.328, quoted in Gaddis, *Russia,
      The Soviet Union, and the United States: An Interpretive History*, p. 149.
119   *FRUS*, Vol. VI, 1949, pp. 1348–9, telegram, Dean Acheson to Franklin C. Gowan at
      Vatican City, 1 September 1949.
120   *FRUS*, Vol. 6, 1949, pp. 1383–7, position paper 'Jerusalem', US Department of State,
      14 September 1949.
121   NAI DFA305/62/1, letter, Joseph Walshe to Seán MacBride, 8 September 1949.

122   Ibid..
123   Jennings and Watts, eds, *Oppenheim's International Law*, p. 157.
124   The United States, for example, grants diplomatic immunity to representatives of governments recognized *de facto*.
125   For example, the Israeli Government, for its delay in granting recognition, chastised India. India did not distinguish between *de facto* and *de jure* in recognizing 'the government of Israel' on 17 September 1950. However, India did not establish diplomatic relations with Israel until after 1966. See Misra, *India's Policy of Recognition of States and Governments*, pp. 50 60. See also Brijesh Narain Mehrish, *India's Recognition Policy Towards the New Nations* (Delhi, 1972), pp. 74–81.
126   NAI DFA 348/117/1, memorandum, 17 December 1948.
127   Ibid.
128   NAI DFA 348/117/1, memorandum, 10 January 1949.
129   NAI DFA 348/117/1, *L'Echo D'Israel*, 2 March 1949.
130   NAI DFA 348/117/1, letter, L. Danon of Tel Aviv to Department of Agriculture, 7 March 1949.
131   NAI DFA 348/117/1, letter, J. Molloy to Department of Agriculture, 27 August 1949.
132   NAI DFA 348/117/1, letter, 27 August 1949.
133   *Department of State Bulletin*, 21, 534 (Washington, DC, 1949), p. 459.
134   Cruise O'Brien, *The Siege*, p. 365.
135   NAI DFA 305/62/1, note, 25 October 1949. Imports from Israel included fresh grapefruit and oranges. Exports to Israel included 'aeroplanes and parts' and potatoes for seed. The trade deficit with Israel was IR£222,397 for a total volume of IR£316,317. NAI DFA 348/117, ST 2718.
136   For a complete record of the Sayers negotiations, see the minutes of the Foreign Trade Committee (FTC) from 14 February 1950 to 22 March 1951.
137   NAI DFA 348/117, letter, M. Palgi to P. Sayers, 13 April 1950. To substantiate his position with the Israeli government, Philip Sayers provided letters to the Irish government, which were copied and inserted into the files.
138   NAI DFA 348/117, letter, M.J. Barry to F. Biggar, 22 March 1951.
139   NAI DFA 348/117, note, J. Molloy to J. Belton, 6 March 1950.
140   Ibid.
141   NAI DFA 348/117, Foreign Trade Committee minutes, 14 March 1950.
142   NAI DFA 348/117, FTC minutes, 14 March 1950.
143   NAI DFA 348/117, FTC minutes, 22 March 1950.
144   NAI DFA 348/117, letter, M. Palgi to P. Sayers, 11 April 1950.
145   NAI DFA 348/117, letter, P. Sayers to G. Meron, 25 April 1950.
146   NAI DFA 305/81 Part 1, extract from Parliamentary Debates (Hansard) House of Commons, Col. 1147/49, 27 April 1950.
147   NAI DFA 348/117, FTC minutes, 5 May 1950. During this time, Lauterpacht's treatise on recognition (1947) was the primary source for defining implied recognition. Lauterpacht did not believe that recognition could be implied without *intent* of the recognizing state, citing the conclusion of treaties (especially bilateral treaties), participation in conferences, accrediting or receiving diplomatic representatives, appointing and receiving consuls, request for an *exequatur*, and the issuance on an *exequatur*. Lauterpacht clearly states that 'the appointment of agents or missions not endowed with diplomatic character does not constitute recognition. The case against implied recognition happening without intent is stronger yet when a state considers its treatment of the unrecognized state as *non-recognition*.' See Lauterpacht, *Recognition*, pp. 368–408.
148   NAI DFA 348/117, FTC minutes, 12 May 1950.
149   NAI DFA 305/81/1, letter, C. Cruise O'Brien to P. Barnicle, 23 May 1950.
150   NAI DFA 348/117, FTC minutes, 25 May 1950.
151   NAI DFA 348/117, teleprinter message, London to Dublin, 26 May 1950.
152   NAI DFA 305/81 Part 1, memorandum, 29 June 1950.

153 NAI DFA 305/81 Part 1, letter, Seán MacBride to Moshe Sharett, 15 June 1950.
154 NAI DFA 348/117, 'Israel wants more Irish trade', *Irish Independent*, 14 June 1950.
155 NAI DFA 349/117, FTC minutes, 25 August 1950.
156 NAI DFA 348/117, letter, Con Cremin to Frank Biggar, 31 August 1950.
157 Ibid.
158 NAI DFA 348/117, FTC minutes, 8 September 1950.
159 NAI DFA 305/81/1, statement made by Seán MacBride at a meeting of the Jewish Discussion Club, Dublin, 30 September 1950.
160 NAI DFA 35/81 Part 1, memorandum, V. Iremonger to T. O'Driscoll, 12 October 1950.
161 NAI DFA 305/81 Part 1, 'Memorandum for the Government – Recognition of Israel', 19 April 1951.
162 NAI DFA 305/81 Part 1, letter, Joseph Walshe to Seán Nunan, 2 May 1951.
163 Ibid.
164 Ibid.
165 NAI DFA 305/149 Part 1, note, Michael Rynne, 8 August 1951.
166 NAI DFA 348/117, FTC minutes, 20 October 1950.
167 NAI DFA 348/117, FTC minutes, 27 October 1950. It is not clear whether 'the Sayer's deal' materialized, but the trade figures for exports to Israel grew from IR£46,860 in 1949 to IR£141,930 in 1950. Ironically, after so much activity between 1949 and 1951 on the prospects of trade, exports to Israel dropped dramatically throughout the 1950s, as low as IR£17,573 in 1957. Exports did not recover substantially until 1964, the year after *de jure* recognition was granted. See Central Statistics Office, *Ireland: Trade and Shipping Statistics* (Dublin, various years).
168 NAI DFA 348/117, note, J.M. Barry, 16 March 1951. Brin's comments were reported to the Foreign Trade Committee, the source of this note.
169 Ibid.
170 NAI DFA 348/117, note, 6 April 1951.
171 NAI DFA 348/117, FTC minutes, 13 April 1951.
172 Statistics compiled by author. *Statistical Abstracts of Ireland, 1948–64*.
173 NAI DFA 305/62 Part I, memorandum, 'Question of *de jure* recognition of the State of Israel', 11 September 1951.
174 NAI DFA 305/81 Part 1, note, Michael Rynne, 20 June 1952.
175 See Lee, *Ireland 1912–85*, p. 322.
176 Keogh, *Ireland and the Vatican*, p. 325. Keogh notes that although Aiken held the portfolio, de Valera 'would remain in personal control of external affairs'.
177 NAI DT S15392A, note, 10 November 1952. See also Chaim Weizmann obituary in the *Irish Independent*, 10 November 1952.
178 NAI DT S15392A, letter, Eamon de Valera to Chief Rabbi Herzog, 11 November 1952.
179 NAI DFA 305/62 Part 1, note, T.J. Horan, 11 November 1952.
180 Joseph Walshe died in February 1956. In an interview with Con Cremin, Keogh wrote: 'Cremin had known Walshe since 1929 and, in retirement, he spoke to me with qualified respect for his former superior. Cremin used an Irish expression – *fear ann féin é* – to describe him, an Irish idiom which literally means "he was peculiar". Cremin did not elaborate, but he repeated the description more than once in our many conversations.' Keogh, *Ireland and the Vatican*, p. 348.
181 See Chapter 2.
182 NAI DT S14330, letter, Leonard Abrahamson to John A. Costello, 8 March 1955.
183 NAI DFA 319/25/9, letter, Immanuel Jakobovits to Seán Murphy, 26 March 1956.
184 Ibid.
185 See Cruise O'Brien, *The Siege*, pp. 381–95.
186 Ibid., p. 384.
187 NAI DFA 319/25/9, letter, J. S. Steinberg to Seán Murphy, 31 March 1956.
188 NAI DFA 319/25/9, memorandum, G. Woods, 12 July 1956.
189 NAI DFA 319/25/9, note, Eoin MacWhite to Seán Murphy, 11 August 1956.
190 NAI DFA 319/25/9, note, Seán Murphy to Sheila Murphy, 15 August 1956.

191   NAI DFA 319/25/9, note, Eoin MacWhite to G. Woods, 17 August 1956.
192   NAI DFA 319/25/9, teleprinter message, Frank Biggar to Seán Morrissey, 21 August 1956.
193   NAI DFA 319/25/9, teleprinter message, Frank Biggar to Seán Morrissey, 3 September 1956.
194   NAI DFA 319/25/9, teleprinter message, G. Woods to Frank Biggar, 14 September 1956.
195   NAI DFA 319/25/9, memorandum, 7 September 1956.
196   Ibid.
197   *FRUS*, Vol. 10, 1955–57, memorandum of conversation, 28 November 1956, p. 643.
198   Ball and Ball, *The Passionate Attachment*, p. 48.
199   Ibid.
200   Ibid.
201   James A. Nathan and James K. Oliver, *United States Foreign Policy and World Order* (Glenview, IL, 4th edn, 1989), p. 171.
202   Ibid.
203   Robert J. Art, 'America's foreign policy', in Roy C. Macridis, ed., *Foreign Policy in World Politics: States and Regions* (Englewood Cliffs, NJ, 7th edn, 1989), p. 144.
204   Skelly, *Irish Diplomacy at the United Nations 1945–1965*, p. 154.
205   Ibid., p. 155.
206   NAI DFA 305/81 Part 1, Frank Aiken, 'Plan for Middle East', *Weekly Bulletin of the Department of External Affairs*, 414 (18 August 1958).
207   Skelly, *Irish Diplomacy at the United Nations*, p. 159.
208   Ibid.
209   Ibid., p. 161.
210   Fanning, '*Raison d'État* and the evolution of Irish foreign policy', p. 324.
211   Cornwell, *Hitler's Pope*, p. 355.
212   Ibid., pp. 356–7.
213   NAI DT S16583, letter, Leo McCauley to Con Cremin, 12 November 1958.
214   Ibid.
215   NAI DFA 305/62/1, note, 17 November 1958.
216   NAI DFA 305/62/1, note, Con Cremin to Frank Aiken, 24 November 1958.
217   NAI DFA 305/62 Part 1, report, D. R. McDonald, 24 March 1959.
218   NAI DFA 305/81 Part 1, memorandum, Con Cremin to John Belton, 15 April 1959.
219   *Oremus et pro perfidis Judaeis: ut Deus et Dominus noster auferat velamen de cordibus eorum; ut et ipsi agnoscant Jesum Christum Dominum nostrum.* Cornwell (1999) also notes Pope John XXIII's omission of the term 'perfidious Jews' from the Good Friday liturgy of the Roman Missal in 1959 and thereafter. Cornwell, *Hitler's Pope*, p. 27 n24.
220   NAI DFA305/81 Part 1, note, Conor Cruise O'Brien to Eoin MacWhite, 6 May 1959.
221   NAI 305/81 Part 1, memorandum, Eoin MacWhite to Conor Cruise O'Brien, 2 June 1959.
222   This term comes from a chapter in Lee, *Ireland 1912–1985*.
223   In a sense, Ireland was quite lucky to escape the wrath of Israel on the non-recognition issue. Apart from the occasional *démarche* at the UN and in Washington, the Israelis did not press Ireland on the matter. The Indian government on the other hand, after granting delayed *de jure* recognition to Israel in August 1958, was severely criticized by David Ben-Gurion in November 1959 for failing to establish diplomatic ties. See the *New York Times*, 13 November 1959. India established diplomatic relations with Israel on 29 January 1992.
224   NAI DFA 305/81 Part 1, draft letter, Con Cremin to Leo McCauley, 5 November 1959.
225   NAI DFA 305/81 Part 1, letter, Con Cremin to Fred Boland, 19 April 1960.
226   NAI DFA 348/117, letter, Department of Industry and Commerce to the Department of the Taoiseach, 28 January 1960. The 'arbitration clause' in the agreement cited the jurisdiction as Tel Aviv, Israel.

227   NAI DFA 305/81 Part 1, note, Con Cremin, 28 March 1960.
228   Ibid.
229   NAI DFA 305/81 Part 1, note, Conor Cruise O'Brien, 22 April 1960.
230   NAI DFA 305/81 Part 1, letter, F. H. Boland to Con Cremin, 6 April 1960.
231   NAI DFA 305/81 Part 1, letter, Con Cremin to F. H. Boland, 19 April 1960.
232   NAI DFA 305/81 Part 1, letter, F. H. Boland to Con Cremin, 26 April 1960.
233   See Chapter 3.
234   NAI DFA 305/149 Part 1, note, Con Cremin, 10 July 1962.
235   NAI DFA 305/149 Part 1, memo, 22 May 1963.
236   See *New York Times*, 26 January 1964.
237   Keogh, *Jews in Twentieth Century Ireland*, p. 229.
238   Jennings and Watts, eds, *Oppenheim's International Law*, p. 198.

Conclusion: Assessment and comparison

The attitude of non-recognition shows that the law, though temporarily shorn of its strength, is a potentially powerful factor so long as there is predominant the sentiment of its ultimate authority. Law is not necessarily disintegrated by impotence; but it is destroyed by unqualified submission to the lawlessness of force. Non-recognition prevents that contingency. For this reason, so long as there is no assurance that international law will be enforced invariably and effectively by ordinary purposes, non-recognition is a legal principle of value.

> Sir Hersch Lauterpacht, *Recognition in International Law*[1]

For some time the definition of a state was not dispositive. A generation or two ago, much law and diplomacy were concerned with issues of recognition... Inevitably, [non-recognized states] created havoc in the world of fact, as states (and the international system) had to accommodate to the existence in their midst an anomalous entity... a child very much alive and well but illegitimate... As was inevitable, other states did deal with such unrecognized entities as with other similar entities, and inevitably the law had to develop fictions, for example '*de facto* recognition'. Recognition is still in the language of diplomats but it does not belong in the language of law... The recognition of governments raises similar issues. Law and diplomacy once struggled with such recognition too. Again, the law has become more realistic. A régime that governs in fact is a government and must be treated as such... International law has not shed all of its fictions, but it is shedding this one.

> Louis Henkin, *International Law: Politics and Values*[2]

In the past fifty years, diplomatic recognition as an international legal concept has faded from the language of diplomats. As Louis Henkin described in the passage above, the tension created by anomalous situations in the Cold War environment has resulted in politicizing recognition issues and decisions. Altogether, using the political process as the core of diplomatic recognition decision-making cannot be seen as a negative aspect. Ireland, in pursuing independent foreign policy after 1949, successfully reconciled the tension of a changing international system. Bipolarity, for all its negative economic and cultural aspects, provided political stability for the system of states in the latter half of the twentieth century, as John Lewis Gaddis and other Cold War scholars have observed. Bipolarity also provided for the evolution of a different approach for smaller governments in diplomatic relations. Pursuing policy based on international law, or an overriding sense of principle, did not always serve the international interests of smaller states, including Ireland. In this study, Ireland pursued the approach of *pro tempora et pro re*, deciding recognition issues within the context of time, or the moment, and circumstance. Today, diplomatic recognition policy may be justified with varying rationales – expediency, morality, economy – approaches that scholars of the pre-Second World War diplomatic environment (such as Sir Hersch Lauterpacht) might have regarded as unwelcome.

THE ANOMALOUS NON-RECOGNITION OF ISRAEL

The Department of External (Foreign) Affairs in Ireland was confronted on a daily basis with recognition issues. These issues were not always apparent to other members of the government, or to the public. Within the workings of the Department, however, diplomatic recognition issues commanded a large amount of time, as the remaining archival evidence of the department shows. If the Department of External Affairs failed in any manner on recognition issues, this study has shown the inconsistency in its policies on one particular case – Israel.[3]

The policy toward Israel was consistently described by the Department as one of *non-recognition* when in actuality, the policy did not constitute deliberate condemnation of Israel – its existence, its governments or its people. Perhaps naively, Ireland's failure to recognize Israel *de jure* for fourteen years, long after the democratic Western states had given full diplomatic approval, was first, an attempt to exact a change in Israel's stance on Jerusalem and the Holy Places. Second, the policy was initiated to foster approval from the Holy See. Third, the non-recognition policy was an attempt to increase Ireland's prestige as a Catholic nation in the world system. Later, with the gradual secularization of Irish foreign policy, non-recognition of Israel became untenable and the members of the Department of External Affairs were uncomfortably aware of the anomaly of Ireland's position. Only with an examination and overhaul of lingering contradictions in recognition policy en masse in 1963 did the department (and the government) quietly recognize Israel *de jure*. The policy toward Israel went virtually unnoticed in the international system, and during the period of the study, while the Israelis actively pursued trade with Ireland, they did not pursue *de jure* recognition.

DE FACTO AND DE JURE REVISITED

The case of Israel highlights the problematic nature of the 'political fiction of *de facto* recognition' to which Henkin refers above. In spite of simplifying recognition with the Estrada Doctrine (1930), international law provided no simple solution for defining *de facto* and *de jure* recognition in practice. In Ireland, the terms were used in an effort to stratify varying degrees of diplomatic contacts within the state system. In their practical usage, *de facto* and *de jure* were used within the confines of the Department of External Affairs to describe how policy should be made toward the state in question. For example, the level of recognition might allow only a trading relationship with the state in question, or recognition might mean complete, formal relations with the state. There was often no legal distinction given between the two variations, not in the sense the Irish Government used them in the period 1949–63, but there continued to be a considerable gap between *de facto* and *de jure* in practice.

For Ireland after 1949, the most effective recognition policy needed to incorporate the 'infinite gradation of relations' of which Louis Jaffe wrote in 1933. Because of changing international interests, Ireland needed the 'grey', flexible policy policies necessary to address many different concerns. As a result, the rationale for recognizing states (and sometimes governments) often stretched to meet changing interests. Ti-Chiang Chen found it instructive in 1951 to describe the modes of recognition,[4] but did not provide a similar guideline for determining rationale in recognition policy. For flexible Irish decision-making, the absolute nature of recognition and non-recognition was not useful. Rather, Ireland pursued diplomatic relationships based on a hierarchy of interests. Recognition in practice paralleled these interests. The levels may be identified as follows:

1. limited recognition to facilitate trade
2. recognition of the state (*de facto*)
3. conditional recognition (*de facto*)
4. recognition of the government (*de facto*)
5. full diplomatic recognition (*de jure*)

At the lowest level, *limited recognition to facilitate trade*, inquiries were conducted by the Foreign Trade Committee with unrecognized states (distinguished often as *de facto* states in Ireland's practice). Contacts were acceptable with citizens of the 'unrecognized' state. Citizens of the 'unrecognized' state were often allowed entry into Ireland to discuss possible trading arrangements. The case studies of Israel and East Germany verify these contacts occurred.

Within the next level, *recognition of the state*, contacts were present as in the trading level. Further, the state was recognized *de facto* but not *de jure*. The state of Israel, for example, was recognized *de facto* from 1949 until May 1963 when *de jure* recognition was granted. Irish policy reflected the idea that recognition of the *state* of China was never withdrawn, nor was it withdrawn from the *state* of Formosa (Taiwan) after 1949. The *state* of East Germany was eventually recognized by most Western governments, including Ireland, after the conclusion of the Basic Treaty with the Federal Republic of Germany in 1972, but diplomatic relations with East Germany were not formally established with the Soviet satellite state.

At the level of *conditional recognition*, trade occurred with the other state and *de facto* acceptance of the state existed. *De jure* recognition was withheld until certain conditions were fulfilled. Withholding *de jure* recognition from the state of Israel and China appears to be the only examples of Ireland's conditional recognition policy. When *de facto* recognition of the state exists for an extended period without change, or without the required compliance of the unrecognized state in fulfilling the conditions necessary, the policy evolves from *conditional recognition* to a policy of deliberate *non-recognition*.

When *recognition of the government* occurs, all prior levels are accepted, as well as accepting the government in power as *de jure*. Relations are intact with the unrecognized state but diplomats have not been accredited, and missions have not been established. This level is very closely related to the last, *full diplomatic recognition (de jure)*, when the *de facto* distinction is discarded and replaced with *de jure*. This level signifies the capacity to enter into diplomatic relations, allowing the exchange of diplomats and missions.

While the classifications listed above reflect the practice in Irish foreign policy, they are purely historical in nature. The difficulty for Ireland during 1949–63 was that the Department of External Affairs and the Taoiseach's office did not distinguish the terms in setting policy, only in practice. For the historian it is not difficult to classify recognition decisions based on these categories, but the decision-makers certainly did not group recognition in this manner. Confusion often resulted in situations involving states that did not have Ireland's full diplomatic recognition. For example, in July 1951, a question arose in the Department of External Affairs over whether Ireland could enter into an air transport agreement with Israel, a state that Ireland recognized *de facto* but not *de jure*. The issue appeared in a memorandum written by a member of Political Section of External Affairs:

> There seems to be no doubt whatever that we could enter into a formal air transport agreement with Israel without committing ourselves to *de jure* recognition. It appears, however, that in keeping with the provisional character of *de facto* recognition the agreement should also be provisional in character... It seems, indeed, to be only common sense – what otherwise would be the use of *de facto* recognition?[5]

Dr Michael Rynne, the legal adviser to the Department of External Affairs since 1932, attached a note of approval to the statement:

I agree with Miss Murphy... that we can make a Trade Agreement with Israel without committing ourselves to recognizing it *de jure*. But in view of our keen desire (inspired largely by Ambassador, Holy See [Joseph P. Walshe]) to avoid doing anything at all ambiguous in this regard, I think we should inform our Israeli delegates, before starting trade or air agreement talks, that in our understanding the conclusion of a trade or air agreement with them will not affect the recognition question.[6]

The ambiguous distinction of *de facto* and *de jure* recognition above is only one of many examples of the political nature of Ireland's recognition policies. In 1948, Hersch Lauterpacht noted that 'according to what is probably still the predominant view in the literature of international law, recognition of states is not a matter governed by law but a question of policy'.[7] In the post-war world, Lauterpacht lamented that international practice would allow recognition to slip away from all legal principle. If Lauterpacht were correct, if recognition in 1948 were simply a matter of policy, then why would the Irish government be concerned about 'doing anything at all ambiguous in this regard'?[8] Lauterpacht provided the explanation:

The answer is that, while denying the quality of law to the act of recognition, some [jurists]... maintain that this act of policy, once accomplished, entails legal consequences... the form and the circumstances of recognition are of legal interest and necessitate the consideration of such questions as the distinction between *de jure* and *de facto* recognition.[9]

The debate distinguishing *de facto* and *de jure* continued in international legal scholarship throughout the 1950s. Philip Jessup, in *A Modern Law of Nations* (1956), argued that '*de facto* is a term used without precision. When properly used to mean the recognition of the *de facto* character of the government, it is unobjectionable and could be identical with the practice suggested of extending recognition without resuming diplomatic relations.'[10] Jessup argued that the usage of *de facto* as a term to connote *conditional* recognition was 'nonsense'.[11] During the period 1949–63 Ireland withheld *de jure* recognition to imply conditional recognition in regard to the State of Israel. *Oppenheim's International Law* clarifies the point:

Recognition, in various aspects, is neither a contractual arrangement nor a political concession. It is a declaration of the existence of certain facts. This being so, it is improper to make it subject to conditions other than the existence – including the continued existence – of the requirements which qualify a community for recognition as an independent state, a government, or a belligerent in a civil war. In fact, the practice of states shows few examples, if any, of conditions of recognition in the proper sense, i.e. of stipulations the non-fulfilment of which justifies withdrawal of recognition. There are...occasional cases in which the recognizing state obtains, as the price of recognition, promises and undertakings given for its particular advantage.[12]

For a young state like Ireland, trying to meet as many interests as possible in one policy decision, the tendency was to categorize all recognition issues under either *de facto* or *de jure*. Although the distinction in *meaning* was clear to the Department of External Affairs when the terms were applied, in *practice* the terms were applied at will for political convenience. The vacillation between *de facto* and *de jure* is arguably one of the more interesting aspects of the history of diplomatic recognition in Ireland. Now, in current international law, *de facto* and *de jure* are not the keywords used in diplomatic recognition policy. As Louis Henkin wrote in 1995, 'an entity that is a state in fact is a state in law. A régime that is a government in fact is a government in law.'[13] The question is no longer, 'when does an entity become a state', but 'whether other governments must establish relations with a new state or a new régime'.[14] In a very unique and subtle manner, the diplomatic recognition policies of Ireland in the period 1949–63 contributed to this new atmosphere of international relations.

NOTES

1   Lauterpacht, Hersch, *Recognition in International Law* (Cambridge: Cambridge University Press, 1947), p. 435.
2   Henkin, *International Law*, pp. 13–15.
3   For an exhaustive discussion on diplomatic recognition of Israel, see Chapter 6.
4   Chen, *The International Law of Recognition*. Chen's modes are: express declaration; bilateral treaties; exchange of diplomatic representatives; establishment of consuls and exequaturs; international conferences, multilateral treaties, and international organizations; *relations officieuses*; and collective recognition.
5   NAI DFA 305/149 Part 1, memorandum, S. Murphy to W. Butler, 18 July 1951.
6   NAI DFA 305/149 Part 1, memorandum, M. Rynne to W. Butler, 20 August 1951.
7   Lauterpacht, *Recognition in International Law*, p. 1.
8   NAI DFA 305/149 Part 1, memorandum, Murphy to Butler, 18 July 1951.
9   Lauterpacht, *Recognition in International Law*, p. 1.
10 Philip C. Jessup, *A Modern Law of Nations: An Introduction* (New York, 1956), p. 57.
11 Ibid, p. 58.
12 Jennings and Watts, eds, *Oppenheim's International Law*, p. 175. In 1911 the United States required written assurances that American interests would be protected before recognizing the Haitian Government; in 1922 the US secured trade advantages in recognizing Albania. Britain required satisfaction concerning treatment of British property in Mexico before granting recognition of its government in 1918. In 1942 the US required assurances about the rights of US nationals before granting recognition to Lebanon.
13 Henkin, *International Law*, pp. 15–16.
14 Ibid, p. *16*.

Appendix 1

Memorandum: Michael Rynne to Frederick H. Boland, 10
February 1949
Subject: *De facto* recognition of Israel

Secretary:
1. We spoke about this and you indicated that the recognition to be accorded
would probably be *de facto* recognition of the Government of Israel. That is, there
would no reference to the State of Israel and *de jure* recognition of both State and
Government would be tacitly reserved.

2. The most obvious and, I think, the best way of handling this matter will be that
adopted already by a number of other Governments, namely, of conveying recognition to the Israeli Foreign Secretary (Moshe Shertok) by replying by telegram (or
letter) to the telegram we received from Tel Aviv, dated 27th May, 1948.

3. The Government's telegram might simply say:
'Referring to your telegram of the 27th May last I desire to inform you that the
Government of Ireland recognises the *de facto* authority of the Government of
Israel. Seán MacBride, Minister for External Affairs.'

4   It will, of course, be realised that the foregoing text represents the virtual
minimum of recognition which it is possible to concede. We could scarcely
reduce it further, in either substance or expression, unless we were to resort to
the improper (though by no means unprecedented) course of attaching some
condition other than one of the implied standard conditions laid down by
international law (e.g. fixed territory, wishes of people etc.)
    If we were to attach, for example a condition about the preservation of the
holy places, we should, I suggest, be going too far below the minimum
prescribed by commonsense and normal practice. Commonsense indicates that,
since *de facto* recognition is recognition of a state of fact, no extra condition or
proviso would ever be relevant in the context.
    A condition, or 'string', to the Government's recognition ought therefore not
to be announced in the actual instrument whereby its recognition is accorded to
the Israeli Government.

5. Notwithstanding these remarks, however, it is clear that if the Government
desires to defend its policy of recognition in the Oireachtas or elsewhere it
would be quite justified in adverting to Mr. Shertok's assurance (contained in his
telegram of last May) that his Government proposes 'to safeguard the sanctity

and inviolability of the shrines and holy places' under its control. Certainly some public declaration or official communiqué ought to be made in any case by the Government following their recognition, if only to inform the interested public of the new situation.

6.   An official press release or Dáil statement could explain, if necessary, why full recognition of Israel is not yet being granted. Nowadays the onus has fallen on Governments to show cause when they with-hold recognition de jure from generally recognised foreign States.

7.   While, naturally, not disposed, nor qualified, to make recommendations on the policy involved in this matter of the degree of recognition to be accorded in this case, (concerning which I am, personally, strictly 'neutral'!), I feel I should, at least, advert to the possibility of the Government deciding to accord full *de jure* recognition to the State of Israel.

Viewing the situation from a strictly legal point of view (that is, ignoring the purely 'political' attitude of Great Britain, France, Netherlands and others who have Moslem and Arab populations to consider), it is not easy to defend mere *de facto* recognition of the Israeli Government at this advanced stage.

That 'Government' is not simply a successfully rebellious faction contesting power in a long-established state (such as General Franco's administration was in, say, 1937), nor a foreign invading régime in an already recognised sovereign entity (such as the Italian régime in Ethiopia in 1935), but a body of persons who claim to rule over a *new international entity*. In other words, the question is *not* whether Ben Gurion's Government is a proper Government, but whether such a State exists in international law (that is, *de jure* exists) as 'Israel'. The answer to this latter question of law would seem to be in the affirmative, if we go back to the United Nations Resolution of 29th November, 1948, when the British League of Nations Mandate terminated, and when we take into account the formal proclamation (by the same people who have just been elected to govern it), of the State of Israel as an independent Republic on the 14th May, 1948, and if we ignore, as we are perfectly entitled to do, the disturbed condition of the country. The state of the country is a question of fact (not unique at present!) and not one of law.

8.   I do not wish to press this point, except to remark that the Jews are not likely to be enthusiastic about our limited recognition, (any more than the Arabs will be!); that we shall possibly feel bound later on to withdraw or complete our recognition as soon as Britain has first given us an example to follow, (which, I feel, will be rather invidious), and that the onus will immediately rest upon us to show why we are going 'thus far but no farther' just now.

9.   As a non-commital gesture to the Israeli Government, – if we grant *de facto* recognition only, – we might consider the expediency of appointing our Honorary Consul General at Beyrouth[1] a 'Special Representative' in Israeli territory.

10.   The following list of recognising countries is about seven short of the complete total (but all I have managed to ascertain); it may serve as a guide:-

Governments which have accorded full *de jure* recognition to the State of Israel.[2]

1. USSR
2. Costa Rica
3. Czechoslovakia
4. El Salvador
5. Finland
6. Guatemala
7. Hungary
8. Nicaragua
9. Panama
10. Paraguay
11. Poland
12. Roumania
13. Uruguay
14. Venezuela
15. Yugoslavia
16. Australia
17. United States of America (after a period during which *de facto* recognition given to the 'Provisional Government' of the 'new State of Israel').

Governments which have recognised *de facto* the Israeli State and/or Government

1. Great Britain
2. France
3. South Africa
4. Canada
5. New Zealand
6. Belgium
7. Netherlands
8. Luxembourg
9. Switzerland

The Scandanavian States, Norway, Sweden and Denmark are said to have decided to recognise Israel (and/or its Government) *de facto* in the near future.

NOTES

1 Beirut, Lebanon.
2 A handwritten note on the file adds Sweden and New Zealand to the list in July 1950.

Appendix 2

The question of *de jure* recognition of the State of Israel[1]

21 March 1956

1.   Before according *de facto* recognition to the State of Israel in February, 1949, we obtained from the Provisional Government of Israel (through its representatives in Washington and London) assurances that it accepted the principle of international control of the Holy Places in the Jerusalem area to ensure their inviolability and freedom of access. *De jure* recognition has since been withheld pending the establishment of such international control.

UNO decision of 1947

2.   The resolution of the UN General Assembly of November, 1947, concerning the partition of Palestine and the establishment of a Jewish State provided that the area of Jerusalem would be put under United Nations administration as an international enclave. This decision was welcomed by the Vatican and the Christian world generally and was accepted by the Jews as the price of their new State.

3.   Threats of armed resistance by the Arab countries decided UNO against any attempt to enforce the partition of Palestine. Upon the evacuation of the British, however, in May, 1948, the Jews themselves declared the State of Israel. In the ensuing hostilities Jerusalem was occupied partly by Jewish and partly by Arab forces. Since then, Israel has remained in control of the New City and Jordan of the Old City. Neither State is prepared to relinquish control and all efforts by UNO to secure their joint agreement to some alternative solution of the problem have been unsuccessful.

4.   Israel maintains that the failure of the United Nations to occupy Jerusalem at the time of the British evacuation has released her from any moral obligation arising out of the acceptance by the Jews of the 1947 resolution. In rejecting territorial control, however, Israel has repeatedly declared her willingness to accept international control limited to the Holy Places and other religious interests in her area and to give any guarantees required to that end. Jordan, however, rejects any form of international control as an infringement of her sovereignty.

5.   Despite these developments the Pope[2] has repeatedly made it clear that

nothing short of full territorial control of the Jerusalem area would be acceptable to the Vatican. A complete deadlock was reached in UNO in 1950, some states refusing to depart from the 1947 decision, while others were in favour of some workable compromise. The position now is still that the 1947 resolution – which was affirmed by the Assembly in 1948 and again in 1949 – still stands, though UNO has no intention of enforcing it.

The question of the status of Jerusalem has not been discussed since 1950 in the United Nations except for incidental references made principally by Arab representatives in discussions regarding the Arab-Israeli conflict.

6.   The State of Israel has been accorded *de jure* recognition by the vast majority of States. We understand that, apart from Ireland, the only European States which have not given full recognition are the Holy See and Spain.[3] Many States, however, excluded the area of Jerusalem as defined in the UNO resolution from the scope of their *de jure* recognition.

In May 1952 the Israeli Government announced that it intended in the near future to transfer the Foreign Office from Tel Aviv to Jerusalem where the other government offices have been functioning since 1949 when Jerusalem was declared to be the capital city of Israel. (The Foreign Office had been left in Tel Aviv because the diplomatic corps could not have been expected to establish themselves in Jerusalem while the future of the city was under discussion by UNO.) On July 10, 1953 the Israeli Government officially notified all foreign diplomatic missions in Israel that the Foreign Ministry would be transferred to Jerusalem within two days and only a liaison office would be left in Tel Aviv to attend to matters in connection with any diplomatic missions remaining there. On the following day the US State Department announced that it would not transfer its Embassy as this would be 'inconsistent with the UN resolution dealing with the international nature of Jerusalem'. A number of States, including Great Britain, France and Turkey also protested and announced that their Missions would remain in Tel Aviv. Six Arab countries, Egypt, Iraq, Lebanon, Saudi Arabia, Syria and Yemen made a formal complaint to the UN on July 16 denouncing the Israeli decision as a violation of UN resolutions. The weekly French language edition of the *Osservatore Romano* describing the move on 7 August as 'a serious and regrettable matter' stated that it 'could offer no effective security to Jerusalem all of which is a holy place'. Subsequently new British and US Ambassadors have presented letters of credence in Jerusalem while keeping their Missions in Tel Aviv. In the first case that of the British Ambassador, who presented letters in Jerusalem, was taken after consultation with the United States and France, on the grounds of 'international courtesy' and, according to a Foreign Office statement the decision had no political implications.

Irish attitude

7.   On 15 June 1949, Mr. MacBride, in reply to a parliamentary question, said that 'the Irish Government strongly support the general demand that the Holy

Places in Palestine should be suitably protected, that the free access to them should be ensured for all religious, and that, with a view to guaranteeing the attainment of these aims, the whole area of Jerusalem should be brought under international control'.

The following week (21 June, 1949) the Irish Hierarchy issued a statement in support of the Pope's appeals 'to secure the just right of Christendom in the Holy Land' and added that there should not be any final recognition of new States until these rights have been secured.

8.   Mr. MacBride referred to the matter again in the debate on the External Affairs Estimates on 13 July, 1949. He explained that the whole question was under discussion by the United Nations and appealed to the Government of Israel 'to meet the just claims of the Christian world for an international régime guaranteeing the safety of the Holy Places and freedom of access to them'. (There have been no further public references to our position in relation to this matter.)

9.   In April, 1951, the then Minister [Seán MacBride] decided that we would no longer be justified in withholding full recognition from Israel and he instructed the Ambassador to the Holy See to explain to the Vatican that we proposed to accord *de jure* recognition in the very near future. The Vatican reacted sharply to this intimation. Mr. Walshe was told by Mgr. Tardini that the Holy See could not regard our change of policy with anything but disapproval. In these circumstances, we did not proceed with the matter.

10.   In April 1952, the Israeli Ambassador in Washington approached Mr. Hearne on the question of *de jure* recognition by Ireland, saying (erroneously) that ours was the only State in the Western Hemisphere that had not given such recognition.

We consulted Mr. Walshe during his visit to Dublin in June, 1952, as to whether there was any likelihood of a change in the attitude of the Vatican. Mr. Walshe thought not, at any rate during the lifetime of the present Pope. He advised against *de jure* recognition by Ireland unless and until there is some very compelling reason in favour of that course.

The Vatican attitude which has not changed since has been re-stated at least twice in the *Osservatore Romano* in 1954. In a report dated 19 January, 1955, Mr. Cremin stated that the Holy See 'stand absolutely by the view that Jerusalem should be under international control'. Mr. Tardini, in the course of the conversation with Mr. Cremin, said that the attitude of the Holy See towards the Jerusalem issue had not weakened but indeed rather hardened.

11.   In January, 1953, the Israel Ambassador to London paid a visit to Ireland and during the course of his stay paid visits to the President, the Taoiseach, and the then Minister for External Affairs, Mr. Aiken. The question of opening direct relations between Ireland and Israel was not brought up officially during his visit as our attitude had been made quite clear to Mr. Elath by Mr. Boland beforehand.

12.   There were no further developments until the 9 March, 1956, when the Israeli Ambassador in Washington called on Mr. Hearne submitting formally a request from the Government of Israel to exchange diplomatic representatives. In the course of this démarche the Israeli Ambassador stated that his Government 'now favours international supervision of the Holy Places'. This is, of course, only a re-iteration of the established Israeli line referred to in paragraph 4.

NOTES

1   The copy of this analysis was found in NAI DFA 305/156.
2   Pope Pius XII.
3   Spain and Greece did not recognize Israel until 1986 and 1991 respectively.

Bibliography

Abbott, Walter M, ed. *The Documents of Vatican II* (New York, Guild Press, 1966).

Abdy, John Thomas. *Kent's Commentary on International Law* (Cambridge, Cambridge University Press, 2nd edn, 1878).

Abrams, M.H., E. Talbot Donaldson, Alfred David, Hallett Smith, Barbara K. Lewalski, Robert M. Adams, George M. Logan, Samuel Holt Monk, Lawrence Lipking, Jack Stillinger, George H. Ford, Carol T. Christ, David Daiches, and Jon Stallworthy, eds. *The Norton Anthology of English Literature* (New York, W.W. Norton & Company, 5th edn, 1986).

Acheson, Dean. *Present at the Creation: My Years at the State Department* (New York, W.W. Norton, 1969).

Adenauer, Konrad. *Memoirs 1945–53* [trans. Beate Ruhm von Oppen] (London, Weidenfeld & Nicolson, 1965).

Akenson, Donald Harman. *The United States and Ireland* (Cambridge, MA, Harvard University Press, 1973).

Albert, Michael. 'Constructing the state extraterritorially: jurisdictional discourse, the national interest, and transnational norms', *Harvard Law Review*, Vol. 103, No. 1273 (1990).

Alperovitz, Gar. 'More on atomic diplomacy', in David Carlton and Herbert M. Levine, eds, *The Cold War Debated* (New York, McGraw-Hill College, 1988).

Ambrose, Stephen E. *Rise To Globalism: American Foreign Policy Since 1938* (New York, Penguin Books, 6th rev. edn, 1991).

Anonymous. 'First thoughts on the debacle of Christian missions in China', *African Affairs*, Vol. 51, No. 202 (1952).

Appleton, Sheldon. *The Eternal Triangle? Communist China, the United States, and the United Nations* (East Lansing, MI, Michigan State University Press, 1961).

Art, Robert J. 'America's foreign policy', in Roy C. Macridis, ed., *Foreign Policy in World Politics: States and Regions* (Englewood Cliffs, NJ, Prentice-Hall, 7th edn, 1989).

Aspaturian, Vernon V. 'Soviet foreign policy', in Roy C. Macridis, ed., *Foreign Policy in World Politics: States and Regions* (Englewood Cliffs, NJ, Prentice-Hall, 7th edn, 1989).

Attix, Cheri L. 'Between the devil and the deep blue sea: are Taiwan's trading partners implying recognition of Taiwanese statehood?', *California Western International Law Journal*, Vol. 25, No. 357 (1995).

Austin, Alvyn. *Saving China: Missionaries in the Middle Kingdom 1888–1959* (Toronto, University of Toronto Press, 1986).

Axelrod, Robert. *The Structure of Decision: The Cognitive Maps of Political Elites* (Princeton, NJ, Princeton University Press, 1976).

Ball, George W. *The Past Has Another Pattern: Memoirs* (New York, W.W. Norton & Company, 1982).

Ball, George W. and Douglas B. Ball. *The Passionate Attachment: America's Involvement with Israel, 1947 to the Present* (New York, W.W. Norton & Company, 1992).

Baring, Arnulf. *Uprising in East Germany: June 17, 1953* [trans. Gerald Onn] (Ithaca, NY, Cornell University Press, 1972).

Barston, R.P., ed. *The Other Powers: Studies in the Foreign Policies of Small States* (London, George Allen & Unwin, 1973).

Bartošek, Karel. 'Central and southeastern Europe', in Stéphane Courtois, ed., *The Black Book of Communism: Crimes, Terror, Repression* [trans. Jonathan Murphy and Mark Kramer] (Cambridge, MA, Harvard University Press, 1999).

Barzini, Luigi Giorgio. *The Impossible Europeans* (London, Weidenfeld & Nicolson, 1983).

Beevor, Antony. *The Spanish Civil War* (London, Cassell & Co., 1999).

Beker, Avi. *The United Nations and Israel: From Recognition to Reprehension* (Lexington, MA, Lexington Books, 1988).

Bell, Coral. 'China and the international order', in Hedley Bull and Adam Watson, eds, *The Expansion of International Society* (Oxford, Clarendon Press, 1984).

Bell, Coral. *Dependent Ally: A Study in Australian Foreign Policy* (St Leonards, NSW, Australian National University, 1984).

Ben-Gurion, David. *Israel: A Personal History* [trans. Nechemia Meyers and Uzy Nystar] (New York, Funk & Wagnalls, 1971).

Bercuson, David J. *Canada and the Birth of Israel: A Study in Canadian Foreign Policy* (Toronto, University of Toronto Press, 1985).

Berman, George A., Roger J. Goebel, William J. Davey and Eleanor M. Fox, eds. *Cases and Materials on European Community Law* (St Paul, MN, West Publishing, 1993).

Bilder, Richard B. 'The office of the legal adviser: the State Department lawyer and foreign affairs', *American Journal of International Law*, Vol. 56, No. 633 (1962).

Bloomfield, Lincoln P. 'China, the United States, and the United Nations', in Richard A. Falk and Wolfram F. Hanrieder, eds, *International Law and Organization: An Introductory Reader* (Philadelphia, PA, Lippincott, 1968).

Bot, Bernard R. *Nonrecognition and Treaty Relations* (Dobbs Ferry, NY, Leyden, 1968).

Boyce, David George. *Nationalism in Ireland* (London, Routledge, 2nd edn, 1991).

Breslin, Thomas A. *China, American Catholicism, and the Missionary* (University Park, PA, Pennsylvania State University Press, 1980).

Brierly, James Leslie. *The Law of Nations: An Introduction to the International Law of Peace* (Oxford, Clarendon Press, 6th edn, 1963).

Brookings Institution. *Major Problems of United States Foreign Policy 1951–1952* (Washington, DC, Brookings Institution, 1951).

Brown, Seyom. 'The changing essence of power', in Ray Maghroori and Bennett Ramberg, eds, *Globalism Versus Realism: International Relations' Third Debate* (Boulder, CO, Westview Press, 1982).

Bull, Hedley. *The Anarchical Society: A Study of Order in World Politics* (New York, Columbia University Press, 1977).

Bull, Hedley. *Intervention in World Politics* (Oxford, Clarendon Press, 1984).

Bull, Hedley, Benedict Kingsbury and Adam Roberts, eds. *Hugo Grotius and International Relations* (Oxford, Clarendon Press, 1990).

Burton, John Wear. *Systems, States, Diplomacy and Rules* (London, Cambridge University Press, 1968).

Byers, Michael. 'Taking the law out of international law: a critique of the *Iterative Perspective*', *Harvard International Law Journal*, Vol. 38, No. 201 (1997).

Calvert, Peter. *The Foreign Policy of New States* (New York, St Martin's Press, 1986).

Calvocoressi, Peter. *World Politics since 1945* (London, Longman, 6th edn, 1991).

Carlsnaes, Walter. *Ideology and Foreign Policy: Problems of Comparative Conceptualization* (Oxford, Blackwell, 1987).

Carlton, David and Herbert M. Levine, eds. *The Cold War Debated* (New York, McGraw-Hill College, 1988).

Carlyle, Margaret. *Documents on International Affairs 1949–1950* (Oxford, Oxford University Press, 1953).

Carr, Edward Hallett. *What is History?* (London, Penguin Books, 2nd edn, 1990).

Chen, Jian. *China's Road to the Korean War: The Making of the Sino-American Confrontation* (New York, Columbia University Press, 1994).

Chen, Jian. *Mao's China and the Cold War* (Chapel Hill, NC, University of North Carolina Press, 2001).

Chen, Ti-Chang. *The International Law of Recognition: With Special Reference to Practice in Great Britain and the United States* (London, Stevens, 1951).

Childs, David. *East Germany* (New York, Praeger, 1969).

Childs, David. *The GDR: Moscow's German Ally* (London, George Allen & Unwin, 1983).

Chiu, Hungdah. 'The international legal status of the Republic of China', *Contemporary Asian Studies*, Vol. 5, No. 112 (1992).

Chomsky, Noam. *The Fateful Triangle: The United States, Israel and the Palestinians* (Boston, MA, South End Press, 1983).

Christie, Kenneth, ed. *Ethnic Conflict, Tribal Politics* (Richmond, Curzon Press, 1998).

Claude, Inis, Jr. *Swords Into Plowshares: The Problems and Progress on International Organization* (New York, n.p., 4th edn, 1984).

Cohen, Jerome Alan and Hungdah Chiu. *People's China and International Law: A Documentary Study*, Vol. 1 (Princeton, NJ, Princeton University Press, 1974).

Cohen, Michael J. *Truman and Israel* (Berkeley, CA, University of California Press, 1990).

Cohen, Paul A. 'Reflections on a watershed date: the 1949 divided in Chinese history', in Jeffrey N. Wasserstrom, ed., *Twentieth-Century China: New Approaches* (London, Routledge, 2003).

Cohen, Warren I. *America's Response to China: An Interpretative History of Sino-American Relations* (New York, John Wiley & Sons, 1971).

Cole, Taylor. *Recognition Policy of the United States Since 1901* (Baton Rouge, LA, Louisiana State University, 1928).

Corbett, Charles H. 'Conditions in Chekiang and Kiangsi', *Far Eastern Survey*, Vol. 12, No. 10 (17 May 1943).

Corbett, Percy Ellwood. *Law in Diplomacy* (Princeton, NJ, Princeton University Press, 1959).

Cornwell, John. *Hitler's Pope: The Secret History of Pius XII* (New York, Viking, 1999).

Cottam, Richard W. *Foreign Policy Motivation: A General Theory and a Case Study* (Pittsburgh, PA, University of Pittsburgh Press, 1977).

Courtois, Stéphane, ed. *The Black Book of Communism: Crimes, Terror, Repression* [trans. Jonathan Murphy and Mark Kramer](Cambridge, MA, Harvard University Press, 1999).

Cox, Terry. *Hungary 1956 – Forty Years On* (Portland, OR, Frank Cass, 1997).

Crawford, James. *The Creation of States in International Law* (Oxford, Clarendon Press, 1979).

Crawley, Aidan. *The Rise of Western Germany: 1945–1972* (London, Collins, 1973).

Cruise O'Brien, Conor. 'Conflicting concepts of the United Nations', in Richard A. Falk and Wolfram F. Hanrieder, eds, *International Law and Organization: An Introductory Reader* (Philadelphia, PA, Lippincott, 1968).

Cruise O'Brien, Conor. *The Siege: The Saga of Israel and Zionism* (New York, Simon & Schuster, 1986).

Cruise O'Brien, Conor. *Memoir: My Life and Themes* (New York, Cooper Square Press, 1998).

Dalai Lama of Tibet. *My Land and My People: An Original Autobiography of His Holiness the Dalai Lama of Tibet* (New York, Warner Books, 1997).

D'Arcy, Michael and Tim Dickson, eds. *Border Crossings: Developing Ireland's Island Economy* (Dublin, Gill & Macmillan, 1995).

De Valera, Eamon. *Ireland's Claim for Recognition as a Sovereign Independent State; Presented Officially to the Government of the United States by Eamon De Valera* (Washington, DC, Irish Diplomatic Mission, 1920).

Delaney, Enda. 'Political Catholicism in post-war Ireland: the Revd Denis Fahey and Maria Duce, 1945–54', *Journal of Ecclesiastical History*, Vol. 52, No. 3 (2001).

Delupis, Ingrid Detter. *International Law and the Independent State* (Epping, Gower Press, 1974).

Dennett, Raymond and Katherine D. Durant, eds. *Documents on American Foreign Relations,* Vol. 13 (Princeton, NJ, Princeton University Press, 1953).

Der Derian, James. *Antidiplomacy: Spies, Terror, Speed and War* (Cambridge, MA, Blackwell, 1992).

Desch, Michael C. 'War and strong states, peace and weak states?', *International Organization*, Vol. 50, No. 2 (1996).

Dolzer, Rudolf. *Encyclopedia of Public International Law* (Amsterdam, North-Holland Publishing, 1987).

Dommen, Edward and Philippe Hein, eds. *States, Microstates and Islands* (London, Croom Helm, 1985).

Drachman, Edward R. *Presidents and Foreign Policy: Countdown to Ten Controversial Decisions* (Albany, NY, State University of New York Press, 1997).

Duanmu, San. *The Phonology of Standard Chinese* (Oxford, Oxford University Press, 2000).

Dulles, Eleanor Lansing. *One Germany or Two: The Struggle at the Heart of Europe* (Stanford, CA, Hoover Institution Press, 1970).

Dwyer, T. Ryle. *De Valera: The Man and The Myths* (Dublin, Poolbeg, 1991).

Dye, Thomas R. *Policy Analysis: What Governments Do, Why They Do It, and What Difference It Makes* (Tuscaloosa, AL, University of Alabama Press, 1976).

East, Maurice, Stephen A. Salmore, and Charles F. Hermann, eds. *Why Nations Act: Theoretical Perspectives for Comparative Foreign Policy Studies* (Beverly Hills, CA, Sage Publications, 1978).

Edwards, P.G. *Prime Ministers and Diplomats: The Making of Australian Foreign Policy 1901–1949* (Melbourne, Oxford University Press in association with the Australian Institute of International Affairs, 1983).

Eisenhower, Dwight David. *Mandate for Change: 1953–56* (Garden City, NY, Doubleday, 1963).

Elder, Robert Ellsworth. *The Policy Machine: The Department of State and American Foreign Policy* (Syracuse, NY, Syracuse University Press, 1960).

Eliot, Thomas Stearns. *Selected Poems* (New York, Harbrace, 1964).

Engel, David. *Facing a Holocaust: The Polish Government-in-Exile and the Jews, 1943–45* (Chapel Hill, NC, University of North Carolina Press, 1993).

Epstein, Lawrence and Richard F. Sherburne, eds. *Reflections of Tibetan Culture: Essays in Memory of Turrell V. Wylie* (Lewiston, NY, E. Mellen Press, 1990).

Evans, Gareth and Bruce Grant. *Australia's Foreign Relations: In the World of the 1990s* (Melbourne, Melbourne University Press, 1991).

Evans, Richard. *Deng Xiaoping and the Making of Modern China* (London, Penguin Books, 1997).

Fain, Haskell. *Normative Politics and the Community of Nations* (Philadelphia, PA, Temple University Press, 1987).

Falk, Richard A. and Wolfram F. Hanrieder, eds. *International Law and Organization: An Introductory Reader* (Philadelphia, PA, Lippincott, 1968).

Fanning, Ronan. *The Irish Department of Finance 1922–58* (Dublin, Institute of Public Administration, 1978).

Fanning, Ronan. '*Raison d'État* and the evolution of Irish foreign policy', in Michael Kennedy and Joseph Morrison Skelly, eds, *Irish Foreign Policy 1919–1966: From Independence to Internationalism* (Dublin, Four Courts Press, 2000).

Fanning, Ronan. 'The United States and Irish participation in NATO: the debate of 1950', *Irish Studies in International Affairs*, Vol. 1, No. 1 (1979).

Feis, Herbert. *From Trust To Terror: The Onset of the Cold War, 1945–1950* (New York, W.W. Norton, 1972).

Fejtõ, François. 'France and China: the intersection of two grand designs', in Abraham Meyer Halpern, ed. *Policies Toward China: Views from Six Continents* (New York, McGraw-Hill, 1965).

Firth, Stewart. *Australia in International Politics* (St Leonards, NSW, Allen & Unwin, 1999).

Fischer, Edward. *Maybe a Second Spring: The Story of the Missionary Sisters of St Columban in China* (New York, NY, Crossroad, 1983).

Fitzgerald, Frances. *Fire in the Lake: The Vietnamese and Americans in Vietnam* (Boston, Little Brown, 1972).

Flynt, Wayne and Gerald W. Berkley. *Taking Christianity to China: Alabama Missionaries in the Middle Kingdom 1850–1950* (Tuscaloosa, AL, University of Alabama Press, 1997).

Foley, Anthony and Dermot McAleese, eds. *Overseas Industry in Ireland* (Dublin, Gill & Macmillan, 1991).

Foster, Robert Fitzroy (Roy). *Modern Ireland 1600–1972* (London, Penguin Books, 1989).

Foster, Robert Fitzroy (Roy). *Paddy & Mr. Punch: Connections in Irish and English History* (London, A. Lane, 1993).

Fraenkel, Osmond K. *A Digest of Cases on International Law Relating to Recognition of Governments* (New York, American Office of Institute of Soviet Laws of the University of Moscow, 1925).

Franck, Thomas M. *The Power of Legitimacy Among Nations* (New York, Oxford University Press, 1990).

Frankel, Joseph. *International Relations* (London, Oxford University Press, 2nd edn, 1969).

Fraser, T.G. *Partition in Ireland, India and Palestine* (London, Macmillan, 1984).

Frey, Eric G. *Division and Détente: The Germanies and Their Alliances* (New York, Praeger, 1987).

Fry, Michael G., ed. *Freedom and Change: Essays in Honor of Lester B. Pearson* (Toronto, McClelland & Stewart, 1975).

Gaddis, John Lewis. *Russia, the Soviet Union, and the United States: An Interpretive History* (New York, Wiley, 1978).

Gaddis, John Lewis, ed. *Cold War Statesmen Confront the Bomb: Nuclear Diplomacy Since 1945* (Oxford, Oxford University Press, 1999).

Gaddis, John Lewis. 'Spheres of Influence: The United States and Europe, 1945–1949', in Charles S. Maier, ed., *The Cold War in Europe* (New York, M. Wiener, 1991).

Gaddis, John Lewis. *We Now Know: Rethinking Cold War History* (Oxford, Clarendon Press, 1997).

Galloway, L. Thomas. *Recognizing Foreign Governments: The Practice of the United States* (Washington, DC, American Enterprise Institute for Public Policy Research, 1978).

Galtung, Johan, ed. *Co-operation in Europe* (Oslo, Scandinavian University Books, 1970).

Galtung, Johan. *The True Worlds: A Transnational Perspective* (New York, Free Press, 1980).

Gardner, Lloyd C. and Ted Gittinger, eds. *Vietnam: The Early Decisions* (Austin, TX, University of Texas Press, 1997).

Garver, John W. *The Sino-American Alliance: Nationalist China and American Cold War Strategy in Asia* (New York, East Gate Books, 1997).

Geldenhuys, Deon. *Isolated States: A Comparative Analysis* (Cambridge, Cambridge University Press, 1990).

Gibbons, William Conrad. 'Lyndon Johnson and the legacy of Vietnam', in Lloyd C. Gardner and Ted Gittinger, eds, *Vietnam: The Early Decisions* (Austin, TX, University of Texas Press, 1997).

Gilbert, Martin. *A History of the Twentieth Century: Volume 2 1933–1951* (New York, NY, Harper Perennial, 2000).

Gilbert, Martin. *Israel: A History* (New York, Morrow, 1998).

Gilpin, Robert. *The Political Economy of International Relations* (Princeton, NJ, Princeton University Press, 1987).

Gilpin, Robert. *War and Change in International Politics* (Cambridge, Cambridge University Press, 1981).

Girvin, Brian. *Between Two Worlds: Politics and Economy in Independent Ireland* (Dublin, Gill & Macmillan, 1989).

Goebel, Julius. *The Recognition Policy of the United States* (New York, Columbia University, 1915).

Goldberg, Louis. 'Historical and political factors in the twentieth century affecting the identity of Israel', in H. Wayne House, ed., *Israel: The Land and the People* (Grand Rapids, MI, Kregel Publications, 1998).

Goldstein, Melvyn C. 'Religious conflict in the traditional Tibetan state', in

Lawrence Epstein and Richard F. Sherburne, eds, *Reflections of Tibetan Culture: Essays in Memory of Turrell V. Wylie* (Lewiston, NY, E. Mellen Press, 1990).

Gong, Gerrit W. 'China's entry into international society', in Hedley Bull and Adam Watson, eds, *The Expansion of International Society* (Oxford, Clarendon Press, 1984).

Graham, Malbone W. *In Quest of a Law of Recognition* (Berkeley, CA, University of California Press, 1933).

Greenslade, Liam. '(In)dependence, development, and the colonial legacy in contemporary Irish identity', in Peter Shirlow, ed., *Development Ireland: Contemporary Issues* (London, Pluto Press, 1995).

Griffiths, Martin. *Realism, Idealism, and International Politics: A Reinterpretation* (London, Routledge, 1992).

Hachey, Thomas E. *The Problem of Partition: Peril To World Peace* (Chicago, IL, Rand McNally & Company, 1972).

Hakovirta, Harto. *East–West Conflict and European Neutrality* (Oxford, Clarendon Press, 1988).

Halpern, Abraham Meyer, ed. *Policies Toward China: Views from Six Continents* (New York, McGraw-Hill Book Company, 1965).

Hammer, Ellen J. *A Death in November: America in Vietnam 1963* (New York, E.P. Dutton, 1987).

Hancock, Donald and Helga A. Welsh, eds. *German Unification: Process and Outcomes* (Boulder, CO, Westview Press, 1994).

Handel, Michael. *Weak States in the International System* (London, Cass, 2nd edn, 1990).

Hanreider, Wolfram. 'German Reunification, 1949–63', in Roy C. Macridis, ed., *Foreign Policy in World Politics: States and Regions* (Englewood Cliffs, NJ, Prentice-Hall, 7th edn, 1989).

Harland, Bruce. *Small Countries in a Tripolar World* (London, University of London, 1991).

Harris, Richard. 'Britain and China: coexistence at low pressure', in Abraham Meyer Halpern, ed., *Policies Toward China: Views from Six Continents* (New York, McGraw-Hill, 1965).

Hederman, Miriam. *The Road To Europe: Irish Attitudes 1948–61* (Dublin, Institute of Public Administration, 1983).

Henkin, Louis. *How Nations Behave: Law and Foreign Policy* (New York, Columbia University Press, 2nd edn, 1979).

Henkin, Louis. *International Law: Politics and Values* (Dordrecht, Netherlands, M. Nijhoff, 1995).

Hepburn, A.C. *The Conflict of Nationality in Modern Ireland* (New York, St Martin's Press, 1980).

Hervey, John G. *The Legal Effects of Recognition in International Law* (Philadelphia, PA, University of Pennsylvania Press, 1928).

Herzog, Chaim. *Living History: A Memoir* (New York, Pantheon Books, 1996).

Hewstone, Miles. *Understanding Attitudes to the European Community* (Cambridge, Cambridge University Press, 1986).

Higgins, Rosalyn. 'Intervention and international law', in Hedley Bull, ed. *Intervention in World Politics* (Oxford, Clarendon Press, 1984).

Hobbes, Thomas. *Leviathan* (London, J.M. Dent, 1914 [1651]).

Hocking, Brian. *Localizing Foreign Policy: Non-Central Governments and Multilayered Diplomacy* (London, St Martin's Press, 1993).

Hogan, Michael J. and Thomas G. Paterson, eds. *Explaining the History of American Foreign Relations* (New York, Cambridge University Press, 1991).

Holmes, John W. 'Canada and China: the dilemmas of a middle power', in Abraham Meyer Halpern, ed., *Policies Toward China: Views from Six Continents* (New York, McGraw-Hill Book Company, 1965).

Holmes, Michael, Nicholas Rees and Bernadette Whelan, *The Poor Relation: Irish Foreign Policy and the Third World* (Dublin, Trocaire, 1993).

Holsti, Kalevi J. *International Politics: A Framework for Analysis* (London, Prentice-Hall International, 7th edn, 1995).

Holsti, Ole R. 'International relations models', in Michael J. Hogan and Thomas G. Paterson, eds, *Explaining the History of American Foreign Relations* (New York, Cambridge University Press, 1991).

Hsiao, Gene T. 'Nonrecognition and trade: a case study of the fourth Sino-Japanese trade agreement', in Gene T. Hsiao, ed., *Asian Studies: Occasional Paper Series* (Edwardsville, IL, Southern Illinois University, 1973).

Hunt, Michael H. *The Genesis of Chinese Communist Foreign policy* (New York, Columbia University Press, 1996).

Ignatieff, George. *The Making of a Peacemonger: The Memoirs of George Ignatieff* (Toronto, University of Toronto Press, 1985).

Inbar, Efraim and Gabriel Sheffer, eds. *The National Security of Small States in a Changing World* (London, Frank Cass, 1997).

Instituto American de Derecho y Legislacion Comparada. *La Opinion Universal sobre La Doctrine Estrada* (Mexico, n.p., 1931).

Inter-American Council of Jurists. *Recognition of* De Facto *Governments* (Washington, DC, Department of International Law, Pan American Union, 1953).

Irani, George Emile. *The Papacy and the Middle East: The Role of the Holy See in the Arab–Israeli Conflict, 1962–84* (Notre Dame, IN, University of Notre Dame Press, 1986).

Jackson, Alvin. *Ireland 1798–1998: Politics and War* (Oxford, Blackwell, 1999).

Jackson, Robert H. and Alan James, eds. *States in a Changing World: A Contemporary Analysis* (Oxford, Clarendon Press, 1993).

Jacobsen, John Kurt. *Chasing Progress in the Irish Republic: Ideology, Democracy and Dependent Development* (New York, Cambridge University Press, 1994).

Jaffe, Louis. *Judicial Aspects of Foreign Relations: In Particular of the*

Recognition of Foreign Powers (Cambridge, MA, Harvard University Press, 1933).

Jennings, Robert and Arthur Watts, eds. *Oppenheim's International Law* (Harlow, Longman, 9th edn, 1992).

Jessup, Philip C. *A Modern Law of Nations: An Introduction* (New York, Macmillan, 1956).

Jian, Chen. *Mao's China and the Cold War* (Chapel Hill, NC, University of North Carolina Press, 2001).

Jian, Sanqiang. *Foreign Policy Restructuring As Adaptive Behaviour: China's Independent Foreign Policy 1982–1989* (Lanham, NY, University Press of American, 1996).

Jones, Roy E. *Principles of Foreign Policy: The Civil State in Its World Setting* (Oxford, Martin Robertson & Company, 1979).

Kaiser, Karl. *German Foreign Policy in Transition* (London, Oxford University Press, 1968).

Katzenstein, Peter J. *Small States in World Markets: Industrial Policy in Europe* (Ithaca, NY, Cornell University Press, 1985).

Keatinge, Patrick. *The Formulation of Irish Foreign Policy* (Dublin, Institute of Public Administration, 1973).

Keatinge, Patrick. *A Place Among the Nations: Issues of Irish Foreign Policy* (Dublin, Institute of Public Administration, 1978).

Kelly, John Maurice, Gerard W. Hogan and Gerry Whyte, eds. *The Irish Constitution: Supplement to the Second Edition* (Dublin, Jurist Publishing, 1987).

Kennedy, Kieran A., Thomas Giblin and Deirdre McHugh. *The Economic Development of Ireland in the Twentieth Century* (London, Routledge, 1988).

Kennedy, Michael. 'The challenge of multilateralism: the Marshall Plan and the expansion of the Irish diplomatic service', in Till Geiger and Michael Kennedy, eds, *Ireland, Europe and the Marshall Plan* (Dublin, Four Courts Press, 2004).

Keogh, Dermot. *Ireland & Europe 1919–1989: A Diplomatic and Political History* (Cork, Hibernian University Press, 1990).

Keogh, Dermot. *Twentieth-Century Ireland: Nation and State* (Dublin, Gill & Macmillan, 1994).

Keogh, Dermot. *Ireland and the Vatican: The Politics and Diplomacy of Church–State Relations, 1922–1960* (Cork, Cork University Press, 1995).

Keogh, Dermot. 'Ireland and "emergency" culture, between civil war and normalcy, 1922–61', *Ireland: A Journal of History and Society,* Vol. 1 (1995).

Keogh, Dermot. *Jews in Twentieth-Century Ireland: Refugees, Anti-Semitism and the Holocaust* (Cork, Cork University Press, 1998).

Keohane, Robert O. and Joseph S. Nye. *Power and Interdependence: World Politics in Transition* (Boston, MA, LittleBrown, 1977).

Keohane, Robert O. 'International relations and international law: two optics', *Harvard International Law Journal*, Vol. 38, No. 487 (1997).

Kirby, William, C. 'The two Chinas in the global setting: Sino-Soviet and Sino-American Cooperation in the 1950s', in Robert S. Ross and Jiang Changbin, eds, *Re-examining the Cold War: U.S.–China Diplomacy, 1954–1973* (Cambridge, MA, Harvard University Asia Center, 2001).

Kissinger, Henry. *Diplomacy* (New York, Simon & Schuster, 1994).

Klieman, Aaron S. and Adrian L. Klieman, eds. *American Zionism: A Documentary History* (New York, 1991).

Knaus, John Kenneth. *Orphans of the Cold War: America and the Tibetan Struggle for Survival* (New York, Public Affairs, 1999).

Knorr, Klaus. *Power and Wealth: The Political Economy of International Power* (London, n.p., 1973).

Kolås, Ashild. 'Tibetan nationalism: the politics of religion', *Journal of Peace Research*, Vol. 33, No. 1 (1996).

Korbel, Josef. *The Communist Subversion of Czechoslovakia, 1938–1948: The Failure of Coexistence* (Princeton, NJ, Princeton University Press, 1959).

Krasner, Stephen D. 'Making peace agreements work: the implementation and enforcement of peace agreements between sovereigns and intermediate sovereigns', *Cornell International Law Journal*, Vol. 30, No. 651 (1997).

Krisch, Henry. *The German Democratic Republic: the Search for Identity* (Boulder, CO, Westview Press, 1985).

Kuppe, Johannes L. 'West German policy toward East Germany: a motor of unification?', in M. Donald Hancock and Helga A. Welsh, eds, *German Unification: Process and Outcomes* (Boulder, CO, Westview Press, 1994).

Kutler, Stanley I., ed. *Encyclopedia of the Vietnam War* (New York, Charles Scribner's Sons, 1996).

LaFeber, Walter. *America, Russia, and the Cold War 1945–1992* (New York, McGraw-Hill, 7th edn, 1993).

Laffan, Brigid. *Integration and Cooperation in Europe* (London, Routledge, 1992).

Lagos Matus, Gustavo. *International Stratification and Underdeveloped Countries* (Chapel Hill, NC, University of North Carolina Press, 1963).

Langer, Robert. *Seizure of Territory: The Stimson Doctrine and Related Principles in Legal Theory and Diplomatic Practice* (Princeton, NJ, Princeton University Press, 1947).

Larres, Klaus. *Churchill's Cold War: The Politics of Personal Diplomacy* (New Haven, CT, Yale University Press, 2002).

Lauterpacht, Hersch, Sir. *The Function of Law in the International Community* (Oxford, Clarendon Press, 1933).

Lauterpacht, Hersch, Sir. *Recognition in International Law* (Cambridge, Cambridge University Press, 1947).

Lauterpacht, Hersch, Sir. 'Recognition of states in international law', *Yale Law Journal*, Vol. 53, No. 3 (1944).

Lee, J. Joseph. *Ireland 1912–1985: Politics and Society* (Cambridge, Cambridge University Press, 1989).

Levey, Zach. *Israel and the Western Powers 1952–1960* (Chapel Hill, NC,

University of North Carolina Press, 1997).

Li, Hongshan. 'Image and perception in U.S.–China relations', Hongshan Li and Zhaohui Hong, eds, *Image, Perception, and the Making of U.S.–China Relations* (Lanham, MD, University Press of America, 1998).

Li, Victor H. *De-Recognizing Taiwan: The Legal Problems* (Washington, DC, Carnegie Endowment for International Peace, 1977).

Lieshout, Robert H. *Between Anarchy and Hierarchy: A Theory of International Politics and Foreign Policy* (London, Edward Elgar, 1995).

Lin, Hua. *A Grammar of Mandarin Chinese* (Munich, Lincom Europa, 2001).

Ling, Oi Ki. *The Changing Role of the British Protestant Missionaries in China, 1945–1952* (Cranbury, NJ, Associated University Presses, 1999).

Linklater, Andrew. *Beyond Realism and Marxism: Critical Theory and International Relations* (Basingstoke, Macmillan, 1990).

Lippmann, Walter. *The Cold War: A Study in U.S. Foreign Policy* (New York, Harper & Brothers, 1947).

Lopez, Donald S., Jr. '*Lamaism* and the disappearance of Tibet', *Comparative Studies in Society and History*, Vol. 38, No. 1 (1996).

Lustick, Ian S. *Unsettled States, Disputed Lands: Britain and Ireland, France and Algeria, Israel and the West Bank – Gaza* (Ithaca, NY, Cornell University Press, 1993).

McCabe, Ian. *A Diplomatic History of Ireland 1948–49: The Republic, the Commonwealth and NATO* (Dublin, Irish Academic Press, 1991).

MacDonald, Ronald St James, Gerald L. Morris and Douglas M. Johnston. *Canadian Perspectives on International Law and Organization* (Toronto, University of Toronto Press, 1974).

McDougal, Myres Smith. *Studies in World Public Order* (New Haven, CT, Yale University Press, 1960).

McFalls, Laurence H. *Communism's Collapse, Democracy's Demise? The Cultural Context and Consequences of the East German Revolution* (Basingstoke, Macmillan, 1995).

McKay, Alex. *Tibet and the British Raj: The Frontier Cadre, 1904–1947* (Richmond, n.p., 1997).

Macridis, Roy C., ed. *Modern European Governments: Cases in Comparative Policy Making* (Englewood Cliffs, NJ, Prentice-Hall, 1968).

Macridis, Roy C., ed. *Foreign Policy in World Politics: States and Regions* (Englewood Cliffs, NJ, Prentice-Hall, 7th edn, 1989).

Madsen, Richard. *China's Catholics: Tragedy and Hope in an Emerging Civil Society* (Berkeley, CA, University of California Press, 1998).

Maghroori, Ray and Bennett Ramberg, eds. *Globalism Versus Realism: International Relations' Third Debate* (Boulder, CO, Westview Press, 1982).

Maher, Denis J. *The Tortuous Path: The Course of Ireland's Entry into the EEC 1948–73* (Dublin, Institute of Public Administration, 1986).

Malekian, Farhad. *The System of International Law: Formation, Treaties, Responsibility* (Uppsala, Uppsala University Press, 1987).

Mann, Frederick Alexander. *Studies in International Law* (Oxford, Clarendon Press, 1973).

Manning, Charles Anthony Woodward. *The Nature of International Society* (London, Macmillan, 1975).

Mansergh, Diana, ed. *Nationalism and Independence: Selected Irish Papers by Nicholas Mansergh* (Cork, Cork University Press, 1997).

Mansergh, Nicholas. *The Unresolved Question: The Anglo-Irish Settlement and Its Undoing 1912–1972* (New Haven, CT, Yale University Press, 1991).

Mathews, R.H. *Chinese–English Dictionary* (Cambridge, MA, Harvard Univerity Press, 1943).

Mathisen, Trygve. *The Function of Small States in the Strategies of the Great Powers* (Oslo, Scandinavian University Books, 1971).

Max, Stanley M. *The United States, Great Britain, and the Sovietization of Hungary, 1945–48* (Boulder, CO, East European Monographs, 1985).

Mehrish, Brijesh Narain. *India's Recognition Policy Towards the New Nations* (Delhi, Oriental Publishers, 1972).

Menon, P.K. *The Law of Recognition in International Law: Basic Principles* (Lewiston, NY, Edwin Mellen Press, 1994).

Millar, Thomas Bruce. 'On writing about foreign policy', in James N. Rosenau, ed., *International Politics and Foreign Policy: A Reader in Research and Theory* (New York, Free Press, 1969).

Milward, Alan S. *The Reconstruction of Western Europe: 1945–51* (London, Methuen, 1984).

Misra, Kashi Prasad. *India's Policy of Recognition of States and Governments* (Bombay, Allied Publishers, 1966).

Moore, John Norton, ed. *The Arab–Israeli Conflict: Readings and Documents* (Princeton, NJ, Princeton University Press, 1977).

Morgan, Joseph G. *The Vietnam Lobby: The American Friends of Vietnam, 1955–1975* (Chapel Hill, NC, University of North Carolina Press, 1997).

Morgan, Roger. *The United States and West Germany 1945–1973: A Study in Alliance Politics* (London, Oxford University Press, 1974).

Morgenthau, Hans J. 'Another 'Great Debate': the national interest of the United States', in John A. Vasquez, ed., *Classics of International Relations* (Upper Saddle River, NJ, Prentice-Hall, 3rd edn, 1996).

Moskovits, Shlomo. 'United States Recognition of Israel in the Context of the Cold War 1945–48', (unpublished PhD Thesis) Ann Arbor, MI, 1982).

Moynihan, Maurice. *Speeches and Statements by Eamon de Valera 1917–73* (Dublin, Gill & Macmillan, 1980).

Nathan, James A. and James K. Oliver, eds. *United States Foreign Policy and World Order* (Glenview, IL, Scott, Foresman, 4th edn, 1989).

Navari, Cornelia. *The Condition of States: A Study in International Political Theory* (Milton Keynes, Open University Press, 1991).

Neff, Donald. *Warriors for Jerusalem: The Six Days That Changed the Middle East* (Brattleboro, VT, Amana Books, 1988).

Neufeld, Mark A. *The Restructuring of International Relations Theory* (New York, Cambridge University Press, 1995).

Newman, Robert P. *Recognition of Communist China? A Study in Argument* (New York, MacMillan Company, 1961).

Norman, Jerry, ed. *Chinese* (Cambridge, Cambridge University Press, 1988).

Northedge, F.S. *British Foreign Policy: The Process of Adjustment 1945–1961* (New York, Praeger, 1962).

O'Connell, D.P. *International Law* (London, Stevens & Sons, 1965).

O'Grady, Joseph P. 'Ireland', in S. Victor Papacosma and Mark R. Rubin, eds, *Europe's Neutral and Nonaligned States: Between NATO and the Warsaw Pact* (Wilmington, DE, S.R. Books, 1989).

O'Halpin, Eunan. *Defending Ireland: The Irish State and Its Enemies Since 1922* (Oxford, Oxford University Press, 1999).

Papacosma, S. Victor and Mark R. Rubin, eds. *Europe's Neutral and Nonaligned States: Between NATO and the Warsaw Pact* (Wilmington, DE, S.R. Books, 1989).

Paterson, Thomas G., ed. *Major Problems in American Foreign Policy: Documents and Essays* (Lexington, MA, Heath, 1989).

Pattison, W. Keith. 'The International Law of Recognition in Contemporary British Foreign Policy', *(unpublished* PhD Thesis) Ann Arbor, MI, 1981).

Pearson, Lester B. *Mike: The Memoirs of the Right Honourable Lester B. Pearson*, Vol. 1, 1897–1948 (Toronto, University of Toronto Press, 1972).

Pfaff, Richard H. 'Jerusalem', in John Norton Moore, ed., *The Arab–Israeli Conflict: Readings and Documents* (Princeton, NJ, Princeton University Press, 1977).

Pfaff, Richard II. *Jerusalem: Keystone of an Arab-Israeli Settlement* (Washington, DC, American Enterprise Institute for Public Policy Research, 1969).

Pollack, Benny. *The Paradox of Spanish Foreign Policy: Spain's International Relations from Franco to Democracy* (New York, St Martin's Press, 1987).

Prachowny, Martin F.J. *Small Open Economies: Their Structure* (Lexington, MA, Lexington Books, 1975).

Preston, Richard, ed. *Contemporary Australia: Studies in History, Politics, and Economics* (Durham, NC, Duke University Press, 1969).

Ray, James Lee. *Global Politics* (Boston, MA, Houghton Mifflin, 1987).

Raymond, R. J. 'The Marshall Plan and Ireland, 1947–52', in P.J. Drudy, ed., *The Irish in America: Emigration, Assimilation and Impact* (Cambridge, Cambridge University Press, 1985).

Reid, George L. *The Impact of Very Small Size on the International Behaviour of Microstates* (Beverley Hills, CA, Sage Publications, 1974).

Reisman, W. Michael. 'International law after the cold war', *American Journal of International Law*, Vol. 84, No. 4 (October 1990).

Reisman, W. Michael and Eisuke Suzuki, 'Recognition and social change in international law: a prologue for decisionmaking', in W. Michael Reisman and Burns H. Weston, eds, *Toward World Order and Human Dignity* (New

York, Free Press, 1976).

Reuter, Paul. *Introduction to the Law of Treaties* [trans. José Mico and Peter Haggenmacher] (New York, Pinter Publishers, 1989).

Reycher, Luc. *Patterns of Diplomatic Thinking: A Cross-National Study of Structural and Social-Psychological Determinants* (New York, Praeger, 1979).

Roberts, J.A.G. *The Complete History of China* (Stroud, Gloucestershire, Sutton Publishing, 2003).

Rosenau, James N. *International Politics Since 1945: Key Issues in the Making of the Modern World* (Aldershot, Edward Elgar, 1991).

Ross, Robert S. and Jiang Changbin, eds. *Re-examining the Cold War: U.S.–China Diplomacy, 1954–1973* (Cambridge, MA, Harvard University Press, 2001).

Rostow, Walt Whitman. *World Economy: History and Prospect* (Austin, TX, University of Texas Press, 1978).

Rostow, Walt Whitman. *The Division of Europe After the Second World War: 1946* (Austin, TX, University of Texas Press, 1982).

Rostow, Walt Whitman. 'Countering guerrilla attack', in Hedley Bull and Adam Watson, eds, *The Expansion of International Society* (Oxford, Clarendon Press, 1984).

Rothstein, Robert L. *Alliances and Small Powers* (New York, Columbia University Press, 1968).

Roy, Denny. 'Ethnic conflict in China: the case of Tibet', in Kenneth Christie, ed., *Ethnic Conflict, Tribal Politics* (Richmond, Curzon Press, 1998).

Rubin, Alfred P. 'Recognition versus reality in international law and policy', *New England Law Review*, Vol. 32, No. 669 (1998).

Ryan, Stephen. *Ethnic Conflict and International Relations* (Aldershot, Dartmouth, 2nd edn, 1995).

Ryan, Thomas F. *China Through Catholic Eyes* (Hong Kong, Catholic Truth Society of Hong Kong, 1942).

Saich, Tony. *China: Politics and Government* (New York, St Martin's Press, 1981).

Salmon, Trevor. *Unneutral Ireland: An Ambivalent and Unique Security Policy* (Oxford, Clarendon Press, 1989).

Schoenbaum, David. *The United States and the State of Israel* (New York, Oxford University Press, 1993).

Schulz, Eberhard, ed. *GDR Foreign Policy* [trans. Michel Vale] (Armonk, NY, M.E. Sharpe, 1982).

Scott, James Brown. *The Catholic Conception of International Law: Vitoria and Suárez* (Washington, DC, Georgetown University Press, 1934).

Scwarzenberger, Georg. *International Law and Order* (London, Stevens & Sons, 1971).

Shakya, Tsering. *The Dragon in the Land of Snows: A History of Modern Tibet Since 1947* (New York, Penguin Compass, 2000).

Shamir, Yitzak. *Summing Up: An Autobiography* (London, Weidenfeld & Nicolson, 1994).

Shearer, Ivan Anthony. *Starke's International Law* (London, Butterfields, 1994).

Shirlow, Peter, ed. *Development Ireland: Contemporary Issues* (London, Pluto Press, 1995).

Sidahmed, Abdel Salam M. *Politics and Islam in Contemporary Sudan* (New York, St Martin's Press, 1996).

Singer, Marshall R. *Weak States In A World of Powers: The Dynamics of International Relationships* (New York, Free Press, 1972).

Skelly, Joseph Morrison. *Irish Diplomacy at the United Nations 1945–1965: National Interests and the International Order* (Dublin, Irish Academic Press, 1997).

Small, Melvin and J. David Singer. 'The diplomatic importance of states, 1816–1970: an extension and refinement of the indicator', *World Politics*, Vol. 25, No. 4 (1973).

Smith, Gary, Dave Cox and Scott Burchill. *Australia in the World: An Introduction to Australian Foreign Policy* (New York, Oxford University Press, 1996).

Smith, Steve and Michael Clarke. *Foreign Policy Implementation* (London, Allen & Unwin, 1985).

Sørensen, Max, ed. *Manual of Public International Law* (London, Macmillan, 1968).

Spence, Jonathan D. *The Search for Modern China* (New York, W.W. Norton & Company, 1990).

Strahan, Lachlan. *Australia's China: Changing Perceptions from the 1930s to the 1990s* (Cambridge, Cambridge University Press, 1996).

Stueck, William. *Rethinking the Korean War: A New Diplomatic and Strategic History* (Princeton, NJ, Princeton University Press, 2002).

Sutton, Paul. 'Political aspects' in Colin Clarke and Tony Payne, eds, *Politics, Security and Development in Small States* (London, Allen & Unwin, 1987).

Symmons, Clive R. 'Irish policy and practice on recognition', *Irish Jurist*, Vol. 28, No. 175 (1995).

Tai, Paul H. *United States, China, and Taiwan: Bridges for a New Millennium* (Carbondale, IL, Southern Illinois University, 1999).

Talmon, Stefan. *Recognition of Governments in International Law: With Particular Reference to Governments in Exile* (Oxford, Clarendon Press, 1998).

Tsou, Tang. *America's Failure in China 1941–50* (Chicago, IL, University of Chicago Press, 1963).

Tucker, Nancy Bernkopf. *Patterns in the Dust: Chinese–American Relations and the Recognition Controversy 1949–1950* (New York, Columbia University Press, 1983).

Tucker, Nancy Bernkopf, ed. *China Confidential: American Diplomats and Sino-American Relations, 1945–1996* (New York, Columbia University Press, 2001).

Tucker, Robert Warren. *The Inequality of Nations* (London, Basic Books, 1977).

Tucker, Spencer C. *Vietnam* (London, UCL Press, 1999).

Ulbricht, Walter. *On Questions of Peaceful Coexistence Between the Two German States* [trans. Intertext, GDR] (Dresden, Verlag Zeit im Bild, 1967).

Unwin, Derek W. *The Community of Europe: A History of European Integration Since 1945* (London, Longman, 1991).

Van Wynen Thomas, Ann and A. J. Thomas, Jr. *Non-intervention, the Law and its Import in the Americas* (Dallas, TX, Southern Methodist University Press, 1956).

Vital, David. *The Inequality of States: A Study of the Small Power in International Relations* (Oxford, Clarendon Press, 1967).

Vital, David. *The Origins of Zionism* (Oxford, Clarendon Press, 1975).

Vital, David. 'Minor power/major power relations and the contemporary nation-state', in Efraim Inbar and Gabriel Sheffer, eds, *The National Security of Small States in a Changing World* (London, Frank Cass, 1997).

von Glahn, Gerhard. *Law Among Nations: An Introduction to Public International Law* (New York, Macmillan, 5th edn, 1986).

Wagner, R. Harrison. 'What was bipolarity?', *International Organization,* Vol. 47, No. 1 (1993).

Walker, Martin. *The Cold War: A History* (New York, Henry Holt, 1993).

Waltz, Kenneth N. *Theory of International Politics* (Reading, MA, Addison-Wesley, 1979).

Warbrick, Colin. 'The new British policy on recognition of governments', *International and Comparative Law Quarterly*, Vol. 30, No. 568 (1981).

Wasserstrom, Jeffrey N., ed. *Twentieth-Century China: New Approaches* (London, Routledge, 2003).

Weizmann, Chaim. *Trial and Error: The Autobiography of Chaim Weizmann* (London, Hamish Hamilton, 1949).

Wells, Samuel F., Jr. 'The defence of Europe', in Wm. Roger Louis and Hedley Bull, eds, *The Special Relationship: Anglo-American Relations Since 1945* (Oxford, Clarendon Press, 1989).

Weston, Burns H., Richard A. Falk and Anthony D'Amato, eds. *Basic Documents in International Law and World Order* (St Paul, MN, West Publishing, 2nd edn, 1990).

Weston, Burns H., Richard A. Falk and Anthony D'Amato, eds. *International Law and World Order* (St Paul, MN, West Publishing, 1990).

White, Robin C.A. 'Recognition of states and diplomatic relations', *International and Comparative Law Quarterly*, Vol. 37, No. 984 (1988).

Wight, Martin. *Systems of States* (Leicester, Leicester University Press, 1977).

Wight, Martin. *International Theory: The Three Traditions* (Leicester, Leicester University Press, 1991).

Wiles, James L. and Richard B. Finnegan, eds. *Aspirations and Realities: A Documentary History of Economic Development Policy in Ireland Since 1922* (Westport, CT, Greenwood Press, 1993).

Wilson, Thomas W., Jr. *The Great Weapons Heresy* (Boston, MA, Houghton Mifflin, 1970).

Woolsey, Theodore Dwight. *Introduction to the Study of International Law* (New York, C. Scribner's Sons, 1864).

Wright, Quincy. 'The Chinese recognition problem', *American Journal of International Law*, Vol. 49, No. 320 (1955).

Wylie, J. A. 'Journey through Central Manchuria', *Geographical Journal*, Vol. 2, No. 5 (1893).

Yasamee, H. J. and K. A. Hamilton, eds. *Documents on British Policy Overseas*, Series 2, Vol. 4 (London, Her Majesty's Stationery Office, 1991).

Yin, Ch'ing-yao. 'The evolution of Communist China's foreign policy', in Yu-ming Shaw, ed., *Mainland China: Politics, Economics, and Reform* (Boulder, CO, Westview Press, 1986).

Zhai, Qiang. *The Dragon, the Lion, and the Eagle: Chinese–British–American Relations, 1949–1958* (Kent, OH, Kent State University Press, 1994).

Zhang, Hong. *America Perceived: The Making of Chinese Images of the United States, 1945–53* (Westport, CT, Greenwood Press, 2002).

Sources

NATIONAL ARCHIVES, DUBLIN

Department of External Affairs
    Common Market Series
    Confidential Reports Series
    Council of Europe and UN Series
    Embassy Series
    Estimates, Administration, and Establishment Series
    Information and Political Series
    Secretary's Series
    United Nations Series

Department of Finance
    General Files

Department of Industry and Commerce
    General Files

Department of the Taoiseach
    Cabinet Minutes
    Government Minutes
    Secretariat Files

IRISH GOVERNMENT PUBLICATIONS

Dáil Éireann Parliamentary Debates, 1922–63
Éire-Ireland. The Bulletin of the Irish Department of External Affairs, Dublin, 1948–63
Seanad Éireann Parliamentary Debates, 1930–63
Statistical Abstracts of Ireland, 1948–63

UNPUBLISHED MEMOIR

Cornelius C. Cremin

PERSONAL INTERVIEW

Gerald Goldberg, Cork, June 1998

NATIONAL ARCHIVES AND RECORDS ADMINISTRATION, WASHINGTON, DC

Declassified Documents Reference System
Presidential Libraries
  LBJ Library, Austin, Texas

UNITED STATES DEPARTMENT OF STATE, WASHINGTON, DC

Foreign Relations of the United States (FRUS) series

JOURNALS AND OTHER PERIODICALS

American Journal of International Law
Cornell International Law Journal
Far East
International and Comparative Law Quarterly
International Law Review
Ireland: A Journal of History and Society
Irish Studies in International Affairs
United Nations Treaty Series

Index

Sayers, Elliseva, 225
Sayers, Philip, 220, 223–6, 229–30,
    250–2
Schoenbaum, David, 217
Schuman, Robert, 123
Schuman Plan, 123
Seanad Éireann, 157
Second World War, 10, 25, 38
secrecy in government, 68–9
self-determination, 12, 18, 28, 163,
    204, 247
Seligman, Eustace, 182
Senate (US), 182
Senegal, 104, 106, 107, 191
Shamir, Yitzak, 204, 209–10
Shanghai, 153, 154, 156, 157, 159,
    192
Shannon Airport, 208
Sharett, Moshe, 207, 216, 226, 261
Shepherd, George, 155
Shertok, Moshe: see Sharett, Moshe
Shien Tao Chen, 157
Sierra Leone, 104, 106, 107
Sikkim, 185
Sinai Peninsula, 235, 236
Singapore, 162
Singer, J. David, 27
Singer, Marshall R., 55
Sinn Féin, 2
Sino-Japanese War, 157
Skelly, Joseph Morrison, 29, 178,
    185, 238
Skocpol, Theda, 22
Small, Melvin, 27
small states, xii, 3, 33–6, 54, 56,
    150, 178, 185, 245, 256; Cold War
    and, 62; constraints on, 21, 22;
    Eamon de Valera on, 25–6
Social Democrats in Soviet Bloc,
    126
Socialist Unity Party of [East]
    Germany, 122
Somalia, 104, 106, 107, 191
Sørensen, Max, 15

South Africa, 36, 107, 159, 263
South America, 5, 92, 159, 207, 210
sovereignty, 118–19, 144
Soviet Bloc, 16, 29, 30, 63, 64, 70,
    71, 74, 130, 135, 159, 172
Soviet Union, 27, 70, 163; and Arab
    states, 236; and Austria, 56; and
    Britain, 121, 172; and China,
    150, 153, 160–1, 166, 169,
    171–3, 175, 179–80, 183, 187,
    189–90; and Cold War, 28; and
    Czechoslovakia, 71, 142; and
    Germany, 13, 28, 37, 78–9, 117,
    118, 120–9, 132–3, 134, 142,
    143, 146, 148; and Hungary, 112,
    135, 177; and Indochina, 92; and
    Ireland, 28–9, 76–8, 87, 89, 107,
    130, 142, 174, 181; and Israel,
    206, 211, 263; and Mongolia,
    106; and Poland, 90, 91; and
    Suez Crisis, 236; and United
    Nations, 74; and United States,
    9–10, 12, 18, 30, 121, 141, 162,
    221; and Yugoslavia, 136
Spaak, Paul-Henri, 52–4, 60
Spain: Britain and, 73, 111; and East
    Germany, 143; Ireland and, 2–3,
    17, 57, 58, 107, 110; and Israel,
    208–12, 217–18, 221, 265, 267;
    and Morocco, 89
Spellman, Francis, Cardinal, 93,
    188
Spence, Jonathan D., 155, 156–7
Sri Lanka, 34, 79, 107, 115, 143,
    180, 190
Stalin, Josef, 120–1, 123–4, 129,
    135, 146, 160, 168, 171, 177
Stasi, 134
State Department (US), 43, 48–50,
    62, 94–5, 161, 182–5, 221, 223,
    236, 250, 265
statehood, 5, 9, 11, 21
states, 13, 22, 255; diplomatic
    recognition of, 3–5, 11, 71, 75, 78,

IRELAND AND THE COLD WAR

IRELAND AND THE COLD WAR
Diplomacy and Recognition
1949–63

PAULA L. WYLIE

Foreword by
DERMOT KEOGH

IRISH ACADEMIC PRESS
DUBLIN • PORTLAND, OR

First published in 2006 by
IRISH ACADEMIC PRESS
44, Northumberland Road, Dublin 4, Ireland

and in the United States of America by
IRISH ACADEMIC PRESS
c/o ISBS, Suite 300, 920 NE 58th Avenue
Portland, Oregon 97213-3644

WEBSITE: www.iap.ie

British Library Cataloguing in Publication Data
An entry can be found on request

ISBN 0-7165-3375-8 (cloth)
ISBN 0-7165-3376-6 (paper)

Library of Congress Cataloging-in-Publication Data
An entry can be found on request

Typeset in 10.5/12.5pt Times by FiSH Books, Enfield, Middx.
Printed by MPG Books Ltd, Bodmin, Cornwall